Table of Contents

Preface

This book is divided into four sections: Network Architecture, Network Implementation, Network Management, and Network Economics. An article may contain material that overlaps sections, but is included in the section seen as the major thrust.

Since the overall concern is for network design strategy, a few articles contain numerical data that is not up to date. But the articles were included because the techniques described were judged to be important and potentially beneficial to the reader.

Some see network design as an art; others see it as a science. Both viewpoints are well represented in this book. In addition, information on standards, software packages, modeling and simulation, maintenance, security, and financial considerations—among others—are covered by their respective practitioners. Several case studies of varying detail are included, to help demonstrate the practical application of the viewpoints cited.

Since a network design is really never finished, some sense of what the future holds for the approaches taken is touched on by many articles. Of course, an implementation that is optimum in one instance may not be so in another. So an attempt has been made to include as many different strategies as possible. No claim of all-inclusivity is made.

Uyless D. Black, Federal Reserve System, Washington, D.C.

Data link controls: The great variety calls for wise and careful choices

Managing the data flow
across a communications link
with software and hardware
at each network site
is no easy task.

The periodic data distortions that occur within a message are the most serious errors that occur in a data communications network. Over the years, many protocols known as data link controls (DLCs) have been developed to handle both these errors and the associated bookkeeping chores that come along with them. These bookkeeping chores are as important as the error handling. For example, the sending site must be assured that data arrives error-free at the receiving site. Moreover, the sending and receiving sites must maintain complete accountability for all messages. This means that in the event the data is distorted, the receiving site must have the capability of notifying the originator to resend the message or otherwise correct the errors.

There are still more tasks for the data link control. The movement of messages to and from the many points within a network must flow in a controlled and orderly manner. This means that the sending and receiving sites must know the identification and sequencing of the messages being transmitted among all users. The connection path between sites is usually shared by more than one user (as in a multipoint configuration). As a result, message-handling procedures must provide for the allocation and sharing of the path.

To do his job efficiently, the data communications user must be familiar with the characteristics of DLCs. Regardless of which of these protocols is under consideration, DLCs consist of a combination of software and hardware and are located at each site in the network. They provide such network functions as:

- Synchronizing the sender and receiver
- Controlling the sending and receiving of data
- Detecting and recovering transmission errors between two points
- Maintaining awareness of link conditions.

A multinode network with intermediate points between two users is a good example of the need for DLCs. User terminal A in San Francisco sends data across the network to user terminal B in Atlanta as part of the user A-B session. The data could, for example, be first passed to an intermediate node in Kansas City (event 1). The DLC in Kansas City then receives the data, checks for errors, and sends a receipt acknowledgment (ACK) of the data to San Francisco (event 2). Kansas City then assumes responsibility for this data. In event 3, Kansas City sends the data to Atlanta, which checks the data and sends an acceptance response to Kansas City (event 4). Thus the DLC relays the message through the network, much like the passing of a baton in a relay race.

The DLC does not provide the user with end-to-end accountability. This means that user A does not receive any indication of data receipt in Atlanta, the end point. Since data link controls do not provide for such end-to-end access and flow control, a higher level of control is required.

Data link controls can be described by either their message format, line-control method, error-handling method, or flow-control procedure. When the message-format classification is used, the DLC is further divided into asynchronous or synchronous categories.

Asynchronous formats originated with older equipment that had limited capabilities compared to what can be done today. But they are still widely used because of their simplicity. Their main disadvantage is the overhead of the control bits. For example, a ratio of 3 control bits to 8 user-character bits is not unusual. Notwithstanding, many variations and improvements have been made to asynchronous protocols. So in spite of the overhead, DLCs with asynchronous formats remain dominant. Asynchronous techniques are found in practically all teleprinter and teletypewriter terminals.

For their part, DLCs with synchronous formats are further distinguished as byte- or bit-oriented formats. The synchronous byte-oriented DLC uses the same string of bits and bytes to represent data characters and control characters. For example, the control field EOT (end of transmission) might occur in a user data stream. In this case, the DLC logic could mistakenly interpret the data as control information. Recent versions of synchronous byte techniques have logic provisions to handle this problem.

The more advanced synchronous DLCs use the bit-oriented approach. In this method, line-control characters are always unique and cannot occur in the user data stream. The logic of the DLC examines the data stream before it is transmitted and alters the user data if it contains a bit configuration that could be interpreted as a control field. Of course, with this approach, the receiving DLC has the capability to change the data stream to its original contents. Such a bit-oriented DLC achieves code transparency. This means that the logic is not dependent on a particular code such as ASCII or EBCDIC.

Master stations

Line control is another method of realizing a DLC. The most common method of line control is through the use of polling/selection techniques. Here a site in the network is designated as the master or primary station. This site is responsible for the sending and receiving of messages between all secondary or slave sites on the line. In fact, the secondary sites cannot send any messages until the master station gives approval.

To understand how polling/selection does its job, suppose site B wishes to send data to site A on the San Francisco master-station line. The master station begins this process by sending a polling message to B (event 1). In effect, the poll message says, "Site B, have you got a message to send?" Site B responds by sending a message to the master (event 2). The master site checks the message for errors and responds back to B with an ACK (event 3).

There are many variations of the polling/selection technique. For example, some vendor implementations allow B to continue sending messages, eventually terminating the process with an EOT message (event 4). Others provide an EOT indicator within the final message itself. This eliminates event 4 and an overhead message.

The selection process begins in event 5. Now the master site informs A that it has data destined for A by sending a selection message. This message means: "Site A, I have data for you; can you receive?" Site A must respond with a positive ACK or negative acknowledgment (NAK), as event 6.

The receiving station may not be able to accept a message. For example, it may be busy or its storage buffers may be full. If A can receive the message, the master site transmits it (event 7). The message is checked for errors at A and an acknowledgment relayed to the master station (event 8). User A could then respond to user B by going through the master

station and executing the process again.

It's useful to compare the two networks described. In the first, for example, the intermediate node in Kansas City controls the San Francisco and Atlanta points. This means that the polling/selection approach allows a site to be a master to one part of the network and a slave to another part. In the second, the master site in San Francisco controls the user terminals within its local environment.

The polling/selection protocol is widely used for three reasons. For one, the centralized approach allows for hierarchical control. Traffic flow is directed from one point, which provides for simpler control than a noncentralized approach. For another, some terminals can be polled or selected more frequently than others. This gives precedence to certain users and their applications. Finally, sites (terminals, software applications, or computers) can be added by changing the polling/selection table within the DLC logic.

There is a price to pay for all these features. The polling/selection DLC incurs a substantial amount of overhead due to the requirement for polling, selection, ACK, NAK, and EOT control messages. On some networks, the negative responses to polls (in which a terminal or user application is solicited for data but has nothing to send) can consume a significant portion of the network capacity. Fortunately, more recent implementations of the polling/selection DLC use some "cleaner" methods to reduce the number of overhead messages.

No response

Timeouts are an error-handling method for the link-control station to check for errors or questionable conditions on the network's transmission line. A timeout occurs when a polled station does not respond within a certain time. The nonresponse condition evokes recovery action on the part of the controlling station.

The timeout threshold is dependent upon three factors. These are the signal propagation delay to and from the polled station, the processing time at the polled station, and the turnaround delay at the polled station (raising the clear-to-send circuit) on a half-duplex line. These three factors are highly variable and depend upon the line type, line length, modem performance, and processing speed at the polled terminals' sites.

A timeout threshold for a network using leased full-duplex lines operating within a distance of 150 miles between the polling and polled sites might range between 30 to 60 milliseconds (ms). The threshold for the same arrangement, but using satellite links, could be as great as 900 ms due to the longer propagation time in such links. In contrast, local networks operating within small confines might use a timeout threshold of a very few milliseconds or perhaps microseconds.

Pass it on

One variation of polling/selection is known as hub polling. This approach is used on a multipoint line to avoid the delay inherent in a polled terminal's turning around on a half-duplex line to return a negative re-

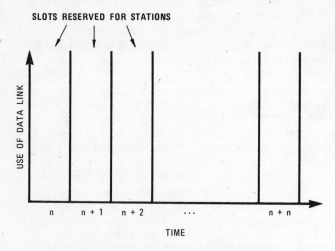

1. Wait your turn. *Time-slot control avoids the problem of one user's signal interfering with someone else's. Network access simply sequences from one user to another.*

SLOTS RESERVED FOR STATIONS

USE OF DATA LINK

n   n + 1   n + 2   ...   n + n

TIME

sponse to the poll. In this operation, the master station sends a poll to the farthest terminal on the line.

If it has data to send, this terminal turns the line around with a message to the master station. If it has no data, the terminal sends the polling message to the next terminal on the line. If this terminal is busy, idle, or has nothing to send, it relays the polling message to the next appropriate station.

The transmission of this poll continues in one direction without additional turnarounds. Eventually, a terminal will be found that has data for the master station. Thus hub polling eliminates the line turnaround time that occurs if each terminal receives a poll from the master station.

No master

Contention is another widely used link control method. It differs from polling/selection since there is no master station. With contention, each site has equal status on the line and the use of this path is determined by the station that first gains access during an idle-line period. Contention DLCs must provide for a station to relinquish the use of the path after an appropriate interval of time. This prevents line domination from one site.

An example of contention controls is provided by a multidropped path with sites A, B, C, and D on the line. Each site, using a line-signal-sensing device, determines if a message is traveling on the path. If there is a message, the sites defer to it. Since the messages are being transmitted at very high speeds, the waiting periods are usually quite short.

Suppose that site D has transmitted a message destined for A. Sites B and C monitor the line, determine that it is occupied, and wait a brief period before sensing again. If both B and C have a message to transmit, each will attempt to gain access to the path after the message from D is received at A. Assuming site C gains access first, site B must wait until C has completed the transmission of its data. Like the polling/selection method, user A will check for errors and send an ACK

or NAK to D when the path becomes available.

The contention control method experiences occasional message collisions. This occurs when more than one site sense an idle line and transmit their messages at approximately the same time as other sites. Now the messages' electrical signals intermix and become distorted. In these situations, the sensing devices must be capable of detecting the collision and must so indicate to the DLC logic. The logic must then direct the sending stations to retransmit the messages that have been distorted.

Contention control is widely used because of its relative simplicity and the absence of a master station. Remember that the polling/selection approach suffers from the vulnerability of the primary site to failure. This could bring down all sites on the link. Since the contention method does not rely on a controlling site, a failed site does not prevent the other sites from communicating with each other. Moreover, the many overhead messages (polls, selections) found in polling/selection methods do not exist in the contention DLCs.

One major disadvantage of a contention DLC is the inability to provide priorities for the use of the transmission path. Since all stations are equal, none has priority over others—even though some user stations and applications may require greater use of the facilities. Since many of the contention DLCs are used on local networks with very high-speed paths, the equal allocation may not be discernible to a station even if it has more frequent access needs than others.

Another potential disadvantage of the contention network is the distance limitation placed on it. For example, if two sites are located at a remote distance from each other, it is possible for both stations to transmit, turn themselves "off" (go to other activities), and never detect the signal or the collision. This is due to the propagation delay of the signals traveling on the line. The contention logic must be designed to handle this situation.

By reserving times of access to the communications path, time-slot control avoids the collision problem found in the contention DLC. For example, in Figure 1 each site or station is given a slot of time on the link. During the period that the station has access to the path, it can send one or a predetermined multiple number of messages. The next station then gains access and transmits its messages across the link.

Time-slot link controls are simple and are found in many applications and networks. Their principal disadvantage is the wasted line capacity that occurs when a station's time slot is not used fully when it has nothing—or nothing more—to transmit. Many time-slot DLCs now avoid this problem with additional capabilities that permit statistical multiplexing.

Error handling

The method of detecting and correcting errors is a key selection criterion for a data link control. Certainly, one option is simply to ignore errors. For instance, the transmission of textual data may not require that every bit of the text arrive error-free. Assuming an error rate of 1 in 10^5 bits, a 400-page book could be transmitted with but 35 Baudot-code characters in error. Such an error rate is not pushing the state of the art by any means. So ignoring errors is a definite option.

On the other hand, many applications cannot afford errors. Financial-data networks electronically transferring funds between customers' bank accounts must have completely accurate data messages arriving at the end point. In these applications, the data link controls must detect and handle any errors that occur on the path.

It is sometimes difficult to appreciate that the reliability and speed of a communications path through a network is appreciably different from the flow of data in a conventional mainframe environment where all components are located in one room or one building. A computer-to-disk channel can operate at data transfer speeds of 10^7 to 10^9 bit/s, with an error rate of 1 in 10^{12} or 10^{13} bits. This is very fast and very reliable. In contrast, a dial-up line transmits data at a rate of 10^3 to 10^4 bit/s, at an error rate of 1 in 10^5 bits. Thus multiplying the bit-transfer rate by the error rate yields ensured bits per second for the inhouse environment that are 11 orders of magnitude better than a dial-up line in a network.

Bit checking

Most methods used to provide for data-error detection usually entail the insertion of redundant bits in the message. The actual bit configuration of the redundant bits is derived from the data bit stream. One common approach, vertical redundancy checking (VRC), is a simple technique. It consists of adding a single bit (a parity bit) to each string of bits that comprises a character. The bit is set to 1 or 0 (zero) to give the character bits an odd or even number of bits that are 1s. This parity bit is inserted at the transmitting station, sent with each character in the message, and checked at the receiver to determine if each character is the correct parity.

If a transmission impairment causes a "bit flip" of 1 to 0 or 0 to 1, the parity check would so indicate. However, a two-bit flip would not be detected by the VRC technique. Thus multilevel modulation (where two or three bits are represented in a signal cycle) requires a more sophisticated technique. The single-bit VRC is also unsuited to most analog voice-grade lines because of the groupings of errors that usually occur on this type of link.

Longitudinal redundancy checking (LRC) is a refinement of the VRC approach. Instead of a parity bit on each character, LRC derives a parity bit (odd or even) based on a block of characters taken from a defined group of characters. This block check provides a method to detect errors "across" characters. It is usually implemented along with VRC, and is then called a two-dimensional parity-check code (Fig. 2). The VRC-LRC combination provides a substantial improvement over a single method. For example, a typical telephone line with an error rate of 1 in 10^5 bits can be improved to a range of 1 in 10^7 with VRC and 1 in 10^9 with the two-dimensional check.

The Hamming Code is a still more sophisticated vari-

2. Minimize errors. *When both vertical and longitudinal redundancy checks are combined, a substantial improvement in the error detection/correction rate may be had.*

CHARACTERS

BITS IN CHARACTERS	1	2	3	n	LRC
1	0	1	0	....	0
2	1	0	0	....	0
3	1	0	1	....	1
4	0	0	1	....	0
5	0	1	0	....	0
6	1	0	1	....	1
7	0	0	1	....	0
VRC →	0	1	1	....	1

ation of the VRC. It uses more than one parity bit per byte or character. The parity bit values are based on various combinations of the user character bits and the parities are inserted in between the bits of the character. For example, in one Hamming code (there are many) a byte of bits $b_1 b_2 b_3 b_4 b_5 b_6 b_7$ carries a 10-bit code as $p_1 b_1 p_2 b_2 b_3 p_3 b_4 b_5 b_6 b_7$. The parity bit p_1 is set odd or even based on the values of $b_1 b_3 b_5$ and b_7. In addition, p_2 is based on $b_2 b_3 b_6 b_7$, and p_3 is based on $b_4 b_5 b_6$ and b_7. The Hamming Code achieves better results than a VRC or an LRC. However, it does carry more overhead.

Several other techniques besides those mentioned are in use for error detection. One that is quite widely used is cyclic redundancy checking (CRC). Figure 3 shows an example of CRC use.

The CRC approach entails the division of the user's binary data stream by a predetermined binary number. The remainder of the number after this division is appended to the message as a group of bits known as a CRC field. The data stream at the receiving site has the identical calculation performed and compared to the CRC field. If the two values of the CRC field are identical, the message is accepted as correct. The divisor polynomial $X^{16} + X^{15} + X^2 + 1$, with a bit-stream representation of 11000000000000101, is often used in cyclic redundancy checking in data communications. It can detect all possible single-error bursts not exceeding 16 bits, 99.9969 percent of all possible single bursts 17 bits long, and 99.9984 percent of all possible longer bursts. This provides for 1 bit error per every 10^{14} bits transmitted, and is much better than the other methods discussed.

Flow control

It should be recognized that a DLC must manage the transmission and receiving of perhaps thousands of messages in a short period of time and move the data traffic efficiently. Communications lines must be evenly used, and no station should be unnecessarily idle or saturated with excessive traffic. Thus flow control is a critical part of the network. Figure 4 depicts the stop-and-wait DLC, which is useful for flow control. This DLC allows one message to be transmitted (event 1), checked for errors with techniques such as VRC or LRC (event 2), and an appropriate ACK or NAK returned to the sending station (event 3). No other data messages can be transmitted until the receiving station sends back a reply. Thus the name "stop-and-wait" is derived from the originating station sending a message, stopping further transmission, and waiting for a reply from the addressee.

The stop-and-wait approach is well suited to half-duplex transmission arrangements because it provides for data transmission in both directions, but only in one direction at a time. Moreover, it is a simple approach requiring no elaborate sequencing of messages or extensive message buffers in the terminals.

Its major drawback is the idle line time that results when the stations are in the wait period. Most stop-and-wait data link controls now provide for more than one terminal on the line. The terminals are still operating under the simple arrangement. They are fairly inexpensive, with limited intelligence. The host or primary station is responsible for interleaving the messages among the terminals (usually through a more intelligent device that is in front of the terminals) and for controlling access to the communications link. Nonetheless, a point-to-point line is underutilized with this approach. In fact, a high-speed stop-and-wait satellite channel may use only 3 to 5 percent of its total capacity.

The simple arrangement depicted in Figure 4 also creates serious problems when the ACK or NAK is lost. If the ACK in event 3 is lost, the master station performs a timeout and retransmits the same message to the secondary site. The redundant transmission could possibly create a duplicate record in the secondary-site user data files. Consequently, data link controls must provide for means to identify and sequence the transmitted messages with the appropriate ACKs or NAKs. Simply put, the logic must have a method to check for duplicate messages.

A typical approach to solve this problem is the provision for a sequence number in the header of the message. The receiver can then check for the sequence number to determine if the message is a duplicate. The stop-and-wait DLC requires a very small sequence number since only one message is outstanding at any time. The sending and receiving stations need only use a one-bit alternating sequence of 0 to 1 to maintain the relationship of the transmitted message and its ACK/NAK.

Figure 5 shows how this arrangement works. In event 1, the sending station transmits a message with the sequence number 0 in the header. The receiving station responds with an ACK and a sequence number of 0 (event 2). The sender receives the ACK, examines the 0 in the header, flips the sequence number to a 1, and transmits the next message (event 3). The receiving station receives and acknowledges the message with an ACK1 in event 4. However, this message is received garbled or lost on the line. The sending station recognizes that the message in event 3 has not been acknowledged. It performs a timeout and retransmits this message (event 5). The receiving station is looking for a message with a sequence number of 0. It discards the message since it is a duplicate of the message transmitted in event 3.

Sliding windows

The inherent inefficiency of the stop-and-wait DLC resulted in techniques for overlapping of data messages and their corresponding control messages. The newer data link controls employ these methods. The data and control signals flow from sender to receiver in a more continuous manner, and several data and control messages can be outstanding (on the line or in the receiver's buffers) at any one time.

These DLCs are often called "sliding windows" because of the method used to synchronize the sending sequence numbers in the headers with the appropriate acknowledgments. The transmitting station maintains a sending window that delineates the number of messages (and their sequence numbers) that it is permitted to send. The receiving station maintains a receiving window that performs complementary functions. The two sites use the windows to coordinate the flow of messages between each other.

In essence, the window states how many messages can be outstanding on the line or at the receiver before the sender stops sending and awaits a reply. For example, in Figure 6A, the receiving of the message-1 ACK allows the San Francisco site to slide its window by one sequence number. If a total of 10 messages could

3. Even better. Cyclic redundancy checking is one of the most efficient error detection/correction schemes. It depends on a comparison of identical calculations performed at the sender's and receiver's sites and is a widely used technique. Most data link control protocols make some form of CRC available to the user.

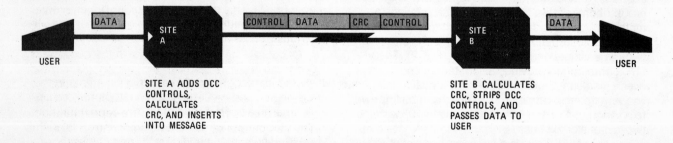

4. Hold it. *The stop-and-wait data link control protocol allows a message to be transmitted, checked for errors, and an appropriate signal to be sent back to the sending station. No other data messages can be transmitted until the receiving station sends this reply. There are many variations to the basic procedure shown.*

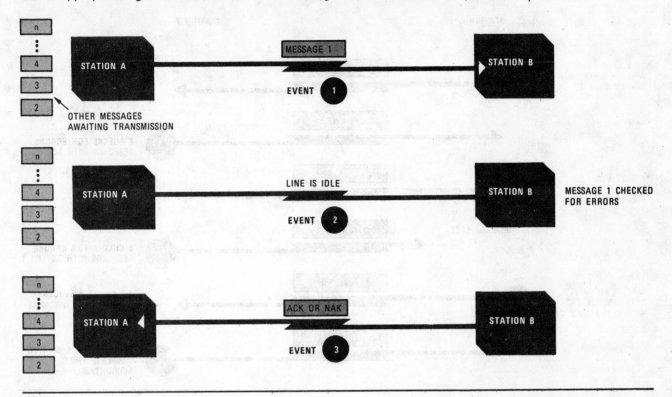

be within the window, San Francisco could still transmit messages 5, 6, 7, 8, 9, 0, 1. Keep in mind that messages 2, 3, 4 are in transit. It could not transmit a message using sequence 2, until it had received an ACK for 2. The window wraps around to re-use the same set of numbers.

Do it again

The "go-back-N" method is a sliding-window technique. It allows data and control messages to be transmitted continuously. In the event an error is detected at the receiving site, the erroneous message is retransmitted as well as all other messages that were transmitted after the erroneous message.

Figure 6 shows the message flow of the go-back-N method. In Figure 6A, messages 2, 3, and 4 are transmitted on the line to Kansas City, and an ACK of previously received message 1 is sent back to San Francisco. Notice the full-duplex transmission scheme. In Figure 6B, messages 4 and 5 are on the path, and Kansas City has now received messages 2 and 3. It determines that message 3 is in error and transmits a NAK to the originating station. San Francisco responds to the NAK in Figure 6C by retransmitting message 3 as well as messages 4 and 5.

The data communications user might question why messages 4 and 5 are retransmitted, since it could mean a duplication of effort and result in wasted resources. These concerns are valid, but the approach also provides a simple means to keep the messages in the proper sequence between the two points. This,

in turn, simplifies the software or chip logic and decreases the length of certain control fields in the message. An error condition on the line (such as a rainstorm on a microwave path) might affect not just one message but the subsequent messages that are traveling down the path as well. For example, a 20-ms distortion on a 50-kbit/s line will distort 1,000 bits, possibly in more than one message. Consequently, these messages may be retransmitted anyway because they are in error.

Almost the same

The selective-repeat method provides for a more refined approach than the go-back-N design. In contrast to the go-back-N, the only messages retransmitted are those that receive a NAK. In Figure 6C, message 3 only is re-sent from the originator in San Francisco. Studies reveal that the selective-repeat DLC obtains greater throughput than the go-back-N.

However, the differences are not great if the comparison is made on a reliable transmission path. The selective-repeat DLC requires additional logic to maintain the sequence of the re-sent message and to merge it into the proper place on the queue at the receiving site. Of course, the message's place in the queue may be gone if subsequent messages have been accepted. The receiving device must be alerted for this. Because of such complications, the go-back-N is found in more data link controls than is the selective-repeat method.

The window size of these data link controls is an important element in the determination of message

5. Enhancement. *To check for duplicated messages, the stop-and-wait data link control protocol may provide for a sequence number in the header of each message. The receiver can check the sequence number to determine if the message is a repeat. Only one message is outstanding at any time so the sequence number is small.*

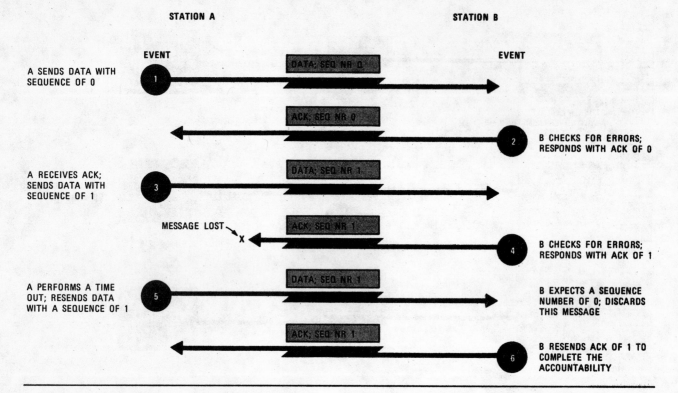

accountability and efficient line use. Due to the delay in signal propagation, a message requires a certain amount of time before all bits of the message arrive at the receiver and the acknowledgment is returned to the sender. The window size should allow for a continuous flow of data. The returned ACKs should arrive before the sender has transmitted all messages within its window. This timing allows the sliding of the sending window and prevents the sender from waiting for the ACK. In other words, the window size should keep the line busy.

Some specific DLCs

To make matters concrete, it is useful to examine three products that use various combinations of the format: line-control, error-handling, and flow-control methods. Since IBM's products are widely used and many other vendors provide IBM-compatible controls, they are used as examples.

The well-known IBM 2740 terminal uses the asynchronous transmission technique. It has options for buffers, but the 2740 logic still provides start and stop bits around each character in the transmission. The 2740 is an old machine, but illustrates an early DLC. It uses an IBM code called extended binary coded decimal (EBCD). This is a six-bit code with a seventh bit inserted for parity checking. In addition, the code provides for functions to control the 2740's print capability—for example, new line, backspace, and uppercase.

The code set is the same for data and control characters. This problem is approached by using special characters to inform the terminal logic that the transmission is either user data or control characters. The EOT (end of transmission) character places the link and all terminals in the control mode, and the EOA (end of address) character places the system in the text (or user data) mode.

The 2740 uses VRC for error detection. The parity bit is turned on to create odd parity of the character. The receiving logic checks each character for an odd number of 1 bits, and signals the transmitter if it detects an error condition. LRC is also used.

This asynchronous method has a considerable amount of overhead. Each character, for example, contains the start and stop bits. Moreover, nine separate transmissions are required to transmit two user data messages, and no other transmissions take place during this process. On the other hand, the approach is a simple arrangement and well suited to low-speed teleprinter applications.

Binary synchronous communications control

BSC is one of the most widely used data link control methods in the United States. Until the advent of SDLC, BSC was IBM's major DLC offering. Many vendors offer a BSC-like data link control. Others offer BSC emulation packages. The product is also called "bisync," a short term for its full title. The method is intended for half-duplex, point-to-point, or multipoint lines.

BSC operates with EBCDIC, ASCII, or Transcode. All stations on a line must use the same code. If ASCII code is used, error checking is accomplished by a VRC

6. Slide over. *The sliding-window data link control proto-col determines how many messages can be outstanding on the line or at the receiver before the sender stops* *transmitting and awaits a reply (A). The go-back-N varia-tion (B) allows messages to be transmitted continually while the selective repeat method (C) allows refinements.*

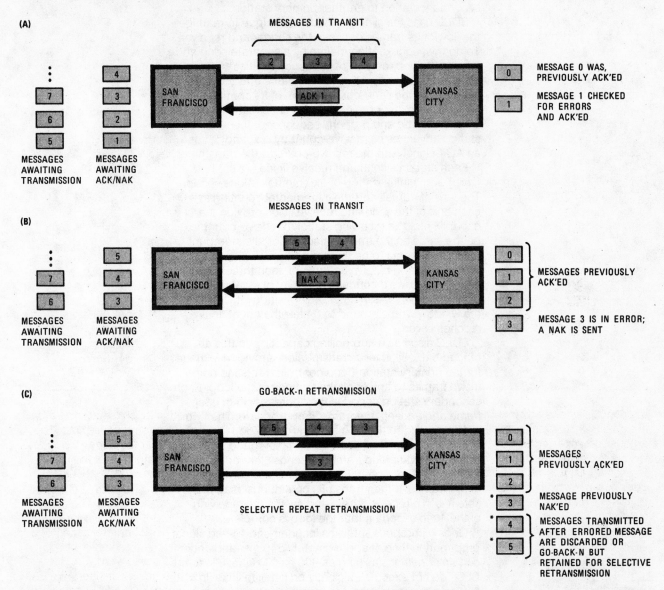

and an LRC. If EBCDIC or Transcode is used, error checking is accomplished by CRC.

BSC uses what is known as the "alternating sequence acknowledgment method." Here the receiving station replies with an ACK0 to the successful reception of even-numbered messages and a ACK1 to odd-numbered messages. A reception of two consecutive identical ACK characters alerts the transmitting station to an exceptional situation.

Up-to-date
BSC was designed in the 1960s. Its early application usually had an operator at the remote station and the half-duplex approach was sufficient. As applications and data communications became more sophisticated, more powerful data link control techniques were eventually needed.

Synchronous data link control (SDLC) is IBM's major DLC offering today. The product was introduced in 1973 to support communications lines among teller terminals in banks. It is widely used in the U.S. and is quite similar to and considered a subset of the international standard HDLC. The product is in many of IBM's communications components and may eventually replace IBM's BSC offering.

SDLC uses the synchronous bit-oriented go-back-N method. It controls a single line configured as point-to-point, multipoint, or loop. It operates on half-duplex, duplex, switched, or private lines. It also provides for duplex multipoint operation in which a station can transmit to another station while continuing to receive from still another.

SDLC uses variations of the polling/selection technique. The primary station is responsible for the control of the line. It initiates all transmissions from the secondary stations with a command. The stations reply with a response. In addition, the primary station can be a secondary station to another primary station.

SDLC uses the sliding-window technique to manage the flow of its frames between the sender and receiver. To do this, each station maintains a separate send and receive "count" as part of its responsibilities. A sending station counts each outgoing frame and transmits the count in the send-count portion of its control field. The receiving station receives and checks the frame. If it is error-free and properly sequenced, the receive station advances its receive-count by one and sends an ACK signal with the receive-count to the transmitter.

Each station's send and receive fields are set to 0 (zero) at the initialization of a communications session. The flow of frames and the incremental counting at each end of the send and receive fields provide the capability for the receiving station's receive-count to be the same as the transmitting station's send-count of the next frame to be transmitted.

The send and receive counts are each three bits long. This allows a counting capacity of eight using binary numbers. As in most sliding-window techniques, the window wraps around to 0 after the count finally reaches seven.

SDLC also has a hub polling capability. In this arrangement, called loop transmission, provision is made for the primary station (loop controller) to send command frames to any or all the stations of the loop. Each secondary station decodes the address field of each frame and accepts the frame, if appropriate. The frame is also passed to the next station (down-loop station).

After the loop controller has completed the transmission of the command frames, it sends eight consecutive 0s to signal the secondary stations of the completion of the frames. It then transmits continuous 1s to indicate it is in a receive mode, and awaits the receiving of the 1s to ascertain that the loop is complete.

Geosynchronous satellites incur an end-to-end signal propagation time of approximately 540 ms, and under certain conditions as long as 900 ms. As a result, some DLCs do not execute efficiently on satellite links. In fact, in some instances, the propagation delay can cause the DLC software to wrap around itself, continuously executing its timeout code waiting for the incoming message.

Additionally, a stop-and-wait technique such as bi-sync would spend a good deal of valuable channel time awaiting the next block of data. But a sliding-window technique such as SDLC is well suited to satellite transmission, due to the continuous sending and receiving of messages between the sites.

Satellite vendors offer components that allow a user to maintain the older data link controls. The components, called delay compensation units, terminate the user's DLC locally and build another data block into a delay-insensitive DLC. The unit responds locally to the terminal or computer as if it were the remote site. ■

This article is adapted from Data Communications, Networks & Distributed Systems, *published by Reston Publishing Co. Inc., Reston, Va.*

Terence D. Smetanka, IBM Corporation, Research Triangle Park, N.C., and Martin A. Reed, IBM Corporation, Gaithersburg, Md.

How to choose between half- and full-duplex SDLC

Model for comparing throughput rates of half-duplex normal response mode and full-duplex asynchronous balanced mode aids a network manager's planning.

The data communications manager makes many decisions when configuring a network. One of the fundamental choices is that of choosing among the many variations of data links and their related protocols. To help make this choice, researchers at IBM have compared, with the aid of a mathematical model, the response time and throughput rates of half- and full-duplex versions of the commonly used serial-by-bit protocol known as synchronous data link control (SDLC). This model of half-duplex and full-duplex point-to-point data links shows that full duplex is usually a better performer.

With the models presented here, the data communications manager can compare the benefits of SDLC full-duplex data links in the normal response mode with SDLC half-duplex links in the asynchronous balanced mode. These are the most common configurations.

Conversely, the models can be used individually to compare various configurations of the asynchronous balanced mode in full duplex or the normal response mode in half duplex. For example, the model can show that a higher-grade link can reduce the bit error rate, in turn, lowering the link response time and raising its throughput.

When in the normal response mode, a secondary station cannot initiate a transmission until directed to do so by the polling primary station. In contrast, in the asynchronous balanced mode the secondary station can initiate a transmission without being requested to do so by the primary station. Also in the asynchronous balanced mode, each station is a "combined" station containing both the primary and secondary station logic. Thus each station can act simultaneously as a primary and secondary station. But in the normal response mode, there is one primary station and one

or more secondary stations per data link.

Before the analytical models can be explained, it is necessary to understand the SDLC frame structure. A data message consists of one or more SDLC frames. Each of these contains up to six fields (Fig. 1). A frame is bounded by opening and closing flags, each of which has the bit pattern 01111110. To ensure the uniqueness of these flags, a zero-bit insertion algorithm is applied to the address, control, information, and frame-check-sequence fields. This means that whenever five contiguous one bits are encountered, a zero bit is inserted into the data stream by the sending station. When the frame arrives at the receiving station, the zero bits are extracted.

The address field differs depending on the SDLC mode. In the normal response mode, the address field contains the address of the secondary station that is receiving and transmitting data. A primary station will only accept frames with addresses of secondary stations that are authorized by the primary station to transmit. In a point-to-point asynchronous balanced mode—the case of interest here—the link stations contain both a primary and secondary station. Either station can transmit commands (acting as a primary) or responses (acting as a secondary). To comply with the CCITT's X.25 standard, the primary station's address is binary 00000001, while the secondary station's address is 00000011. There are, of course, many other such bit specifications for the X.25 fields, but they are not of interest here.

The control field also varies depending on the SDLC mode. In general, the control field contains the commands and responses required to control the data link. For example, each station maintains a sending and receiving sequence number, designated as $N(s)$ and $N(r)$, respectively. The control field contains both the current count of frames sent, N(s), and the number of the frame that the sender next expects to receive from the receiver, N(r). To ensure correct bookkeeping, N(r) is incremented upon receipt of each error-free frame, only when the received N(s) matches the N(r) count. In the comparisons made in this analysis, an extended control field is assumed. This means that up to 127 frames may be outstanding (unacknowledged) at one time. This is said to be a modulo count of 128 in the N(s) and N(r) subfields. (It is important to note, however, that IBM's Model 3705 communications controller running the network control program does not currently support SDLC modulo 128 or the asynchronous balanced mode. But IBM experiments show that, apart from extreme cases, there are instances where the performance of the normal response mode, supported by the company's network control program, and the asynchronous balanced mode is similar.)

A transmission error is detected when an N(s), N(r) mismatch occurs. In the half-duplex normal response mode, this mismatch can be detected without the use of a reject supervisory frame. In contrast, in the full-duplex asynchronous balanced mode a reject supervisory frame is sent by the receiving station in order to cause the transmitting station to begin the retransmission of data. The retransmission of SDLC frames for both the normal response and asynchronous balanced modes of operation is one whereby the frame in error and all subsequent frames are present.

The control field also contains the poll/final (P/F) bit. This bit is used in the normal response mode to synchronize the transmission of frames. The P bit is used by the primary station to poll a secondary station for input, while the F bit allows the secondary station to inform the primary station when a frame is the last one sent in a transmission.

In the asynchronous balanced mode, the P bit is used to solicit a response frame with the F bit set "on." This P/F bit cycle provides a backup technique for detecting frames received in error as a result of data-link transmission errors in the asynchronous balanced mode. Once a "combined" station sends a command with the P bit set to one, a timeout sequence is started. When the timeout expires—prior to the receipt of a response frame with the F bit set—retransmission of the frame with the P bit is initiated.

Perhaps the most important part of the frame from the data communications manager's viewpoint, the information field contains user data to be transferred across the data link. Any type of code (EBCDIC or ASCII, for example) may be conveyed. The content and format of this data is transparent to the SDLC protocol. The information field may also contain supervisory information required by higher levels of a layered network structure such as IBM's systems network architecture (SNA).

For example, in SNA the user data is prefixed by a 26-byte transmission header, a 3-byte request/response header, and an optional function-management header. It is important for the data communications user to remember that information

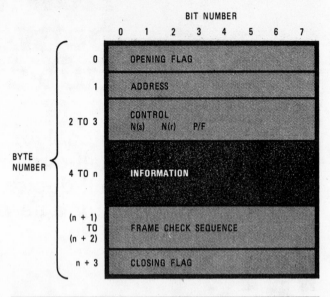

1. Extended frame structure. *IBM's SDLC is a subset of the ISO's high-level data-link control protocol. The opening and closing flags are identical.*

frames are the only type of frame that contain both the N(s) and N(r) counts in the control field.

The last field, the 16-bit frame check sequence, is used to provide a cyclic redundancy check. All the bits contained between the opening and closing flags are included in the cyclic redundancy check, except any that may have been inserted by the zero-bit insertion algorithm. If the frame check sequence indicates a transmission error, the receiving station will not increment its N(r) count.

Analysis

The setting up of the models for the SDLC networks for either the full-duplex asynchronous balanced mode or the half-duplex normal response mode, while not difficult, is no easy task. It should be set up by a systems analyst who is capable of translating the actual networks into models that can be analyzed by the describing equations (see "Setting up the model"). These equations are then programmed for computer solution. Only then can a sensitivity analysis be undertaken by varying any one model input or their combinations. Thus the link error rate, SDLC modulo, frame size, message size, link speed, and round-trip delay can be varied. Round-trip delay should include all the components of response time other than the actual frame transmission time. Thus modem transit delay, modem turnaround time, acknowledgment transmission time, central processing unit or network control processor time, and propagation delay of the link, among others, are considered. The model output can be either the link response time or the link throughput, as either of these variables is of interest to both the network designer and the network user.

Figure 2 is a good example of the results that can be achieved by using IBM's analytic performance model. The independent variable labeled "maxout" is

2. Which is better? *The half-duplex response time is longer than that of the full-duplex, regardless of the maxout, a measure of the number of frames outstanding.*

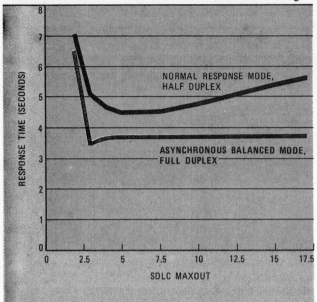

the SDLC modulo. The dependent variable, or output, is the data-link response time. The link analyzed in this example is 9.6-kbit/s terrestrial with an error rate of one bit in 10^4. The frame consists of 128 user data bytes and 36 SDLC and SNA header bytes. The round-trip delay is 0.25 second while the asynchronous-balanced-mode timeout is 0.5 second. The message size is approximately 2,048 bytes. This is about the size of an IBM 3270 full screen.

For the half-duplex normal response mode, an optimal data-link response time of 4.4 seconds is achieved when the modulo count is 6. For all maxout

cases, the full-duplex asynchronous-balanced-mode data-link response time is less than that of the half-duplex normal-response-mode data link. In fact, a response time of just 3.6 seconds is possible for the full-duplex asynchronous-balanced-mode data link. Of course, other networks with different parameters will give their own range of calculated response times.

Another variation

With the use of IBM's advanced communications function release 3 architecture, more than one physical link can be associated with a logical link, known as a transmission group, for links between two nodes governed by an IBM network control program (Fig. 3). Data in SNA communications (logical connections between two network-addressable units) is thus capable of being transmitted over more than one physical link spanning two network control programs as long as the links are a member of one transmission group. There is no physical limit to the number of links that can be combined into a transmission group. Only the 3705 hardware limits the transmission-group size. Figure 4 shows the results of using the analytical model to predict the performance of a variable number of satellite links combined into the transmission group spanning the network control programs shown in Figure 3.

When a transmission group has more than one SDLC data link, the individual frames of the message may be sent over any link in the group. To reconstruct the message, the receiving station simply reorders the frames received. By assuming that a message's bits are equally distributed over the transmission group's data links, the SDLC model can be applied to a transmission group consisting of more than one link. This is usually a valid procedure.

In this configuration, the analysis is performed by

3. Multiple links. *With appropriate software, more than one physical link can be associated with a transmission group, with no limit to the number of grouped links.*

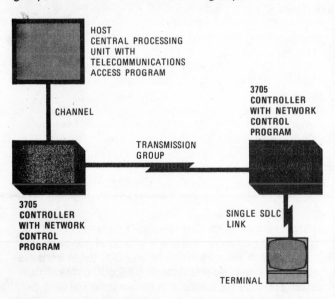

4. Difference. *The asynchronous balanced mode in full duplex has a greater throughput, regardless of the number of node links. Each message contains 25,600 bytes.*

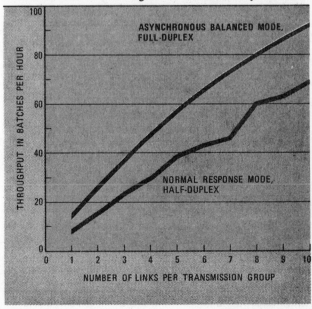

Setting up the model

IBM does not provide services to model customer's networks with the procedures that result in the information shown in Figures 2 and 4. But this can be done by appropriately trained personnel. The defining equations presented here are most easily programmed in PL-1 and APL, although Fortran can also be used.

The two dependent variables of interest—regardless of the network being in the half-duplex normal response mode or the full-duplex asynchronous balanced mode—are designated as N and τ. N is the mean message response time in seconds, and τ is the data link throughput in messages per second.

Following is information needed to calculate these two quantities:

B = number of user information bytes per frame.
BER = bit error rate (randomly distributed).
BPS = transmission rate of the link in bits per second.
D = round-trip delay in seconds.
DF = D/X.
j = particular level of transmission, 1 to L,
    (half-duplex normal-response-mode model only).
K = particular frame, 1 to n,
    (half-duplex normal-response-mode model only).
L = total number of transmission levels considered,
    (half-duplex normal-response-mode model only).
M = SDLC modulo (maxout).
n = number of frames per message.
p = probability of an error in a frame.
q = probability of an error-free frame.
S = 8(B + 36); frame size in bits.
TO = time-out internal in seconds (full-duplex
    asynchronous-balanced-mode model only).
X = S/BPS; frame transmission time in seconds.

There are several assumptions and definitions that are needed. Since the BER is assumed to be random, we have $p = 1-(1-BER)^s$. We define 0/0 to be 1 whenever it occurs. Moreover,

$$\sum_{i=a}^{b} \Phi(i) = 0 \text{ if } b < a.$$

And finally, we define $a\Gamma b$ = the larger of a and b; aLb = the smaller of a and b; Γa = the smallest integer greater than or equal to a; and La = the largest integer less than or equal to a.

In the half-duplex normal-response-mode model, we have $N = N_F X + N_L D$ and $\tau = 1/N$. Here N_F denotes the average number of frames transmitted. This figure includes frames retransmitted because of errors. N_L denotes the mean number of transmission levels required. It is also necessary to define

$$N_F = \sum_{j=1}^{L} E_j \qquad \text{and } N_L = \sum_{j=1}^{L} V_j \qquad \text{where}$$

$$E_j = \begin{cases} (M-1)Ln & j = 1 \\ \sum_{K=1}^{n} (P_{j-1,K} + P'_{j-1,K})[((M-1)Ln)-(K-1)] & j > 1 \end{cases}$$

$$V_j = \begin{cases} 1 & j = 1 \\ \sum_{K=1}^{n} (P_{j-1,K} + P'_{j-1,K}) & j > 1 \end{cases}$$

distributing the message size equally over the transmission group. Thus, if the actual message size is x frames per message and the transmission group contains n links, the model is applied with a message size of x/n frames. The fact that x/n may not be an integer is the cause of the perturbations seen in the

normal-response-mode half-duplex results in Figure 4. These slope changes are not a source of concern.

In Figure 4, the batch size of 512,000 bytes consists of 20 messages, each containing 25,600 bytes. This batch size reflects a facsimile transmission of an 8.5-by-11-inch page scanned at 8 lines per millimeter. Each

$$P_{jK} = T_{jK}p^j q^{K-1}$$

$$T_{jK} = \begin{cases} \sum_{a=0}^{(\Gamma(K/M-1))-1} (-1)^a (C_{j+1-a,\,a+1})(C_{j,\,K-a(M-1)}) & \text{for } K < M + (j-1)(M-2) \\[12pt] 0 & \text{otherwise,} \end{cases}$$

and $C_{jK} = \dfrac{(j+K-2)!}{(K-1)!(j-1)!}$. Finally,

$$P'_{jK} = \begin{cases} \sum_{a=1}^{\Gamma\left((K-M+1)+(M-1)\right)} (C_{j+1-a,\,a+1})(T_{j-a,\,K-a(M-1)})p^{j-a}q^{K-1} & \text{for } M-1 < K < M + (M-1)(j-1) \\[12pt] q^{K-1} & \text{for } K = j(M-1)+1 \\[8pt] 0 & \text{otherwise} \end{cases}$$

Note that the total number of transmission levels (L) must be set to a practical finite value such that levels $L+1, L+2, \ldots$ can be neglected. A suggested value is one whereby the number of frames transmitted on level L is less than 10^{-5}.

Another set of equations is needed for the full-duplex asynchronous-balanced-mode model. Here $N = T + W$ and $\tau = 1/N$. Then

$$T = nX + D + \left[\left(\Gamma\frac{n}{M-1}\right) - 1\right]\left[0\Gamma X(DF - (M-2))\right] \quad \text{where}$$

$$W = \begin{cases} \dfrac{nXp[1+q(DF+1)]}{q^2} + \left[\dfrac{q\,TO - X(1+q\,DF)}{q^2}\right]\sum_{i=1}^{n} p^{\zeta(i,1)} & \text{for } DF \le M-2 \\ & \text{or } n \le 1 \\[16pt] \left[\sum_{i=1}^{n}\sum_{a=1}^{iL(M-1)} R(i,a)\left\{\dfrac{Xp}{q}\left[1+q(DF+1)\right] + p^{\zeta(i,a)}\left[TO - X(DF+1) - \dfrac{Xp}{q}\right]\right\}\right] + \\[16pt] \left[\dfrac{nXp^2[1+q(DF+1)]}{q^2} + \left[\dfrac{pq\,TO - pX(1+q\,DF)}{q^2}\right]\sum_{i=1}^{n} p^{\zeta(i,1)}\right] & \text{for } DF > M-2 \\ & n > M-1 \end{cases}$$

$$\text{and } R(i,a) = \begin{cases} 1 & \text{for } i=1, j=1 \\[8pt] \left[pq^{a-2}\,\mathbf{L}\sum_{v=0\Gamma(2-a)}^{\frac{i-a-1}{M-1}} q^{v(M-1)}\right] + q^{i-2}\left[\mathbf{L}\,\mathbf{L}^{\left(\frac{i-a}{M-1}\right)}_{\frac{i-a}{M-1}}\right] & \text{for } 2 \le i \le n \\ & 1 \le a \le (M-1)Li \\[8pt] 0 & \text{otherwise} \end{cases}$$

In all cases, $\zeta(i,a) = (n - (i-1))L(M-a)$.

Once the equations for the half-duplex normal-response-mode and the full-duplex asynchronous-balanced-mode models are programmed, they may be called by the data communication manager at any time. He can change any or all of the input variables to see their effects on network throughput and response time. Thus the comparison of alternate implementation schemes will be both straightforward and inexpensive since the computer simulation is the equivalent of a prototype network.

message must be sent in its entirety before the next message of the batch is transmitted. The frame size is 256 user data bytes plus 36 SDLC and SNA overhead bytes. The individual links in the transmission group were satellite links at a 19.2-kbit/s rate with an error rate of one error in 10^6 bits. The SDLC modulo was assumed to be 8, a typical case. As expected, the transmission groups in the full-duplex asynchronous balanced mode can sustain a higher throughput than the same transmission groups operating in the half-duplex normal response mode, and a greater number of links per group allows a higher throughput. ■

Harold C. Folts, data communications consultant, Vienna, Va.

Coming of age: A long-awaited standard for heterogeneous nets

Open systems interconnection, a forthcoming international standard, is a solution to the problem of linking incompatible computers.

Builders agree that a structure designed to weather the ages must have a sound, orderly architecture. The same tenet applies to the data communications industry. In the development of early data communications networks and the formulation of ensuing standards, little consideration was given to the relationship between the existing standards, proprietary protocols, and system architectures. This was due partly to a lack of foresight, but also to vendors' deliberate efforts to gain a competitive edge.

Awareness of this dilemma and its ramifications peaked in 1977 when the International Standards Organization's (ISO) Technical Committee 97 established a subcommittee, SC 16, to address the problem. The subcommittee was chartered to develop an architec-

ture that would be the framework for defining standards for linking heterogeneous computer networks. Its proposal—the open systems interconnection (OSI) reference model—provides the basis for interconnecting "open" systems for distributed applications processing. The term "open" denotes the ability of an end-system of one manufacturer (or design) to connect with any other end-system conforming to the reference model and the associated standard protocols. When OSI is completed, end-system application processes will be able to communicate through the resulting open systems interconnection environment.

Because of the diversity of today's complex networks, these application processes can be correspondingly diverse. They might include, for example, a person

16

operating a manual keyboard-entry terminal, a credit-checking program, an industrial production-line-control program or sensor, or an endless range of distributed processing applications.

In the OSI model, these application processes, or APs, could be one or a group of activities that execute a specific set of procedures according to a computer's instructions. In distributed applications processing, it is frequently necessary for APs to communicate in order to perform a larger, more complex task than they could perform individually. Communications is likewise required for geographically dispersed computers that need to operate as a cooperative unit.

The OSI reference model addresses the interconnections and communications among the end-user APs of a spectrum of systems, regardless of their manufacturers and internal designs. Its universally applicable logical structure serves as a bench mark for analyzing the areas where standards are needed, determining the adequacy of existing standards, and enabling the orderly evolution of technology.

Collective effort

Since the ISO SC 16's first meeting in March 1978, its efforts have accelerated with intense participation from many countries. Active participants include the national standards bodies of the United States (ANSI, for one), Canada, the United Kingdom, Japan, France, the Netherlands, and the Federal Republic of Germany, as well as the European Computer Manufacturers Association (ECMA), a trade organization. In addition, the International Telegraph and Telephone Consultative Committee (CCITT) recognized the significance of such a reference model to the design of new public data networks and related services. CCITT therefore appointed a special group to develop a compatible reference model for international data communications services.

By the ISO subcommittee's second meeting in June 1979, the architecture had developed significantly. A working draft (version 2) of the OSI reference model, known as document ISO/TC 97/SC 16 N227, was published and widely distributed for further study and comment. The CCITT special group continued its work, using N227 as a basis, and advanced its efforts at joint meetings with ISO in May and October of 1980. This past November, the ISO SC 16 completed the third version of the OSI reference model, which was considered mature enough for the ISO to start soliciting letters of approval from member nations.

The OSI reference model will have a profound impact in the very near future on all facets of data communications and distributed applications processing. Since the subject is complex and the model is evolving into its advanced stages, an overview of the architecture's basic structure is necessary for a fundamental understanding of this effort.

Layering by function

There is a continuum of functions involved in an OSI communication. Consequently, ISO chose the principle of layering through partitioning, or logically grouping the necessary functions, as the method of defining the

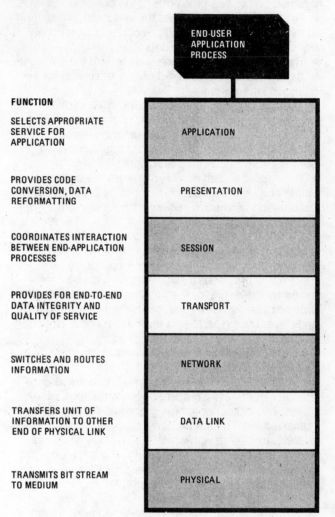

1. Functional layering. *ISO has solidified a seven-layer structure for OSI. Each layer is composed of functionally separate units that provide specialized services.*

reference model. Because there are several viable ways of doing this, the subcommittee structured the architecture by following some basic premises.

The functional partitions should not be too narrow, or each layer will be more complex than it needs to be. On the other hand, the functional groupings should not be so large that they can no longer be reasonably managed. The layers should contain the functions that work most logically together and complement each other. Additionally, the partitioning should ensure that the largest range of present and foreseeable applications can be accommodated. Lastly, the arrangement must be acceptable to those users and vendors whom it will affect. The solution, therefore, is not only technical but political as well.

Although there is still some disagreement among ISO members as to the finer details of the reference model's individual layers, the firm basis of seven layers is now accepted. These seven layers, as illustrated in Figure 1, can be described as follows.

■ The physical layer provides for the transparent transmission of the bit streams to the connecting physical transmission media.

■ The data link layer handles the transfer of a unit of information between the ends of the physical link.

■ The network layer governs the switching and routing of the information to establish a connection for the transparent delivery of the data.

■ The transport layer assures end-to-end data integrity and provides for the required quality of service for exchanged information.

■ The session layer coordinates the interaction between the communicating end-application processes.

■ The presentation layer provides for any necessary translation, format conversion, or code conversion to put the information into a recognizable form.

■ The application layer directly serves the communicating end-user application process by providing the distributed information service appropriate to the application and its management.

Figure 2 illustrates a logical grouping of functions that is identified as a specific layer N. A function is a logical entity that accepts one or more inputs (arguments) and produces a single output (value) determined by the nature of the function. Functions can be grouped in a collective unit that is then defined to be an N layer having an N + 1 layer as an upper boundary and an N − 1 layer as a lower boundary.

In addition, one or more functional units within a layer can provide a set of services to the N + 1 layer, facilitating the OSI communication. There are also interactions between adjacent layers in the form of requests and indications (or responses). These are called primitives (B). The interaction primitives can have associated parameters with which they convey additional information between layers. Finally, there is a peer protocol (C) that provides the necessary procedures for the functional units within a specific layer to interact with each other and exchange information. These structural concepts, which ISO has incorporated in OSI, help to explain the interrelationship of the layer services, primitives, parameters, and functions.

The OSI environment
How does the OSI reference model fit into the overall communications scheme? Within an "open system," the OSI users are application processes, which are shown in Figure 3 as "X" in end-system I and as "Y" in end-system II. These are each located within their respective local system environments (LSEs).

When an AP in one end-system wants to communicate with an AP in a distant end-system, the interconnection is performed by the OSI environment (OSIE), or open communications environment (OCE), as it is called in the current CCITT proposal. The local system manager (LSM) provides the control for invoking the OSIE functions to create the interconnection and facilitate the desired communications.

The APs communicate through the application layer window and the underlying layers along the path shown. A peer protocol for each layer controls and coordinates the designated functions between the communicating end-systems. Within the OSIE are the

seven functional layers and their respective peer protocols. Outside the OSIE are the end-systems containing the LSMs and the APs. The physical transmission medium, incidentally, is also outside the OSIE. By themselves, LSEs are "closed" systems. They become "open" when they communicate through the OSIE.

The interaction between the functional layers and protocols and the LSM is detailed in Figure 4. Each OSIE layer has a layer-management function to control its operation (such as layer activation/deactivation, monitoring, and error control). The system-interconnection-management functions, shown as part of the LSE, monitor the various resources and their status, using specific management protocols. These protocols are outside the scope of OSI.

The system-interconnection-management functions control the local system activation/deactivation, the resources used, and the data transfer (within the local system). They coordinate the interaction primitives between the layers and manage the performance of the functions and peer protocols. The resulting services collectively enable the APs to communicate.

Local system interface
The application layer directly serves the AP and provides the window through which the communications move in and out of the OSIE. The layer provides distributed services to the AP for its management and performs the functions that initiate the overall interconnection and data transfer. Also, user-specified parameters are made known to the OSIE through this layer.

Examples of services that will probably be provided by the application layer to the AP user are:
■ Identification of intended communications partners
■ Agreement on privacy mechanisms
■ Authentication of intended communicants
■ Determination of cost of the allocation methodology
■ Determination of adequacy of required resources
■ Determination of the acceptable quality of service
■ Agreement on responsibility for error recovery
■ Information transfer

The interaction primitives for this layer are presently undefined. A typical example might be an INTERCONNECTION REQUEST from the AP, with parameters giving the name/address of the destination AP, the minimum error rate required, and the nature of the outgoing communication. For an incoming communication, there might be an INTERCONNECTION INDICATION to the AP, with parameters supplying the name/address of the communications source.

At this time, the functions performed by the application layer are only basically identified and require further definition. They include, however, initiation of the interconnection, termination of the interconnection, synchronization, commitment of resources, tasking, and information transfer.

Peer protocols for the application layer fall into three general categories: system management, applications management, and user application. The system-management protocols include activation/deactivation management, monitoring, error control, and recovery. The application-management protocols provide for

2. Primitives and protocols. *Services are provided by subjoining layers to higher layers. This is done with primitives and parameters, exchanged between layers, that indicate certain conditions and activate the layer's functional entities. Additionally, a peer protocol handles interaction between units of the same layer.*

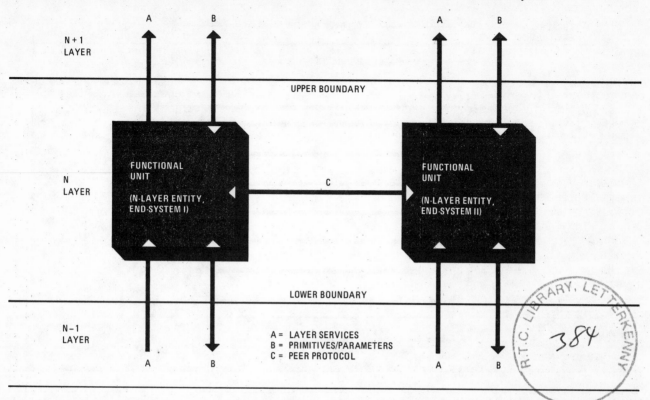

authentication, access control, accounting, deadlock recovery, and commitment. The user-application protocols enable remote job entry, subprocess selection (specific module within an application), and file access. Additional user-application protocols may be industry-specific, such as for banking or airlines operations.

Presentation functions

The presentation layer provides services that the application layer can request to interpret the meaning of the data being communicated. These services manage the entry, exchange, display, and control of structured data in a form appropriate for the AP. This includes code and format conversion.

Services that this layer would typically provide to the application layer are:

■ Data transformation: code and character set translations
■ Information formatting: modification of data layout
■ Syntax selection: initial selection and subsequent modification of the transformations and formats used

An example of a primitive at this layer could be PRESENTATION CONNECTION REQUEST. The associated parameters would include coding and formatting information required for the communication. As with the application layer, the finer details of the primitives and their parameters are still under study.

To accomplish all these services, the presentation layer may need to perform a number of specific functions, such as presentation-service establishment, service initialization, image negotiation, information transformation and formatting, and presentation-service release. The initialization functions perform the start-up of operations, while the image negotiations determine the necessary conversions interactively with the peer functions at the distant end, in order to deliver data that can be interpreted by the receiving AP. Negotiations would normally occur at the beginning of the connection, but they could also be conducted during the connection if some characteristics need to be changed.

Three types of peer protocols have been identified for the presentation layer and are currently under active development within standards organizations. The first of these, the virtual terminal protocol, will handle a number of terminal classes and parameter profiles to accommodate different applications. In addition, a virtual file protocol will enable the formatting of file-store commands, communication of file information, and code conversion. Finally, a job transfer and manipulation protocol will provide for control of record structures and related devices, command formatting, and data formatting.

Session control

The session layer, subjacent to the presentation layer, is the last layer concerned with high-level functions not directly involved with the networking mechanisms. Its services coordinate interactions between the presentation-layer entities at each end of the connection. A cooperative relationship, called a "session," is set up between the end-presentation functional units. Although the session layer can be composed of several

3. Structured message flow. *A message generated in one local system enters the OSI environment through a window of the applications layer. After being processed by each of the seven layers, a formatted message traverses the transmission medium. The process is then repeated in reverse at the destination local system.*

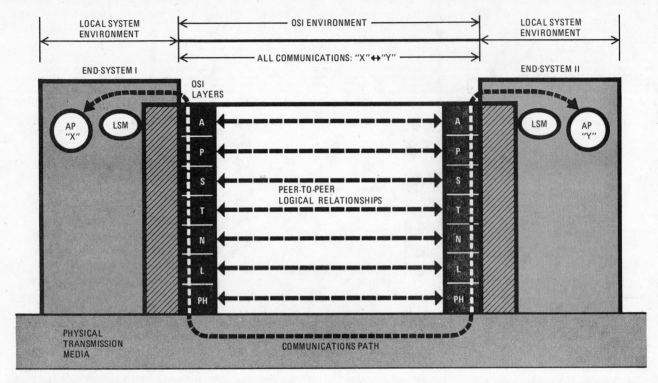

session functional units, all operating separately, there is only a one-to-one correspondence between each presentation-layer entity and a session-layer entity. There is no multiplexing between the two.

The session layer provides these services to the presentation layer:

- Session-connection establishment and termination binds and unbinds the two presentation entities in a cooperating relationship.
- Session-connection management enables the presentation entities to determine cooperatively the unique values of the operating parameters.
- User data exchange supports the transfer of a unit of data and prevents the receiving presentation entity from being overloaded with data.
- Data quarantine affords the sending presentation entity explicit control of data units to be delivered to the receiving presentation entity. The sending entity may also request that "quarantined" data be discarded before delivery.
- Interaction management is the dialog control used to establish a two-way simultaneous interaction, a two-way alternate interaction, or a one-way interaction (send-only from one end and receive-only at the other end). It provides for identification of the type of dialog, initial first-turn to send, and both voluntary and involuntary exchange of transmission opportunity in the case of two-way alternate transactions.

Although the interaction primitives (requests and indications) are not yet well defined, they can be rationalized in the context of the associated services.

For example, with two-way alternate operation, a SEND DATA REQUEST primitive would establish the appropriate direction of dialog for the communication. Also, a parameter might identify a unit of data as being expedited, giving it precedence in any queues en route and priority over any data sent subsequently.

Many functions within the session layer are readily implied by the services being provided. A few others, not so obvious, include mapping session connections into transport connections provided by the subjacent layer, flow control, and connection recovery.

Some preliminary work has been done in developing protocols for this layer, but none is very advanced at this time. The new Bell System version of the CCITT X.25 packet-switching protocol (called BX.25), for example, has described a session layer protocol to work with X.25 network services, but it includes combined functions associated both with the above presentation layer and the underlying transport layer. Further standards work in this area will accelerate soon.

The transport layer is intended to provide a network-independent transport service to the upper layers that is transparent to the types of underlying network services. It would ideally optimize use of the available communications services and ensure the requested quality of service for the communications by providing any needed enhancements.

The services provided by the transport layer to the session layer are:

- Connection establishment between one or more session entities within each end-system. The connec-

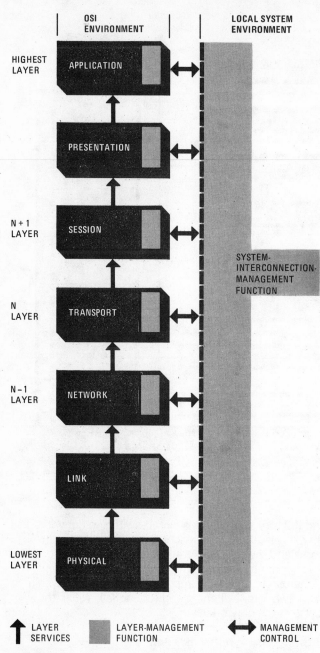

4. Local system interaction. *Each OSI layer contains a layer-management function that interacts with correspondent management applications in the local system.*

OSI ENVIRONMENT | LOCAL SYSTEM ENVIRONMENT

HIGHEST LAYER — APPLICATION

PRESENTATION

N + 1 LAYER — SESSION

SYSTEM-INTERCONNECTION-MANAGEMENT FUNCTION

N LAYER — TRANSPORT

N – 1 LAYER — NETWORK

LINK

LOWEST LAYER — PHYSICAL

↑ LAYER SERVICES   ▮ LAYER-MANAGEMENT FUNCTION   ↔ MANAGEMENT CONTROL

tains several parameters, including calling and called addresses, required facilities (operational services), and the quality of service required. A CLEAR INDICATION notifies that the transport connection has been terminated. Parameters for this primitive would contain information as to the reason for a session's termination, such as network failure. There are many more primitives that can be readily conceived, and these will be listed as the reference model matures.

The transport layer's functions include selecting the appropriate network service, multiplexing transport connections on a single network connection (to optimize the cost of transmission), establishing an optimum data unit size for the underlying services, mapping the transport addresses onto the network connection, detecting errors in received data (including loss, corruption, duplication, misrecording, or misdelivery), bypassing flow control for expedited data, and purging data along the transport connection to facilitate recovery from an abnormal situation.

Work in the area of transport peer protocols has advanced further than that for the upper layers. CCITT has finalized and approved a transport layer protocol in Recommendation S.70 for its new Teletex services (an office-oriented text-transmission service). In addition, work in ISO and ECMA is advancing rapidly and now includes CCITT S.70 as a class of operation. The Department of Defense's ARPA (Advanced Research Projects Agency) transmission control protocol (TCP, version 4) is one example of a functionally rich protocol that provides an extremely high quality of service.

Switched network support
The network layer provides the means to establish, maintain, and disestablish switched network connections. Additionally, it provides for exchange of data units between transport entities over the established network connections. The control of network connections at this layer applies equally to circuit-switching as well as to packet-switching networks. Earlier versions of the reference model excluded circuit-switching call establishment from this layer, but the functionality was recognized as being the same, regardless of the implementing technology.

These services are provided by the network layer to the transport layer:
■ Network connection sets up a transmission path through a switched network.
■ Connection endpoint identification provides the transport layer's functional unit with a unique identification of the associated network connection.
■ Error notification indicates unrecovered errors to the transport layer to enable any recovery action.
■ Sequence control is an optional service maintained by the network layer on request from the transport layer. A datagram network service, alternatively, does not provide for sequencing of data.
■ Data unit delivery confirmation notifies the transport layer that a particular data unit has been delivered and acknowledged by the distant transport entity.

There are several interaction request and indication primitives identified in the latest CCITT version of the

tion will not necessarily be broken if services supplied by the underlying layers are disrupted, thus affording the opportunity for recovery.
■ Data transfer.
■ Flow control. With this service, the session layer can dynamically request to limit data delivered from the transport layer. This would be accomplished through the peer protocol controlling the flow from the other end of the connection.

The CCITT, in its latest draft, has identified a number of interaction primitives, called "elements," for this layer. A CONNECTION REQUEST from the session layer con-

5. Frame construction. *The application-process data unit is appended with a control header (containing information defined in the peer protocol) by each of the seven functional layers. The original data, combined with the header of a specific layer, is viewed by the subjoining layer as an integral data unit.*

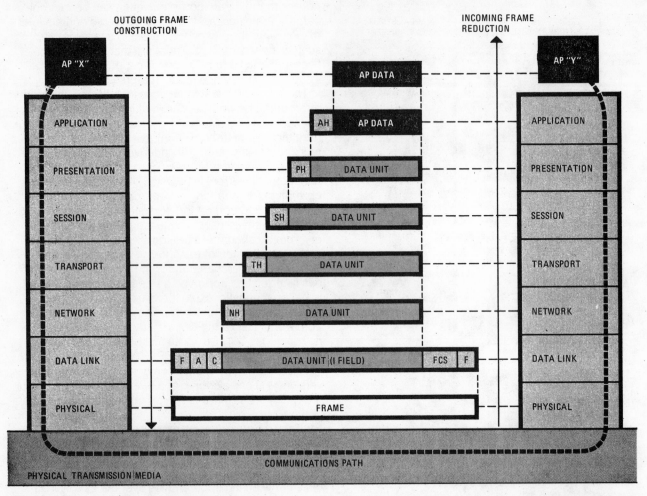

reference model. These include ESTABLISHMENT REQUEST with address, facility, and class of service parameters, RESET REQUEST for reinitialization of a connection to recover from a fault situation, and RECALL REQUEST to change some of the network-connection parameters during an established communication.

Functions delegated to this layer include routing and switching, reset, termination, recall, upward multiplexing, segmenting and blocking, error detection, error recovery, mapping network addresses with the transport addresses, resource management, and relaying. Though many of these functions are similar to those for the other layers discussed above, relaying is a unique function and has been included in the latest draft of the CCITT version. Relaying provides for transparent forwarding of data units from one network entity to another. This is an important concept for multinodal connections and tandem networks where there is either routing or monitoring of the network-layer functions during the communication.

Several protocols for this layer are already available. There is the well-known CCITT Recommendation X.25 for packet-switching services on public data networks

and X.21 for synchronous circuit-switching networks. There is also X.20 for asynchronous public data networks and the RS-366-A auto-calling procedure for the telephone network. Any protocol that deals with exchanging addressing and control information within the network for switching and routing falls within the scope of the network layer.

Framing and synchronization

The data link layer provides the functional and procedural means to activate, maintain, and deactivate data links between network entities. It effects reliable data transfer across a physical link by providing the frame synchronization, error detection, and possibly error recovery for the transmitted data.

These functions are performed by the data link layer for the network layer:

■ Data link establishment creates a logical association between the ends of the physical link and provides for the transfer of data units between network entities.

■ Data unit transfer identifies the beginning and end of a transmitted frame.

■ Error notification, like other similar higher-layer services, indicates unrecovered errors that occur between ends of the transmission medium to the above network layer for further recovery action.

■ Flow control regulates the flow of the data units across the link.

■ Downward multiplexing provides mulitple link capabilities for a single network entity, thereby facilitating a higher reliability and graceful degradation as transmission links fail.

The primitives associated with this layer are similar to those for higher layers. Among the many functions delegated to this layer are activation, mapping of addresses onto physical connections, delimiting and synchronizing data, error detection and recovery, and resource management.

There are two well-known and widely used protocols in this layer. The first, known internationally as basic mode, is a character-oriented link protocol defined in ISO 1745 and ANSI X3.28. A more commonly known subset is the IBM binary synchronous communications (BSC) protocol. The other protocol is the bit-oriented international HDLC (high-level data link control) of ISO (and ADCCP, the advanced data communications control procedure, of ANSI). The LAP/LAP-B portion of X.25 can also be considered a link-control-layer type of protocol. IBM's SDLC (synchronous data link control) is yet another example.

The bottom rung of the OSI ladder is the physical layer providing the electrical, mechanical, and procedural characteristics to activate, maintain, and deactivate a physical connection. The connection activation/deactivation procedures are analogous to the off-hook/on-hook functions associated with traditional telephony.

Earlier versions of the reference model specified call-establishment for circuit-switching networks at this layer. However, it was later determined that this conflicted with the function of the network layer. Thus, the latest versions include all switched-network call-establishment procedures at the network layer.

Services provided by the physical layer to the data link layer include:

■ Physical connection.

■ Data unit transmission. This service provides, however, only for the bit transmission of data. A data unit at this layer is a single bit.

■ Fault-condition notification.

Primitives and associated parameters are fairly obvious for these services. Typical examples include CONNECTION REQUEST for outgoing communications and CONNECTION INDICATION for incoming data. The primitive FAULT INDICATION may include a parameter specifying the nature of the fault.

Among the few functions relegated to this layer are activation, deactivation, upward multiplexing, and fault detection. There are no mechanisms for recovery, as it is the most basic and simple layer. The only fault that can be detected is the loss of the physical connection or a loss of power in the equipment.

Standards at the physical level are well-established and implemented. The Electronic Industries Association (EIA) RS-232-C has been in use for many years, al-though it is now being replaced by RS-449 (with much higher performance). For public data network applications, CCITT has established Recommendation X.21, which specifies the physical layer elements (in addition to the network-layer circuit-switching protocol) and uses the smaller 15-pin connector of ISO 4903. In the future, X.21 will be the base for further enhancements.

A scenario

How do the various components of the reference model fit together to operate efficiently and in harmony? A description of a basic point-to-point configuration in an X.25 packet-switching network illustrates an OSI communication.

Referring to Figure 3, assume that application process "X" in end-system I requests the LSM to establish a connection with AP "Y" in end-system II. With the request, AP "X" provides the parameters required for the communication. These may include the address (or identification) of the destination AP, the maximum acceptable error rate, the desired throughput, and any other requirements. The LSM determines the availability of the OSIE and initializes the layer entities with the appropriate request primitives.

The connection to end-system II is then constructed starting from the physical layer. The physical circuit is first activated, and then the data link layer is notified by an indication primitive. The data link entity then establishes its logical relationship, using the data link protocol, with the data link entity in the network. This enables the network protocol to establish a connection through the packet-switching nodes in the network.

On completion of the network connection to the destination, the transport layer is notified with a CONNECTION ESTABLISHED primitive. The transport protocol then establishes an end-to-end transport connection with the corresponding transport entity at the other end. In the same way, each remaining layer establishes itself, using the layer peer protocol, with its peer entity at the distant end of the interconnection. The peer entity handshakings for each layer need not be done sequentially. They may be done concurrently, for example, with the transmission of one composite block of information during network call establishment.

Once the OSIE is fully established, full communication of data can proceed. Some data from the AP may have already been passed to the destination AP during the establishment phase, but in this example, data exchange will commence only after the connection is fully established.

Referring to Figure 5, the unit of data (AP data) from AP "X" is passed to the application layer where an application header (AH) for the peer protocol is attached. The AH contains the control information for the peer application entity at the destination. The combination of the AH and the AP become the data unit that is then passed to the presentation layer.

Likewise, a presentation header (PH) is added to convey control information to the peer presentation entity. A functional unit in the presentation layer performs any code or format conversions needed to facilitate understanding or further translation by the application process at the destination end.

Sequentially, the data unit, with the concatenated header, is passed to the next-lower layer for further processing. At any given layer, the data unit is the AP data with the headers of each above layer attached. Each header conveys to the peer entity the necessary control information to facilitate the defined functions of every layer.

Continuing at the network layer, an X.25 data-packet header will be added. Then, at the data link layer, the opening flag (F), address (A), and control (C) information are appended to the front of the data unit (referred to as the "I" field in the LAP B specification of X.25), and the frame check sequence (FCS) and closing flag are attached at the end. Next, at the physical layer, the total package appears as a single frame, which is passed on bit-by-bit to the transmission media.

At the destination, the frame enters the physical layer, where it is passed directly to the data link layer. As the data unit is passed to the next-higher layer, the first layer's header is stripped off and processed by the layer's functional unit. Finally, at the application layer, the application header is removed, acted on, and the AP data is passed on to AP "Y."

The APs may continue to pass data back and forth in this manner during the connection. When they are finished, a request is made, typically by the initiating AP, to terminate the connection and to free the re-sources for subsequent communications.

This scenario is only an example of a possible OSI communication using the reference model. Other scenarios can be drawn, and many can become very complex. Although a number of system dynamics and operating phases come into play, it is the ISO's goal that the reference model accommodate as many application processes as possible.

Still to go

The ISO's work is advancing rapidly to produce a basic reference model shape that can be used for planning by those who intend to become a part of future OSI-based communities. Additional refinement is necessary before all details are fully established, but that should not preclude immediate use of what will probably be a cornerstone of tomorrow's standardization effort.

The major task ahead is the development of protocols for the layers, particularly at the upper layers where there presently are no established standards. As the technology evolves, however, protocols at different layers will be able to be revised or replaced without affecting the other layers. Then, as new applications arise, they can likewise be designed to conform to the reference model.

Yet it should not be presumed that the reference model is absolutely rigid. To make it so would preclude the incorporation of unforeseen advances. ∎

Richard H. Sherman, Melvin G. Gable, and Anthony Chung,
Ford Motor Company, Dearborn, Mich.

Overcoming local and long-haul incompatibility

**After the higher layers
of the OSI models are defined,
then what? Ford researchers
discuss the trials and tribulations
of developing end-to-end control.**

There are long-distance data networks—
composed of switched or leased facilities, point-to-point, or multipoint connections—and now there are local networks. Most agree that the two will have to interconnect, and some progress is being made in this area. But it remains unclear how this can be done while retaining end-to-end network efficiency, reliability, connectivity, and cost-effectiveness.

A network protocol layer is needed that can adapt to the evolution, operation, and interconnection of such diverse networks. The network should accommodate computers that implement different network protocols, and the network components, such as interfaces and computers, should be as easy to install as modems—without requiring communications or computer specialists. Some modems, for example, can now sense the data rate and modulation scheme and automatically adapt. Whole networks should be able to merge with or separate from other networks as easily as individual network components are added and removed.

In view of this, an experimental network has been developed at Ford in an attempt to implement these evolutionary and operational objectives. Different types of networks were interconnected using a uniform network protocol layer developed to perform measurement and control functions.

The Ford experimental network combines a unique local network architecture with a store-and-forward network called Distributed Computer Network, or DCNet. The local network architecture, using packet-switching technology, is a high-bandwidth (1-Mbit/s) multiaccess contention network. The contention technique is called feedback carrier-sense multiple access with collision detection (FB/CSMA/CD). The medium is standard coaxial cable. The network technology is packet switching, with each packet broadcast to all

local interface locations. Local network interfaces (LNIs)—microprocessor-based communications interfaces—implement an interprocess communications and synchronization (IPC) function that actually connects the computer or terminal equipment with the network services.

Local network applications are often simply an economical replacement of point-to-point wiring using a single coaxial cable. A terminal-emulation module in the Ford LNI is used to implement a direct device connection. This application requires short delays and features fast recovery from error conditions. The LNI also provides various connection modes that accommodate terminals, programmable controllers, and microprocessor-based equipment.

There are three different types of access methods to an LNI which are selected using LNI commands. An access method is a protocol between a host (DTE) and an LNI (DCE). The LNI commands can be entered by the attached host DTE or from any other host in the network. The characteristics of the LNI for each type of access method are shown in Figure 1. They are:

1. The terminal emulation mode, wherein the LNI provides a reliable transport service, including flow and error control, between two processes. This mode emulates point-to-point-type links. The LNI permits data transmission ranging from character-at-a-time to more efficient block data transfers.

2. The virtual-circuit mode provides the same service, but the host DTE is involved in multiplexing the circuits. A process may employ commands to create a new virtual circuit, and the LNI provides connection-control services in this case. Moreover, a connection requires that the local-network packet address and sequence numbers match.

3. In the datagram mode, the LNI provides reliable

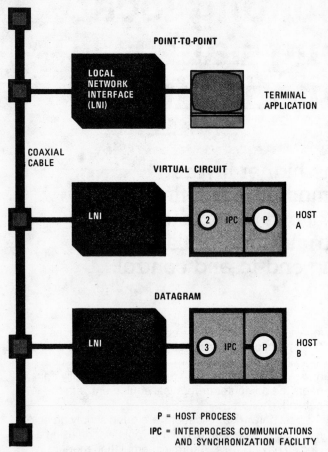

1. Triple interface. *Local network interface (LNI) handles point-to-point circuits, virtual circuits, and datagrams. IPC links host processes (P) with network services.*

P = HOST PROCESS
IPC = INTERPROCESS COMMUNICATIONS
AND SYNCHRONIZATION FACILITY

transport of packets, but no connection-control service. Each packet can be individually addressed, and capabilities exist for both broadcast and selective group addressing. With datagrams, different reliability and delay behavior (under noisy or congested conditions) is possible by adjusting an upper limit on the number of retransmissions.

The Distributed Computer Network, DCNet, is a datagram packet-switched network based on the federal government Department of Defense internetwork protocol (IP). The DCNet supports several host services including virtual terminal, file transfer, and electronic mail. DCNet hosts are connected with point-to-point dedicated or switched links. DCNet employs a uniform operating environment with a naming scheme for all hosts, networks, and services. Names are symbolic representations of logical addresses. In DCNet, each host performs a store-and-forward routing function.

The Ford local network architecture is integrated into DCNet by using datagram access to the LNI for the transport of internetwork packets. The IP provides a uniform packet format that allows the transport of packets across the networks. Further, the transport layer consists of either a reliable end-to-end protocol, known as TCP, or a datagram protocol called UDP.

Both are implementations of the IPs developed by the Defense Department.

Comparison with OSI

The functional layering of the ISO model for open systems interconnection (OSI) can be used to illustrate the host organization in this experimental network (Fig. 2). A process corresponds to the application, presentation, and session layers. Each process has a unique name, which is a symbolic representation of the process port identification. The IPC facility contains the transport, network, and link layers.

The transport layer provides primitives (command statements) for sending and receiving messages on either a character-by-character basis or on an individual message basis. Synchronization occurs for the establishment of connections and for handling urgent requests. Buffer management is provided in this layer so that processes do not require communications buffers. In addition, end-to-end flow control, connection establishment, and error conditions are performed by the transport layer.

The link layer contains drivers for controlling the physical links between hosts and local networks. On the link level, not all hosts can be reached over the same link. For example, in Figure 3, host C cannot be reached from host A on link 1. A table in each host contains the necessary connectivity information.

The network layer dynamically probes the underlying network to determine the network's properties. These properties include host connectivity, network delay, data rate, and time synchronization information. Although these properties may be known at any given time, changing network conditions and host locations make a fixed configuration unacceptable. The determination and measurement of these properties provides a means for network control of disturbances (see Glossary). Based on this information, resultant actions are taken, such as decisions on routes, linked delays, clock updates, device resets, and host resets.

The network layer accommodates networks with a wide range of interconnection properties. For example, a point-to-point link of 2.4 kbit/s can have the same delay properties as a 1-Mbit/s satellite channel, although the maximum data rate (throughput) is much different. From a link-control point of view, there are three types of ports:

1. A point-to-point port provides the ability for a driver process to send to only one other driver process. From a user point of view, however, this port can provide access to several hosts in a store-and-forward network. Note that a permanent virtual circuit qualifies as a point-to-point port since intermediate processing units, if any, only retransmit messages, including acknowledgments used in error control.

2. A switched port allows connections with multiple driver processes. However, only one particular driver process is addressed at a time. Again, at the user level, this port may appear simultaneously to access multiple hosts. On the link level, however, the selection time can vary depending on the underlying network (for example, on the dialing procedure over the telephone

2. Layered architecture. *Network-control features in the Ford experimental network are compared with the ISO model for open systems interconnection (OSI). Network* *and transport layer functions are performed by the Ford interprocess communications and synchronization (IPC) facility, which includes several different protocols.*

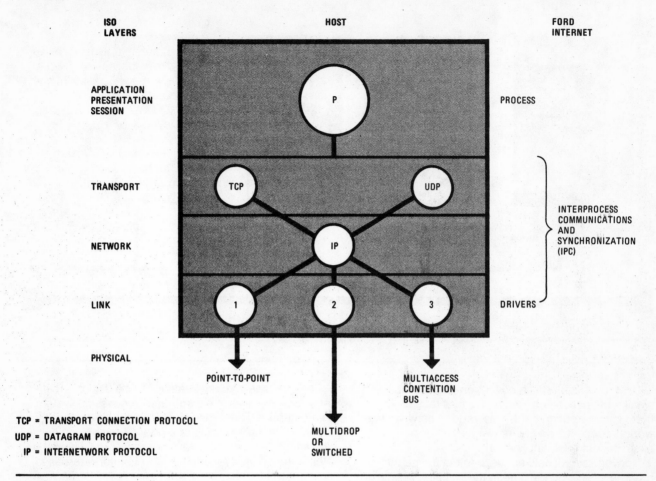

TCP = TRANSPORT CONNECTION PROTOCOL
UDP = DATAGRAM PROTOCOL
 IP = INTERNETWORK PROTOCOL

network or the call-request procedure on X.25 packet-switching networks).

3. A multiple-access port provides the ability for the driver process to send messages to a number of other host driver processes at any time; for example, an HDLC primary station sending messages to a secondary station. The host with a secondary station port, however, views connections as point-to-point since it can only address the host that is the primary station.

Since these port types have been defined abstractly, one must be careful to consider the appropriate protocol layer when applying the definitions. For example, a datagram access layer can be implemented on top of a virtual-circuit network; the switching is performed on each message or else several open connections are maintained simultaneously.

A further distinction in multiple-access ports is required when one considers addressing capability. Two types of broadcast are possible:

1. Broadcast messages can be sent by explicitly addressing all hosts reachable via the port.

2. Broadcast messages with a group, or all-party, address may be sent, with response messages returned by each individual host.

Response time can be measured through the use of broadcast messages, which requires a further distinction in the type of port. The broadcast-message delay to a shared-bus local network would probably be identical for all hosts. Otherwise, message delay could be a function of specific host locations, such as in a ring local network.

If the broadcast messages arrive at different times at the destination hosts, the response-time calculation requires a copy of time-stamp values provided by the remote hosts. In a multiaccess contention bus, the response time can be calculated as the sum of two local-port delays.

Small network, fast broadcast

The broadcast mechanism is also used to perform tasks such as the readdressing of all hosts on the network. In this way, the addresses of all hosts on one network can be changed to another network. In the Ford local setup, several different local networks can reside on the same multiaccess contention bus.

The speed at which measurements are made and controls are performed depends directly on the time it takes to perform a network broadcast. In general, assuming a constant host broadcast overhead, the smaller the network the faster the broadcast and the

3. Port arrangement. *In order to access local and long-haul facilities efficiently, different drivers need to be incorporated in each host's communications interface.* *Depending on user requirements, not all driver types need to be included with each host. In this case, a local network driver is not required for host C.*

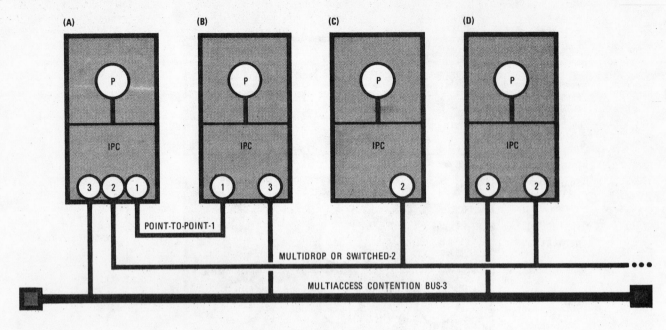

1,2,3 = DRIVER   P = PROCESS   IPC = INTERPROCESS COMMUNICATIONS

faster the network can recover from disturbances. The smaller the network, however, the less redundancy there is for rerouting data. This tradeoff between network broadcast time and network size needs to be examined for each application.

Network broadcasts are used to determine the round-trip delay to each host, the hosts reachable on each link, and the optimal route to a host, as well as to synchronize a network clock. Delay measurement is useful in detecting changes in links and link interface speeds. As a separate function, absolute time synchronization can be used for network instrumentation and to maintain a total ordering of transactions on a higher-layer distributed database.

Separation of function
The network-layer functions have been designed to be modular for ease of development and operation. These include an assortment of measurement and control functions. Specific network measurements include:
- Link delay to each host.
- Network absolute time measurement.
- Host and network connectivity (for instance, status and availability).
- Data-transfer rate of a port.

In addition, there are control functions that offer the following capabilities:
- Calculation of minimum-delay route.
- Network clock synchronization.
- Generation of control messages.
- Congestion-control mechanisms.

Link delay to each host is computed relative to a host clock without the need for clock synchronization.

A network time synchronization can be useful in relating process events in a distributed processing system to a centralized time record. This might be used, for example, in the changing of a public encryption key.

Meanwhile, queuing delays are measured within the higher transport layer and can be used for rate-based flow-control techniques.

Host and network autonomy
In the Ford internetwork, hosts are autonomous and may be connected to the network only on a temporary basis. A host enters the network with no prior configuration information assumed, except for its own resources. The host then informs the network of its existence by sending a "hello" broadcast with its own address. The hello is sent to each driver port serving the host. Measurements of link delay, network synchronization time, and data rates are then obtained by the host from responses received.

This procedure works well on all port types because the hello message is encapsulated into each specific link-level protocol by the driver. Using this procedure, for example, the same host (see Glossary) can then be brought up somewhere else on the network on different computer hardware.

The network broadcast is also used to propagate "public" information throughout the network. When a disturbance is detected, the entire network must agree on the condition and on what to do about it (usually reconfiguration). For consistency in routing, a host should be known to all the other hosts on the network as inaccessible before it appears at a different location.

After that, the broadcast packets are passed on by

each individual host until all network hosts have received this information.

Faulty processors are assumed not to pass on any bad information. This assumption is made because of two design factors. First, the broadcast uses the same table-lookup mechanism as the data packets. Therefore, failures in forwarding data packets can also be sensed as failures to forward a network broadcast packet. Second, individual broadcast packets are often responses to earlier broadcasts. The feedback of public information on broadcasts, therefore, can be used to check consistency and to protect against the propagation of bad information.

Delay measurement

The procedure for measuring delay involves the port type. The delay measurement for point-to-point ports is performed by exchanging hello packets and measuring round-trip delay. For store-and-forward networks, this procedure is repeated at each intermediate host. For switched or virtual-circuit links and multiaccess ports (without broadcast), the procedure is repeated for each host in succession.

The delay between hosts depends on the specific communications facilities employed in the network. Consider, for example, two communications facilities: a local-network point-to-point port and a direct-wire point-to-point port. Even though the local network employs a high-bandwidth medium, there is still a measurable delay between hosts accessing the local network. This is because the transfer rate of a packet between the host and the LNI is dependent on both the serial-data rate and the host operating-system performance for asynchronous parallel access. Also, the transmission between the source and destination LNIs may experience a contention delay depending on the utilization level of the local network. Finally, the transfer into the destination host depends on its interface rate. The result is that a local network represents more delay than a direct-wire connection with corresponding throughput (data rate).

For the local network, the objective is to measure the delay of the link port and add this delay to the delay each host encounters on the link port. A broadcast hello is sent with a time stamp to the port. After that, all network hosts, including the originating host, receive this hello packet. Finally, when the hello is received from the local-network medium, the calculation of port delay is then made.

Network delay also includes the contention delay inherent in local networks, along with buffer delay in the host-to-LNI interface. After receiving a hello message, other hosts respond with broadcast hellos containing their respective port delays. The round-trip delay, therefore, is the sum of the originator link delay and the remote-host port delay.

A reduction in overhead is achieved by only sending hellos on startup for hosts with only a single network port. These are called nonbridge hosts. A bridge host is defined as a host with more than one port. Nonbridge hosts receive broadcasts from bridge hosts to keep network status rapidly updated. When a non-

bridge host comes up, a single hello can be sent that measures the port delay and informs the other hosts of its state.

Time synchronization is achieved throughout the internetwork by comparing the absolute clock values. The interaction of hello packets is used continually to feed back clock information. This is particularly fast on a multiple-access network because the same hello packet is received by all hosts within microseconds.

Names and addresses

A naming scheme exists for use in referencing local networks, hosts, processes, and data files and records. A name process resides in several hosts and is used to translate symbolic names to addresses. The name-table search is hierarchical. If a name is not found in the local context, the global context is searched. When multiple addresses exist for the same name, other qualifiers must be used to designate a unique name.

Internetwork addresses are composed of four bytes, each referring to a specific network, subnetwork, host, and subhost. Process names are identified with generic service-port numbers that are used consistently throughout the network, in conjunction with specific local-port numbers.

The local network behaves like an associative lookup table when a local-network address is received by the destination LNI or group of LNIs. The address mapping is shown in Figure 4. The Net-ID byte is used to locate the network, the subnet byte is used to locate the subnetwork, and the Host-ID byte is used to locate the host. In addition, a host port indicator defines the route to a logical host. If a port is connected to a local network, the host table is used to determine the local network address.

For addresses derived from a network, an inverse address map is made. A hello arriving at a host port results in the updating of mapping tables. The logical port is then recorded in the host table, and the local network address is derived from the source internetwork-packet address.

The address-mapping procedure is adequate when hosts are using the same interprocess communications and synchronization (IPC) procedures. A complication in addressing occurs when different types of driver ports are using the same LNI—say, when LNI address changes for datagram applications have to be tracked by point-to-point or virtual-circuit connections. One solution is to use separate LNIs for each type of application, but this involves a proportionate increase in network component cost. Another approach is to include the local-address header with all data packets, with an additional expense in host overhead. The local address can be used to identify the packet source and could also be included in the address map.

Determining the path

Routing is accomplished with the use of logical host address tables. Each host table contains several other host names, the associated port number, the round-trip delay to that host, and a status of when the last update was received. This information is used in the store-and-

4. Addressing scheme. *A consistent addressing scheme is the key to the interconnection of multiple, diverse networks. Addressing is hierarchical; the first address byte designates the destination network, the next denotes the subnetwork, and so on. Local-network addressing is easier, and uses an abbreviated procedure.*

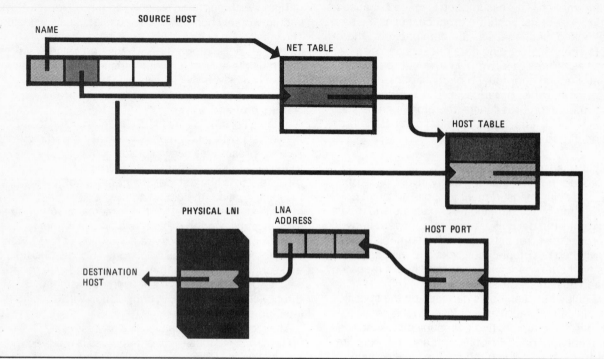

forward routing of data packets in the network.

Routing is direct on the local network. LNI and link interface faults, however, can be bypassed with the use of delay measurements. For example, if two local network hosts cannot communicate because of attenuation problems, but a host in between the two hosts can still communicate to both hosts, then a path is established. Unfortunately, a store-and-forward host also hears collisions that are undetected by other hosts, and the contention scheme loses some degree of performance.

Broadcasts are implemented using a reverse path-forwarding technique. A host forwards a broadcast packet it has received on each port except the incoming port. When a broadcast packet is sent to a local network, a broadcast destination address is used.

A "selective" broadcast can be implemented through an address-filter function in the LNI. The local network destination address contains the "all-parties" broadcast address (defined in HDLC), which has a standard representation. The address filter is then used to discriminate on this or any other portion of the address. The LNI port address represents the LNI on the shared local-network medium, while a segment address byte is used to designate the particular virtual network or network application.

Convenient network tools are desirable in measuring performance and tracking individual component problems. Such measurements are particularly important at Ford, considering the complexity of large data networks. Special-purpose instruments, such as oscilloscopes and data analyzers, do exist for specific diagnostic purposes, but these have not yet been integrated into a general diagnostic setting.

Some valuable diagnostic tools include the network statistics gathered during network operation experiments. These can be used in examining selected network components. Since a virtual-terminal service can be used remotely to obtain access to a host, delay measurements can be retrieved and viewed at a remote site. When certain conditions are sensed, such as an increase in delay between a host and the local network, statistics on the host's local-network driver can be gathered and displayed. Host-interface hardware faults, as well as buffer overrun conditions, can also be identified in this manner.

The host local-network driver program collects statistics gathered by the LNI during the course of its operation. These include hardware errors, buffer-overrun conditions, and a packet-retry summary based on the last 100 packets sent.

For collecting network statistics, there are several procedures that can be performed. The controlled data loops that can be examined are:

■ Internal loopback within one host computer.
■ Host-generated loopback to its attached LNI.
■ Host-generated loopback to its attached LNI, which in turn loops back externally through the shared local-network medium.
■ Host loopback over the local network to a remote LNI on the local network. Data is looped back through the remote LNI without disturbing data flow to the remote host attached.
■ Host-generated loopback to a remote host.

Data-delay statistics can be collected and displayed in a graph of delay versus frequency. A typical delay

Glossary

Internetworking involves the identification of network properties and the isolation of applications from network operation. This is done through the use of virtual host and network concepts. Considering the present variety of communications technology and practices, network terms need to be clarified. The following glossary is provided to aid the reader in understanding the concepts and principles discussed in this article.

disturbances network changes due to failures in either communications or computer facilities. Operators can cause disturbances as a result of their autonomous control actions.

driver a communications process associated with a physical I/O device. Multiplexing of messages through a driver, for example, is made possible by supervisor synchronizing commands, or primitives, which permit several sender processes to send messages to a single-receiver process port associated with the driver.

end user an application process or a person interacting with processes through a human interface.

gateways hosts used to interconnect networks. Two fundamental types of gateways may exist:

1. gateway has capability to perform routing functions when interconnected networks have a consistent message format.

2. gateway may have to translate services between interconnected networks when hosts use dissimilar message formats. In this case, the internetwork can only support services that can be mapped between the two dissimilar networks. End-to-end flow control is lost with this type of gateway.

host an abstraction of an operating environment wherein a set of processes interacts with a supervisor. The supervisor contains system processes and manages the operating environment, which includes input/output (I/O) devices, directories, and file systems. A host is a convenient boundary for containing specific resources desired by other hosts. A host is virtual, and several hosts may reside on the same computer.

internetwork a collection of networks with an IPC facility such that hosts on any network appear immediately accessible to hosts on any other network. Externally, an internetwork appears as a single network, with hosts on interconnected networks appearing as interconnected hosts. Internally, an internetwork is composed of heterogeneous networks with different message formats and protocols.

IPC for interprocess communications and synchronization facility; provides the capability for transmitting variable-length messages from any process in a host to any other process in the same or different hosts.

local network a network which is geographically local, such as in a plant or office. Examples include local loops and multidrop and multiaccess contention buses.

message consists of header and data; is an informational unit sent by a process to a named interface, such as a port.

network a collection of hosts and an IPC such that any host in the network appears immediately accessible to any other host. One requirement of a network is that there exist a consistent message format with a uniform addressing scheme for the hosts present (actually or potentially) in the network. Network functions may include data-flow control, error control, connection control, and routing.

network-layer process handles disturbances in topology and variations in data transfer rates.

port interface between a process and a communications connection. A process has at least one port used by the supervisor to identify the process.

process a single activity containing procedure code, data storage, and an interface for communication with other processes.

routing the process of finding a path to a host. To route, a host must decide on which of several ports to send a message. Routing is hierarchical in an internetwork. A host in an internetwork must know which port to use, and whether to send messages to another host or a gateway. For example, host P knows the direction to host Q when P and Q are on the same network. Otherwise, host P knows that gateway G knows the direction to host Q when P and Q are on different networks. The use of gateway G to denote the address of host P is an indirect reference which permits autonomy and efficiency in internetworking.

histogram on a local-network host-to-host loopback contains frequency peaks corresponding to the local-network retransmission cycle. There is another characteristic delay that occurs when hellos are being processed because of the multiplexing of packets through one host port.

The Ford internetwork experiments have resulted in some very definite conclusions. The control and measurement features used in the Ford test have been invaluable in evaluating internetwork efficiency and in performing system diagnostics. Such capabilities, it is believed, will have to be incorporated into commercially available internetworking products. Another feature found to be both useful and implementable is the use of alternative data paths in the design and operation of local networks.

The local network architecture has fit remarkably well into this internetworking scheme, primarily because of dynamic, hierarchical addresses and a link protocol that adapts to various host requirements including point-to-point links, virtual circuits, and datagrams. The local-network packet format is efficiently used in point-to-point link applications and is flexible enough to support the internetwork communications and synchronization required for the maintenance of virtual hosts and networks. ∎

Mike Neighbors, Associated Technology Consultants, Huntsville, Ala.,
and Francis Lane, Science Applications Inc., La Jolla, Calif.

Applying network architecture to data acquisition

Remote analog measurements may be brought directly to a CPU, but use of a distributed network can be more cost-effective

Recent technological advances have made digital approaches to acquisition and analysis of data from analog measurements cost-competitive with older approaches. Data in digital form also offers considerably better resolution and fidelity. But the primary reason for replacing old analog techniques with digital ones is to combat the so-called information explosion. Large-scale experiments produce too much data to analyze manually, making the extensive use of digital computers necessary to scan selected data for more detailed analysis.

In recent years, the evolution of data communications as a reliable and powerful tool has led to a variety of data acquisition architectures. To better understand them, the user should first examine the basic architectural approaches to computer-control design.

The primary difference between computer systems for data processing and those for instrumentation applications is the number and variety of data communications interfaces to the outside world. In a data processing system, interfacing requirements are generally restricted to a relatively few digital data devices such as local terminals, printers, and mass storage units. These devices invariably rely upon well-defined, high-level digital interfaces such as transistor-to-transistor logic (TTL) levels or RS-232-C standard data levels. In addition, to justify the usually high cost of a data processing installation, the user generally wants to maximize the data transfer rate between the computer and its peripheral devices to maintain computational operations as a high percentage of the overall functions.

Instrumentation applications, in contrast, usually involve interfacing signals of many different types and levels (see Table). Since the data transfer rates in these applications are, for the most part, limited by the physical process being measured rather than by the speed of the computer, there is little need to maximize the interface speed in relation to the speed of the computer. Other differences include lower computing speed and capacity requirements resulting from the more dedicated nature of the application; greater ease of use, since the user will not be a staff of trained computer specialists; and a lower cost, since the device will be used in one application and not companywide.

Figure 1 illustrates an architecture that both typifies a central computer system and is similar to those of most current minicomputer-based — data acquisition systems. Key to this architecture is a group of high-speed interconnection buses linking the elements of the system. Although this type of architecture maximizes data transfer rates between the elements, it also imposes a heavy burden with respect to bus interface logic that each interface must maintain. Also, since the buses operate at the full processor speed — often several megahertz — all bus interfaces must utilize high-speed, high-capacity components. Careful attention must be given to the physical layout and termination of the buses themselves, since the frequency spectrum of the signals can reach several megahertz, introducing signal reflections and crosstalk.

Adapting this architecture to instrumentation systems results in the development of overly fast, expensive interfaces that, because of minor differences in bus implementation for various computer models, must be custom-designed for each model.

There are additional problems associated with the central approach:

■ Sensor signals are often transmitted 1000 or more

feet from their source to the control room. The electrical environment in a typical industrial plant is often severe; therefore, the possibility of error due to induced noise is very high when transmitting low-level signals over long distances.
- Expansion is often difficult because of the limitations of computer room size, machine speed, and mass storage capability.
- Cost of field-wiring all sensors back to a central point becomes very expensive when sensor signals are routed more than a few hundred feet. A typical estimate is $10 to $20 per foot of installed sensor cable.
- Application software for the entire project must reside in and share a single computer.

Sharing a computer may cause more problems:
- System implementation may be quite expensive in terms of software-development manpower and time.
- Response to access requests or commands may be

Sensor outputs

DEVICE	OUTPUT
THERMOCOUPLE	VOLTAGE
STRAIN GAUGE	VOLTAGE OR CURRENT
BRIDGE	VOLTAGE
THERMISTOR	VOLTAGE
TACHOMETER	VOLTAGE
TTL GATE	VOLTAGE LEVEL
SWITCH CLOSURE	VOLTAGE-LEVEL CHANGE
TTL = TRANSISTOR-TO-TRANSISTOR LOGIC	

slower than anticipated unless care is taken in establishing memory partitions and task priorities.
- System flexibility may be limited, since a simple modification to existing routines or the addition of new tasks tends to increase in difficulty as the size of the software complex grows.

Many experts feel that the need for a central processor will never disappear entirely. Users still believe that the central site must participate no matter how extensive distributed data processing becomes, because there are some common functions that are better managed centrally. According to these proponents, even if a large data acquisition system does not start out with a central mainframe, it will eventually require one.

To circumvent the disadvantages of conventional architecture for data acquisition systems, while maintaining the generality necessary to the creation of a product line, several companies have created the architecture shown in Figure 2. At first glance it may seem similar to a conventional architecture, but the use of a measurement-and-control computer interface unit (CIU) and a secondary bus for measurement and control interfacing gives these important advantages:
- Compatibility with conventional computer architecture is maintained. The data acquisition system is essentially processor-independent, and the user can take advantage of existing hardware and software.
- All the computer bus interface logic resides in the CIU. This overhead does not have to be repeated on each measurement and control interface.
- The CIU may contain considerable power and intelligence, allowing its cost to be spread over many simple, relatively inexpensive interface cards.
- The CIU allows implementation of a secondary bus optimized for measurement and control applications. Since the CIU is a critical node, its failure would have wide impact. A design trade-off between speed and simplicity is normally required; higher-speed operation requires additional hardware, increases complexity, and reduces reliability. For maximum availability, it is better to opt for simplicity and reliability.

Evolving to a network
The evolution of instrumentation systems away from sensors directly connected to computers leads to the simple multiplexed distributed data acquisition architecture, where the only master assumed is the central processor. In such an arrangement, the data acquisition devices are remote and connected to the central computer through some form of data communications multiplexers. The protocol can be completely and simply managed by the single processor. Operator consoles and other devices are usually controlled directly by the processor in such a network.

Evaluation of reliability, backup, and operation of the network in a graceful degradation mode quickly leads to the need for more distribution than remote multiplexing allows. Hence the trend in distributed networks has been moving toward a 1-Mbit/s data "highway" and a limited number of modules using the highway for gathering or transmitting data. The essential feature of this architecture (Fig. 3) is that more than one module can become master, or controller, of the highway, initiating communications with other modules.

The connection of a computer to a data highway eliminates the need for that computer to have a unique interface. All information stored in the individual controllers is then available over the data highway for use by the computer and instrumentation systems. Serial data highway communications in conjunction with microprocessor-based instruments has changed the techniques of integrating a control computer with instrumentation systems. The separate interface unit has been replaced by the more-integrated approach of a computer interface to the data highway.

The design of a data highway network is based on several criteria:
- The amount of information and sampling rates needed
- The distribution distance of the instrumentation
- Error checking to ensure the data security in environ-

1. Conventional acquisition. The architecture of this data acquisition network is similar to that of most current minicomputers and typifies a central-computer system.

Critical to this architecture is a group of high-speed interconnection buses that maximize data transfer rates between the linked network elements.

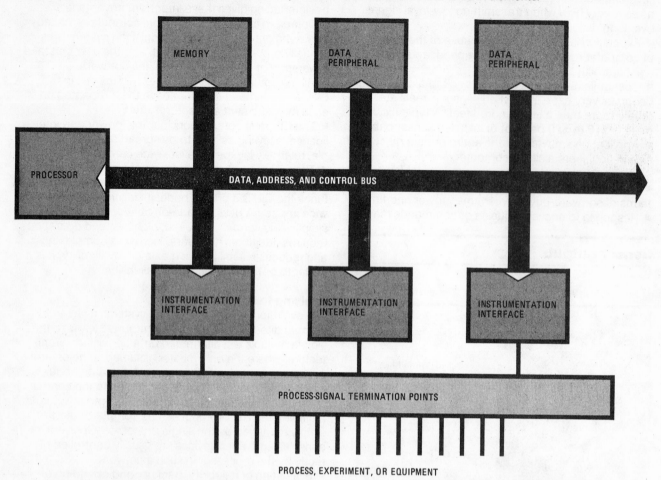

PROCESS, EXPERIMENT, OR EQUIPMENT

ments that are electrically noisy

The multidrop link is best suited as a simple, efficient, and low-cost means of distributing the controllers and data acquisition devices in a network. But the multidrop approach is generally not designed as a communications tool between disk-based supervisory systems or as a communications medium between two network nodes. The complex task of controlling communications between mainframe CPUs normally requires a more comprehensive and flexible set of tools in the form of software packages. As a means of distributing production-line devices and terminals, the multidrop link has several advantages over the more software-intensive radial links:

■ Wiring costs are lower. Terminals and other devices may be connected to the host via a single cable.

■ Hardware communications control requires less of both host-processor load and communications-software development, and frees up memory at remote subsystems. Also, expansion is easier, usually requiring minimal software modification.

■ The well-designed multidrop link enables a reduction in host processor overhead. The load on the host is further reduced by block data transfers. In addition to

controlling communications along the bus, the hardware communications controller "steals" computer bus cycles to access memory without CPU intervention. Data is therefore transmitted in block form, with access requests generated only after a full data block has been successfully sent or received.

The multidrop link evolves readily into a minicomputer network. The network's outstanding benefit is that processing power is distributed at the right locations, thereby improving response times while reducing the host's work load. Many organizations have developed hierarchical networks like the one in Figure 4.

The upward flow of sensor-based data fits well into the structure of many large data communications systems. Another justification for networking is the high degree of reliability attainable by spreading the monitoring-and-control function across many small computers and by providing one or more levels of backup for each network node.

The host processor often ties the network together by supervising and controlling its operation. The bulk of the supervisory-management and software-development functions is the responsibility of the host, which supports common peripheral devices—such as mass-

2. Advantageous interface. A way to overcome some disadvantages of conventional central-computer architecture is to insert a computer interface unit (CIU) and a bus optimized for measurement and control applications. All the computer bus interface logic resides in the CIU, thus eliminating repetitious measurement overhead.

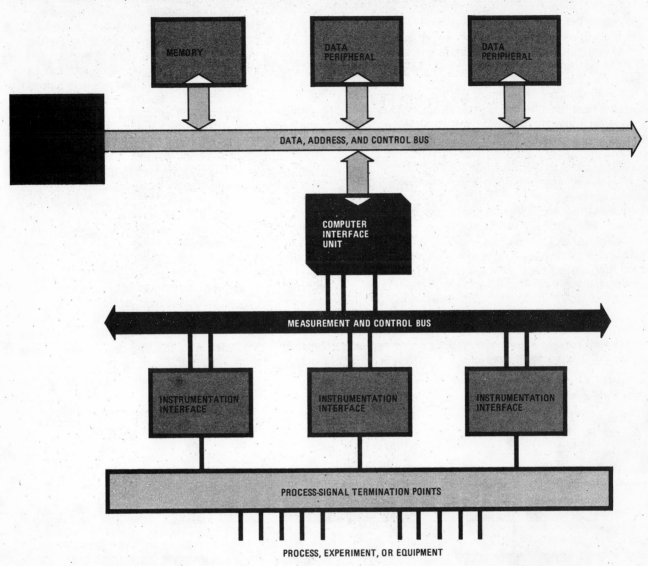

storage disks—that are shared by the remote devices. The host also maintains a complete database on current network conditions to provide up-to-date information on ongoing operations and to optimize productivity by making dynamic scheduling decisions.

Seeking an optimum network
Different architectures have been proposed for distributed data acquisition networks. All are similar in that they interconnect modules with some type of digital communications and distribute the computing power. Details of the architectures vary considerably, however, ranging from single- to multiwire buses, ring networks, and others. Furthermore, the controlling protocols differ greatly. As a consequence, different architectures use different message lengths, different methods for devices to access the communications network, and different error-checking and recovery procedures.

Figure 5 shows a multilevel data acquisition architecture that represents a trend found in process control environments. Supervisory communications is between minicomputers, with data acquisition and control at the local processors.

As an overall approach to instrumentation, a minicomputer network offers several significant advantages over a single central processor:

■ *Less expensive initially.* Network members share resources, such as mass storage devices, terminals, and processing power, as well as programs and program data. Installation costs such as field wiring and computer room space are usually lower.

■ *Improved availability.* Response to access requests or alarm conditions is improved since each remote computer has a specific application. Plus, response by the host processor to requests for management information, control parameter updates by operators, and access requests for program development are significantly improved, because the high-priority process-related tasks are off-loaded to remote computers.

■ *Ease in implementation.* The software breaks down to a more manageable series of functional tasks with well-defined partitions. Since the network can be built, tested, and put into service one leg at a time, portions of it can operate before the complete software complex is running.

■ *Ease in expansion.* Distributing the processing load frees the host to support a greater number of applications. New applications can be added without major modifications to existing host software.

■ *Increased reliability.* Each leg of the network can provide backup to other legs. Therefore, the loss of one computer, even the host, is not catastrophic to total operation. Also, backup can be built in much more efficiently, since the need for redundant computers or analog instrumentation is reduced.

Because of increased emphasis on reliability in many data acquisition systems, loosely coupled multicomputer architectures are preferred to tightly coupled multiprocessor ones. This advantage hinges on the inherent reliability in loosely coupled networks.

Multiprocessor systems have integrated software working on a single-input data stream. Main memory and most other hardware resources are accessible to all processors. In a multicomputer system, however, each computer has its own operating system working on a separate data stream, memory is seldom shared, and little data transfer occurs between like computers.

Multicomputer networks are distributed intelligence systems ideally suited to applications where it is possible to segregate independent subsystems that require relatively little interaction. Dedicating a computer to each subsystem permits the software for each computer to be custom-tailored to a specific task, resulting in improved system throughput. Each computer in a multicomputer network performs jobs that are specifically partitioned to minimize computer interaction.

Most manufacturer-supplied minicomputer systems use elaborate protocols. The vendors are less concerned with speed of communications than with error control and exchange of multiple messages between processors not directly connected. For example, better commercial networks use one level of protocol to communicate between adjacent network nodes in an error-free manner. Synchronous (SDLC) and high-level

---

3. On the road. *The need for greater distribution than remote multiplexing allows has brought about the data highway. The essential feature of this architecture is that* *more than one device can become master, or controller, initiating communications with other devices that use the highway for gathering and transmitting data.*

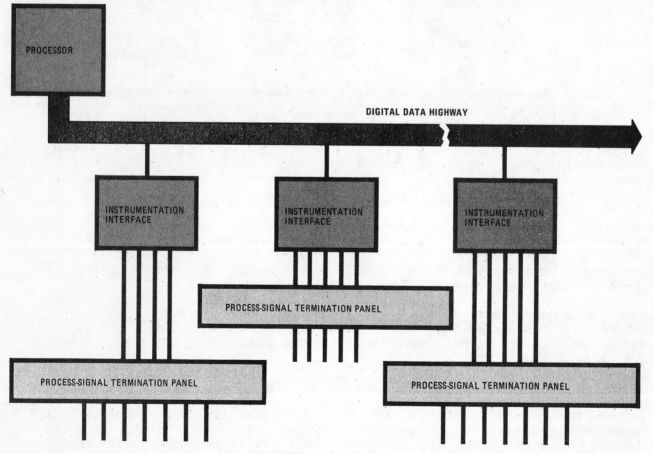

DIGITAL DATA HIGHWAY

INSTRUMENTATION INTERFACE

INSTRUMENTATION INTERFACE

INSTRUMENTATION INTERFACE

PROCESS-SIGNAL TERMINATION PANEL

PROCESS-SIGNAL TERMINATION PANEL

PROCESS-SIGNAL TERMINATION PANEL

PROCESS, EXPERIMENT, OR EQUIPMENT

PROCESSOR

4. The centralized approach. *Typical of the hierarchical architecture, this network's operation is tied together by the central processor's supervising and controlling the remote processors. Processing power is placed at the required locations, thereby improving response times while reducing the work load of the host processor.*

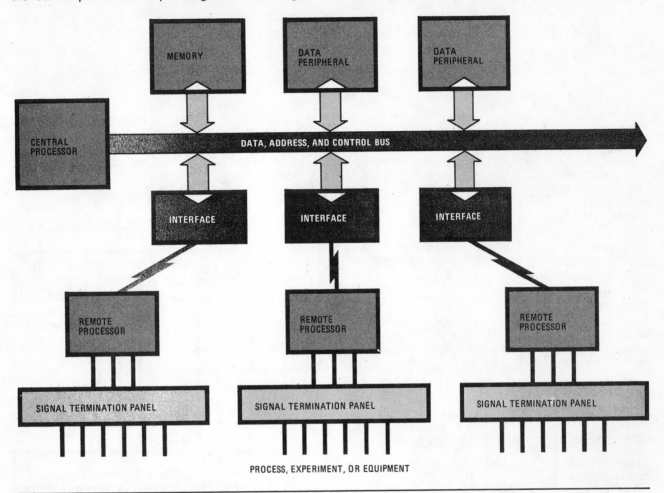

(HDLC) data link controls, and Digital Data communications message protocol (DDCMP) are examples. Messages from nondirectly connected processors use a second level of protocol containing source and destination addresses plus sequencing and control information, all of which are transmitted from node to node using the first-level protocol.

At a third level, a protocol exists to allow an application in one computer to "converse" with an application in another computer. Each message in the conversation is carried out using the second-level and first-level protocols. The net result is a general communications environment that is considered reliable and error-free but relatively slow compared with speeds used at the data acquisition and control level of the network. Some current examples of data network communications include Digital Equipment's Decnet, Modcomp's Maxnet, and the packet-switching network described in the X.25 standards.

Regardless of the protocol used, modern communications networks have four basic characteristics: (1) Information is transmitted digitally; (2) The network accepts a message and delivers it to a specified destination; (3) The network either delivers the message to the destination without error or informs the sender that the message cannot be delivered; and (4) Formats and protocols are assumed to be optimized.

Other desired features

Several characteristics which users want but seldom find include:

■ *Dynamic message routing.* The network constantly monitors the communications paths. When a transmission fails, the network retries until the transmission succeeds or until the network determines that the communications path has been broken. In the latter event, the network automatically reroutes the message.

■ *Best-path message routing.* The network monitors the communications lines and automatically selects the best path—which optimizes a user's selected algorithm based on time or priority.

■ *Logical address.* A user of any network node can access the resources of any other node (files, processors, or other physical devices) without regard to the physical location of the resource. To the user, the network appears to be one large set of computer resources rather than a collection of separate devices.

■ *Simple programming interface.* The communications

5. On the level. *A significant step toward an optimum architecture is the multilevel data acquisition network. At the supervisory level, there is communications between* *minicomputers. At the local processor level, there are data acquisition, control, and operator communications. Process control often uses this architecture.*

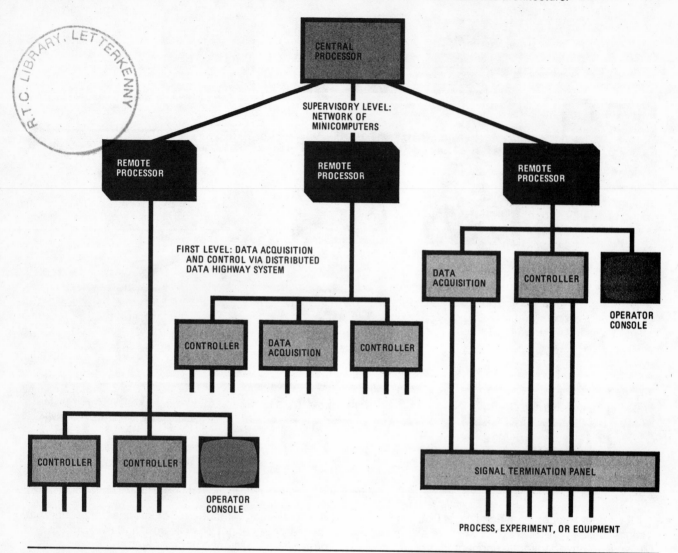

CENTRAL PROCESSOR

SUPERVISORY LEVEL: NETWORK OF MINICOMPUTERS

REMOTE PROCESSOR

REMOTE PROCESSOR

REMOTE PROCESSOR

FIRST LEVEL: DATA ACQUISITION AND CONTROL VIA DISTRIBUTED DATA HIGHWAY SYSTEM

DATA ACQUISITION

CONTROLLER

OPERATOR CONSOLE

CONTROLLER

DATA ACQUISITION

CONTROLLER

CONTROLLER

CONTROLLER

OPERATOR CONSOLE

SIGNAL TERMINATION PANEL

PROCESS, EXPERIMENT, OR EQUIPMENT

subsystem should free programmers from dealing with a cumbersome telecommunications access method.

■ *End-to-end protocol.* End-to-end protocol ensures the integrity of messages from source to destination regardless of the number of intervening nodes and resources used in the message transmission.

Networks may be structured as a series of layers with different interfaces sandwiched between. But the interfaces in a data communications network depend on whom you are talking to. The applications programmer writes calls to communications subroutines in a high-level language. The computer engineer must connect his serial port to a modem, probably employing RS-232-C. For him, this is the interface. Not all interfaces need to be standardized, as when layers on both sides of the interface are supplied by the same vendor.

The nature of computer communications is usually highly application-dependent; that is, implementation requirements vary widely from installation to installation. Specific parameters include data rate, error rate,

signal levels, and modulation techniques.

Implementation of networks for data acquisition and control may be even more varied than for character-oriented data terminal equipment. Even though it may not be technically feasible to standardize the communications system itself, interfaces to such communications systems can be standardized.

Remote multiplexing

The desire to simplify installation and decrease the costs of multiple wire runs from sensors and actuators to centralized minicomputers and process control equipment also has led to the desire to distribute the data acquisition.

Hence the current trend among most users is toward distributed data acquisition and control at the first levels, with minicomputers communicating in a more general network arrangement for the upper levels. This trend leads to multiplexing the remote inputs.

The cost benefits of remote multiplexing of sensor

signals will multiply in the future, mainly because of the continuous rise in labor costs on the one hand and the continuous decline of multiplexing and microprocessor equipment costs on the other. The benefits improve for applications that don't require directly wiring transducers to annunciators and displays in the central control room. These sensor signals, therefore, can be remotely multiplexed, and the annunciators driven by the host computer.

Software versus hardware
In recent years, hardware has become extremely fast and efficient, while software has remained relatively difficult to manage. In fact, the two have completely reversed their positions: whereas hardware was once the major development cost item, software is now by far the more expensive. One result of this is the reordering of priorities to reflect the importance of software in large data acquisition and control applications.

One major drawback of a network is the complexity of putting together a software package to control communications. Effective network control is critical to project success. Thus the availability of personnel to develop and support the network becomes an important design consideration. The use of vendor-supplied network tools—either hardware- or software-oriented—can alleviate this problem to some extent.

When considering a data communications software package, the user should look for the following:
■ A well-established communications protocol
■ A high-level language interface between nodes
■ Direct memory-to-memory data transfer
■ The ability to down-line load data files, application tasks, and commands from a terminal at the host
■ The ability to write, debug, and compile programs at the host and install them in a remote processor
■ The ability, from any remote processor, to use host resources such as mass storage and terminals

The higher-level need
It is likely that the industrial community will adopt higher-level (above assembly level) vendor-independent languages in the near future for data acquisition and process control. (See "Building a higher-level language to use in data communications," DATA COMMUNICATIONS, August 1979, p. 51.) Until such data-acquisition and process-control languages are widely used, certain guidelines should be observed:
■ To minimize the cost of software development and avoid project delays, employ high-level language programming whenever possible.
■ Careful segmentation of the measurement process with an eye toward balancing the processing load on each remote computer can pay high dividends.
■ Use a hardware-controlled communications link between the host and remote computers if possible.
■ To the extent that assembly-level programming is necessary, the job can be made easier by selecting a supporting computer system in which the instruction set and operating system are subsets of those used on the host.

Many higher-level languages have been used to

some extent in large data acquisition networks. The list includes the more common numerical-computation-oriented languages: Fortran, Basic, Pascal, PL/1, Forth, and "C." In most applications they significantly decrease software cost.

If it were only a matter of hardware, large data acquisition networks would probably shift to distributed networks overnight. The problem is that sophisticated network-control software is unavailable because of its high developmental costs—estimated to be as much as nine times the expense of programming equally complex batch applications. This is so because extensive message formatting and editing logic are required: programs must be modular (functionally segmented) and reentrant (programmed so multiple users can access them concurrently); testing, debugging, and run-in is considerably more complex; and program maintenance is more frequent and more difficult.

Part of the problem is that users tend to demand networks that are custom-designed around their own specific needs, making it impractical for vendors to produce a standard program and spread its development over many user companies. Because of the lack of sophisticated distributed data processing software, the mainframe processor remains central to most data communications configurations.

Managing the database
In large data acquisition networks two methods of database management are generally used. First is the traditional instrumentation recorder. This recorder is often analog, frequency modulated (FM), pulse-code modulated (PCM), or a combination. Secondly, there is a data processing-oriented database used for data reduction and analysis. This generally resides on disk or magnetic tape.

Progress in optical recording will possibly make three design objectives realizable within two years: projected cost per bit should reach 0.01 cents/Mbit, with data rates of 100 Mbit/s, and access time of 100 milliseconds. Archival life may exceed 10 years.

Presently, the most common method of saving real-time data is the instrumentation tape recorder. Using the tape recording as a transmission and storage medium has these merits:
■ The convenience of capturing total real-time high-speed data
■ Physical transport of tapes where other means are impractical
■ Slow playback to "stretch" data for a more-detailed analysis
■ Playback "off-line," which allows repeated tape passes for in-depth analysis
■ Ability to provide historical records
■ Capacity as a back-up data collector

FM versus PCM
When a large data acquisition network is being considered, the question of whether to use FM or PCM often arises. A review of the functional requirements will, at times, indicate which approach to pursue. But sometimes the answer is not so obvious.

With many factors to consider, there is no simple formula for a direct comparison, although the two techniques can be compared in general ways. One of the most important points to consider is system accuracy. Typical end-to-end accuracies for PCM and FM systems are 0.1 percent and 1 percent, respectively. Therefore, where accuracy better than 1 percent is required, PCM has a definite advantage.

Where large numbers of channels are required, PCM also has advantages, chiefly in size, weight, and lower per-channel cost. These advantages, however, are offset by the frequency of the data. Generally, FM systems can pack more high-frequency channels into a given bandwidth than can PCM. For instance, to handle many channels of high-frequency vibration data, a constant-bandwidth FM system is a likely choice. PCM is also better for use with low-power, low signal-to-noise transmission links, because the digital form is easier to distinguish in a noisy environment.

Perhaps the greatest fear of all large computer systems users is that the database is down. Therefore the safeguards for database integrity should be carefully examined. When data is received from remote locations, end-to-end protocols make sure that data transmissions are received correctly. The safeguards for data integrity in a distributed database should be examined closely. Database integrity at each site is just as important as accurate data transmission throughout the network. A single corrupted database can quickly contaminate the entire network, because the data at one site is typically based on data from other sites.

Critical to efficient operation is database size, since computers and database-management software vary greatly in their amounts of storage. Planning for growth is often difficult. If a database needs 200 megabytes of storage now, the user should choose at least two or three times that amount to provide for expansion.

Looking in the crystal ball

The evolution of large data acquisition architectures shows a trend toward multicomputer networks that provide allocatable computation power and higher availability. Such future networks will partition functions such as database management, display, front-end processing, data analysis, and message switching.

On the front end, increased computer intelligence will affect the design of signal conditioners, filters, and multiplexers. Signal conditioning with automatic calibration, data compression, and digital filtering are expected as hybrid microprocessor technology matures. Multiplexer technology now in its infancy for large data acquisition networks will evolve to support the requirements of increased flexibility, reliability, and maintainability. Digital filtering as a technology is well established; its increased use is inevitable. The filter price-performance trend, predictable in recent years, may be upset by advances in a new, embryonic technique: reverse-switch capacitor technology.

In the area of network communications, data highways' new interest is in products which offer 25- to 50-Mbit/s data rates—to supplant the current products with a 1-Mbit/s limit. ■

Aspects of database design in a distributed network

Mary E. S. Loomis, University of Arizona, Tucson, Ariz.

Applying an extensive knowledge of several information systems, this author illustrates approaches to creating a successful database.

The challenges of meeting information systems' needs are being tackled by computer networking and distributed data processing technologies. The potential for supporting databases in future distributed environments is promising, but there is tremendous room for discovery, development, and innovation in this area. As distributed databases assume a greater role in distributed data processing, their success will depend largely on users' abilities to integrate them and data communications concerns.

Each information system requires distinct strategies for user queries and for the update, replication, and distribution of data. Data communications planners are adapting the various distributed data processing technologies for their networks. More and more they are using databases designed for distributed environments in an effort to give users sufficient control and to keep communications costs manageable.

Distributed data processing (DDP) is not a new solution to handling data. When computerization was young, the physical distribution of information for processing was common; DDP was the original means of replacing manual functions. To understand the evolution of DDP and databases, it is helpful to look at their development in a typical organization, Company Q.

Originally, the functional responsibility and activities for handling information, albeit manual, were clearly distributed throughout the organization. As depicted in Figure 1A, each user group (five are shown) satisfied its own data-handling needs and maintained and controlled its own data files. Communication with other groups to share information was via telephone, mail, or conference. Eventually, one of these distributed processing groups (in Company Q's case, the accounting department) procured automated equipment to facilitate its manual efforts. Why was the accounting group seemingly so innovative and forward-looking? Because, for one, the processing requirements were well-defined. Second, the cost savings were relatively easy to identify.

Thus, Company Q entered what is called the initiation stage of data processing development. A computing center grew under the auspices of the accounting department. Looking on, other groups began to identify applications that could benefit from similar automation. At this point, company Q entered what is termed the contagion stage: while the computing center was still under the control of the accounting department, new programs and systems were designed and implemented using an applications-oriented approach. For example, each new application controlled its own set of data files, dictating field formats, file contents, file organization, data-editing requirements, and accessibility. The applications depicted in Figure 1B were supported by a central computer, which had evolved from the accounting department's facility but was moved out of that particular group. In Company Q's case, the facility became the corporate data center.

Several related problems can arise if such an applications-oriented approach results in a proliferation of

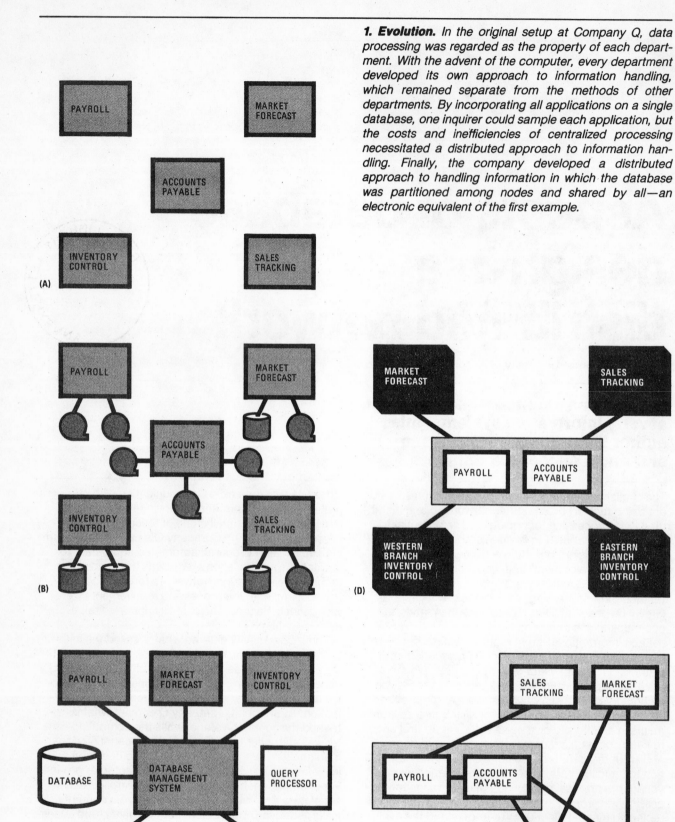

1. Evolution. *In the original setup at Company Q, data processing was regarded as the property of each department. With the advent of the computer, every department developed its own approach to information handling, which remained separate from the methods of other departments. By incorporating all applications on a single database, one inquirer could sample each application, but the costs and inefficiencies of centralized processing necessitated a distributed approach to information handling. Finally, the company developed a distributed approach to handling information in which the database was partitioned among nodes and shared by all—an electronic equivalent of the first example.*

standalone programs and special-purpose files. First is the problem of data replication across applications. As identical data is stored in more and more files, chances of keeping all copies of that data consistently updated plummet. The generation of inconsistent reports often indicates synchronization problems. For example, if reports generated for the district sales offices do not balance with reports for the regional sales office, or if data input to the market forecasting program is supposed to match outputs from the sales tracking program but does not, then the problem may be data replication with inadequate synchronization.

Second, it may not be possible to integrate data across applications. For example, management's request to correlate salesmen's salaries and billable revenues for each region may be no mean programming task, depending on file organizations, coding schemes (such as, how is each salesman identified?), willingness of payroll and sales tracking to provide file access, and differences in update cycles.

Third, because of a lack of standardization, and because data processing control ultimately might reside in the hands of each application programmer, there may be gross duplication of effort in data-management activities. Each new program requires data definition, file organization, data manipulation, security, recovery, and integrity logic and controls to be established and coded, even though the method of data manipulation may be the only distinguishing factor.

Solutions to these problems become evident if users take a data-resource approach, which means controlling and managing data as they would any other important company resource. One tool for this purpose is a database management system (DBMS). There are numerous DBMSs on the market today. Cincom's Total and IBM's Information Management System (IMS) are two examples representing today's DBMSs.

DBMS software provides an interface between the applications programs and the data resource, or database, as depicted in Figure 1C. This interface is responsible for data definition, file organization, as well as security, recovery, and integrity functions. It relieves the applications programs (and application programmers) of data-manipulation tasks. Because the database is a shared resource, the need for data replication in order to support multiple applications generally disappears. A degree of standardization is required, since some data-management concerns, such as data description, security authorization, and recovery protection, that were the responsibilities of individual applications programs, are now governed by the common, shared DBMS interface. The DBMS thus provides the centralized control that was lacking in the applications-oriented approach.

By focusing on the data as the resource, information management can be designed around that most stable aspect of the system: the data structure itself. Applications requirements can change, and applications programs can be changed without modifying or degrading the data resource. Users gain additional benefit from using a query processor (see lexicon) that enables unanticipated, interactive, natural-language-like access to the database. This capability has proven to be instrumental in increasing responsiveness to users and in eliminating the development of one-time-only applications programs.

Upon successfully implementing a DBMS and the converting and integrating of its applications programs to access the database (or databases), Company Q could be said to have passed through the third stage, that of control, into the fourth stage of data processing development: integration. And into the fifth stage called data administration.

Concomitant with the development of the database approach is a tendency toward centralization, in part because DBMS software has traditionally required significant computing resources in order to run efficiently. Additionally, an organization's database-administration expertise is generally considered a corporate resource and is centralized with corporate data processing.

However, centralizing the data processing activities and the database is not without its problems. Especially in a company with decentralized operations, profit-center accountability, and distributed responsibilities, centralized data processing may not fit at all well into the organizational structure. Users may be frustrated over increasing data processing costs and feel that they have little or no control over these costs. They may suffer poor response from heavily utilized central computers. They may perceive a lack of understanding or empathy from the data processing center's staff and see a lack of responsiveness to their requests for new systems and support. They might want private control over their own data and may commonly refer to "DP's system" rather than "our system."

On the other side, the data processing staff may actually be having difficulties managing a large central computing facility and may welcome the opportunity to offload applications from the central facility to remote sites. DP personnel may realize that they can quench users' criticisms to some degree by distributing processing capabilities and responsibilities.

DDP's re-emergence
Distributing function back to local areas has in most cases been fueled by an applications orientation. Specific applications have been offloaded from the central processor to local facilities. New applications have been designated as either appropriate for distribution or for the central site. The central site has sometimes been removed altogether. Based on two fundamental facts — (1) different computers are good at different kinds of jobs and (2) communications costs can be controlled by localizing resources — DDP approaches the complex data processing problem by dividing it into manageable parts. Data processing solutions can then be tailored to the problems in each part, with the promise of relief from the constraints and the expenses of the centralized approach.

However, continued strong centralized control is necessary to ensure that DDP remains a useful management tool. Centralized coordination can guarantee the compatibility of remote computing facilities and of distributed software and data. Data communications solutions must be centrally managed to effectively tie together the DDP components as well as to accommodate future growth.

The configuration depicted in Figure 1D was developed at Company Q. The four local nodes and one central node provide an example of both functional and geographic distribution: functional by inventory control versus market forecasting versus sales tracking versus payroll and accounts payable; geographic by eastern versus western branch inventory control.

Yet, a distributed-applications orientation may very well lead to the same kinds of problems that arose with the centralized-applications orientation. Even if each node implements its own applications, the user needs to be able to integrate his distributed data resources. The problems that the centralized DBMS was supposed to solve persist despite distribution. Moreover, they are complicated in that the user must now deal with the integration of multiple databases. Each database tends to be more complex than the relatively simple

Implications of distributed DBMS

1. AVAILABILITY OF INTERACTIVE QUERY LANGUAGE TO SUPPORT TERMINAL ACCESS

2. AVAILABILITY OF BATCH-REPORT WRITERS TO SUPPORT LARGE-VOLUME ACCESS

3. AVAILABILITY OF COMMUNICATIONS-MONITOR SOFTWARE COMPATIBLE WITH DBMS SOFTWARE AND OPERATING SYSTEM

4. AVAILABILITY OF INFORMATION TO SUPPORT DECISION-MAKING PROCESSES

5. AVAILABILITY OF DISTRIBUTED DATABASE SUPPORT (UNDER DEVELOPMENT)

6. INTEGRATION OF APPLICATIONS THAT SHARE DATA

files of the centralized-applications-oriented approach.

The communications problems that must be addressed in DDP are exacerbated by the difficulty of accurately predicting demand in a distributed database system. As shown in the table, the communications implications of database systems all indicate increasing demand. Many DBMS vendors now offer compatible software to control or supervise data communications. For example, Cincom's Total uses the Environ/1 communications monitor; Informatics' Mark IV uses the Intercomm package; MRI's System 2000 has TP 2000 monitor software; Cullinane's IDMS employs IDMS/DC; and Software AG's Adabas is compatible with Com-Plete communications monitor software.

Decentralizing storage
The distributed database is defined as a shared data resource whose components have been appropriately divided to enhance local access and control while providing integrated applications support. Some potential

advantages of distributed database systems are:
■ Lower communications costs and transmission delays by designing for localization of resources
■ Improved response times through access to smaller and less complex databases
■ More flexibility and adaptability from customizing the structure of the local database partition (the subset of the entire database that is stored at a node), the interfaces, and the contents to the local requirements
■ Improved reliability because of the successive back-up or fail-soft characteristics of distributed systems
■ Increased user accountability for the system's success as users identify more with the local resources and experience growing feelings of local control
■ Increased shareability achieved by standardization of interfaces between database partitions
■ Increased integrity through reduced data replication across databases and controls for consistency

It should be emphasized that distributing databases does not imply a lack of central coordination among the database partitions. In order to effectively integrate (or even design) the partitions, there must be an overall corporate plan and data-administration authority. This plan may follow a DBMS vendor's architecture for distributed databases, or it may be home-grown. In either case, it must be shaped by the characteristics of the organization and its management philosophy.

The design context
Understanding the significant costs in operating distributed databases will help in analyzing and designing future distributed database environments. There are at least six major areas of expense.

The first is the hardware costs of the physical network, that is, data processors, communications processors for interface and switching management, communications media, primary and secondary memories, and peripherals for input/output support. Next, there is a series of development and maintenance costs for software that:
■ Controls data sharing, including locking and signaling mechanisms to avoid read and/or write of inconsistent data and solutions to the usual deadlock, mutual exclusion, and synchronization problems
■ Initiates and coordinates parallel processes, including logic to identify potential parallelism within transactions and to schedule and coordinate results from related parallel activities
■ Handles update problems to ensure good update protocols and logic for updating redundant data
■ Accesses directories and determines where resources are located in the network and then, if necessary, controls the movement of objects between nodes
■ Manipulates the database for specific applications (traditional programming costs)
■ Maps the logical database to physical data structures, handles memory-management problems, schedules resource access, provides security and recovery tools and protocols, monitors performance, and manages resource reorganization and restructuring (traditional operating system and DBMS functions).

The third major cost category is creating, accessing,

Lexicon of distributed database terms

Cluster directory. A table stored at a cluster-controlling node containing the names and addresses of shareable objects stored in all nodes of that cluster.

Database. An integrated, structured collection of logically related records, which provides shared support of multiple applications.

Database administrator (DBA). The person responsible for managing data activity, database structure, database support, system maintenance, and tuning.

Database management system (DBMS). The software support for creating, maintaining, and protecting databases and for providing the means for various types of access, including database interrogation.

Directory. A table that provides a mapping of logical addresses (names of shareable objects) to physical addresses (object locations at the processors).

Directory-driven. When a directory manager of a distributed database system has primary responsibility for interfacing both the DBMS and the user interfaces to the communications manager and network-operating system.

File. A collection of logically related records, usually of the same type.

Global directory. A table that comprises the names and nodal locations of all shareable objects in the distributed data processing network.

Local directory of node N. A table, stored at node N, containing the names of N's shareable objects.

Logical database. The functional structure of a database, with no regard for the objects' locations.

Object. Any software resource data located at the nodes in a distributed system, including data, programs, and directories. The term refers to these entities as generic items, without regard for size, scope, or use.

Partition. A subset of the database; that is, the part of the overall database that is located at a node.

Physical database. A representation of database structure that includes physical considerations such as the layout and formatting of records and linkages on storage devices.

Query processor. Software that supports interactive, natural-language-query access to files or databases throughout the network.

Shareable object. An object that can be referenced and accessed by users at multiple nodes.

Shielding. Removing one part of a system from another part's concern, such as shielding users from implementation details.

Update synchronization. Reconciling the contents of replicated copies of objects to ensure that all updates are accurately represented.

---

maintaining, and controlling the distributed database. It includes the costs of transmitting commands and objects (see lexicon) between network nodes.

Category four covers computation costs from creating, accessing, maintaining, and controlling the distributed database, that is, the costs of CPU usage for database manipulation. Fifth are costs for storing software and data for access by processors or for delayed input/output. The final category includes personnel costs incurred in interfacing with the database and administering the database and its controls.

Which of these costs categories will be most significant in future systems? If current trends continue, the component costs of the hardware of the physical network should be relatively inconsequential. This is exemplified in the popular design axiom: plan for zero-cost hardware. On the other hand, the software costs of distributed databases are likely to be significant. For instance, packet-switched communications services were selected for the Arpanet and subsequent value-added networks because of their greater flexibility, higher effective bandwidth, and lower cost provided over leased-line or circuit-switched communications services. Yet packet-switched communications require more-sophisticated software control than their circuit switched counterparts.

Several conclusions can be drawn from these projections. First, if hardware costs will not be a major factor, then devising exotic techniques to distribute databases within given storage or line-capacity constraints will not be necessary. In many cases, more memory or higher bandwidth could provide a relatively low-cost solution to these problems.

Second, the significance of software development and personnel costs implies that the use of high-level database interfaces, not only for query access but also for update and maintenance operations, must be given high priority. As mentioned earlier, benefits are already being gained from natural-language-like query processors. The database research community is presently tackling the problem of appropriate nonprocedural, nonrecord-based update and maintenance interfaces. This will mean increased transparency to the database user and computer-communications network, plus improved utilities and tools for data-administration.

Third, there are important operational problems in distributed databases. Until good methods can be developed to control and schedule shared access, updates, resource location, recovery, security, and the like, distributed database technology will remain in an underdeveloped state.

Fourth, the problem of allocating database resources among network nodes is significant and of interest. Communications costs are affected by the distribution of objects among processing nodes: if data or software are not directly accessible where they are to be processed, then transmission is required. Minimizing communications costs should clearly be a goal in designing distributed database systems.

Allocating database components

One aspect of distributed database design that can have a serious impact on communications costs is the allocation of database components among network

2. Choices. *There are two fundamental options for allocating data. The first distributes information geographically—proximity to the source is important. The second, functional distribution by usage, places items usually requested simultaneously at the same node.*

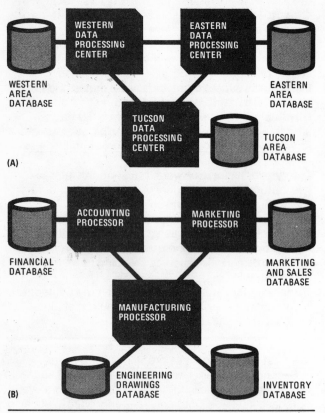

(A)

(B)

WESTERN DATA PROCESSING CENTER

EASTERN DATA PROCESSING CENTER

TUCSON DATA PROCESSING CENTER

WESTERN AREA DATABASE

EASTERN AREA DATABASE

TUCSON AREA DATABASE

ACCOUNTING PROCESSOR

MARKETING PROCESSOR

MANUFACTURING PROCESSOR

FINANCIAL DATABASE

MARKETING AND SALES DATABASE

ENGINEERING DRAWINGS DATABASE

INVENTORY DATABASE

nodes. There are two basic tenets that guide data-distribution efforts, each with the object of minimizing communications costs and improving responsiveness:
1. Locality. At least 80 percent of database requests that originate at a node should be able to be serviced by the local partition.
2. Clustering. Database items that are normally requested together should be available in the same partition (Fig. 1E).

If these were the only considerations, users could completely replicate the database in each partition, thereby making all database contents local everywhere. However, a third tenet must also guide data-distribution efforts:
3. Consistency. If there is replication of a database object across partitions, then updates to that object must be reflected in all those partitions in a manner that matches the user's needs for database consistency.

Two fundamental approaches to allocating objects to partitions are (1) geographically by usage and (2) functionally by usage, as depicted in Figure 2. In either case, the idea is to improve responsiveness by locating the data where it will be requested. In some cases, the two approaches are equivalent. In order to decrease communications costs, the user could copy the data and make an object local to multiple nodes.

Operational problems are compounded with data

replication. For example, which copy of a file should be accessed if copies are stored at three nodes? For inquiry purposes, only one copy need be accessed—most likely the closest copy. But how is "closest" defined? Is it more accurate to think in terms of geographic distance, or line-traffic conditions, or processor-loading conditions, or most recent update? Moreover, how is the node that processes a particular transaction selected? The choice may be based on processor specialization, closeness to the request, closeness to the data, or some other criterion. It is desirable for the user if these decisions do not involve the operator.

There are several options for update resolution. The update transactions may be transmitted to appropriate nodes where they are processed to update affected data, or copies of updated data may be transmitted to appropriate nodes where they replace old information. Affected nodes may be notified that updates have occurred and be expected to request details of the updates when convenient. Finally, multiple versions of the database may coexist. One copy is designated as a master and is kept current, while other copies are flagged as out-of-date and subsequent requests are routed to the master copy.

Database characteristics and user requirements determine the appropriate strategy for balancing communications costs and the need for consistency. It is important to understand that controlling database replication becomes a problem only with respect to update activity. With a database that is often queried but very seldom updated, data could be replicated everywhere without inconsistency.

Finding database components

How can distributed data be found once it is allocated? One option is to build an object's node location into its access key, or logical address. Another option is to maintain at each node a directory that maps data objects to node locations. Consider two different approaches to using directories in processing database requests. First, a user's request is handled by the local DBMS, which supervises directory look-ups and may pass the request on to the DBMS at a remote node. Alternatively, a user's request is handled by the local directory manager, who supervises directory look-ups and may pass the request on to the directory manager at a remote node, who in turn presents the request to the remote DBMS. A distinct advantage of the second approach is that it is directory-driven: directory managers rather than DBMSs communicate across nodes, as depicted in Figure 3, facilitating the interfacing of heterogeneous DBMS packages.

A subsequent design issue is the scope of the directories stored at each node. If each node is a global directory containing mapping information for all objects and nodes, then it has all the advantages and disadvantages of complete replication. Alternatively, each node may store a directory. One directory manager can send requests to other nodes by broadcast or by successive communications with neighbor nodes.

A third option is to use cluster directories. Here, each node has a local directory, and each cluster of "close" nodes has a master directory of data stored on every node in the cluster. The cluster directory then routes requests within that cluster. Clearly the scope of directory contents affects communications costs. A directory is in itself a specialized database; determining directory scope is basically the same problem as allocating database components to partitions.

It must be possible to share data across partitions. In order to respond to a given user's request, data from multiple partitions may need to be aggregated or compared. The primary constraints on integrating mechanisms appear to be heterogeneity and shielding.

Heterogeneity means that dissimilar DBMSs must be able to communicate with each other. Shielding requires that the differences among DBMSs be transparent to those DBMSs. For example, it should be possible for Total to process a request for Company Q's national sales trends over a range of products without regard for the fact that the needed sales data is stored in, say, four database partitions in IMS, IDMS, Total, and System 2000 models, respectively.

One approach to achieving shielded integration is to introduce a standard interface. This approach is also used to interface heterogeneous hardware to a common communications network. Each interface processor communicates with the others in a standard format and with its host in a specialized way. It is important to recognize that the directory managers in Figure 3 serve one part of the DBMS interface function and the communications managers provide the rest.

The administration of distributed databases encompasses a broad range of responsibilities and provides database security controls, recovery mechanisms, performance monitors, and reorganization utilities, and supports design, implementation, query, and update activities. Much of what has been learned in the context of centralized databases may also be applied to distributed databases. Caution is needed, however, since some solutions to problems in the centralized context work poorly in the distributed environment.

In fact, distributed database administration is further complicated by attempts to distribute human administrative functions. Hierarchic structures will most likely evolve to enable local administrative control under the umbrella of corporate direction.

Design sample
To illustrate the complex problems of distributed databases, consider several successful and very familiar information systems and compare their characteristics of data and directory allocation, query and update operations, and administration.

The Bible is certainly an established distributed database of information. There is rampant replication of this database; some persons even have several copies. All partitions have the same global contents, although it is possible to procure a copy of, say, a given testament or a set of verses. Actually, there are multiple versions of the database, but this inconsistency is generally tolerated. Query access is universally available, but update is evidently by special authority. A requester generally queries the closest copy (geographically),

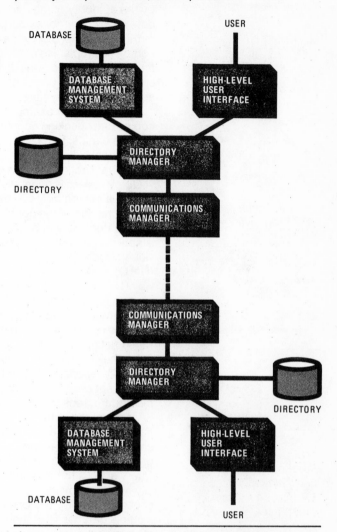

3. Distribution. *The architecture of a distributed database support system stresses the physical similarity of the resources used by geographically separate users. Transparency is important to smooth operation.*

although he may occasionally reference a more distant version. The ratio of query to update is essentially infinite. How are updates resolved? Copies of a new version are made available, and a user chooses to either ignore the update or replace or augment his collection.

There are copies of the telephone directory nearly everywhere. But rather than each copy having global contents as the Bible, each partition contains local contents, where locality is defined in geographic terms. It is assumed that this arrangement satisfies most local inquiries. Actually, a user may make his own subset of this database containing numbers frequently called (and often crossing geographic boundaries) and/or numbers not to be forgotten. In addition to the local database partitions, there is a cluster partition defined in geographic terms by area code.

Query access is generally to the closest copy. However, when a user needs to find a number that is not in his local database partition, he routes his request to the appropriate cluster directory. There is significantly more querying than updating. Actually, contents are changed, items are deleted and added continually, and these updates are reflected soon thereafter in the authority's cluster directories. When a person attempts to use a number that has been updated, he is notified by the authority of the update. The user then can update his own database partition to reflect the results of the transaction. Updates are resolved annually by completely replacing each local copy. (A given user may replace his personal copy at a different interval, such as when the pages are full or when the copy falls apart and recovery takes place.)

To give another example, there are usually two copies of a checking account register—the customer's and the bank's. Each copy contains local contents, where locality is defined in terms of time. The most recent transactions are the ones usually queried.

Query access is generally to the closest copy, although a person may sometimes need to query the bank's version or the contents of an old register. The relative frequency of query (Q) and update (U) activity is approximately equal, depending on whether the individual writes checks without consulting the balance (U > Q), consults the balance and writes a check anyway (U = Q), or consults the balance and puts the register (checkbook) back in his pocket (U < Q). Updates actually happen asynchronously: the customer updates his balance when he executes the transaction (or sometime thereafter); the bank updates its version when the check clears. This asynchronous update is generally reconciled monthly. The authority distributes a copy not only of the processing results but also of the update transactions.

Consider the common use of the credit card in which there is only one record maintained of the current balance—the credit agency's. The user is offered copies of the transactions but may or may not retain them. Query access to the credit limit and balance is generally not made by the cardholder but by another type of user: the store. The credit agency may actually have multiple database partitions, geographically distributed. A user's request is generally routed to the geographically local partition, from which it may be routed to a remote partition if the cardholder is out of his home area. There is usually more update activity than query activity, although some of us may be declined update privileges as a result of query. The agency may update its copy of the cardholder's balance either when the transaction is processed, that is, when the sale is made, or when it later receives notice of the transaction. The authority periodically distributes a copy not only of the processing results but also of the updates.

As these examples show, the relative frequency of query and update are important in determining replication and update strategies.

Distributed database design is but one aspect of setting up a distributed information system. It is, however, of extreme importance in determining communications costs, responsiveness, and reliability as seen by the user community. The various system components must fit into an integrated whole, yet it is important to shield the details of the various components from each other. ■

Robert Holland, Holland Systems Corporation, Ann Arbor, Mich.

Distributed databases: decisions and implementations

A strategic corporate plan is needed to successfully implement distributed databases. The plan must consider approaches, problems, and company database organization.

The proliferation of computers and computerized information, in conjunction with the diversification and isolation of products and services, will result in greater emphasis on distributed databases. The major concerns in distributed databases involve overall corporate strategies that can be employed to make reliable decisions regarding distributed database approaches, the problems caused by distributing databases, and possible solutions to these problems.

Problems in distributed database environments frequently involve invalid updates, slow performance, excessive computer overhead, and synchronization anomalies such as deadlock. Many of these problems are still unresolved or are resolved only at great cost and overhead. Others are avoided by an overall strategic database and data management plan to control and manage a company's data.

A strategic plan must take into account the location of business activities that require the data, types of business transactions, traffic patterns, and physical characteristics of the data. It also must consider the logical organization of the company's databases, how to integrate them with different types of corporate and departmental activities, and the ability of the databases to communicate with each other. Clearly, a decision to decentralize data, as well as how to do it, requires the cooperative inputs of communications specialists, company management, and data processing experts.

One of the first decisions that must be faced when decentralizing data is that of determining how much data to distribute and where. In considering the degree of distribution, it is necessary to strike a balance between transmitting data and storing it in peripheral units. A rule of thumb here may be stated as follows:

The more widely dispersed corporate data locations are, the more attention must be paid to the actual transmission costs and reliability of the transmission facility between the locations. On the other hand, the more geographically close the data locations, the more attention must be paid to the peripheral devices in which the data resides.

Using that rule and considering only cost, it is possible to investigate the tradeoff between dispersed storage units and transmission to a centralized unit of data.

Figure 1, which indicates these tradeoffs, can be used to show that in North America it is more cost-effective to centralize data since transmission is relatively efficient and inexpensive. On the other hand, in many foreign countries transmission is fairly expensive and often breaks down. This would generally lead foreign corporations to decentralize their data. Since storage and transmission costs are both decreasing, the relative arguments of decentralization versus centralization of data will probably remain the same over the coming decade. Therefore, it is necessary to consider other factors when making a distributed data decision. For example, properties exist for data which may lead naturally to decentralization while other properties of data lead users to gravitate towards centralization. The following properties lead to decentralization:

■ Data is primarily used at one peripheral location. To transmit such data for storage at remote locations may be unnecessarily complex and expensive. Therefore, if technology costs permit, it makes sense to store the data where it is used.

■ Accuracy, privacy, and/or security of data is a local responsibility. Under these conditions, more accurate, private, and safe data might be maintained if the data is stored near those people responsible for its safekeeping. Such people are generally intimately acquainted with the requirements of the data, the appli-

1. Cost considerations for degree of data distribution.
When considering whether or not to distribute data and how much to distribute, it is necessary to strike a balance between transmitting the data to a centralized location and storing it in multiple peripheral units. Cost and reliability factors must be considered.

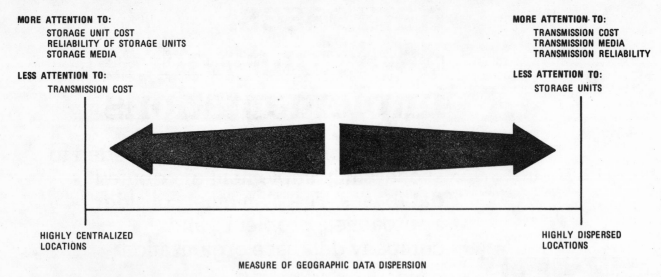

MORE ATTENTION TO:
    STORAGE UNIT COST
    RELIABILITY OF STORAGE UNITS
    STORAGE MEDIA

LESS ATTENTION TO:
    TRANSMISSION COST

MORE ATTENTION TO:
    TRANSMISSION COST
    TRANSMISSION MEDIA
    TRANSMISSION RELIABILITY

LESS ATTENTION TO:
    STORAGE UNITS

HIGHLY CENTRALIZED
LOCATIONS

HIGHLY DISPERSED
LOCATIONS

MEASURE OF GEOGRAPHIC DATA DISPERSION

cations that use it, and the means for safekeeping.

■ The databases or files are simple and used by few applications. In this case, there may be no reason to use database-management-system software that requires large computing resources at a remote site.

■ The update rate for the databases involved may be too high for a single centralized storage of the data. The individual smaller databases in a distributed network may make updating of data a simpler task.

■ Remote databases may be interrogated or manipulated with an end-user language such as engineering graphics, statistical analysis routines, linear programming packages, or other methods that result in unique and highly specialized uses of the data. In these cases, too many end-user operations on the data can destroy performance characteristics needed by all users of a centralized system. Data may be better located in a remote database environment where end users are responsible for their own usage and costs in analyzing the data through special-purpose software packages.

There are also major factors that strongly lead to centralization of data. For example:

■ The data may be used by centralized or shared applications such as payroll, accounting, material requirements planning, or production scheduling. In these cases, the shareability of data across multiple applications is so important that a distributed facility would be costly and unwieldly to invoke because of all the protocols needed to support such an environment.

■ Users in all functional areas of the company may need access to the same data but also require current or up-to-the-minute versions. To support this need, the data must be frequently updated. Only centralization prevents the real-time synchronization problems that occur in environments with high update levels for multiple copies of data that are used by multiple organizations within the company.

■ If corporate users require data from many separate locations, it may be less expensive to centralize their data than to use a switched data network.

■ Searching geographically scattered data is very time consuming. This is because software and hardware for efficient searching in response to ad hoc queries requires secondary indices (means of finding particular data using any one of several identifiers). However, such indices refer only to the data stored in one location. Thus database-management-system software operates today on centralized rather than geographically scattered data. This is expected to change during the latter part of the 1980s, but corporate strategies today must consider the current capability of a database management system to handle its data.

■ If a high level of security through standardized security techniques is to be maintained over data, data should be centralized. Protection may be achieved through a centralized data administration that has knowledge of both the data and security techniques to invoke data authorization at the data element level (smallest unit of meaningful data); segment, set, or relational level, record level, and/or database level. In other words, data administration in the organization today must fully learn about these security techniques before decentralizing such knowledge. However, if security includes catastrophe protection for a corporation's data, distributed data should be considered. In these cases, decentralization is primarily for backup and recovery from a possible disaster rather than for decentralized usage of the data on a daily basis.

■ Some companies require very large data-storage areas. They use marketing or design techniques that require millions of customer records, product-design records, and research experiments. In these cases, economies of scale that take advantage of centralized bulk storage are desirable.

■ Most network operations are more easily audited when their detail usage is centralized. Auditing often requires detail transaction audit trails that are better stored in large centralized archival storage units.

Such pros and cons of centralization and decentralization are concerned with the technological and control aspects of data within a company. Human-oriented factors should also be considered. For example, the degree to which a company distributes data should also depend upon the sophistication level of its data processing staff. As the company decentralizes its data, it needs professionals with a background in communications protocols, and in database and integrated-software technologies. Since the data processing and data communications industries are growing so fast, such talent is difficult to acquire or maintain. Because of this situation, many companies should consider centralizing their data. Exceptions to this rule are the banking industry, travel agencies, and customer service industries in which distributed data is a major part of the business. These companies will have to train or hire the right computer professionals to do the job.

For their part, database management systems (DBMSs) are designed to exist in a single computer or computer environment. A database management system controls, among other things, the amount of redundancy in a database, querying of the database, and independence of the database from the applications that use it. This independence allows either a company's database or application to be changed without having to also change the other.

A DBMS in one CPU facility generally has no direct control over DBMSs in other facilities. Exceptions to this include Cullinane Corporation's Integrated Database Management System (IDMS) with resident and virtual monitors, and Computer Corporation of America's System for Distributed Databases (SDD.1). These database management systems employ a local data manager that controls the conventional functions of the DBMS and a separate network manager that does not access the data itself but determines the access strategy for handling distributed data operations.

These systems are representative of how close the software industry has come to implementing distributed database management systems. Even these systems, however, exert strong centralized control over distributing the data and handling the communications protocols that are necessary. Therefore, an easy to implement capability that allows different types of communications between nodes in a nondirected fashion does not exist and is a limiting factor in distributing data.

Distributing the data

Databases may be distributed in four basic, different ways. In the first, a user input device communicates directly with the remote processor. The processor, in turn, either singly requests data for each transaction, or batches the transactions for request to the central processor that houses the DBMS (Fig. 2). Access validation, security checking, and the return of data to the user is carried out by the DBMS through the communications network and the remote processor.

In the second (Fig. 3), applications can reside in multiple processors within the company. Each processor needs a directory that indicates the location of data subjects of interest (such as employee, vendor, or customer) in other processors as well as its own. A user requirement for data can then be directed through a communications network to the correct processor.

Protocols exist for transferring either a single record or an entire file between database management systems. If the data in one machine at a time are read-only, rather than write or update, the protocol procedure is relatively straightforward. If on the other hand the data is updated on all machines within the network, care must be taken to avoid file, record, or even data element lockouts (locking of data so that only one transaction at a time can access it), which may occur with today's database management systems.

A third method of distributing data involves a centralized DBMS but uses remote physical storage (Fig. 4). This method is frequently used to take care of special security considerations, audits, and archival data, or to take advantage of mass-storage systems. In the latter case, the same physical data may be read by users but not written by them. Examples of such databases include library abstracts, stock market data, and econometric databases. These are typically used by companies that sell data or data-oriented services to their customers.

Finally, in the fourth method, a well-organized data directory is needed to support the remote processor environment shown in Figure 5. In this case, the user requests a logical record (a record based on data as seen by the user or programmer rather than based on physical organization seen by the computer). The re-

2. Remote processor environment. *A user input device communicates directly with the remote processor, which, in turn, either singly requests data for each transaction or batches the transactions for request to the central processor that houses the database management system. Security is carried out by the DBMS through the network.*

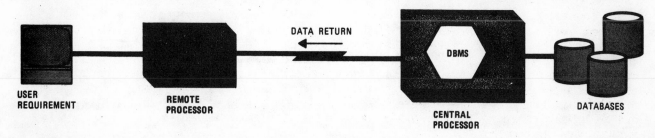

USER REQUIREMENT   REMOTE PROCESSOR   DATA RETURN   DBMS   CENTRAL PROCESSOR   DATABASES

3. Multi-database management system network. *Applications can reside in multiple processors within a company. A directory in each processor indicates the* *location of data subjects in other processors as well as its own. A request for data can thus be directed through a communications network to the correct processor.*

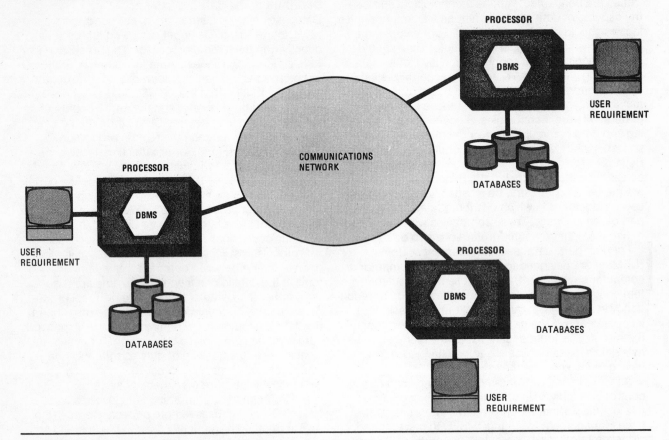

quest is made through a remote computer or an intelligent terminal that is normally too small to house a DBMS. The request goes to a parent database management system on a distributed database network. Through the directory, the DBMS then finds the data that was requested and returns it to the end user. Much effort and many computing cycles may be wasted if the directory is not kept up to date in a synchronized fashion and distributed to the processors at all locations that house DBMSs. In all four of the cases, shown in Figures 2 through 5, readers should note that while it may be easier to implement databases in a remote fashion, it is most difficult to control, synchronize, and create concurrency among the distributed databases.

To obtain a clearer understanding of the distributed database environment, and how to take advantage of it in the corporate setting, it is important to think of a three-level database. Such a stratum identifies a number of characteristics of users and applications that will support the business activities of the organization.

Data on the Level
Each stratum level contains a database and database management system (DBMS) geared to different types of access methods, queries, and how fast a response is needed (see table). The upper levels contain subsets

4. Remote physical storage. *A centralized database management system that uses remote physical storage is frequently used to take care of special security considera-* *tions, audits, and archival data, or to take advantage of mass storage media. In the latter case, the physical data may be read by users but not written by them.*

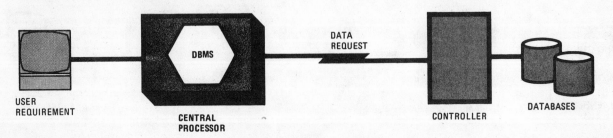

5. Remote processor DBMS network. *The user requests a logical record through a remote computer or an intelligent terminal that is too small to house a database management system. A parent database management system receives the request and, through a directory, locates the requested data and returns it to the end user.*

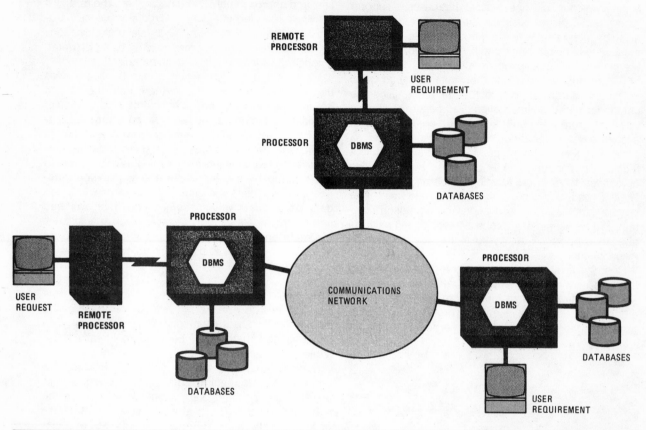

of the level directly below.

Level 1 consists of subject databases only. These are databases created based on subjects of interest to a company, such as personnel, products, and customers, instead of applications such as payroll, inventory control, and cash management. They contain groups of data, called entities (employees, suppliers, and contracts are examples), that are grouped to meet overall business activities for a company's integrated database environment (see "Planning databases"). Grouping techniques indicate the need for 20 to 30 subject databases to support all integrated business functions.

Level 1 contains a company's most stable and protected databases. To maintain these databases' stability and integrity, a database at Level 2 or 3 is never allowed to replace a database in Level 1. Instead, databases that occur at Level 1 are synchronized by receiving transactions from Levels 2 and 3. The Level 2 and 3 databases are then rederived (completely replaced) at some quiet point in processing (Fig. 6).

If it is economically justifiable, a company can have synchronization on a transaction-by-transaction updating of the Level 1 databases as well as any Level 2 updates that exist. Few applications require total synchronization among the different database levels—that is often more a desire than a business necessity. However, if the need exists, it can be done. For example,

update of customer-transaction databases within the banking environment must be achieved through total synchronization. This is because banks are required by law to keep track of activities in branches as well as the central offices so that the auditability of various cash positions is available at all times.

The subject databases of Level 1 are formulated in such a way that they support all activities of the company by allowing subjects to be derived for multiple applications. As such, they are likely to be used for companywide centralized operations. In contrast, Level 2 databases, which are derived from Level 1 databases, are more operational in an on-line environment because they are able to combine subjects in order to achieve fast performance objectives. This makes them likely candidates for distribution to remote sites where they can provide instant responses to queries and interactively produce reports for decision making. The fast performance achieved by recombining and structuring of subjects is also required for high-volume transaction applications commonly found at remote sites. In contrast, the Level 1 databases are oriented toward more routine production applications.

To avoid many of the lockout and synchronization problems that can exist with multiple levels of updates going on within a computing environment, Level 2 databases should be "read only" as much as possible. When an application must update a Level 2 type of

Planning databases

A company normally has multiple databases to support its different types of business activities. The databases must be integrated with each other so they can communicate with each other and be combined, in various ways, to support application requests.

One of the first decisions that must be faced when defining a database plan is that of determining the criteria for database integration. Databases may be set up to integrate with each other based on, for example, a company's applications, departments, divisions, or some combination of criteria. A popular approach in a multidivision organization is to create corporatewide databases for support functions such as accounting, finance, and personnel, but use division-based integrated databases for production and marketing functions. To be useful, the databases established must be able to support all applications that are needed by these functions.

Once the level of database integration is established, the company must develop a "strategic data model" for the functions defined for the integration. In such a model, each business function is broken down into a group of actions that must occur in order to perpetuate

(A) STRATEGIC DATA MODEL

BUSINESS FUNCTION: PRODUCTION

BUSINESS PROCESS: MANUFACTURING PRODUCT "A"

ACTIVITY: DETERMINING QUANTITY
PURCHASING RAW MATERIALS
SCHEDULING PRODUCTION
DETERMINING PRODUCT SPECIFICATIONS

ENTITY: CONTRACT
PRODUCT
EMPLOYEE
SUPPLIER
INVENTORY

the function (Fig. A). Additionally, each business process has a set of business activities that must be completed on a continuous basis in order to achieve the objectives of a process.

Finally, the activities are broken down into groups of data, called entities, that support the business activities. When a map is provided to associate entities to business activities and processes, and finally to business functions, as defined in the integration plan, this results in a strategic data model.

Typically, a strategic data model for both large and small companies consists of about 30 business functions, 250 business processes, 1,000 business activi-

ties, and approximately 200 data entities. The business activities specified in Figure A directly influence hardware, software, and data- and telecommunications plans. The data is merely raw material being delivered among the various functions in an organization.

Most companies implement application databases that are designed by a design team from the bottom up, in order to fulfill the requirements of a particular application. Unfortunately, as new company applications that require existing data are developed, the old application data structures never seem to fit the new application requirement. As a result, it is not unusual to see a company develop 75 to 100 application databases over a six-year period. Redundancy in these databases causes very substantial computer overhead and destroys data integrity. A more efficient solution is to create and implement what are known as subject databases—databases based on subjects of interest in a corporation.

The ID job

The first task in establishing subject databases is to identify the subjects of interest in a corporation. The strategic data model can be used to identify these subjects of interest.

Subject databases actually consist of groups of a company's data entities. Statistical techniques are used to group homogeneous entities into the same subject database. The goal is to maximize intradatabase associations and minimize interdatabase associations based on a company's business activities and distributed database requirements.

Once the entities are clustered into each subject area, they are named. Each entity is subdivided into two or more data elements. A data element is the smallest unit of meaningful data. Vendor name, vendor address, and employee salary are all data elements. Finally, entity-to-entity relationships are established within and between each database (Fig. B). Relationships may be defined that are uni- or bidirectional and that relate one element to one other or many others.

The identification of subject databases from the strategic data model provides a quick, top-down blueprint of the data groups needed to support a company's business activities. The data elements that comprise the entities need not be established at subject database identification time. All data elements and their detailed relationships should be developed bottom-up as project designs are necessary. Thus, database success requires top-down design of databases to the subject database level, as well as bottom-up design for the detail data element relationships.

database, these applications should be batched together and sent to the Level 1 database for updating. In the Level 1 environment, the transactions are run through various screens and edits that help ensure the integrity of the data at the subject database level. The

company is able to rederive the Level 2 database or provide backup and recovery of these databases in the event that they are harmed. In the case where such backup is needed, the company can invoke the last derivation of the Level 2 database plus the transaction

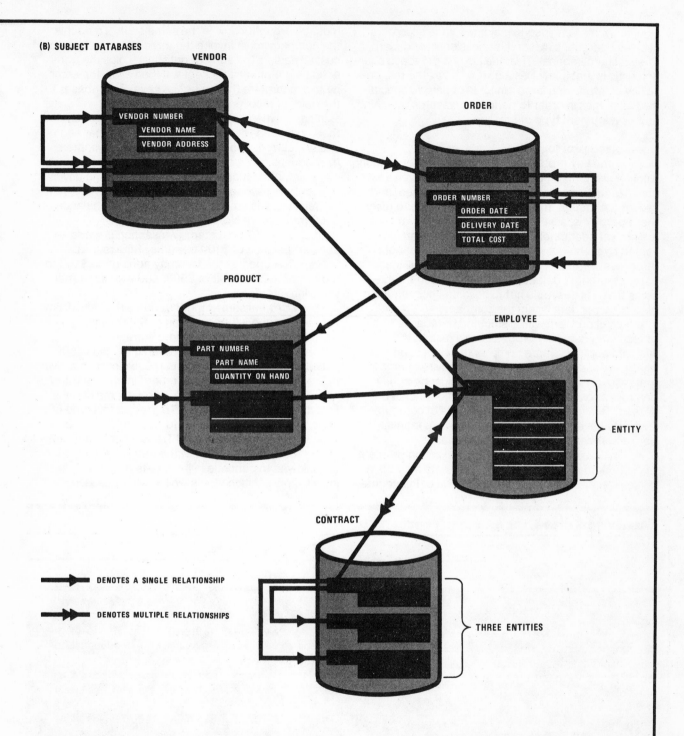

(B) SUBJECT DATABASES

VENDOR

VENDOR NUMBER
VENDOR NAME
VENDOR ADDRESS

ORDER

ORDER NUMBER
ORDER DATE
DELIVERY DATE
TOTAL COST

PRODUCT

PART NUMBER
PART NAME
QUANTITY ON HAND

EMPLOYEE

ENTITY

CONTRACT

THREE ENTITIES

→ DENOTES A SINGLE RELATIONSHIP

⇒ DENOTES MULTIPLE RELATIONSHIPS

An advantage of subject databases is that they are particularly easy to maintain. All information about employee, contract, or supplier, for example, is within its own subject database. It is not necessary to split entities within the database as new applications arise. Instead, subject databases can be implemented on a piecemeal basis and new data elements can be established as needed without changing the old ones. Good subject database environments may be established with only 20 to 30 subject databases. However, they vary in content, size, and relationships based on the type of company that they are intended to support.

log that has occurred since the last derivation.

Level 3 is primarily used for research and development endeavors in a company. Databases at this level are required to be interfaced with fourth-generation languages (very-high-level English-like query languages instead of machine, assembler, or common programming languages) so that users can do their own structuring, manipulation, and demand reporting from specialized analyses of the data. The class of user for a Level 3 database environment includes graphics designers such as engineers, major resource allocators such as operations research professionals and market forecasting personnel. Thus the Level 3 database characteristic is that it involves a user who has the responsibility of interfacing large amounts of data to specialized packages in order to perform a research, planning, and development type of function.

Unresolved problems

Many of the key problems that can occur when working within a distributed database environment involve synchronization, error recovery, protocol overhead, and security. Although attempts have been made to resolve these problems, several are only partially solvable or are not yet adequately resolved. Still others are prevented by techniques such as the development of the three-level database concept. From an overall standpoint, distributed database problems are so troublesome that it is desirable not to have an unconstrained distribution of data within the company.

A typical problem with distributed databases is that of recovery. Recovery processes in a distributed environment are much more complex than in a centralized one. The concern in distributed data environments is that recovery after a network failure must be tightly controlled so that updates are not lost or double processed. The increasingly large amounts of computerized data have resulted in situations where manual backup processes may not be possible.

In addition, because of the synchronization problem of distributed data, multiple copies of data may be in different states of update. After a period of failure, they must be brought back to the same state. To do this, the company must invoke the three-level stratum discussed earlier. The subject databases plus the transaction log that must be kept will then allow the company to synchronize the Level 2 or Level 3 databases to the point of recovery initialization.

In cases where transactions update distributed data, the transactions may interfere with each other and cause incorrect updates. For example, two or more transactions may be updating the same data file, segment, set, or relationship on a remote storage device. The following sequence can occur:

Step A: Transaction A reads an account balance of $100 from record No. 1.

Step B: On the next step, Transaction B reads an account balance of $100 from the same record.

Step C: A updates the value by adding the $100 to the customer's deposit of $500, and writes the final value into storage.

Step D: At the same time B updates the value from yet another deposit transaction of $300, making it $100 plus $300 and writes it into storage.

The final result should have been $100 plus $500 plus $300. However, Transaction B, which was allowed to read and handle the same record in parallel with A, has overwritten Transaction A's update, making the final answer $100 plus $300. To prevent this type of error, most DBMSs today perform some type of partial lockout of Transaction B until Transaction A has completed the use of that part of the database. Only then is B allowed to continue in its update mode. This seemingly simple solution works well when updates involve

Stratified database characteristics

CHARACTERISTIC	STRATIFICATION LEVEL		
	LEVEL 1	LEVEL 2	LEVEL 3
DATA ORIENTATION	SUBJECT	COMBINED SUBJECTS	APPLICATION
ACCESS PURPOSE	PREDETERMINED BATCH UPDATE TRANSACTIONS	READ ONLY OR MINIMAL UPDATE TRANSACTIONS	TOTAL USER CONTROL FOR AD HOC DATA USE AND DESIGN
OUTPUT REPORTS	PREDETERMINED PERIODIC REPORTING	EXCEPTION SPECIAL DEMAND REPORTING	SPECIAL DESIGN REPORTS
DBMS TYPE	PRODUCTION ORIENTED DBMS	LIMITED AD HOC QUERY DBMS	FOURTH GENERATION LANGUAGE DBMS
TRANSACTION FEEDS FROM	LEVEL 1 USER LEVEL 2 USER LEVEL 3 USER	LEVEL 2 USER	LEVEL 3 USER
DATABASE REPLACEMENT FROM	BACKUP DATABASES ONLY	LEVEL 2 PLUS TRANSACTION LOG	LEVEL 2 OR LEVEL 1 PLUS TRANSACTION LOG
DISTRIBUTION TENDENCY	HIGHLY CENTRALIZED	DISTRIBUTED BY APPLICATION REQUIREMENT	HIGHLY DECENTRALIZED
DATA ADMINISTRATION AND DICTIONARY JURISDICTION	YES	YES	YES

6. Stratified database characteristics. *Each Level of a three-level database configuration contains a database and database management system geared to different users and applications with different types of access methods, queries, and response time requirements. The upper levels are subsets of the levels below.*

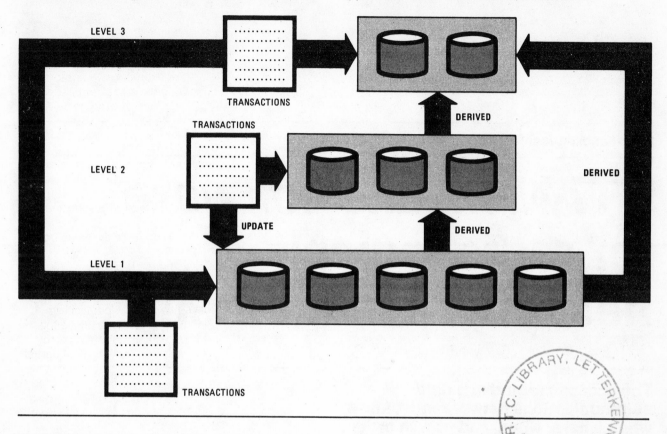

a single record. But more complex solutions are required for transactions that cause data to be searched in multiple or distributed databases before updating occurs. Simple solutions may give rise to further synchronization problems and excessive overhead.

Distributed data environments may cause inconsistent reads and use of the data. This happens because when more than one copy of data is used, the company stands the chance of generating reports from multiple sources that are unsynchronized. In these cases, because of timing problems, data that should agree may not. This problem can be prevented with appropriate locks of the DBMS. Additionally, synchronization protocols can be implemented to ensure integrity.

Locking distributed databases, as DBMSs do to prevent update interference or inconsistent reads, can often cause deadlocks. A deadlock may occur if two or more transactions attempt to read or update the same two or more records. It occurs as follows:

Step A: Transaction Y locks Record 1.
Step B: Transaction Y reads Record 1.
Step C: Transaction Z locks Record 2.
Step D: Transaction Z reads Record 2.
Step E: Transaction Y tries to read Record 2, but it is locked.
Step F: Transaction Z tries to read Record 1, but it is locked.

Both transactions wait for the records they want to be unlocked, but neither will unlock its record until it

has read both records. Deadlock has occurred. Most DBMSs today are programmed to back the transactions out of a deadlock. However, overhead is a problem since many compute cycles are lost while the system is backing out of the deadlocked transactions.

The protocols needed to prevent invalid updates and inconsistent reads as well as deadlock can cause excessive overhead within the distributed database environment. Moreover, when transactions handle data in multiple locations the chances of deadlock occurring can be significantly increased. The best way to cope with this extra overhead for synchronization problems is to avoid it by planning and classifying user applications in conjunction with developing and distributing the three-level database concept.

Finally, protection of the security, privacy, and auditing functions within the company are difficult in a distributed database environment. It is difficult to determine who did what to different records of the data at different times. In additiion, security controls and privacy protection are often poor on distributed database systems because of the total lack of control over the DBMS in a distributed environment. Until better methods of handling integrated distributed environments are developed, such as by a controlling directory or integrated dictionary, this problem will plague distributed database systems. Meanwhile, special attention must be paid to this area by a data security officer within the company. ∎

VTAM means software for more logical network management

Sam D. Scott, IBM Corp., Research Triangle Park, N.C.

The access method in a data communications network must know what, where, when, and how in order to move data in and out of a host computer

IBM's Virtual Telecommunications Access Method (VTAM) has been a boon to data communications users because it increases growth potential by providing session services between the host's application programs and the terminals in the network. By doing that, VTAM decreases the adverse effects of changes on applications-program investments. Because IBM's data communications host software products (IMS, CICS, TSO, etc.) have a VTAM interface, a single access method for an entire network provides an economical means of supporting many different on-line requirements. Here is how VTAM works.

VTAM implements Systems Network Architecture (SNA) in IBM 370 or 303X host computers. As an SNA access method, VTAM uses SNA's data formats, data transfers, protocols, and operational sequences to control data communications. The data communications applications programs and VTAM provide the three layers of communications function as defined in an SNA host: applications, function management, and transmission control. Applications are implemented by programs written by the application developers or obtained through IBM. Function management is implemented through VTAM's application program interface. Transmission is implemented by VTAM.

The primary responsibilities of VTAM include start-up, recovery and termination (network control), dynamic connection and disconnection of terminals and applications, and the routing of data between terminals and applications (application services). A terminal can be connected to one application at a time, but has the flexibility to alter this connection should the user choose to communicate with another application in the same host that also uses VTAM. With the Advanced Communications Function (ACF), the responsibility of VTAM is increased to include managing the dynamic connection and disconnection of terminals that have applications running on different hosts. However, the other hosts must also use the ACF versions of the access methods, either ACF/VTAM or ACF/TCAM.

VTAM is designed to take advantage of a host computer that provides virtual-storage (VS) capabilities. VTAM starts itself, based on terminal and application definitions supplied in the form of tables stored on a direct-access storage device (DASD). VTAM can add new definitions while it is running so that additional applications and terminals can become active participants in the network. Thus VTAM adapts itself to supporting both small and large networks. Growth is manageable because additional terminals can be brought into the network as needed. The applications-program interface is supplied in the form of VTAM macros that are compatible across all VS operating systems, such as Disk Operating System (DOS), VS1 and VS2. By using VTAM as a common applications interface, developers of data communications application can concentrate their efforts on delivery of function instead of exhausting their resources on the physical network.

Applications-program interface

The VTAM applications-program interface is in the form of macro instructions that are coded within IBM-supplied programs. IBM programs such as Customer Information Control System (CICS), Information Management System (IMS), Virtual Storage Personal Computing (VSPC), as well as some types of systems control programming (SCP) such as the Time Sharing Option (TSO) and the Job Entry System (JES), have been written to use VTAM. A user-written data processing applications program can be designed and written to use a high-level language, such as COBOL, for its major part. Additional subroutines can be written in assembler language to provide the VTAM interface.

The VTAM data communications macros that provide data transfer between terminals and applications programs are implemented in two forms. The first form consists of macros to support channel-attached IBM 3270 terminals and start-stop and binary synchronous remote terminals controlled by an IBM 3704/3705 communications controller with a Network Control Program/Virtual Storage (NCP/VS). The second form consists of record-mode data communications macros to support channel-attached IBM 3270 and 3790 terminals, remote SNA terminals on switched or leased SDLC lines, and binary synchronous 3270s controlled by NCP/VS. The record mode data communications macros are designed to provide the end-user-to-end-user protocols defined in SNA. These protocols manage data between host applications and intelligent SNA terminals in the network. In addition, the record mode data communications macros in the ACF version of VTAM manage data transferred between two applications programs in either the same host computer or different hosts.

The flexibility of VTAM with terminals is demonstrated by postulating a Multiple Virtual System (MVS) with IMS/VS, TSO, and JES2, using VTAM to support remote IBM 3790, 3270, and 3770 terminals dropped on the same SDLC link. Using the intelligence built into the 3790 cluster controller, one 3790 with multiple display stations can support remote job entry with JES2, on-line applications with IMS/VS and TSO, and off-line user applications executed in the 3790. The 3270 terminals on the same SDLC link can have access to either IMS/VS or TSO along with the 3770 terminals being used for remote job entry. One of the benefits of VTAM is that a given terminal can have access to more than a single host application (like IMS/VS and TSO), thereby reducing data communications line costs and avoiding duplicate terminal costs.

With the advent of ACF, and the ability to network multiple hosts, an application that could not be justified previously because of a limited number of users now becomes possible because more users in the corporate network have access to the program in question.

The interface to VTAM for the remote physical network is provided by NCP/VS in the IBM 3704 or 3705 communications controller, while the start-up of the network is controlled and coordinated by VTAM through NCP/VS. VTAM issues commands to the NCP/VS to start the network in an orderly fashion. The commands issued by VTAM for network start-up can be controlled by user definition and by the VTAM operator facilities. VTAM thus allows the user to activate only that portion of the network requiring access to applications available in the host. Also, terminal-user access of host applications can be controlled based on resource requirements at the host (such as on-line file availability). Similarly, VTAM operator commands allow any part of the remote network to stop receiving services. VTAM, in this case, issues shut-down commands to NCP/VS, which quiesces the portion of the network that no longer requires host services.

VTAM-NCP interface

To control and pass terminal messages between VTAM and NCP/VS, a well-defined interface is used. That interface is currently implemented in two formats, one for NCP/VS-attached SNA terminals, and one for NCP/VS-attached start-stop and binary synchronous terminals. For data transfer between VTAM and NCP/VS, multiple messages for both SNA and non-SNA terminals may be handled in a single input-output operation. VTAM input-output logic for inbound messages for applications programs is driven by an interrupt created by the 370X communications controller.

A user-defined number of VTAM input-output buffers receive one or more messages from the NCP/VS. Thus, during one I/O operation, multiple messages from different terminals may be received by VTAM for distribution to one or more host applications. For outbound messages from applications within the host, VTAM schedules and initiates I/O to transfer one or more messages to the 3704/3705 NCP/VS. Upon completion, the VTAM I/O operation is structured to read any inbound messages the NCP/VS may have received during the VTAM-to-NCP/VS data transfer.

Handling inbound and outbound messages in this fashion provides host efficiencies for attaching terminals by means of older communications controllers that could support only single-terminal message transfers during an I/O operation. The older hardware-oriented methods left all the link protocol responsibilities (polling, addressing, etc.) to the host access method, such as the Basic Telecommunications Access Method (BTAM).

VTAM and the 3704/3705 NCP/VS manage data transfers between themselves by using two different controls. The object is to give better performance and a more uniform response time for inquiry terminals in the network. Either type of control may prompt the 3704/3705 hardware interrupt to inform VTAM that data is formatted in NCP/VS ready for VTAM processing. The first type of control operates through an attention delay that is specified by the user in NCP/VS. The attention delay value, specified in units of tenths of a

1 Dynamic connection

Sessions. At any one time, a terminal may be attached to only one applications program in the host computer. However, each applications program can be simultaneously attached to several terminal users. These connections, through the use of VTAM, can change dynamically from minute to minute, depending on the user's needs.

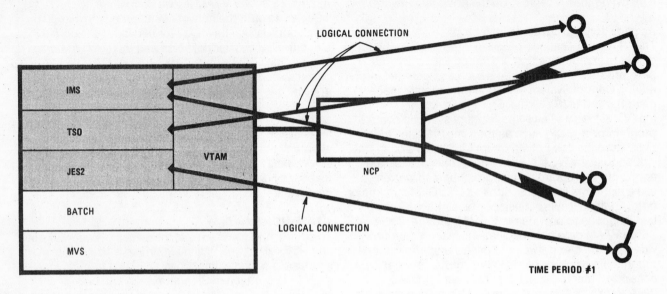

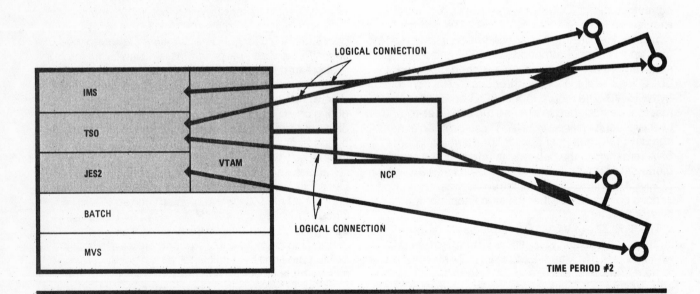

second, controls the maximum time inbound messages can be held in NCP/VS before the communications controller provides a hardware attention interrupt to the host computer. The other type of control is a user-specified maximum number of VTAM message buffers to be used in a single input-transfer operation from NCP/VS to the host. When the NCP has data for VTAM equaling or exceeding the capacity of the buffers before the end of the attention-delay time, the 3704/3705 will provide a hardware interrupt to notify the host of data in the NCP. The ability to buffer and transfer multiple messages in a single input operation from the NCP to VTAM by using the attention delay contributes to upgrading the host's performance.

The ACF has enhanced VTAM by allowing its applications, in the same or different hosts, to communicate with each other. Two widely used applications programs, CICS/VS and JES2, give the user an application-to-application capability when used with ACF/VTAM. JES2 (MVS) is currently available to provide that function for job networking, which is the ability to enter batched data from a remote job-entry terminal. The system then routes the data to the proper host and relays any batched output back to the terminal upon completion of processing.

CICS-to-CICS data communications using ACF/VTAM can be done in the same host or between multiple hosts—the added application-to-application

2 ACF session capability

Extension. *The Advanced Communication Function allows a network of hosts and terminals with similar access methods to act as one user resource. Host-to-host* *data communications, along with multi-host access from any terminal in the network, can provide the traffic load to justify previously uneconomic program expansion.*

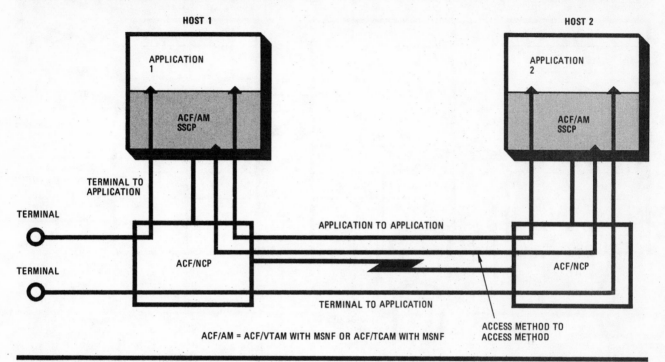

ACF/AM = ACF/VTAM WITH MSNF OR ACF/TCAM WITH MSNF

data communications capability between two IBM hosts is provided by functions added in the Multi-System Networking Feature for ACF/VTAM and in ACF/NCP.

In addition to supporting remote terminals via the 3704/3705 communications controller, VTAM supports the local (channel-attached) IBM 3270 and 3790 terminals, where it performs all the physical I/O operations for data transfer and error recovery.

VTAM services
Network services are performed by specific logic — called the system services control point (SSCP) — within VTAM. The SSCP is responsible for such things as network start-up, recovery, and termination, as well as for dynamically connecting (and disconnecting) each terminal to a given application in the IBM host.

The SSCP becomes active when VTAM is started by the computer operator. Through user definitions, the control point is logically informed of the network resources (which include one or more NCPs with attached links and terminals, channel-attached terminals, and applications eligible to use VTAM). Also through user definitions, all or part of the data communications resources can be put into operation. VTAM reports any failures at network start-up time and continues to bring up as much of the network as possible. After VTAM start-up is complete, the SSCP will service VTAM operator commands. These commands allow a computer operator to define for the SSCP other data communications resources, such as another NCP or a new

data communications application. These new data communications resources are defined using VTAM tables that are placed on a direct-access storage device (DASD) before the computer operator enters the VTAM command to use the new definitions. If the definitions are not found on the DASD, VTAM will inform the operator.

For network recovery, VTAM reports terminal outages to the applications programs and to the computer operating system, then automatically attempts to recover the physical network. VTAM informs the host application program of any permanently lost terminal connections in the network. This keeps the applications program informed of the status of its connections and allows message resynchronization after reconnection has been made.

Another major service is performed by VTAM's SSCP. It monitors connection requests, which can be made by an applications program or by a terminal user. A connection can be made if each data communications resource is available; that is, if the application is running in the host and the terminal is not currently logged onto an application. When an applications program requests a connection to a terminal already logged onto another application, VTAM will inform the application currently connected to the terminal of the pending request. The application, in turn, can honor the request by terminating its connection or it can deny the request.

Thus a single terminal, such as a printer, can be shared by two applications and data can be sent to

3 VTAM inbound message flow

Upstream. Messages bound for a host application program are first buffered in the communications controller, then in either a real or virtual buffer under the control of VTAM. VTAM also has the option of placing the message in a secondary storage device before it is finally sent to its destination in the application's work area.

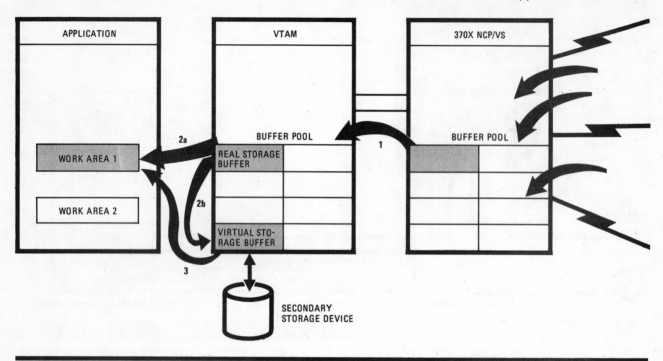

the terminal as it becomes available to the host. Failure to make a connection is reported to the requesting resource, either the applications program or the terminal user. The connection of the terminal user with the application is called a session. Only one session exists for each end user (terminal operator), but concurrent sessions can exist between an application and an SNA terminal with multiple end users (IBM 3790). As in the example described above using MVS with IMS/VS, TSO, and JES2, multiple sessions can exist for terminals residing on the same link. Those connections can change dynamically, based on the terminal user's requirements (Fig. 1).

The ACF has extended the capability of the systems services control point in VTAM. With the Multi-System Networking Feature, the ACF/VTAM SSCP has the ability to communicate with other ACF/VTAMs and ACF/TCAMs that have the Multi-System Networking Feature and that are running in other hosts. This host-to-host communications allows a total network of many hosts and many terminals to be managed in an orderly fashion. (Fig. 2).

Data flow
Before discussing the flow of message data between VTAM and an application, a description of VTAM's message buffers should be reviewed. The message data buffers are created by VTAM at start-up time. The size and number of buffers are specified by the user. However, the program will automatically assign a predetermined amount of buffer space if that information

is not given by the operator at start-up time. Two different message-buffer pools are created: the virtual-storage buffers; and the real-storage message buffers that are used to achieve fast message processing.

For input messages from terminals in the network (Fig. 3), the NCP will physically collect the messages in its storage. Upon 3704/3705 hardware notification, VTAM will read these messages into separate real-storage buffers. Each separate message will start in a new buffer; multiple VTAM buffers will be chained together if the message length requires more than a single buffer. For those applications that have issued a VTAM applications-program message-receive operation (receive or read), VTAM will move the message into the application's message-work area and then designate those buffers available for reuse in its real-storage buffer pool. For those applications that have not issued a VTAM message-receive operation, VTAM will move the message into the virtual-storage buffer pool so that messages become eligible for paging onto a secondary storage device. VTAM keeps track of the messages moved to virtual-storage buffers, so when the application does request message input, VTAM will move the message from the virtual-storage buffer pool to the application work area, where, in this case, the system designates buffers that can be paged as eligible for reuse.

Messages outbound from applications programs to terminals (Fig. 4) are moved from the application's message-work area into VTAM's real-storage buffer pool. VTAM prefixes the message with the proper SNA

4 VTAM outbound message

Downstream. *Data flow management for messages being returned to a terminal in the network begins by moving the data from the applications program's work area to a buffer in VTAM. VTAM sends the message to a buffer in the communications controller, where the message waits until it contains enough bits to form a complete message.*

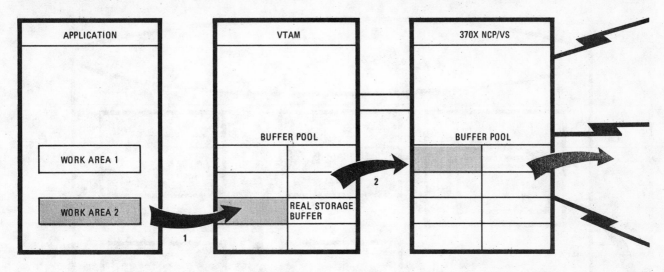

routing control. Multiple messages may be collected from the same or different applications before VTAM schedules the output operation to the NCP. In this way, VTAM can send multiple messages from the host to the NCP in a single transmission. When the NCP indicates that all messages have been received correctly, VTAM designates the real-storage buffers used for output as reusable in the buffer pool.

Since VTAM runs asynchronously with the data communications applications, multiple messages will enter and exit the communications access method, providing more throughput overall. To enhance the flexibility of the buffer management for terminal messages, ACF/VTAM has been designed to allow dynamic buffering. This user-controlled technique, implemented in ACF/VTAM, allows VTAM to add or reduce buffers to accommodate message volume, which results in greater flexibility in determining the number of VTAM buffers required to service message traffic. The technique also permits reduction in the memory requirements for the real-storage message buffers. Although the number of message buffers can grow dynamically, ACF/VTAM can control the number of messages an SNA terminal can send to the host, using a control feature known as inbound pacing.

VTAM generation
Users who need VTAM must have it specified in the operating system (the ACF version of VTAM is an IBM program product and must be ordered separately). As a result of this process, the VTAM code will be placed in a library on a DASD ready to be executed.

The user then creates the proper network definitions that will be used by VTAM at start-up time. There are five different types of definitions that can be classified: (1) NCP terminals, (2) channel-attached terminals, (3)

switched SNA terminals, (4) application lists, and (5) VTAM-only parameters (Fig. 5). The NCP/VS definition is the same source definition that is used to create an executable NCP. Channel-attached and switched SNA-terminal definitions, plus application definitions, are tables created by the user. The VTAM-only parameter definition is composed of a few customized parameters for the access method, the most important of which is the buffer allocation. As mentioned in the section on data flow, ACF/VTAM is enhanced to allow dynamic buffer allocation so that the access method can react to different loads. VTAM-supporting documentation provides a formula for calculating the number of buffers required to service the network and its message traffic. In addition to creating the tables for VTAM definitions, the user builds a simple procedure for starting VTAM. All those tables and the start-up procedure for VTAM are stored on a direct-access storage device.

Running with VTAM
VTAM execution begins in the host computer by initiating the start-up procedure. This loads into a partition (region or address space) the VTAM-executable code that begins reading the definitions from the DASD, builds buffers, creates the necessary control blocks, and activates the network. Network activation is implemented in VTAM to provide multiple concurrent network operations that allow VTAM and the NCP to activate the physical network in a quick and orderly fashion. After VTAM is started, host applications may identify themselves to it, and terminal connections can proceed.

VTAM commands exist to display meaningful information about the network. They are used by network operations personnel to determine the status of such data communications resources as terminals, lines,

5 VTAM definitions

Network configuration. The user prepares his system to properly handle VTAM by defining those elements of the network that will work with the access method. Eligible VTAM-related configuration elements include NCP terminals, local peripherals, terminals on the network, applications lists, and VTAM-only parameters (buffer allocation).

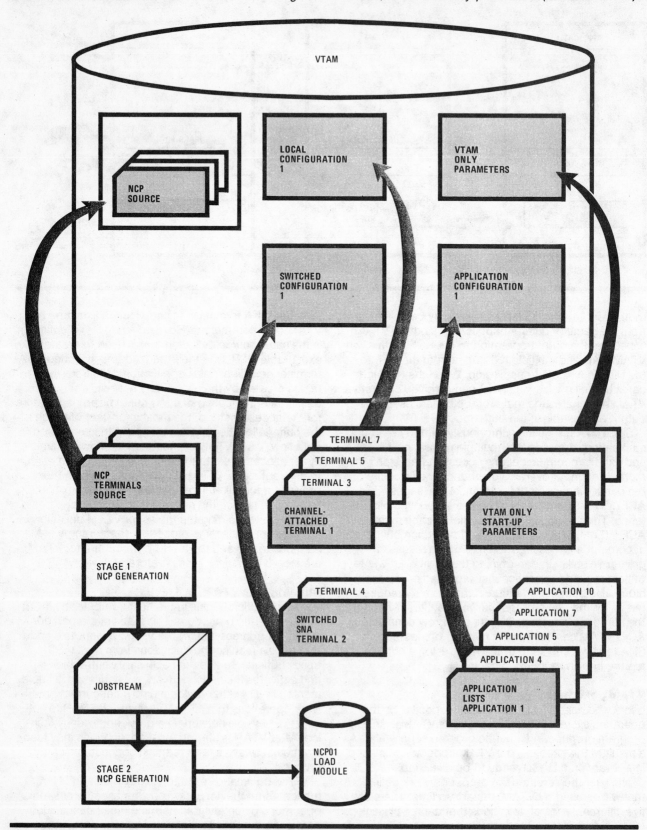

Applications support

APPLICATION	OS	API	TERMINALS
CICS/VS	DOS, VS1, SVS MVS	RECORD	SNA + 3270*
IMS/VS	VS1, SVS, MVS	RECORD	SNA + 3270
TSO	MVS	RECORD	SNA + 3270
POWER/VS	DOS	RECORD	SNA + 3270
JES/RES	VS1	RECORD	SNA
JES2	MVS	RECORD	SNA
JES3 (SCHEDULE RELEASE 9/78)	MVS	RECORD	SNA
IIS	DOS, VS1, SVS MVS	RECORD READ/WRITE	SNA + 3270 2741, TWX
VSCP	DOS, VS1, MVS	RECORD READ/WRITE	SNA + 3270 1050, 2741, TWX

THIS TABLE SUMMARIZES CURRENT VTAM APPLICATIONS SUPPORT

*THE IBM 3270 TERMINALS SUPPORTED INCLUDE THE SNA, BINARY SYNCHRONOUS, AND CHANNEL-ATTACHED MODELS.

NCPs, and applications. The console operator at the host enters the commands, and then documented VTAM messages are displayed (or printed) in response to them. In addition, a VTAM-programmed operator interface exists to allow VTAM commands to be submitted to the access method for processing. A VTAM application using the programmed operator interface can let a terminal in the VTAM network enter VTAM commands to aid in data communications systems management. By doing that, the operator can monitor and act on the VTAM network without interference from system-console messages relating to the operation of the data communications system.

Shutting down the VTAM network is relatively simple. When a console operator calls for an orderly shutdown, VTAM allows all sessions to end normally before terminating execution in its partition. In the case of a quick shutdown, which is designed for emergency situations, halting VTAM execution takes precedence over loss of terminal connections and data.

Service aids
Included with VTAM are several service aids that have been designed to assist in installing and maintaining the network. VTAM has the ability to trace data moving between any terminal or remote application and any application within the host. This data can be captured and written to a host sequential file for printing and diagnosis. Both inbound and outbound data can be captured at the host's interface to the communications controller and at the applications program's interface. Also, the buffer usage in VTAM (operating system type only) can be monitored by using trace facilities, which

help in tuning VTAM buffer usage. The traces can be started and ended by using VTAM operator commands. In addition, the ACF version of VTAM has been enhanced to allow data to be captured in the host for use in tuning the user-defined parameters, such as attention delay, which affect I/O transfer between VTAM and the NCP.

VTAM is designed to take care of malfunctioning network elements. It attempts to detect and handle problems before they become serious. If there is an error, VTAM sends the console operator a message and attempts recovery. If recovery is not possible, VTAM notifies the console operator and automatically provides error records to assist in identifying the problem and its cause.

Migration
VTAM is made to co-exist in the same host with other data communications access methods, such as BTAM and TCAM. Thus VTAM can be brought up or implemented independently in each host, a process that is called migration. Here is one migratory approach.

Given that the data-center host has one IBM 3277 display station attached to a local peripheral IBM control unit, VTAM testing can begin without bringing up an NCP in a 370X communications controller. This gives the system operators experience in: (1) defining VTAM parameters (exclusive of the NCP), (2) providing the VTAM interface in a test application, and (3) operationally starting, managing, and stopping VTAM execution in the virtual operating system. Once that phase of migration has been completed, the installation can use VTAM as the access method to communicate with all channel-attached IBM 3270s. An advantage may immediately be gained by migrating all the channel-attached 3270's to VTAM, because new testing can then begin for a second VTAM-supported application. The channel-attached 3270 terminal has access to multiple applications, such as TSO and IMS running on a MVS-based host.

As a follow-up in this total migration plan, the NCP can be introduced as the next test element. A single data communications link can be used as a test vehicle to obtain experience with VTAM and the NCP. Additional links can then be brought up on the NCP to move the remote network to VTAM/NCP control. To test the stress on VTAM and the applications programs before going into production, a simulator like the program product, called the teleprocessing network simulator (TPNS), can be considered. In addition to providing a production-like environment, TPNS indicates the response time that can be expected under load.

VTAM can also support the central-site management of intelligent terminals. SNA provides architectural compatibility among the access methods that use ACF with the Multi-System Networking Feature. That allows VTAM in one host to communicate via the NCP with TCAM in the same host or with VTAM or TCAM in another one.

SNA adds new capabilities to VTAM, which, by design, can continue to deliver new functions based on rapidly changing technology. ∎

How to access a network via IBM's TCAM

Larry Esau, IBM Corp., Research Triangle Park, N.C.

Software that is designed to grow as user needs change must be flexible enough to accommodate new demands, as well as specialized to fill networking needs

Since 1969, TCAM has proved itself to be a reliable access method to which additional functions and terminal types can be added with relative ease. Its flexibility has made it a strong bridge between the old and the new, protecting the user's investment in application programs and terminals while providing a clear path to the systems network architecture environment.

TCAM—for telecommunications access method—is IBM's primary queued access method that provides high performance, high-level-language-application interface, and comprehensive capabilities for the very large as well as the small teleprocessor user. It supports binary synchronous, start-stop, local attachment, and synchronous data link control terminals, and operates under such IBM programs as operating system/virtual storage 1, single virtual storage, and multiple virtual storage.

Installation of TCAM occurs at system generation time. By specifying that TCAM is required, which is a system generation parameter, TCAM macrocodes and module libraries are created and placed on disks.

The message-control program (MCP), which is executed like any other program in the operating system, is then assembled and control responsibilities are assigned. The MCP can be started and restarted with job-control language statements from the system job queue or by a START command from the system console. Once the MCP has been initiated, TCAM becomes active. The TCAM system programmer can design the MCP in such a way that the network control programs (NCPs), the communications lines, and the terminals will all be brought on line in an active state, or TCAM can require operator control procedures for bringing them up individually. The system programmer can allow the operator to override some start-up parameters by having TCAM request them from the operator. At activation, TCAM builds the required control blocks and opens the required memory areas for handling communications line groups, NCPs, periodic status records, permanent records, and the storage area required if disk queuing is requested.

In many early installations, users were primarily interested in using TCAM's timesharing option (TSO) subsystem. As these customers grew, they began using other facilities available under TCAM; for example, message switching, data collection, and simple inquiry response. Once they started writing TCAM applications, they found the key to TCAM design—the way in which it shields the application programmer from terminal-dependent coding. Also, TCAM allows its application programs to be coded in assembler, Cobol, or PL/1 languages. The application coder retrieves

1 TCAM network components

TCAM components. *Along with its own user-defined tables, the message control program includes such TCAM modules as TP interface routines, message handlers, queuing routines, buffering routines, checkpoint routines, operator control, application interface, logging, service aid, and random-access storage in memory devices.*

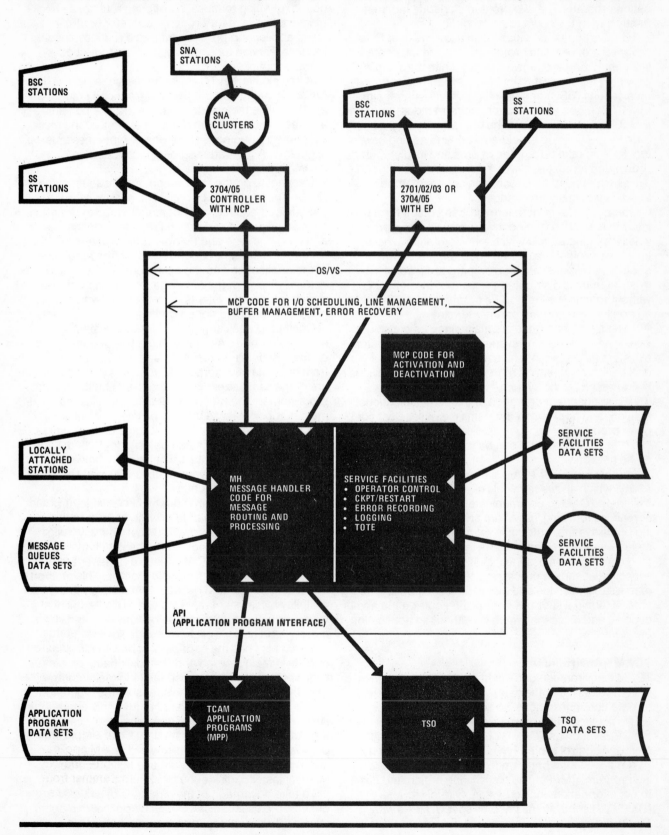

messages and writes messages back to the terminal in the same way a programmer reads and writes to a sequential disk or tape file. That feature allows the separation of the network control performed by TCAM from the message processing performed by the application program. The two programs operate independently and at their own rates of speed.

TCAM is unique because it can allow the user to take advantage of new line protocols (synchronous data link control and systems network architecture) while providing full support to its binary synchronous communications (BSC) or start-stop terminals under either IBM 270X mode (or emulation program mode) or under IBM 3705 NCP. This gives the user an easy migration path by maintaining his old network and adding new functions to take advantage of SNA and its distributed processing terminals.

Being a queued teleprocessing access method, TCAM offers many advantages:

■ Operators at a remote terminal can enter information into the network at their convenience. Queuing provides a staging area in which the information is held until the recipient—either an application program or another terminal—has been prepared to receive it.

■ Information is distributed throughout the network without forcing the input to be synchronized with either an application program or other terminals.

■ If queues of messages are maintained on a disk device, the teleprocessing system can be restarted after a system failure. Maintaining message queues on a disk device also permits retrieval of messages previously processed by the system.

■ The independent operation of the communications network and application programs increases host computer productivity because application programs can use prestored input and can be tested independently of the network.

Another facility of TCAM is its transaction routing ability, which allows terminals or applications controlled by TCAM to communicate with each other. Other reasons for using TCAM are as follows: checkpointing of the system; automatic retransmission of messages when errors occur; warm restart capability; logging of complete messages; multiple routing of messages; independent processing of messages; queuing of messages; service and maintenance capability; extensive terminal support; data-editing outside the applications; and message switching without an application program.

TCAM's environment

TCAM's environment, as illustrated in Figure 1, consists of items external to the central processing unit—such as data communications hardware, telephone lines, and disks for storing messages—and items internal to the CPU—such as TCAM's control program, called message control program (MCP), and roll your own (RYO) application programs, called message processing programs (MPP). The timesharing option and customer information control system/virtual storage (CICS/VS) subsystems become special MPPs with TCAM.

The MCP (Fig . 1) consists of a combination of user code and user-defined tables together with TCAM-provided modules and control blocks. The major programming components of the MCP are the teleprocessing interface routine, message handlers that are user coded, queuing routines, a buffering routine, a checkpoint routine, a restart routine, operator control routines, application-program interface routines, logging routines, service-aids routine, and random-access-storage routines.

A key element of TCAM is the message. TCAM uses buffers to handle messages sent from one point to another while they are in the network. The buffer size and the message length determine whether the message transmitted consists of one or more message segments. A message segment is that portion of a message that will fit into a buffer.

Depending on the application, a message may consist of a header, text, or both. The header, which actually is not required, may contain control information such as origination and destination terminal names, and message type and number. The header's length, format, and content depend solely on the requirement of the application and the user's preference, and are entered as part of the message text, a different procedure from that of systems network architecture headers. The two should not be confused.

Once messages enter the computer system, they are handled by TCAM through the use of buffers and queues. Buffers and main-storage queues are built from units of main storage. All the units in main storage are of the same size, which is specified by the system programmer. The programmer also specifies the maximum number of these units to be used for buffers and for main-storage queues. The storage units assigned to main-storage queues can be used for buffers if the message traffic warrants it. The reverse, however, is not true. TCAM will never use units assigned to buffers as message-storage queues.

Because message sizes are highly variable, it would be inefficient to assign buffers large enough to fit the largest message. Instead, TCAM dynamically builds buffers from the unit pool during the sending or receiving operation. When TCAM needs a buffer or a queue, it is built by linking units of main storage. This method of building buffers and queues from units gives the user flexibility in his use of main storage. This flexibility allows efficient accommodation of both long and short messages in heavy or light message flow.

TCAM also has the capability of having message queues in main storage and on a disk data set. Messages are, of course, queued faster in main storage than they are on disk. For this reason, the main-storage queue is ideally suited for fast inquiry-reply operations. However, the main-storage queue has the disadvantage of tying up storage that might be used for other purposes. Thus a store-and-forward or a data-collection-type operation should not use main-storage queues; instead, disk queuing should be considered.

To take advantage of the strengths of all types of queues, the user can select which applications or terminals will use what type of queue, whether main stor-

2 Routing via DMH and AMH

Message handling. The message from the terminal is examined by the incoming group of the device message handler and is passed through a queue to the outgoing group of the application message handler. The application program processes the message and passes it back through the AMH, queue, and DMH, in reverse order.

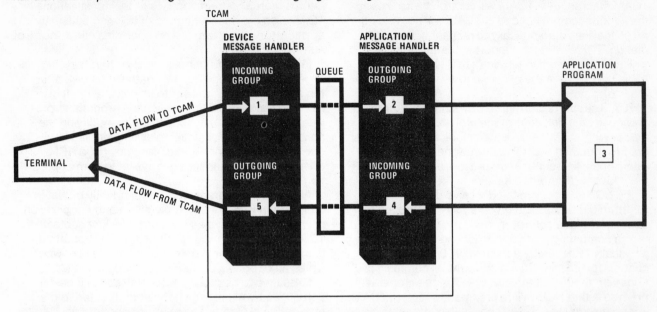

age or disk. In fact, a combination of main-storage queues with disk-queue backup can be used to take advantage of both types of queuing methods.

The facility in TCAM that controls the flow of messages from buffers to queue to destination is a message handler (MH). Message handlers are TCAM's functional management layer. They control the message (data-flow control) from the arrival at the host processor until it reaches its final destination.

MHs are used to isolate the application programmer from device-dependent coding and error-handling code. Separate message handlers can be designed for each group of terminals with similar characteristics.

There are basically two types of message handlers: device (DMH) and application (AMH). The processing of these message handlers are divided into two groups: incoming and outgoing. Figure 2 illustrates how the two types of message handlers work together.

Each of the groups in Figure 2 is further divided into subgroups:

■ An inblock subgroup—handles incoming physical transmissions before they are divided into logical messages.

■ The inheader and outheader subgroups—handle only the headers of incoming or outgoing messages (first buffer only).

■ The inbuffer and outbuffer subgroups—handle all message segments.

■ The inmessage and outmessage subgroups—specify actions to be taken after the entire message has been received or sent (for example, checking for specified errors and sending an error message to the source or destination).

A major source of message-handler flexibility is

TCAM's option-field capability. These user-defined fields can be set and examined by TCAM to control the path or subgroup to be executed. For example, a user may want to identify, through the use of an option field, whether the terminal is a printer or a screen device.

The user can design and code a message handler to perform different functions on each type of message. The user codes the message handler through the use of TCAM- provided macrocodes. An assembler code can be added to perform functions not provided in a TCAM macrocode, but it cannot be used in the inmessage and outmessage subgroup.

Message handlers can perform the following functions: determine message origin and destination, check and assign sequence numbers, determine message priority, edit message, remove and insert device-dependent code, gather statistics, log message, insert time and date, test for transmission errors, cancel message, generate new messages, and hold message to send later.

Terminal interface
TCAM allows the user to choose whether the terminals are to be controlled through the IBM 270X or emulator program (EP) on the IBM 3705 or through the use of the network control program (NCP). No matter which is selected, TCAM manages the network.

In the EP mode, TCAM supports both start-stop and BSC line protocol. BSC is used for higher-speed data transmission between the central computer and the remote computer or terminal and requires more sophisticated electronics to control the line discipline. The TCAM programmer does not need to be concerned with the differences in transmission techniques except to know the control characters being used to regulate the flow of data on the communications line.

In the MCP, the TCAM programmer develops tables to describe the network to TCAM through the use of TCAM macrocodes. TCAM will control the lines using the information provided to it. TCAM will poll and address the lines automatically to request or send information. TCAM will also support automatic answer, which allows switched terminals to dial the host to retrieve messages in the queue or to send messages to the host.

TCAM supports start-stop, bisynchronous, and synchronous data-link control line protocols in the NCP mode. With NCP, the 3705 communications controllers are programmed control units designed to assume many of the line-control and processing functions for the network (distributed function). The primary function of the NCP is to transmit and receive data as well as to do limited processing on data passing through the communications controller.

The communications controller and the host are physically attached by a System/370 input/output channel, over which TCAM performs all communications with the rest of the network. The basic operating premise is that NCP will be prepared to receive TCAM information as long as NCP has buffers available, regardless of line or terminal availability. However, when NCP has information for TCAM, it presents an attention interrupt over the channel to the host. The host cannot be forced to read from the communications controller, but does acknowledge the attention interruption when ready by issuing a READ command. NCP holds the data ready until TCAM reads it over the channel.

NCP/VS and TCAM communicate over the channel by exchanging information. This information contains control data and, optionally, message data. The control data directs NCP to perform a specific operation. When the operation is completed, NCP responds with corresponding control data, message data, and the completion status of the operation. Thus TCAM directs NCP/VS, which, in turn, controls the network operation and provides TCAM with its resulting data and status information.

In an operating network, NCP receives data from TCAM and remote terminals concurrently. NCP collects the data in communications controller buffers and routes it to its destination when line availability and other conditions permit. Control information and data intended for TCAM are sent to the host processor in a storage-to-storage transfer across the channel. Consequently, TCAM is able to direct the network at channel speeds, while the NCP and the communications controller assume responsibility for line control and data transfer.

Application-program interface
Although free of many real-time network responsibilities, TCAM still must know the structure of all resources that are in the network. This information is provided for both TCAM and the NCP at their respective generations. With TCAM, the network is described through the use of GROUP and TERMINAL macrocodes.

Messages can be generated, or terminal messages processed, through application programs written by the user. TCAM passes messages and inquires to the application programs for processing via a queue and returns messages or responses to their destinations. TCAM also provides a method of tailoring buffers to application programs and handles line control automatically.

In addition, TCAM permits the user to retrieve a message from a message queue's data set on disk after the message has been sent to its destination. It also has facilities to allow the application program to provide network control by examining or modifying the contents of a control block, releasing messages queued for a terminal, and closing down the NCP. All operator control functions are available from application programs.

Application programs run independently of, but in conjunction with, the MCP, usually in another partition or region, but always as a separate task or subtask. If TCAM application programs are not in a separate region or partition, they are attached by the user who writes an operating system macrocode in the MCP.

Messages to be processed are placed in a destination queue by a message handler and routed to the application program. The messages are obtained from the destination queues and transferred to user-specified work areas, where they are processed by application programs. A response message may be returned to the MCP for transmission to a terminal, a list of destinations, or another application program. Application programs are capable of concurrently processing several transactions, using multiple interfaces.

Regardless of the type of processing required, there are several ways to design application support:
■ One common method is to code a separate program for each application, thus each application will have its own interface with the MCP. As shown in Figure 3-A, the message is processed by the appropriate AMH, which, in turn, passes it on to its application program.
■ In another situation, it may be more efficient to process the message through a single application program having a single interface to TCAM to perform all of the data processing. As can be seen in Figure 3-B, one AMH is used to pass the message on to the application program, which analyzes the message and routes it to the appropriate processing subroutine.
■ Another possibility is shown in Figure 3-C, where an application program is used primarily as a message router to other application programs in the same or other regions. It performs this function by returning the messages to the MCP via a PUT or WRITE macrocode. The AMH in the MCP then routes the message to the next application program. The amount of data transferred from the MCP to an application program by a single GET or READ macrocode of from an application program to the MCP by a single PUT or WRITE is called a work unit. The work unit is processed in an application program's work area. A work unit can be an entire physical message or a record whose length is defined

3 TCAM application design

Application support. *A separate program for each application results in an interface for each program. A single application that performs all processing has one interface* *with the application message handler and three subroutines. Another possibility is to let one program act as the interface as well as the router for all other applications.*

(A)

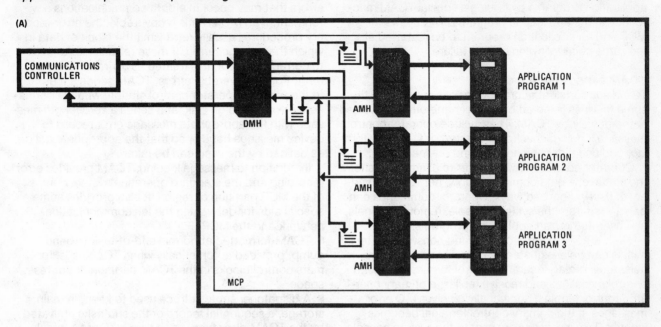

(B)

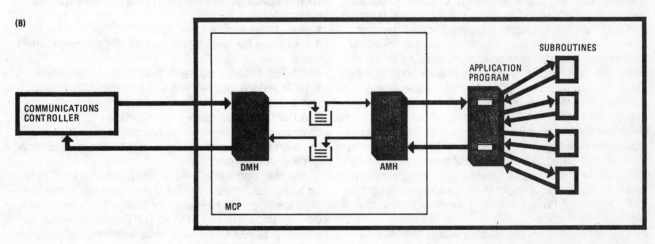

(C)

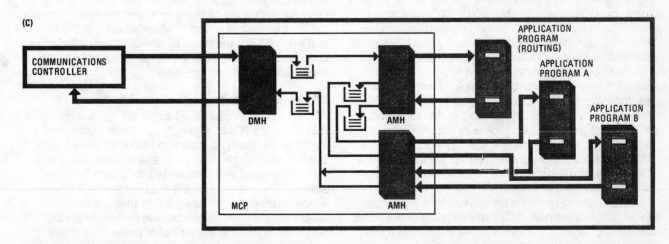

by such delimiter characters as END-OF-BLOCK. A specifically defined amount of data (a work unit) can also be a portion of a message that fits into the work area.

The TCAM checkpoint of the MCP can be coordinated with operating system checkpoints of TCAM application programs by issuing a special TCAM macrocode in the application programs. This allows the MCP and an application program to be restarted at the same point following system failure.

TCAM service facilities

TCAM supports data communications networks with some facilities selected by the user and others provided automatically by TCAM. They include operator control, message logging, checkpoint/restart, I/O error recording, additional debugging aids, and on-line testing.

Operator control allows the user to examine or alter the status of a data communications network in a variety of user-authorized ways. Operator commands can be entered from the system console, remote terminals, and user-authorized application programs.

Various application programs and nonswitched terminals can be designated as operator control terminals. A secondary operator control terminal can send control messages and receive replies; a primary operator control terminal additionally receives I/O error messages. If the primary control terminal becomes inactive, I/O messages are sent to the system console, even when it is defined as a secondary control terminal.

TCAM's message-logging facility enables the user to keep a record in a sequential storage area of either messages or message segments handled by an MCP. Message logging can be useful in accounting, for long-term backup, or for collecting data for exceptional cases. In message switching, the logging of incoming headers may supply all the information needed. In more sophisticated applications, it may be necessary to log complete messages. By determining the flow patterns of message traffic, a programmer can more efficiently allocate the resources of a data communications network. Logging can also aid debugging by allowing the programmer to trace the flow of a message through an MCP.

The checkpoint/restart facility allows the MCP to be restarted after a shutdown or system failure by using information periodically recorded on the status of each station, destination queue, terminal table entry, and invitation list in the system. Upon restart, the terminal table, option table, invitation lists (optional), and internal control blocks associated with stations and lines are restored to the condition they were in before shutdown or system failure. Outgoing message traffic to each destination resumes with the message with the highest priority. Checkpoints of the MCP can be coordinated with operating-system checkpoints of TCAM application programs, so that the entire TCAM system can be restored to its condition at the time of shutdown or failure.

If checkpoint/restart is to be used for a 3705 communications controller, TCAM maintains a checkpoint memory area that provides a series of checkpoint records that correspond to incident records. A record is written each time the status of a link or of a terminal changes in the 3705.

The TCAM MCP or the 3705 communications controller includes a comprehensive set of error-recovery procedures for dealing with the various types of I/O errors that may occur in a data communications environment. If an I/O error is recoverable, the error-recovery procedures usually retransmit the block of data in which the error occurred. If these retransmissions fail to correct the error, it is treated as an irrecoverable error. For irrecoverable errors, TCAM sends a message to the primary-operator control station, writes a permanent error record on disk, and sends a zero-length message with the appropriate message error record to the device message handler so that the appropriate action, as defined by the user, can be taken.

In addition to message logging, TCAM provides error recording and the standard operating system dumps of the MCP partition or region. It also provides some special aids for debugging the telecommunications network and the MCP (Fig. 4).
■ TCAM-formatted abnormal end-of-task (Abend) dump, provided automatically when TCAM fails, formats control blocks in the TCAM partition or address space.
■ A dispatcher subtask trace used to keep, in main storage, a sequential record of the subtasks activated by the TCAM dispatcher each time a TCAM subtask is dispatched.
■ Subchannel trace for an IBM 3705.
■ I/O trace for local 3270s or IBM 270X-mode control units.
■ A trace of buffer contents and status information.
■ NCP service aids—line trace and path information unit trace.
■ A dump of the message queue data set, dynamically invoked by a separate TCAM facility, which formats the data set for immediate printing or directs it to tape or disk for later printing.

The teleprocessing on-line test executive (TOTE) is an attached subtask of TCAM that controls the selection, loading, and execution of on-line tests for many devices supported by TCAM. TOTE provides a link between TCAM and device tests written to diagnostic architecture. TOTE schedules and controls the test, conveys messages to the user about the test, prompts the user when requested or when an error in the format of a test-request message is detected, and allows the user to enter changes to the configuration data stored in a configuration storage area.

TCAM message flow

All that has been discussed so far are the components that make up TCAM. Figure 5 ties these components together by tracing a message through TCAM.
Steps 1 and 2: The input message is prepared at a remote terminal and transmitted on a data line.
Step 3: The message enters the host and is stored in a main-storage buffer assigned to that line for input. TCAM inserts chaining addresses and other control information into the stored buffer prefix field of the message. This allows the message to fill multiple buf-

4 Debugging aids

Control traces. *Various line and device traces aid the user in determining the nature and extent of networking problems when a TCAM-controlled component fails to* *function properly. Aside from sleuthing routines, TCAM provides the operator the ability to dump all information for examination when there is an abnormal condition.*

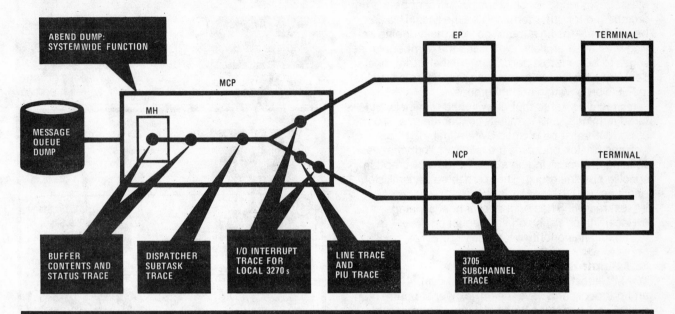

fers that TCAM will chain together to form a message.
Step 4: The incoming message is passed—a buffer at a time—through the message handler's incoming group, which performs the user-selected functions and destination selection.
Step 5: After the message is processed by the message handler, it is forwarded to a destination queue for either an application program or an accepting terminal.

If the message requires no further processing and the destination queue is a terminal, the next operation is Step 13.

The destination queue consists of message segments on direct-access storage devices or in main storage. If the destination queue is located on disk, the buffers are released; if in main storage, the buffers are used to contain the message in the main storage queue.
Steps 6, 7, and 8: The message from a destination queue for an application program is placed in main storage buffers, passed through the outgoing group of an AMH, and kept in a read-ahead queue until the application program requests the buffer or message with a READ or GET macrocode.
Step 9: TCAM passes message data to a user specified work area in the application program. TCAM removes the prefix, which it attached to the buffer, and the application processes the message. The application may return a response message using a PUT or WRITE macrocode to a terminal or another application program for further processing.
Steps 10 and 11: TCAM moves the data from the application program work area into an MCP buffer, in which header or text prefixes are created, and chaining ad-

dresses and other control information are inserted by TCAM. The response message generated by the application can be of any length. After the buffer is filled, it is handled by the incoming group of the AMH assigned by an MCP macrocode.
Step 12: If further processing of the message data by another application is required, the message is queued for that destination and steps 5 – 11 are repeated. If not, TCAM places the processed message on the destinations queue of a terminal.
Step 13: The destination queue for a terminal is like that of an application queue. It is part of the message queue data set and can be either in main storage or on disk. TCAM obtains message segments from the destination queue in first-ended, first-out (FEFO) order within user-defined priority groups
Steps 14 and 15: The message segment is placed in a buffer, and the outgoing group of the DMH for the line or terminal processes the message. The message in this DMH can be translated into the receiving terminal line code, and the required line code inserted along with any other required functions.
Step 16: TCAM transmits the message, minus the buffer prefix it attached, to the destination terminal. As each buffer is transmitted, its units are returned to the buffer unit pool for reuse.

TCAM allows the user to assign priorities to messages and their queues. These priorities will influence the flow of messages within a TCAM system.

Outgoing messages can be queued by destination line or terminal. When queued by line, messages for all stations on the line are placed on one queue. Messages are taken off the queue and sent to the destination on the line in the order received within priority

73

groups. Thus all messages of one priority class on the queue are transmitted before any of the messages on a lower priority queue can be delivered.

When outgoing messages are queued by terminal, one queue is created for each terminal on a line. All messages queued for one terminal are sent before any are queued for other terminals on the line. (This can be modified—using a macrocode in the outgoing device message handler—by limiting the number of messages to be sent to a particular terminal during one contract.) Messages on a queue are sent to a terminal in FEFO order within priority groups.

It should be noted that all switched terminals, buffered terminals, and terminals connected to a 3705 using NCP must be queued by terminal.

Transmission priority is the relative priority between sending and receiving on a line. This is a user option specified by line group. There are three transmission priorities:

- Host receiving has priority over host sending.
- Receiving and sending have equal priority.
- Sending has priority over receiving.

TCAM growth

TCAM's latest versions manage their own SNA formats and protocols and have their own layer structure managers. SNA has three types of network addressable units (NAUs), which are resources in the network addressable by TCAM: the system services control point (SSCP); a physical unit (PU); and a logical unit (LU).

In SNA, a session is a formally bound pairing, or logical connection, established between two NAUs to allow communication between them. A session is identified by a pair of network addresses identifying the origin and the destination NAUs.

Once TCAM is active, the SSCP initiates an SSCP-PU session with each PU in the network (Fig. 6). This session remains established until the PU is deactivated.

After the SSCP-PU session has been established, the SSCP can initiate a SSCP-LU session with the LUs contained within that PU. These sessions also remain established until the LUs are deactivated. Once these two types of sessions are established, an LU can initiate an LU-LU session with another eligible active LU.

Basically, TCAM has three types of primary LUs (Fig. 6). The first type being the TCAM MCP, also called the TCAM LU. If a session is established with this type of LU, the appearance of the SNA terminal will be similar to a BSC or start-stop terminal in that the DMH specified by the GROUP macrocode will be used.

The next type of LU is the device message handler (DMH). Using this type of LU, the user can request a session with any eligible DMH. If a terminal is able to use multiple DMHs, such as one for CICS and another for TSO, the user must use this LU level.

The third type of LU definition is an eligible Tprocess queue. A Tprocess queue is nothing more than a message queue assigned to an application program. Using this type of LU, the DMH should not forward the message. The message will automatically be forwarded to the Tprocess queue that was named in the session request. The device message handler used in this case

5 TCAM message flow

Data flow. TCAM is composed of components, all of which work together to get the job done. Buffers, queues, message handlers, and interface programs all play a part.

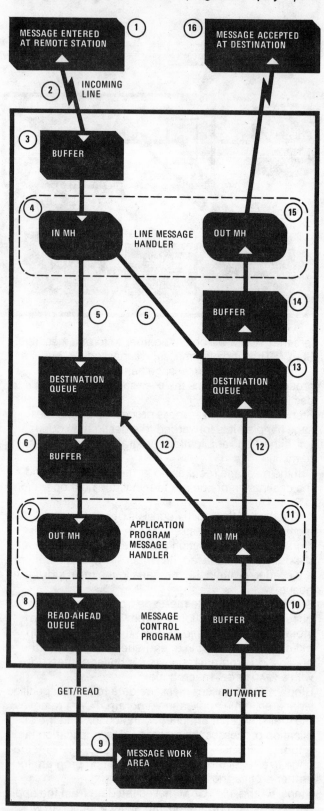

6 TCAM SNA sessions and LU

Sessions. *In the SNA, a session is a formally bound pairing, or logical connection, between any combination of the three different types of network addressable units.*

7 Sessions with transaction routing

Routing. *TCAM can forward messages from a logical unit to an application program independently of sessions, freeing the operator from logging on and off the terminal.*

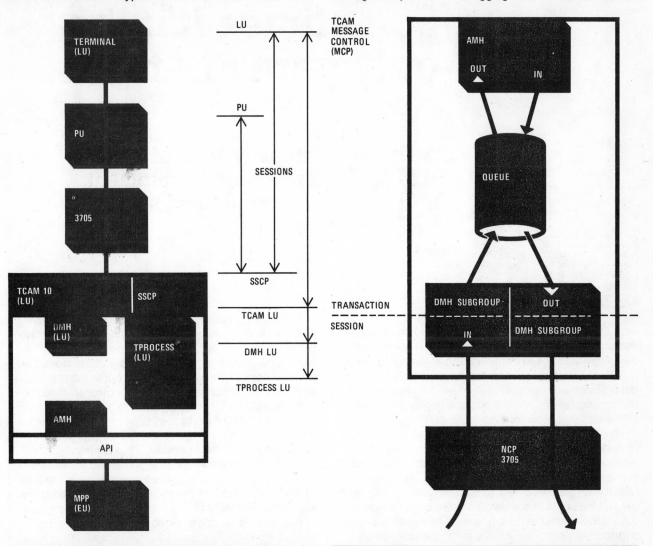

is the DMH specified on the GROUP macrocode.

A secondary LU can establish a session with any of the three types of primary LUs in TCAM (MCP, DMH, or Tprocess). Of course, before an LU-to-LU session can be established, the SSCP-to-PU and the SSCP-to-LU sessions must have already been established.

One of the unique features of TCAM is that even with LU sessions, TCAM still has the full routing capabilities that it had with BSC and start-stop terminals (Fig. 7). If the session is established with either the TCAM LU or a DMH LU, TCAM can forward the message to any application or terminal (SNA, BSC, or start-stop). This routing occurs independently of sessions. In other words, the operator will not have to log on and off the terminal. (TSO users are an exception in that they must log off the TSO MH and log on to a non-TSO MH to gain access to a non-TSO application.)

Termination of a session can occur as follows: the

LU's queue is exhausted and the session had been initiated by TCAM; the DMH executes a "stop session" macrocode, and the terminal operator logs off.

ACF/TCAM

Advanced Communication Function (ACF) for TCAM is available as a program product and runs under the following operating systems: SVS, MVS, and VS1. Previous versions of TCAM permitted only a single-host network configuration, referred to as a single-domain network. ACF/TCAM, with its networking feature, additionally supports a multiple-host-network configuration, called a multiple-domain network.

ACF/TCAM's base product supports only a single-domain network. By ordering the multisystem network facility, which runs with the ACF/TCAM base, ACF/TCAM will support both single- and multiple-domain networks. ■

George R. Fisher

Migration to SNA: Sometimes it's the only game in town

A large oil company, user of both
IBM and other vendors' equipment,
is changing its star networks
to SNA in six stages.

At one of the world's largest oil companies, data communications applications have almost become ubiquitous. The ability of these applications to communicate with each other at all network software/hardware levels, from all locations, is not. For this corporation, with a large amount of IBM and other gear, the solution to this problem is IBM's systems network architecture (SNA).

The need for networking and distributed processing is immediate and SNA is considered to be the "only game in town," because of the way it addresses the company's requirements with available equipment. Still, the firm is well aware that SNA currently addresses only a small part of the data communications world. Future SNA releases can, however, be expected to expand SNA's scope. What's more, public network offerings and private carrier services will expand the scope even further. The effect on the user at the company and elsewhere will be easier access to computer power, at less cost.

While the company is migrating from its separate star networks to an SNA network, it is encouraging its non-IBM vendors to provide an SNA interface. At the same time, the company doesn't look solely to IBM for the solution to its data communications/processing problems. The CCITT's X.25 protocol and the open systems interconnection software/hardware layers are being studied and used where applicable.

The company's goal in migrating its existing networks to SNA is the realization of a corporate "utility" data network. A utility data network is the computer analogue of the familiar telephone network. In a telephone conversation the location of the telephone is unimportant and the facilities over which the conversation travels are invisible. The user simply dials the telephone number and the connection is established.

In a similar manner, in a utility data network, a user at a terminal can access any information, in any computer on the network, by entering the equivalent of a telephone number on the keyboard. Furthermore, two or more applications can establish communications with each other for data transfer, distributed data processing, master-file update, and the like.

Currently, at the company, prior to the implementation of a utility network, access to and application requires dedicated mini-network. Thus access to more than one application is cumbersome and expensive. Since multiple application communications is the goal of SNA migration, it's fair to say that, at the company, the installation of SNA is a first step toward the goal of a unified data/voice/video utility network using shared facilities.

SNA has many advantages as a utility data network, and these are well known. They include increased productivity, cost-effective sharing of computer resources, and better backup of critical configurations. However, SNA has its problems, and the change in the data communications environment at the company, the network's complexity, and the need for planning and training are all prices that must be paid.

At the company, the migration to SNA is a six-stage process. This implementation is separate from the equally profound conversion problem of existing application programs to support SNA. The migration problem is the only subject of concern in this article.

Evolution to unification

There are six stages involved in migrating to full SNA networking support. The purpose is an evolutionary one, beginning with several pre-SNA networks and ending with a single unified network. Although the objective of implementing an SNA network is to provide

1. First stage. *Moving dissimilar applications into SNA is not an easy task. In this network, for instance, SNA must accommodate information management system develop-* *ment (IMND), test (IMNZ), and production (IMNP), along with CICS and TSO. In addition, the network has a virtual-storage operation system VSAPL and ROSCOE).*

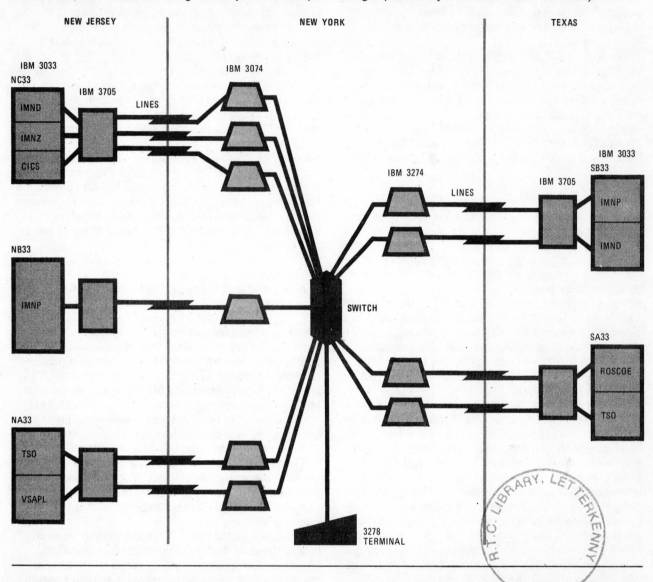

a framework for new and enhanced functions, the functions existing prior to the SNA realization must be supported throughout the migration. Of course, this support need not be provided in the same manner. Clearly, however, any disruption of service to existing users must be avoided except where obvious benefits can be gained.

To demonstrate the aspects of the company's migration to SNA that are relevant to the data communications user, a fictitious IBM 3278 video display terminal that is located in a New York City database administration (DBA) office is ideal because most migration procedures apply. Assume that the terminal requires access to six interactive applications at a computer center in New Jersey and four at a computer center in Texas (Fig. 1). The access provided to the user is the same throughout the example that is discussed in the rest of this article. This means that the network configurations change but not the basic service.

Remember that in the pre-SNA environment every application has its own network. In order to provide access to ten applications from one terminal, which is the case in the company's 3278 video display terminal example, individual facilities must be provided for each of the ten applications. This means ten communications lines, twenty modems, ten 3274 terminal control units, and a ten-way switch to select a control unit (and therefore an application).

Although there is only one terminal in this example, from the perspective of a pre-SNA network operator at a computer center, there are 10 terminals. Each has different names, different characteristics, different control commands, and different problem-determination procedures as dictated by the application it takes care of. What is more, since each line is controlled directly by the application, network control tends to be distributed among several operators. Thus one operator knows information management system (IMS), which is one of IBM's database management systems; another knows time sharing option (TSO), an application that provides time-sharing services; and a third is good with modems and communications lines. Clearly, providing service to a user under such conditions is a difficult proposition.

Network design and implementation before an SNA implementation is also difficult. Because applications cannot share facilities, no matter how poorly utilized those facilities may be, entirely new facilities must be installed to support a new application or a new user. Issues such as floor space and vendor delivery times play a significant role in pre-SNA network design. Perhaps worse, backup can be complex and expensive.

Intra-CPU
The second stage in the migration to SNA networking has three parts (Fig. 2). There are the implementation of the virtual telecommunications access method (VTAM), a program in the host computer that provides SNA support to an application; the implementation of network control program (NCP), an SNA communications controller program that runs on an IBM-3705 communications control unit) and, finally the conversion of the applications to support VTAM. At this stage of implementation a switch is necessary only to select a specific CPU, not individual applications within each CPU. Once the CPU has been chosen, the particular application in the CPU can be selected via a log-on request to the network.

When these three parts have been completed, there is no longer such a thing as a "TSO controller" or an "IMS line." Simply put, all terminals, and the physical facilities connecting the terminals to a CPU, become SNA resources to be allocated to individual applications based upon user log-on requests. The network now controls the allocation of terminals. With this approach, the terminal requests connections to an application, or one application can request connection to another application.

Suppose the DBA user wants to access the IMS development subsystem (identified as IMND, in this example) running in the IBM NC33 (a local designation for a 3033 computer). To do this chore, he sets the switch to select NC33 (at the top of Figure 2), types I-M-N-D at the terminal, and presses the ENTER key. Since the terminal is under the control of the network, this message is received by VTAM. This reception, in turn, established a session between the terminal and IMND and turns control of the terminal over to IMND. Once a session has been established, anything entered from the terminal will be received by the IMND subsystem.

Now suppose the user wants to access IMNZ (an IMS test subsystem). This is also running on the NC33 computer. So the user logs off from IMND. When he does this, control of the terminal is returned to the network. Anything entered at the keyboard at this point will be received by VTAM and interpreted as a log-on request. Thus, to log-on to IMNZ, the user simply types I-M-N-Z and presses the ENTER key. VTAM then established a session between the terminal and IMNZ.

At the end of this SNA implementation stage, a com-

prehensive, standardized network-monitoring methodology must be in place. This is necessary because later stages of the implementation will not be successful without constant monitoring. This monitoring takes the form of network-operator watchfulness and daily reports generated from a database created on-line by the network components.

It's also important that, by this stage of implementation, significant progress has been made toward the establishment of network operations control. Although this article deals primarily with the implementation stages of SNA networking, it is important to note that once intra-CPU networking is in place, the network will succeed or fail on the strength—or weakness—of network operations. Finally, the initial cut at a network-standards manual should be well under way before the next stage is begun. The group responsible for network management must take the initiative in ensuring that standards are formulated and adhered to by all users and centers.

Intra-center
The third stage in the migration to SNA provides networking among CPUs within the same computer center (Fig. 3). To do this the 3705 routes messages (data) from one computer to another. The DBA user in our example still needs a switch to select computer centers, but network log-on requests entered from the terminal will select an application within a center. The intra-CPU facility described here is implemented with MSNF—the multisystem networking facility of VTAM.

It is at this stage that network interactions begin to get complex. Not only are the applications interacting with the network through VTAM, but VTAM in each CPU is in communication with every other CPU in the center. To accomplish this, the NCP serves as a traffic policeman. It communicates with several CPUs on one side, and numerous lines, controllers, and terminals on the other.

At this stage, the network begins to take on more of an SNA identification. Everything from the VTAM interface of an application in a computer to the user interface at the terminal (inclusive) is a shared network resource. Thus a communications line may carry data for sessions to several different applications simultaneously (to different terminals), on the same CPU or on different CPUs.

The control of the network management people must be well-established now. Standards must be in place, monitoring must be routine and the network operators must be familiar with all of the network components and their control.

Direct attachment
The fourth stage in the migration to an SNA network provides intercenter communications (Fig. 4). This means that one or more lines comprising a 3705-to-3705 link (trunk) provide a path between the centers over which data for multiple sessions can be routed. The implementation of this stage requires careful coordination to ensure compatibility between the centers. It is at this stage that the operation, not just the imple-

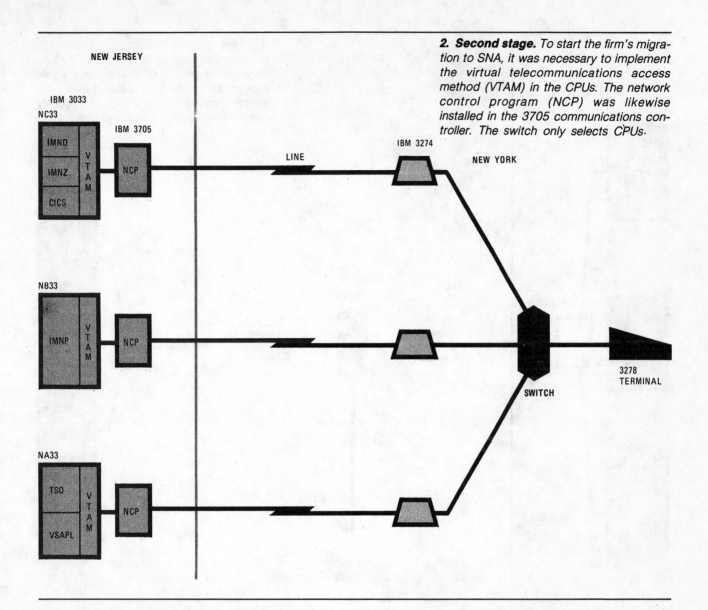

2. Second stage. To start the firm's migration to SNA, it was necessary to implement the virtual telecommunications access method (VTAM) in the CPUs. The network control program (NCP) was likewise installed in the 3705 communications controller. The switch only selects CPUs.

NEW JERSEY

IBM 3033

NC33

IMND
IMNZ
CICS
V T A M

IBM 3705

NCP

LINE

IBM 3274

NEW YORK

NB33

IMNP
V T A M

NCP

NA33

TSO
VSAPL
V T A M

NCP

SWITCH

3278 TERMINAL

mentation, of the network becomes a global rather than a local concern. The user at this stage is truly a network user, rather than a center or application user.

The DBA user can now log onto any application in the network by entering a network log-on request. For example, to access TSO on the SA33 computer, the user types T-S-O-S-A on the keyboard and presses the ENTER key. The network interprets the log-on request, locates the application, establishes a session between the application and the terminal, and turns control of the terminal over to TSO. After working on TSO for a time, the user might decide to test a new transaction under IMND on the NC33 machine. To do so he logs off TSO to return control of the terminal to the network and then logs on to IMND by entering I-M-N-D. The network then creates the session and turns control of the terminal over to IMND.

This direct attachment stage has two major tasks. The first is the implementation coordination of inter-center communications and managing the operational difficulties that arise. The second is the conversion of all non-SNA devices to full SNA support. Actually, this

stage of direct attachment is a watershed. Either control and coordination are well established prior to this stage, or the network will not function properly. If everything has been carefully planned, the network will now function as a full SNA network during normal network operation. But the user is still dependent on the services of a particular center. And backup and concentration have not yet been addressed.

Concentration

The fifth stage in the SNA migration involves the utilization of communications controllers located at a site remote from the computer center (Fig. 5). In this network the communications controller is located in New York. The user's terminal is attached directly, not to a center, but to a concentrator which has links to the centers. Better still, the concentrator of the not-too-distant future will also provide local-processing capabilities as well as network functions. There are several advantages to this more sophisticated arrangement over a stage-four network. These are backup, reduced line costs, higher-speed local devices, and improved

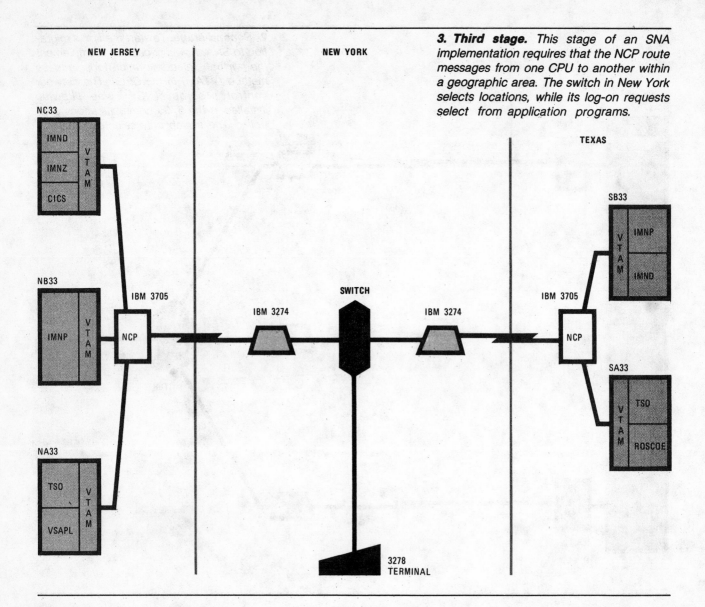

NEW JERSEY

NEW YORK

3. Third stage. *This stage of an SNA implementation requires that the NCP route messages from one CPU to another within a geographic area. The switch in New York selects locations, while its log-on requests select from application programs.*

TEXAS

NC33
IMND
IMNZ
CICS
VTAM

NB33
IMNP
VTAM

IBM 3705
NCP

NA33
TSO
VSAPL
VTAM

IBM 3274

SWITCH

IBM 3274

3278
TERMINAL

IBM 3705
NCP

SB33
VTAM
IMNP
IMND

SA33
VTAM
TSO
ROSCOE

throughput.

Of course, the use of concentrators does not preclude the direct attachment of users to the computer center's communications controller. Any such terminals, however, would not gain the benefits of attachment to a concentrator.

The first of these benefits, operational backup of lines, is effected through the use of multiple-line links (transmission groups) between the concentrator and the centers. If one line is out, throughput may be reduced, but service continues without interruption. Operational backup of terminals or control units can be done either by having redundant equipment or by simply using a different terminal. In this approach, the network log-on request procedure is the same for all terminals and any terminal can access any application.

Contingency backup of a computer center is simply a matter of ensuring that the application can be supported at the backup center. No special network backup is required. This means that if the Texas center is required to provide backup for New Jersey's IMNP, user access is automatic as soon as the application is

started on the backup CPU and its location identified in the network's session-routing tables. This movement of applications can also be done in a normal network environment to provide CPU load balancing.

The reduced line costs benefit accrues because users in the same building as the concentrator have no need for lines or modems since they are directly connected to the concentrators. Moreover, nearby user sites need a line only to the concentrator, not to a computer center. Thus the DBA user's terminal in New York is attached directly to the concentrator. A terminal in Boston only needs a line to New York to gain access to both New Jersey and Texas.

Higher speed is another part of the benefits picture. It can be achieved for some devices that have a special adapter to allow direct attachment to a 3705. Some devices will run 50 to 100 percent faster when attached directly to a 3705 than when attached through a modem—for example, the IBM 3777 remote job entry (RJE) station.

Finally, the last of the benefits, higher throughput, is a result of the better utilization that can be made of

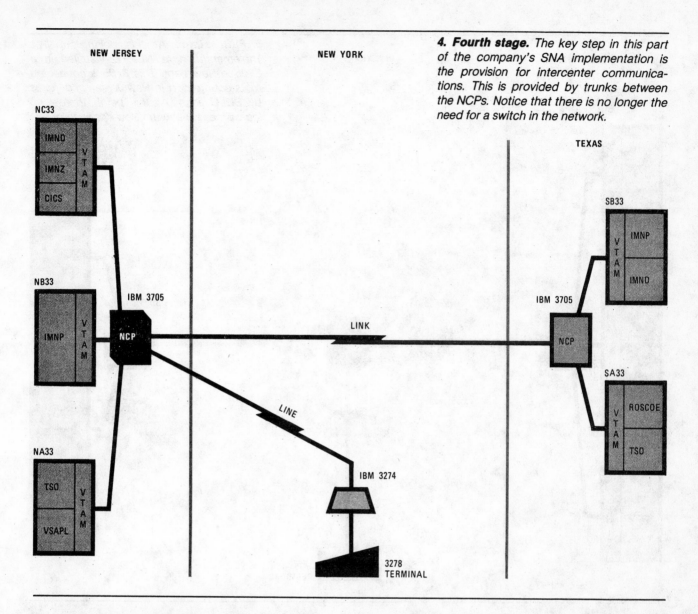

NEW JERSEY   NEW YORK

4. Fourth stage. *The key step in this part of the company's SNA implementation is the provision for intercenter communications. This is provided by trunks between the NCPs. Notice that there is no longer the need for a switch in the network.*

NC33
IMND
IMNZ
CICS
VTAM

NB33
IMNP
VTAM

IBM 3705
NCP

LINK

LINE

IBM 3274

3278 TERMINAL

NA33
TSO
VSAPL
VTAM

TEXAS

SB33
VTAM
IMNP
IMND

IBM 3705
NCP

SA33
VTAM
ROSCOE
TSO

the lines comprising the 3705-to-3705 trunks. Since the trunks provide a "pipe" with built-in operational backup, line speed, link overhead, propagation delay, and error retries are no longer bottlenecks between the center and the user site.

Network management
The last stage in the migration to full SNA networking support involves the creation of centralized network operations (Fig. 6). In this stage, communications network management (CNM) is the IBM term used to describe the separation of production and network functions. And communications management configuration (CMC) refers to the configuration, shown in the figure, that allows the achievement of communications network management.

One of the underlying objectives of the migration to SNA is this separation of network and application functions. The reasons for this separation are to allow network independence of applications or CPUs, and to off-load network processing from the application-processing computers. To accomplish these chores, the

CMC permits the network operation to be wholly separate from the processing of the production-oriented workloads that the network serves. In other words, the separation of these functions permits achieving the goal of a unified utility network—the objective of the SNA implementation.

The sixth stage makes complete the separation of the network and application functions. Network operations and data-flow control that are wholly network functions are controlled by a computer (a 4300, for example) dedicated to the CMC. The center's operations staff is thus relieved of network coordination responsibilities, and the processing computers are relieved of much of the network processing. Centralized control also ensures better coordination of the numerous interacting network components.

It's important to remember that the implementation of a CMC does not imply that local network operations control will no longer be needed. On the contrary, each computer center will be responsible for moment-to-moment operations control of the resources within its domain. It is the coordination and control of the net-

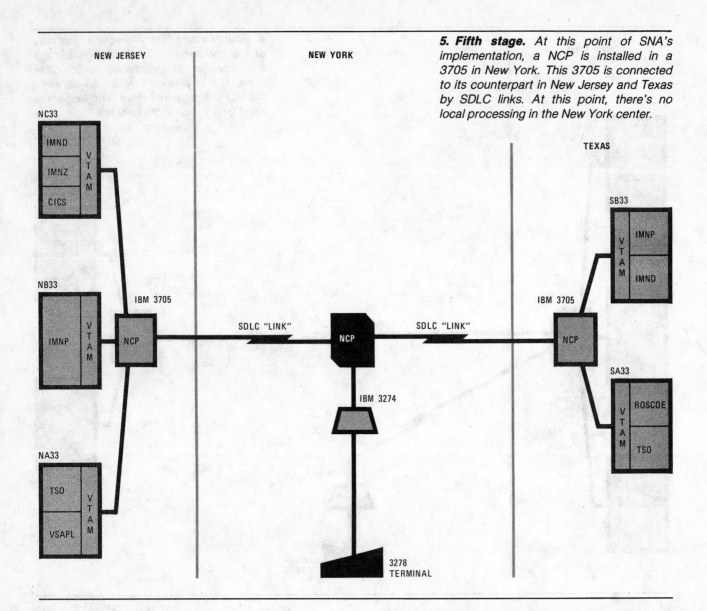

NEW JERSEY

NEW YORK

5. Fifth stage. At this point of SNA's implementation, a NCP is installed in a 3705 in New York. This 3705 is connected to its counterpart in New Jersey and Texas by SDLC links. At this point, there's no local processing in the New York center.

TEXAS

NC33

IMND
IMNZ
CICS
VTAM

NB33

IMNP
VTAM

IBM 3705

NCP

SDLC "LINK"

NCP

SDLC "LINK"

IBM 3705

NCP

SB33

VTAM
IMNP
IMND

IBM 3274

NA33

TSO
VSAPL
VTAM

SA33

VTAM
ROSCOE
TSO

3278
TERMINAL

work as a whole that will be performed by the CMC operations staff.

At this stage, many of the responsibilities of the SNA network management group might be given to a group in charge of the communications management configuration. The SNA network management group can continue to exist, but its role will become more strategic rather than operational. The network standards document should be well established by this point, and the network monitoring and coordination responsibilities should be assumed by the CMC group.

Impact
What has been described is the migration to a new network environment for the company. In this environment, not only is the concept of a TSO controller obsolete, the concept of a user is changed. The users, under SNA, are users of network services, not users of a particular center or application. This is in contrast to pre-SNA networks with well-defined user communities. There, a single user might access several networks to more than one center, but each network was discrete.

And the center was the hub of each specialized network, regardless of its function.

The SNA view of the network, wherein computers are not the hub but the periphery, has several implications as mentioned earlier. SNA implementation implies an extraordinary increase in internal network complexity, and requires a re-education and re-orientation of network support personnel, users, and management.

Perhaps worst of all as far as implications are concerned, the improper installation or malfunction of any component in an SNA network affects the entire network. For example, imagine an interactive terminal and an RJE station attached to the same concentrator in New York. The terminal operator is accessing an application running on a computer in New Jersey, and the RJE station is communicating with an application running in Texas. If improperly defined, the data traffic to the RJE station could flood the concentrator, resulting in throughput degradation to the interative terminal without a similar throughput degradation to the RJE station. Determining the source of the interactive terminal's trouble would be impossible using pre-SNA

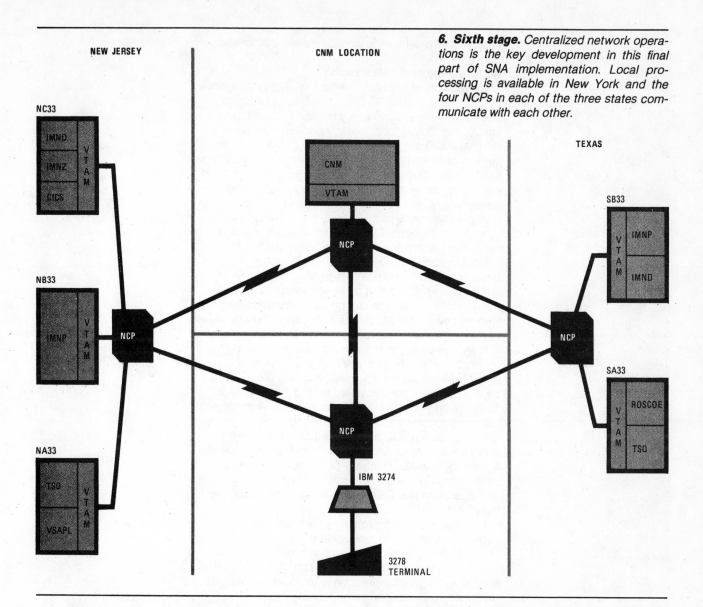

NEW JERSEY CNM LOCATION

NC33

TEXAS

SB33

SA33

NB33

NA33

6. Sixth stage. *Centralized network operations is the key development in this final part of SNA implementation. Local processing is available in New York and the four NCPs in each of the three states communicate with each other.*

techniques or procedures.

There are still other problems. For example, one irony of decentralized/distributed information processing is that its complexity requires centralized control to ensure compatibility between the numerous interacting components and organizations. Research about the technology of the approach must yet be done. And standards must be set, enforced, and modified as a result of performance monitoring. Furthermore, as the complexity of technology increases, "reinvention of the data communications wheel" becomes more and more expensive and centralized documentation and coordination must be used to help alleviate this.

Network operation must also be done from a centralized vantage point, not just from the perspective of one node. This means that the tuning of the network must strive for global rather than local optimization. This is more difficult than it was in a pre-SNA network since those components that constitute the network are more numerous.

Not only does an SNA implementation result in centralized control—it generates problems with access

security and load-level control. This happens because any user will have access to all of the computer and information resources in the network. What's more, the number of users, compared to those in the pre-SNA environment, is likely to increase significantly. The issues of security and load control become very serious in this environment.

Security is usually the repsonsibility of the application program or operating system. Thus most large applications such as IMS or TSO require that all authorized terminals be defined for them, and that authorized users identify themselves with a password. Of course, SNA provides an encrypt-decrypt facility. For those devices that support it, data can be encrypted on a session basis or on a block basis, at the discretion of the application.

For its part, load level is usually controlled by determining the maximum number of users that can be accommodated and restricting the number of users to that amount. This implies that a more active role must be played by the performance-monitoring and operations staffs to ensure that demand on the various processors in the network is approximately distributed.

Redundancy and catastrophe

The two kinds of backup, operational and contingency, are of great import in an SNA network. Operational backup provides redundancy in case of component failure. In contrast, contingency backup provides for the major catastrophes that destroy entire computer centers or user sites. SNA makes both types of backup easier. Operational backup is easier because the hardware complexity of the network is reduced and redundancy is simpler and cheaper. Between 3705s, the multiple-line trunks provide built-in and transparent operational backup. This means that if one line in a trunk fails, others are available to carry the load.

Contingency backup is easier because the concentrators located at the user site provide access to all computer centers. If one computer center is disabled, the critical applications can be run at the backup site with no new or special facilities required. The user need not even know that the application has been moved.

SNA also provides many facilities for improving the network's reliability and availability. Unfortunately, these facilities are largely invisible to the user. This is because reliability and availability are "dissatisfiers." They are only noticed in their absence. SNA implementation will increase the user's ability to access information, and, as a result, the demand for access to information will increase. As the number of users increases, the reliability and availability of the network will become more critical and the role of the network support and operation that SNA supplies will become increasingly important.

Finally, there is the problem of response time. Response time is usually more affected by non-network factors than by network factors. In most networks, application design, CPU load, and channel contention have a much greater effect on response time than such things as transmission line utilization. This is not to suggest that networks should not be monitored and tuned. It just means that a perfectly tuned network can have poor or erratic response times. Network-support personnel must work closely with the computer-support and application-design personnel to ensure a responsive network. This emphasizes again the requirement for centralized coordination.

In the future

It is unlikely that an entire network of private leased lines will ever be economically feasible. Even with the advent of full-screen edit support under SNA, and the lower charges expected from private carriers such as Satellite Business Systems, certain locations will not be able to justify direct access to a private network.

In those cases, public network offerings will be very useful in extending the reach of an SNA network. As a step in this direction, IBM has recently announced support for X.25 links in the United States.

As an additional link-level technology that will help extend private networks, X.25 is another variable to be mixed into the data communications user's least-cost/best-response analysis. ∎

2 Network Implementation

Building block approach shows structure of network programs

Alan P. Rosenberg, Securities Industry Automation Corp., New York

Handling and processing information from points in a network is done in discrete stages, and each step has its own software component

Understanding software, especially the programs for an entire data communications configuration, can be a difficult task the first time out. But, despite the extensive and esoteric customization that is often necessary, any data communications software system contains certain minimum and necessary modules. A discussion of these modules will perhaps aid in the understanding of what has come to be recognized as a vital part of the data communications picture.

The design of complex computer software is still very much an art, although system builders commonly rely on a scientific approach and on a variety of concepts and methods provided by computer science. Often, however, system design depends critically upon past experience and on creative use of resources. The nature of system design as "art-vs-science" probably applies nowhere more strongly than in the area of data communications.

This has historically been the case in the software area for several reasons:
■ users' needs in data communications vary greatly across terminals, disciplines, and applications, and thus require significant customization;
■ in the development of standard software products, data communications stood well behind language processors, general-purpose operating systems, and ap-

plication packages in the priority schemes of hardware manufacturers because of the relative newness of data communications compared with other areas of computer use;
■ user demand for standardized data communications software became significant quite late in the overall expansion of the software marketplace. Hardware vendors were generally slow to realize the marketing value of data communications software as an aid in selling processors, which left early communicators with the task of developing their software on a customized basis.

A major effect of this history is that the fundamental concepts of data communications software are not widely understood. What follows is an introductory description of the basic software components which make up a typical data communications system. While there is much room for variation in the specific set of building blocks, the essential pieces discussed will be found in any data communications processing system.

In order to describe the software components of a typical data communications system, it is necessary to define some basic terms.

A *line* or *circuit* is any physical link connecting communicating devices; neither the physical nature of the medium (copper, microwave, satellite) nor its relative

1   Idealized network structure

Environment. *Data communications software operates in a network which is a set of stations controlled by a central computer. Stations may be terminals, terminal controllers, or computers. The links that connect various stations to the central computer may have diverse physical characteristics and may be leased lines or the switched network.*

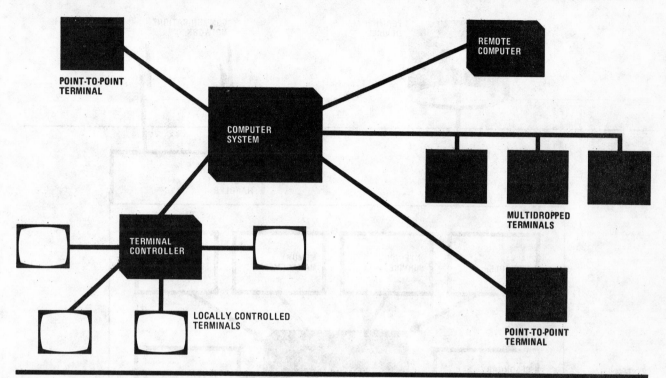

permanence (leased, switched) is important to this discussion. A *station* is any device capable of receiving and/or sending data via a line. A station may be a terminal, a terminal controller, or a computer.

A *network,* for the purposes of this discussion, consists of a set of stations and lines linked to and controlled by a central computer system. While it is understood that certain stations may be computers, and that the central computer functions may be physically dispersed, it is convenient here to view this universe (or network) as a star, in which all stations connect to the (single) central computer. Figure 1 shows a schematic of an idealized network.

A *transaction* is the basic unit of information traversing the network. Examples of transactions include messages in a store-and-forward switching system, inquiries to a remote database, and data in a remote-job-entry or data collection application. A transaction always originates at one station, passes to the central computer, and eventually results in information being transmitted to one or more stations (possibly including the originator). The number of distinct outputs produced as part of processing a transaction is called the explosion factor, and is usually a key input in determining the maximum throughput of the system (the maximum number of transactions which can be serviced in unit time).

Data communications systems are typically characterized by:
■ the random arrival through the network of incoming

requests for transaction service;
■ the requirement to service multiple users (i.e. stations) simultaneously;
■ the requirement to hold and possibly process in-transit transactions within the computer system, often without a pre-definable limitation on the maximum volume of traffic to be accommodated and;
■ the requirement to protect in-transit traffic from loss or duplication.

Thus, such systems are usually implemented via real-time, event-driven, multitask software. These terms mean that the system operates in response to external demands for service (events), at a rate consistent with the arrival frequency of such demands (in real time), and in a manner which permits several processing functions (tasks) to run concurrently by capitalizing on the fact that internal processing speeds are orders of magnitude faster that input/output speeds, which are, in turn, orders of magnitude greater than actual line transmission rates.

Figure 2 shows, in block diagram form, the major components in any data communications software system. It should be noted that the operating system component is the heart of the model, providing the connecting links to and among the network, computer peripherals, system-support software, and applications. In many cases, the support software supplied by computer manufacturers is structured so that the lines of demarcation (between operating system and communications services, for example) are blurred.

2 Communications system software structure

Functional divisions. The operating system provides the connecting links among network, computer peripherals, system support software, and applications. Communications services move data across the network. Message management handles transactions within the system. Network management monitors performance.

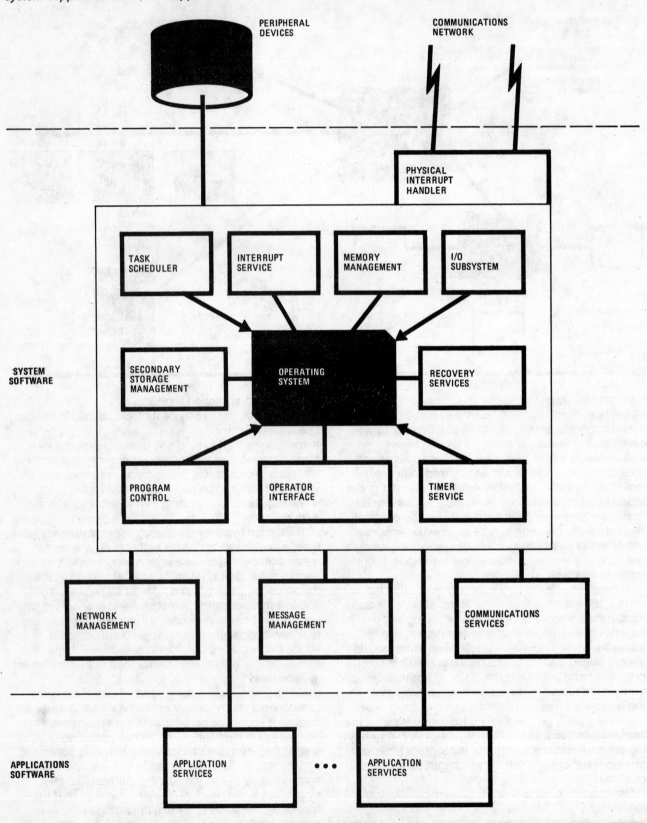

Nonetheless, closer examination will always allow each of the major areas shown in the diagram to be assigned to appropriate portions of the software.

Operating system

The operating system is the manager of such critical system resources as the main memory, the central processor, and the input/output subsystems. An operating system may be either general-purpose, in which case the special requirements of data communications functions are provided by add-on program modules (either purchased or user-developed), or special-purpose, in which event many of these functions will be included.

The major subsystems within the operating system are:

■ Task scheduler—distributes use of the processor among system functions according to demand and priority of operation.

■ Interrupt service—provides the hardware level response to external events, specifically input/output operations. With certain general-purpose operating systems, special physical interrupt handlers may be needed, as illustrated in Figure 2.

■ Memory management—controls the assignment and release of main memory for use as a temporary data residence and work-space. This dynamic use of memory significantly reduces the quantity of storage which might otherwise be required.

■ I/O subsystem—provides for data transfer between software and peripheral devices, usually including communications interface controllers.

■ Secondary storage management—obtains and releases space on disks or other mass storage devices for user information, in-transit message buffering, data-base structures, transaction logs, and the like.

■ Recovery services—provides for the generation of checkpoints and other records to be employed if system failure occurs. The degree and cost of protection for in-process transactions and data files depends heavily on the particular application.

■ Program control—governs the loading and execution of system and user software modules, including overlay structures used to accommodate programs whose overall size would exceed the amount of memory available.

■ Operator interface—allows external monitoring and control of all system functions.

■ Timer service—allows event initiation based on elapsed time or time of day.

Most operating systems include various additional aids to program development, testing, and maintenance. These include, among others, on-line dumps and traces, and file services.

Communications services

The communications services component of a typical data communications software system is responsible for all activities concerned directly with moving data across the network (i.e. between the central computer and its remote stations). In effect, the communications services subsystem functions as a software front-end between the network with its users and all other software within the system (including the application programs which perform the actual transaction processing operations).

It is usually desirable to design the communications services subsystem with as few dependencies as possible on either the specific applications or the specific types of terminal devices to be used. While this goal can very seldom be completely met, an attempt to reach independence usually simplifies later maintenance and modification of the software. It should be noted, however, that in certain cases considerations such as system-response overhead or development cost may militate against the ideal of maximizing application and terminal independence.

The most important software subsystems within the data communications service area are:

■ Initiation of network service—this includes, on the input side, polling terminals on multipoint lines, answering calls on switched lines, and responding to incoming traffic on contention or freewheeling lines. On the output side, it includes transmission initiation by calling multidrop stations, dialing for switched stations, and sending appropriate bid sequences on contention lines.

■ Message assembly and disassembly—data moving across the network typically appears as a serial stream of characters, and the transmission format is often inconvenient from the perspective of the user application program. Thus, this subsystem provides a logical transaction-oriented interface between the rest of the software and the network, and can remove the need for programs within the system to be concerned with the idiosyncracies of terminal operation or data format. Message assembly occurs upon input from the network and involves composing the data in one logical message or transaction into a standard internal format for subsequent processing. Message disassembly is the same process in reverse. This function also accounts for disparities of terminal type such as code set and text blocking. When data lengths in messages exceed one or two hundred characters, or when transmission speeds are very slow, data will be placed piecemeal in secondary storage to make more efficient use of main memory. In-transit traffic will be moved back and forth between the appropriate processing programs and secondary storage (a technique called staging) when secure message recovery is a requirement, as in a store-and-forward switching application (Fig. 3).

■ Protocol services—this function provides the specific control sequences, data framing, and block construction and interpretation required for communication within the various protocols currently in use. Although modern data communications hardware has assumed many of these tasks (redundancy checksum generation and validation, synchronization-character stripping and insertion, and others), the significant decisions concerning successful receipt and delivery of data traffic must still be made by software. As could be expected, the level of programming to support a complex full-duplex protocol such as IBM's synchronous data link control (SDLC) is usually significantly greater than

3 Staging in-transit traffic

Message management. *The message management subsystem treats transactions as logical units of information. It receives incoming messages from the network via communications software and an initial buffering stage. Messages are queued until they are processed by the applications program and re-delivered to the network.*

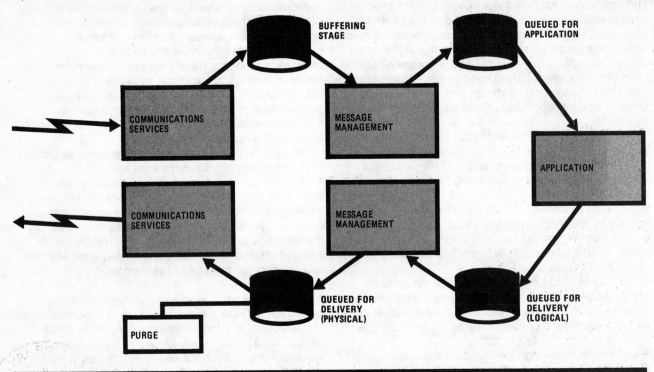

that required to support a teleprinter interface. However, hardware manufacturers seem to be simultaneously increasing the share of protocol handling done by hardware while expanding the functions provided by their standard data communications software facilities.

■ Error detection and retry—the data communications subsystem is typically charged with recognizing network errors, and with initiating appropriate retry measures. Because the expected frequency of errors on a telephone line can be several orders of magnitude greater than that for a computer peripheral (such as a disk drive), network errors are usually treated under a threshold approach. This means that an error or malfunction (such as a parity error or invalid block checksum) is not considered to be a true or "hard" error until a predefined number of retry attempts have likewise failed. The threshold method allows a line or station suffering a transient problem to self-correct without human intervention. Even when a fault condition fails to clear up within the threshold limit, the software may continue its attempts at re-establishing service, although at a lower retry rate to avoid wasting system resources. Of course, any hard failure and its eventual correction will be reported to the operator as part of the network management function.

Message management refers to the portion of the system which handles messages or transactions as logical units of information, generally without regard to actual text content. The message management function receives incoming messages from communications

services and controls their movement through the system (including any processing by applications programs) to the point of presentation to the communications function once again for delivery to the final physical or logical destination (Fig. 3).

Since transaction arrival is a random phenomenon, all data communications software systems are designed so that message service in the network and message processing in the central computer can occur asynchronously.

The software device providing this capability is the *queue,* a first-in, first-out chained list which permits messages to be serviced by the various components of the system at their respective speeds and without the need for complex interlock mechanisms. Hence, the most important message management function is the maintenance of a queuing service for receiving input, processing it, and holding it for output until delivery to the indicated destination is possible. Queue structures often provide two or more priority levels within a queue, so that urgent traffic is not delayed behind normal messages. One of the most significant benefits of a queuing scheme is that application programs can often be designed to operate in a batch-like manner: the program simply obtains the next transaction from an input queue, processes it, directs any output to appropriate delivery queues, and then requests the next input once again. This approach allows applications programs to be developed and tested with a minimum of awareness of the actual on-line nature of the rest of the software. Other message management functions of significance include:

■ Routing—selecting the proper destination(s) for arriving transactions. A destination may be a physical station (as in a message-switching application), or an application program within the central computer (as in an order entry or database inquiry application). The routing function also provides for placing outbound messages on queues for subsequent delivery by the communications services component in accordance with the specified destination station(s). It should be noted that transaction routing information may be explicitly carried as part of the message, or may be implied by transaction type, origin, or other parameters. For example, traffic in a message-switching system usually carries explicit destination station identifiers; transactions in a database update application may carry no routing information at all, with implied routing of the input message to an application program and implied routing of the response back to the inquiry originator.

■ Validation—the extent to which validation of transaction syntax and content is performed will vary among systems. In general, this function will tend to be included in the message management area when a strong standardization in format is required. A case in point would be large-scale message switching. In other instances, most of the validation required for incoming traffic will be highly application-dependent and thus will most sensibly be incorporated into the individual application functions.

■ Purging—since storage for in-transit transactions is usually limited, the removal of transactions from active storage once processing and delivery are complete is a critical function, and it is usually included in the message management area. The purging function commences when a message has been delivered to its eventual destination(s). Any space occupied by the message in the in-transit area (main or secondary storage) is released for subsequent re-use. Depending on the specific application, the purged message may be entered into a historical log for archival storage or redelivery if required later.

Network management

The network management component of a typical data communications software system provides facilities to monitor the performance of lines, stations, and the central computer, and to modify the assignments and functions of the elements of the network. Network management also provides the main operator interface into the system, and is the vehicle for human control over its operation.

Performance monitoring is chiefly concerned with recognition of errors and unusual occurrences. As mentioned previously, errors on communications facilities are much more frequent than on data processing facilities, and hence the threshold approach to error handling is used. The network management subsystem is charged with maintaining accurate error statistics, generating logs of true (i.e. hard) failures, and keeping an updated picture of the state of all central-site and

network equipment. Many network management software systems provide video displays of lines and stations that are not operating correctly, a feature of great benefit to operations personnel when the network is extensive.

Network management software can also detect network-wide problems (such as an unusually large number of messages waiting for delivery in in-transit storage) and can take immediate action or inform the operator with appropriate alarm notifications.

The second major function of network management is control of the network, i.e. providing the operator with the ability to modify the operation or use of any network component. Typical functions provided would include the ability to:

■ allow or disallow service to a particular line or station;
■ change frequency or order of service;
■ establish or remove alternate routing assignments;
■ transmit test messages;
■ enable or disable selected message or transaction types and;
■ display network traffic statistics, error statistics, and equipment status.

It is usually good practice for network management to produce a hard-copy log of all significant events relating to system operation, including operator commands, system failures, network errors, and so on. This kind of documentation can prove extremely useful should problems arise or if detailed studies of the system are required.

Applications

The applications portion of a data communications software system might best be described as the "useful work" part. Everything else is the "overhead" of bringing transaction traffic in and results out. Obviously, the ease of defining and developing applications software depends directly on the facilities provided by the operating system. The applications designer will need to know the manner in which applications receive incoming traffic from the network and pass outbound traffic back, the nature of the database management facilities for user files, and the level of transaction and file recovery supported by the underlying operating system software.

As noted earlier, it is usually advantageous to structure applications modules as serial processing elements which obtain new messages from an input queue and present output to other queues for delivery. If it is necessary to have multiple application paths in parallel, several of these serial modules can be operated simultaneously. The goal is to make the application programs as simple and straightforward as possible, since experience indicates that this is the area of the system most susceptible to change.

The key to intelligent acquisition of data communications software, whether by purchase or development, is complete definition of functional and capacity requirements, and a corresponding understanding of the capabilities of the proposed system. The breakdown into functional areas outlined in the article may be useful in performing the necessary analysis. ■

A programming language for networks

Paul A. D. de Maine, Pennsylvania State University, University Park, Pa.

**Researchers have built a truly transportable language.
Programs written in it execute on any computer, and
the compiler can make any language transportable.**

*Contrary to what many software vendors say, there is
no portable programming language. Moreover, the
word "portable" is used irresponsibly by both vendors
and users. Users assume a portable program is one
that will compile and execute on different computers.
Actually, such "portable" programs may compile on
different machines, but if they execute at all, they may
do so incorrectly. A close look at available portable
software shows that it is portable only after the user
purchases a software-conversion package for his
machine. Another common marketing term is "very
nearly portable" software, which means a user must
know intimately both the program and the executing
machine to make the proper code changes.*

*Even programs in a language such as Cobol, which is
more standardized than most, will not execute properly
from one machine to the next. The reasons are that the
machines may differ in size and architecture and each
vendor implements the Cobol compiler differently.*

*Confusion arises, then, when users or vendors use
terms such as "portability," "transferability," and
"transportability" interchangeably. The difference is
that a transportable program can compile and execute
without error and without change over a range of small
to large machines, while portable and transferable programs either compile but do not execute or cannot
specify their environment well enough to execute correctly. Since high-level languages make assumptions
about machine-dependent characteristics, such as
word and byte size, programs written in those languages cannot be transportable.*

*But all is not lost. Researchers at Pennsylvania State
University have built a prototype of a high-level transportable programming language (TPL) and a compiler
coded in that language. This language and compiler
allow the same programs to be correctly executed on
all machines in any heterogeneous network.*

*The key to a language's transportability lies in its
ability to respond to programmer-specified information
such as a particular machine's word and byte size,
orientation (byte or word), and maximum amount of
core memory. Furthermore, any language can be standardized if its compiler is transportable.*

*A compiler is a program that translates an input
program, called the source program, into an output
program, known as the object program, or object
code. The object code can be machine language,*
*assembler language, or a high-level language that is
closer to machine language than the source program
language. Although compilers are not usually transportable, the TPL-coded compiler operates over a
range of machines.*

*The TPL compiler takes any TPL program and pro-
duces Fortran, a language available on most computers. Fortran for different computers is not the same;
however, since the TPL-coded compiler understands
the machine-dependent characteristics specified by
the programmer, the Fortran it produces is the Fortran
for that particular machine.*

*TPL compilers can also be written to translate other
high-level languages to TPL. They can also translate a
nonportable compiler program, coded in Fortran
instead of TPL (but eventually coded in any language),
into a transportable one. To do this, the user's nontransportable compiler is fed twice into the TPL compiler. The first time, the TPL compiler flags nontransportable statements and advises changes; the second time,
it takes the altered compiler and the specified machine
characteristics and produces the user's original compiler coded in the Fortran for the user's machine.*

*Some vendors sell a "preprocessor" to make their
software transportable. A preprocessor functions similarly to the TPL compiler, which is a sophisticated
preprocessor. The major difference is that a preprocessor is not transportable. The TPL compiler, which recognizes dynamically specified machine-dependent
characteristics for a range of machines, is transportable and needs to be coded only once.* —WR-H

Until recently, there has been no portable software
language for data communications users' programs.
Every language touted as transportable from one machine to another has actually needed a software-conversion package to make it operate correctly. But now,
the prototypes for a new transportable programming
language (TPL) and its compiler, both developed at
Pennsylvania State University, promise to deliver real
transportability.

TPL is transportable because it responds to pro-
grammer-supplied information such as word and byte
size and the amount of core memory for a particular
machine. Once the machine characteristics are specified, the TPL compiler can convert a TPL program into

the Fortran designed for a user's machine.

To understand TPL, it is necessary to understand the nature of a transportable language, how its compiler is organized, and how the language adapts to a computer's architecture. Then the data communications user will be able to decide what degree of transportability he needs in his application and whether or not a vendor's offerings are useful to him.

A programming language for writing operating systems and user software that will execute on any machine needs efficient, flexible, easy-to-use numerics and nonnumerics. In particular, the language's numerical computations must be independent of computer word size and hardware instruction sets, and its character manipulation must be independent of hardware character sets and machine-addressing modes.

These capabilities require that the language allow variable-precision arithmetic (different machines compute to a different number of decimal places) and contain a machine-independent character-variable type. A programming language with these two features is said to be machine-independent.

The language must also compensate for changes in

ticularly Fortran, are the most transferable. However, transferability does not mean a program will execute on a range of machines. Frequently programs will compile on several machines with different architectures but will either not execute or execute incorrectly.

The second factor, portability, is a measure of the control a language can exert over its environment during execution and compilation. This includes the ability to reserve memory space, to specify word or byte instructions, and to control the machine's registers. Assembler languages are the most portable, but they are also the least transferable. To be transportable, a language must be both transferable and portable.

Transportability can be achieved in one of two ways: the new-language approach or the extended-language approach. Pennsylvania State University's TPL is an example of the latter.

The new-language approach decrees transportability by requiring that any language and compiler be built according to standardized specifications (see "Failed attempts at standardization"). The goals of this method are desirable but unrealistic. All attempts to come up with a standard for language transportability

1. Software chain. *The user's high-level language program is the source code for its compiler that is coded in TPL. The Fortran object code outputted by the TPL compiler is the source code for the vendor-supplied Fortran compiler. This Fortran compiler generates optimized machine-dependent code for the user's machine.*

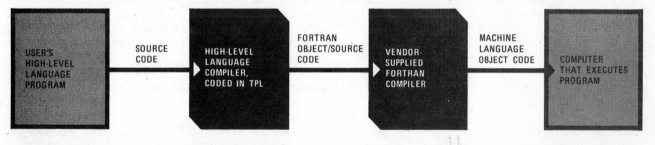

the amount of primary memory available to a program through some form of virtual memory so that the same program can be implemented on both small and large computers. Virtual-memory software contains instructions for swapping information stored in primary memory with information stored on a disk. As a result, large programs, which contain more information than can be accommodated in a computer's primary memory, can still execute on that computer. A programming language with this characteristic is said to be configuration-independent.

Finally, to be transportable across the range of computers in a heterogeneous network, the language must be easily learned and easily used. Programs coded in the language must also be efficient with respect to the execution time and the use of computer resources.

Two factors determine whether a language is transportable: transferability and portability. The first factor, transferability, is simply a measure of the compilability of a program by different machines' compilers. In other words, it indicates the degree of syntactic standardization of the programming language and the support provided for its compilers. High-level languages, par-

in the past 20 years have failed, even though large organizations, such as the Department of Defense and IBM, have supported them.

The second approach for creating a transportable programming language, the extended-language approach, has great potential for success, as evidenced by TPL. This transportable language is an open-ended, natural extension of a parent high-level language already implemented in a particular range of machines. The compiler must be coded in the transportable new language. Its source code is the parent high-level language for which a vendor-supplied optimizing compiler geared to the user's machine already exists.

For example, suppose a machine already has a compiler for a particular Fortran dialect. The transportable compiler can translate the code the programmer is writing into that computer's version of Fortran. This compiler's Fortran output program is the source code for the vendor-supplied Fortran compiler that both translates the Fortran code to machine or assembler language and optimizes the program to produce fast, efficient code for execution.

Researchers at Pennsylvania State wanted to begin

2. Conversion. *The user's nontransportable compiler is the source code for the TPL compiler. The TPL compiler flags all nontransportable code, which the user changes to TPL code. The TPL-coded compiler is fed again into the TPL compiler after the machine's characteristics have been specified. The output is the machine's Fortran.*

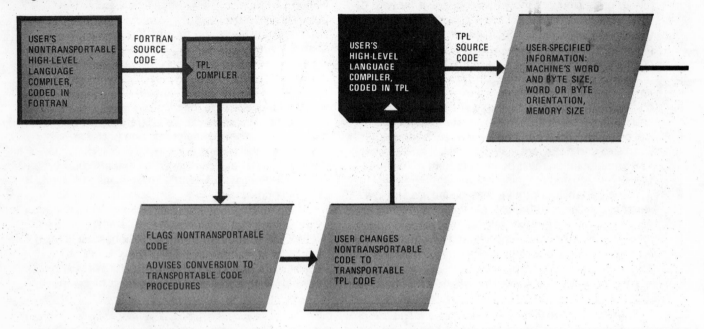

with a language that could run on the greatest possible number of computers. So, they chose the ubiquitous Fortran as the parent language for TPL. Fortran differs from computer to computer; however, since the TPL-coded compiler understands the machine-dependent characteristics specified by the programmer, it produces the Fortran for that particular machine, such as the IBM 370/3033 at the university.

Features of the language

TPL consists of a subset of declarative and executable Fortran instructions that are fully transportable for a desired range of machines. In addition, it contains new declarative and executable instructions that either replace nontransportable Fortran instructions or provide a special capability not present in most Fortrans.

Since TPL has been designed to appear as a simple and natural variant of Fortran, a large part of the TPL syntax has been obtained directly from Fortran. Moreover, TPL features have been designed, whenever possible, as natural extensions or generalizations of conventional Fortran instructions.

TPL's Fortran subset was obtained from a comparative study of seven versions of Fortran: ANSI-standard (American National Standards Institute) Fortran IV, IBM 360/370 Fortran G and H, Control Data Corporation (CDC) 6000 series Fortran IV, Univac 1108 Fortran IV, Digital Equipment Corporation (DEC) PDP-11 Fortran IV, DS Sigma 5/7 Fortran IV, and Honeywell Information Systems 6000 series Fortran. Fortran instructions were classified as to transferability and portability. Only transportable instructions are included in TPL.

However, information about transferable instructions that are not portable is used by the TPL compiler for testing and converting nontransportable statements

to transportable ones. The replacements for nontransportable instructions were obtained by reconfiguring input/output and I/O-related instructions so that both the simplest and the most sophisticated options appear as natural variants. All extensions of ANSI-standard Fortran particular to a vendor's version of Fortran were eliminated, and constraints were imposed to scale down various features of different versions of Fortran to a common level.

The salient features of TPL are a virtual-array capability, variable-precision numerics, variable-size kernels for working with strings, flexible I/O capabilities, data compression/decompression capabilities during I/O operations, and several modular control structures to make the language more like Algol and PL/1. Some of these control structures have been added to Fortran 77. However, Fortran 77 is not transportable.

The virtual-array capability

Array are considered virtual if they have more than three dimensions (as may occur in an inventory program) or if the amount of primary memory is insufficient to contain all elements of the array. Every virtual array must be specified by a special nonexecutable statement. Also, the data type (real or integer) and the dimensional structure and total size of the virtual array must be specified. These are dynamic quantities that are set by the programmer during program execution.

A virtual array is referenced in the same way as conventional arrays. All executable TPL instructions that allow conventional-array references also allow virtual-array references.

Flexibility of the virtual-array capability is enhanced since the programmer can redefine an array without destroying information stored in it. Programmers can

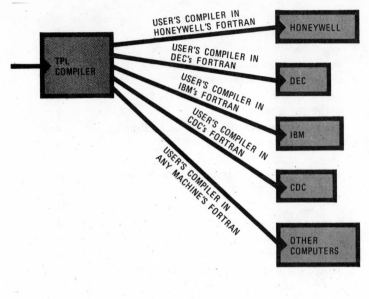

USER'S COMPILER IN HONEYWELL'S FORTRAN

USER'S COMPILER IN DEC's FORTRAN

USER'S COMPILER IN IBM's FORTRAN

USER'S COMPILER IN CDC's FORTRAN

USER'S COMPILER IN ANY MACHINE'S FORTRAN

TPL COMPILER

HONEYWELL

DEC

IBM

CDC

OTHER COMPUTERS

Failed attempts at standardization

The new-language approach has not been successful in the past because the ANSI committees and major user groups, such as the Department of Defense (DOD), have found that it is impossible to impose rigid specifications for a language and a compiler. This method ignores the fact that programmers are not prepared to learn a new language when a familiar language is "nearly adequate."

In addition, the new-language approach does not take into account the many programs in widely used languages that will ultimately have to be translated to the new language. This means that, to be successful, the new language must be capable of facilitating the translation of these programs.

For these reasons, the several attempts to market new languages, such as IBM's PL/1, have not succeeded. In fact, with the possible exception of Cobol, which at best has been only partially successful—and then only because of its primary user, the DOD—all attempts to specify standards for high-level languages have failed.

The current work on the Ada language is yet another effort to instantaneously create a widely used transportable programming language. The DOD plans to standardize the language, by imposing strict specifications, and the compilers, by testing them for validity. It will meet the wide support problem by providing support tools and service programs. An extensive educational program will convince prospective users of the desirability of using the new language. However, the DOD is ignoring the difficulty of recoding existing programs.

also specify the way an array is stored (for example, by column or by row) and whether it is to be retained after program execution.

Variable precision

Since the word or byte size may vary from machine to machine, if a language makes assumptions about the word or byte size, it cannot be transportable. To make the language machine-independent, TPL contains two numeric variable types not found in conventional Fortran: variable-precision real and variable-precision integer. Any variable in a TPL program can be defined as variable-precision. The degree of precision may be set during program execution.

Conventional or virtual variables and subscripted or simple variables can be variable-precision and used like real variables. For example, they can be used in I/O statements or passed as subprogram arguments, which eliminates the need for programmers to work directly with local, machine-dependent packages.

For character and string manipulation, TPL contains a nonnumeric variable called the kernel. Like numeric variables, kernel variables must be defined by a specification statement. The kernel size, which is the actual number of bits making up one kernel, can be specified by the number of bits per kernel or by English-like characters or words. This variable-size capability eliminates dependency on machine architecture (such as character or word sizes).

Although kernel arrays, either conventional or virtual, must be defined before they are referenced, the number of dimensions, subscript ranges, total array size, and kernel size can be defined or altered during program execution. Kernel arrays are referenced in the same way as conventional arrays.

Input/output

The I/O in TPL is a generalized form of that found in most conventional Fortran dialects but with new features. For example, TPL allows three ways, instead of the normal one way, of specifying I/O, storage, or communications devices. Users can implement I/O by specifying the I/O task number, the device-type number, or the device-unit number.

The I/O task number indicates the type of I/O task to be performed. Each of six different tasks is assigned a number from 1 to 6. The tasks include read/received operations from the input device specified for system use, the same operation with the input device specified for user's use, a write/transmit operation with the output device specified for computer use, and the same operation with the output device specified for user use. Other task numbers specify read or write operations to be performed on a direct-access storage device, either permanently allocated or temporarily assigned for TPL. Information on permanent direct-access devices is saved at the end of each program.

I/O can also be specified by assigning numbers to all devices of a particular type that are similarly accessed. For example, all card readers are assigned one device-type number, and all disks with the same characteristics are assigned another. So far, TPL identifies about 20 types of devices.

The unit number, assigned to a particular device, is still another way to specify I/O. For example, a certain card reader might be assigned the number 18.

Initialization information supplied to TPL contains formats, error messages, and both the device type and the unit numbers for devices assigned for use with every value of I/O task. Other TPL I/O features that make TPL more efficient at execution time, more user friendly, and machine-independent include block transfer of data with or without format control to or from conventional and virtual arrays, and format-specification codes to allow for I/O of variable-precision variables and kernels. Moreover, data compression/decompression and operations such as encode/decode and stream-oriented I/O are provided in TPL, as is a conversion of hardware character codes into a special machine-independent character code set.

Besides the computational and control instructions derived from the TPL's Fortran subset, generalized control structures such as WHILE, UNTIL, FOR, and CASE are supported. A BEGIN-END type of statement, analogous to that in Algol and Pascal, can be used. These structures make the language more modular, which makes it easier to write and debug programs.

The compiler and transportability

To make programs transportable, the compiler must be given five parameters for any local machine on which a program is to execute:
- The maximum size of a program module, exclusive of the storage needed for arrays
- The maximum amount of core memory available for executing a program
- Two parameters that together specify both the sizes of bytes (or characters) and words and the orientation (byte or word) of the machine
- The kernel size, which is either an integral fraction or a multiple of the basic data unit (byte or word)

The maximum program-module size has been arbitrarily set equal to 5,000 bytes or, for small machines, to 2,500 sixteen-bit words. The other four parameters are set by the user when TPL is installed.

The compiler operates in two modes: transportability testing and compilation. To transport Fortran programs from one machine to another, the compiler, operating in the transportability test mode, checks the source program to find out what size word or byte it is geared to. At compilation time, the compiler uses this information to convert that source program to an object program with the word and byte length necessary for a user's machine. This requires only a minimum of special procedures, functions, or subroutines.

The compiler can also aid in translating existing programs in other languages to transportable versions for a user's machines. For example, a user might have a program written in Ada or in Cobol for an IBM computer but want to add a Honeywell, a DEC, and a CDC computer to his network. Since he wants the program to execute on all these computers, he needs a transportable compiler, such as TPL's.

Suppose this user's compiler is coded in Fortran,

3. Troubleshooter. *The TPL compiler flags statements 5, 6, 7, 8, 9, 16, 18, and 20 to 22 with advisory messages so the programmer can convert them to transportable form.*

```
C      Program I.                                              1
C      This program reads up to ulimit double precision        2
C      numbers, two at a time, then computes and prints        3
C      both the average and the standard deviation.            4
       INTEGER ULIMIT/1000000/, COUNT/0/                       5
       REAL*8 VALUES (1000000), AVERAGE/0D0/, STDDEV/0D0/       6
       DO 100 I=1, ULIMIT, 2                                    7
       READ (5,1000, END=200) VALUES (I), VALUES (I+1)          8
1000   FORMAT (2D25.16)                                         9
       COUNT = COUNT + 2                                       10
       AVERAGE = AVERAGE + VALUES (I) + VALUES (I+1)           11
100    CONTINUE                                                12
C                                                              13
200    IF (COUNT.LE.1) GO TO 400                               14
       AVERAGE = AVERAGE/COUNT                                 15
       DO 300 I=1, COUNT                                       16
300    STDDEV = STDDEV + (VALUES (I) - AVERAGE)**2             17
       STDDEV = DSQRT(STDDEV/COUNT-1) )                        18
C                                                              19
400    PRINT 2000, COUNT, AVERAGE, STDDEV                      20
2000   FORMAT ('0', 5X, 'NO OF VALUES =',I8, ' AVERAGE=',      21
       1D25.16,' AND STANDARD DEVIATION =', D25.16)            22
       STOP                                                    23
       END                                                     24
```

C INDICATES COMMENT.
NUMBERS ON LEFT ARE PROGRAM LABEL NUMBERS.
NUMBERS ON RIGHT ARE READER REFERENCE NUMBERS.

which is not transportable. Therefore, as shown in Figure 2, the user feeds his Fortran compiler through the TPL compiler, which flags all nontransportable code and informs the user how to convert it to transportable code. The nontransportable statements are then changed to TPL statements. As a result, the Ada or Cobol compiler is coded in transportable TPL.

To allow the program to execute on the Honeywell machine, the user now specifies Honeywell machine characteristics, such as the word size and byte orientation, to his TPL compiler. Once again, the Ada or Cobol compiler, now coded in TPL, is fed through the TPL compiler. The TPL compiler produces as object code the Ada or Cobol compiler in the Fortran geared to the Honeywell machine. The user employs the compiler to compile all his Ada and Cobol programs for that computer.

To produce compilers and execute programs for the DEC and CDC computers, the user follows the same procedures, setting the word and byte sizes for those machines. The TPL compiler then produces the user's high-level language compiler in Fortran suitable for the DEC or CDC machines. Thus, one software package can be used over all machines in a network. This capability allows programmers to continue using their favorite nontransportable languages while developing new fully transportable programs.

The TPL compiler is table-driven (information necessary for operation is in parameter tables), and three of its key tables are the transportable code table, the transferable code table, and the I/O device table. The transportable code table comprises the entire instruction set for the TPL language, which includes the fully transportable subset of Fortran instructions. The transferable code table contains all nontransportable Fortran instructions that are transferable. The I/O device table contains information about the unit, device type, and I/O task numbers for a local installation.

Transportability testing mode

Parameters such as maximum amount of core memory, byte and word size, machine orientation, and kernel size, as well as the I/O device table, are affected by changes in a local installation. The local managers must update these parameters whenever the configuration or machine is changed.

The TPL compiler uses the maximum value of the program-module size and the information in the transportable code table to flag all nontransportable instructions and advise how to convert them to transportable ones. The programmer then alters all the flagged statements. Figure 3 shows an IBM-Fortran-coded program that reads data and computes average and standard deviations. The TPL compiler can convert this program into its transportable form. In this case, statements 5, 6, 7, 8, 9, 16, 18, and 20 to 22 will be flagged with appropriate messages. Figure 4 shows the programmer-produced transportable version.

In the transportable version, the precision of the integer (IIP) and real (IRP) variables must be set either before compilation or when the program is executed. Otherwise, they will default to a precision of 6 and 7 figures, respectively. The ALLOCATE statement stipulates that the real variable-precision virtual-array "values" have one dimension and length, Ulimit. The read and print operations are performed with the default devices allocated for user use (I/O task = 3 and 4). RPSQRT is the variable-precision equivalent of the real square-root routine. In the format statements, skip = 1 means skip a line; RP19.10 is a real variable-precision field of width 19 and with 10 significant figures; and IP8 is a variable-precision-integer field of width 8.

Because the conversion of Fortran to TPL is mechanical, the transportability testing mode of the TPL compiler can eventually be fully automated.

Compilation mode

In the compilation mode, the TPL compiler uses the values for the computer parameters and the information in the transportable code, transferable code, and I/O device tables to produce Fortran versions of TPL programs that are optimal for a local installation. A primary goal of the compiler is to minimize calls to the special routines in the TPL library by using, whenever possible, transferable Fortran code in place of the unique TPL instructions. For example, for the program in Figure 4, if IIP = 8 and IRP = 10 and there is sufficient core memory, then the TPL compiler will convert the TPL program in a way particular to a machine. For IBM machines with 21-bit words, variables will be defined as in the original program and the virtual array will be changed to the conventional double-precision array. For CDC machines with 48-bit words, single-precision variables will be used and the virtual array will be eliminated.

This means that the run-time efficiency of a TPL program is ultimately determined by the efficiency of the vendor-supplied Fortran compiler. Thus, a TPL program can never be less efficient than the parent Fortran program specifically altered for a particular machine.

The compilation mode of the TPL compiler has three major functions:

1. Translating the unique TPL syntax into Fortran instructions. In the best-case situation, where there is sufficient core memory and no need for special routines in the TPL system library, only transferable instructions are used and the translation is straightforward. In the worst case, a single TPL instruction is replaced by several Fortran instructions, additional variables are created and initialized, and calls to one or more routines in the TPL library are issued.

2. Processing the Fortran subset of TPL instructions. In the best case, such instructions are not changed. In the worst case, which occurs when calls are issued to the TPL library, certain instructions might be replaced by several instructions. For example, if virtual arrays are used, references to them must be followed by the computation of the actual in-core location and, if necessary, by the paging of information from secondary storage such as disks.

3. Performing selected types of reconfigurations of the object program to produce a more efficient Fortran version of the input TPL program. Such modification includes substitution of conventional memory-resident

---

Software terms

Compiler. A program that translates a high-level language input program into machine language, assembler language, or another high-level language that is closer to machine language.

Source code. The input program to be processed by a compiler.

Object code. The processed output code from a compiler.

Interpret. To decode a program and execute it statement by statement.

Compile. To decode a program as one logical unit before executing it.

Preprocessor. A nontransportable program that converts a high-level language program to a format accepted by a compiler.

Virtual memory. The appearance of more memory than actually exists. This concept is implemented by storing some information in primary memory and some in secondary storage, such as a disk. During program execution, data addresses are calculated and recalculated so information can be exchanged between primary and secondary storage.

---

4. Corrected program. *The IBM Fortran nontransportable program is converted to its transportable form by both the TPL compiler and the programmer.*

```
C     Program I.                                              1
C     This program reads up to ulimit (precision IIP≤8)       2
C     real numbers (precision≤10), two at a time, then        3
C     computes and prints both the average and standard       4
C     deviation. If IIP and IRP are not set via a             5
C     constant statement the compiler will use the            6
C     defaults for integer(=6) and real(=7) precision.        7
      INTEGER*IIP ULIMIT/1000000/, COUNT/0/,I                 8
      VIRTUAL VALUES                                          9
      REAL*IRP VALUES AVERAGE/0/,STDDEV/0/                   10
      ALLOCATE VALUES AS DIMEN = (ULIMIT)                    11
      DO 100 I=1 TO ULIMIT BY 2                              12
      READ(IOTASK=3,FMT=1000,END=200)VALUES(I),VALUES(I+1)   13
1000  FORMAT (2RP25.16)                                      14
      AVERAGE = AVERAGE + VALUES(I) + VALUES(I+1)            15
      COUNT = COUNT + 2                                      16
100   CONTINUE                                               17
C                                                            18
200   IF (COUNT.LE.1) GO TO 400                             19
      AVERAGE = AVERAGE/COUNT                                20
      DO 300 I=1 TO COUNT                                   21
300   STDDEV = STDDEV + (VALUES(I) - AVERAGE)**2            22
      STDDEV = RPSQRT (STDDEV/ (COUNT-1) )                  23
C                                                            24
400   PRINT (IOTASK=4,FMT=2000) COUNT, AVERAGE, STDDEV      25
2000  FORMAT (SKIP=1,5X,'NUMBER OF VALUES=', IP8,'          26
1AVERAGE=',RP19.10,'AND STANDARD DEVIATION=',              27
2RP19.10)                                                  28
      STOP                                                  29
      END                                                   30
```

C INDICATES COMMENT.
NUMBERS ON LEFT ARE PROGRAM LABEL NUMBERS.
NUMBERS ON RIGHT ARE READER REFERENCE NUMBERS.

arrays for selected virtual arrays and restructuring of DO loops (loops beginning with the statement DO) and I/O statements to increase their efficiency, particularly if TPL library routines are called. Various forms of execution-time error checking may also be introduced.

Other TPL components

In addition to the TPL language and compiler, a TPL package includes a TPL library that supplements the local operating-system library of routines with functions and services not normally available to all machines. The library is coded in TPL, and its Fortran-coded version for each different machine is generated at local network installations by the Fortran-coded version of the compiler.

Also part of the TPL software is a small machine-support package that permits programs designed for large computers to execute on computers with smaller amounts of primary memory. Chief among these pro-

grams is an "overlay" monitoring routine that contains instructions for moving different parts of a program in and out of main memory whenever the entire program cannot reside in core.

Most of this package is coded in TPL. However, some parts must be coded in assembler language and recoded for machines with different assemblers.

Development of a library is a conventional method of increasing program transportability by extending a high-level language with a package of special routines. However, this approach is usually only partially successful at best, because the complex procedures for calling many of the special routines tend to discourage even the most dedicated programmers from using them. In addition, to achieve wide transportability, the programs must be coded for the worst-case (least-core-memory) machine. However, since optimizing such programs with respect to their run-time efficiency is determined by the amount of core memory, kinds of peripherals, and architecture of each local machine, the optimization of programs for each local installation is inefficient and time-consuming.

Installation of TPL

The minimum hardware needed to install TPL on any computer is at least 10,000 bytes of core memory that can be used to execute TPL programs. In addition, sufficient direct-access storage for load modules for the TPL compiler, for the TPL library, for the small-machine support package, for TPL programs, and for virtual arrays is needed. Storage for the I/O devices for communicating with the machine is required as well.

The software needed to install TPL is a noninterpretative Fortran compiler. In other words, the Fortran compiler resident on the computer must be one that decodes the program for execution as one logical unit instead of decoding and executing each statement in turn. The usual loaders that prepare the machine-language program for execution and other system resource routines are also necessary.

To install a TPL package, users select the system parameters—maximum program module size, maximum amount of core memory for a program, byte and word size, orientation (byte or word) of the machine, and kernel size—then describe the I/O device table. The installer then uses the manufacturer-supplied compiler to compile a "primitive" TPL compiler. This primitive compiler, which produces nonoptimum Fortran code for a minimal machine, without using the small-machine support package, generates optimum Fortran code for the TPL compiler, the TPL library, and the small-machine support package.

This optimum Fortran code is tailored for a particular installation. Compiling the primitive compiler might involve the literal translation of, at most, two I/O instructions in the TPL library to the local Fortran dialect.

If the small-machine support package is used, the parts coded in assembler language must be recoded for the particular installation. If an installation is reconfigured, values for the computer parameters will have to be reset, the I/O device table reconstructed, and some modules recompiled. ■

Software packages for solving network puzzles

B. R. Konsynski and W. E. Bracker, University of Arizona, Tucson

How do you choose a computer aid for troubleshooting or designing a network? The authors discuss many available software packages and how to select one.

The process of designing, implementing, and controlling present and planned data communications networks is rapidly exceeding our manual capabilities. Network managers and designers are looking more to computer resources to manage the volume of traffic information, develop and evaluate network configurations, and even assist in allocating and placing control functions among the network processors.

The sheer number of network alternatives is increasing so fast that the demand for network optimization—both in private network design and in the interface to, and use of, public network facilities—can be satisfied only through computer aids. These aids range from simple scratch-pad memory systems that store and compile network statistics to complex traffic simulators, design configurators, and software for data-distribution modeling. Purchase prices also vary widely—from $4,000 to $50,000.

How does one select from among these packages? Before choosing a product, the potential user should pinpoint the primary objectives of his network analysis/design and prepare a list of desired package features, including (1) system capabilities such as inputs and outputs and (2) characteristics such as ease of use, price, and applicability to a particular design problem (see "Network-design-system checklist"). There may not be a single product that can satisfy all these criteria, and some characteristics, such as ease of use, may require subjective rather than objective evaluation. With these points in mind, the user can begin comparing several of the available packages.

Effective network-design aids take into account several problem areas that have traditionally plagued network designers/planners:

■ Complexity of the design process. The proliferation of advanced hardware, software, control features, and facilities has created a wide range of design choices. Data communications networks have evolved from simple multiple-terminal, single-CPU configurations to large multiapplication systems with distributed data processors and sophisticated message structures and routing strategies.

■ Seat-of-the pants design techniques. Traditional design methods based on rules of thumb and past experience can no longer handle either the complexities or the volume of information necessary to effectively plan today's networks.

■ Over-design of networks. When planners/designers lack the expertise required, they tend to over-design the network in regard to user needs. Often they evaluate very few alternatives, and each with only a cursory cost-benefit analysis.

■ User interface. Users frequently make unreasonable demands on the network and seldom have a feel for the cost-performance. Little is ever done to educate users in this regard.

Most computer-aided network-design tools consist of libraries of modules that perform different—and specialized—subordinate operations, such as those outlined in Table 1. Several representative capabilities are generating and analyzing traffic patterns, compiling tariff information, providing node locations, plotting and graphically displaying outputs, designing the network topology, partitioning the network, evaluating overall network requirements, simulating traffic load, and maintaining a database of network statistics and directory information.

The optimal network design, of course, meets all design constraints and user requirements, and has the lowest possible cost. Furthermore, it provides answers to these questions:

1. What are the best message formats and transmission schemes?

2. What kinds of concentrators, multiplexers, or front-end configurations are needed, and where should they be located?

3. What combination of lines (dial-up, point-to-point, multipoint, and other transmission facilities) should be used, and what are the optimal line speeds?

4. How sensitive is the design's performance to variation in traffic loads, equipment availability, and other parameter changes?

5. What size buffers will keep the message-blocking probability within specified design limits? Also, how will buffering relate to message statistics and outgoing trunk capacity?

6. What are the time delays (response times) expected under varying traffic and message conditions?

7. What would be the effect of adopting dynamic buffering (variable-length buffers under software control) or using message block storage?

A quick and comprehensive answer to these and other questions is still far from reach with existing design packages. Network-design questions are generally attacked one at a time and interactively.

The problem of topological design (the actual physical layout of the network), although fundamental to least-cost network design, is so complex that it precludes generating a truly optimal design that incorporates all desired performance criteria in a single step. Network design must be carried out interactively. For example, a network planner might first determine the best location and linkage of concentrators, then eval-

uate the best message-routing paths, and finally find the least-expensive way to link terminals to each concentrator. He will repeat the battery of design questions as different alternatives and parameters are injected (Table 2).

For truly complex cases, search routines can perform a series of repetitive procedures and derive, say, a minimum-cost or class of minimum-cost networks. This approach uses algorithms and heuristics (generalized rules) to arrive at optimum (or nearly optimum) solutions in a reasonable number of iterations.

The many diverse tools and methods needed to make optimization decisions may be classified as:
■ Informational. Packages simply supply information about available tariffs and line types.
■ Statistical. Software analyzes existing data and produces summary profiles on traffic and network use.
■ Heuristics. Software routines apply generalized rules in solving particular design problems.
■ Mathematical models. Analytical software produces generalized models.
■ Simulation. Discrete-event-simulation software evaluates and analyzes network functions.

A network-design product, in general, should plot a set of performance data for an existing or proposed network. It can generate, and regenerate, these performance curves in response to changes in critical design parameters, such as protocols, line capacity, concentration points, host processor capability, and message-routing techniques. Since the network planner must determine cost-performance trade-offs for a fixed set of design parameters, he needs the network-design package to evaluate these trade-offs in light of expected network functions. For this reason, there generally evolves a close relationship between the planner and the design package.

However, even such an interdependence will not guarantee optimum solutions for every design problem. Many areas in the design process do not lend themselves to automation, so the designer will frequently introduce his own judgment (and possible biases) into the design procedure with the assistance of the software package.

Several state-of-the-art network-design products are compared in Table 3. All are currently available either as general offerings or as proprietary packages that use and evaluate the vendor facilities.

DMW offerings

The DMW Group's Advanced Network Design and Management System (ANDMS) is an interactive software package used for the design and analysis of IBM 3600 processing networks. Figure 1 shows the overall ANDMS structure and its relationship to DMW's other design packages. There are three major ANDMS modules: database manager, network design, and performance analysis.

The database module operates on the file structure representing the network database. Each record in the database contains information on equipment location, hardware, traffic characteristics, and general network parameters and event statistics. The design module

---

Network-design-system checklist

Before selecting a software design package, network planners should consider these factors.

- ☐ Ease of use and amount of training required
- ☐ Interactive or batch mode
- ☐ Design models supported
- ☐ Readability of output reports
- ☐ Vendor consulting support
- ☐ Sensitivity analysis
- ☐ Ease of update for network changes
- ☐ Modifications to support customer requirements
- ☐ Ease of network parameter specification
- ☐ If installation is on in-house computer:
  - ☐ CPU and disk storage requirements
  - ☐ Source language
  - ☐ Operating system required
- ☐ Protocols supported

Table 1 Design package inputs/outputs

INPUTS

TERMINAL/LINE CONNECTIONS AND LOCATIONS

PROTOCOLS

ERROR RATES

TERMINAL-OPERATOR CHARACTERISTICS

TARIFFS

HARDWARE CHARACTERISTICS

NETWORK CAPACITY

OUTPUTS

TERMINAL/LINE STATISTICS

ACTIVITY ANALYSIS

SENSITIVITY ANALYSIS

QUEUING ANALYSIS

LINE COSTS

MULTIPLEXER/CONCENTRATOR CONNECTIONS

DELAY ANALYSIS

POINT-TO-POINT PRICING

TARIFF COMPARISONS

NETWORK TOPOLOGY

CPU REQUIREMENTS

BOTTLENECKS

OVERALL NETWORK COST

SERVICE TIMES

Table 2 Design criteria

CONSTANTS

NUMBER AND LOCATIONS OF PROCESSORS

NUMBER AND LOCATIONS OF REMOTE TERMINALS

INFORMATION FLOW

TRANSACTION TYPES

TRAFFIC VOLUMES

INFORMATION PRIORITY

ERROR RATES

FUTURE GROWTH

RELIABILITY AND AVAILABILITY

VARIABLES

TOPOLOGY

LINK TYPES

TYPES OF FACILITIES

TRANSMISSION SPEEDS

TERMINAL TYPES

MULTIPLEXERS/CONCENTRATORS

ERROR CORRECTION

NETWORK SOFTWARE LOCATIONS

determines concentrator (or controller) locations, as well as standalone locations for terminals. The software also selects both the sites and the candidate devices for connection to high-speed data links, based on a minimum-cost analysis. The performance-analysis portion of the software uses the network response-time characteristics to compute traffic rate tables for various design configurations.

Other DMW software packages include the batch-mode NDMS; Response, which provides data on response times; and the On-Line Tariff Guide, a database that stores information on current tariff rates.

MIND (Modular Interactive Network Designer), a product of Network Analysis Corporation (NAC), represents the conversion of several of NAC's internal-analysis tools for general use. The software analyzes and integrates information on throughput, line utilization, message-response-time constraints, system sensitivity, and reliability measures.

The package minimizes the cost-objective function and provides a set of design alternatives and performance-cost trade-offs. Among its major components

is the editor, which maintains a database of node linkages and associated properties. With this module, the user may create a new network description or modify an existing one.

Specialized function

Another component, the MPL (multipoint-line) module, computes tariff charges for leased point-to-point and multipoint communications lines. The topological optimization module (TOPO) analyzes various design topologies. Inputs to TOPO include terminal traffic estimates, line-use factors, and potential concentrator/multiplexer locations. Outputs (Fig. 2) include reports on line and termination costs for multipoint lines, as well as concentrator/multiplexer analyses.

MIND also contains a multipoint line simulator (MLS). Inputs include message-length distributions, message-arrival frequencies, terminals per line, and line protocols. Outputs provide estimates of message-response times, potential bottlenecks, network sensitivity to input changes, load limits, and saturation levels.

Another NAC analysis package, Grinder, is a set of

Table 3   State-of-the-art network-design products

VENDOR COMPANY ADDRESS/CONTACT	PACKAGE NAME	OPERATIONAL MODE	SOURCE LANGUAGE	COMPUTERS SUPPORTED
IBM CORPORATION 1133 WESTCHESTER AVE. WHITE PLAINS, N.Y. 10604 (914) 696-1900 DAVID E. BENEVIDES	CICS NETWORK-ACTIVITY SIMULATOR	BATCH	ASSEMBLER (MACRO CALLS)	360/370 DOS, DOS/VS OS/MFT, OS/MVT OS/VSI, OS/VS2 CICS, CICS/VS
THE DMW GROUP INC. 2395 HURON PKWY. ANN ARBOR, MICH. 48104 (313) 971-5234 CASEY MAUCH	ON-LINE TARIFF GUIDE	INTERACTIVE	FORTRAN	TYMSHARE IN-HOUSE COMPUTER
	ANDMS	INTERACTIVE	FORTRAN	COMMERCIAL TIMESHARING VIA TYMSHARE
	NDMS	BATCH	FORTRAN	COMMERCIAL TIMESHARING VIA TYMSHARE
	RESPONSE 1 RESPONSE 2	BATCH OR INTERACTIVE	FORTRAN	TYMSHARE IN-HOUSE COMPUTER
NETWORK ANALYSIS CORPORATION 130 STEAMBOAT RD. GREAT NECK, N.Y. 11024 (516) 829-5900 DAVID A. RUBIN	MIND	INTERACTIVE	FORTRAN	DEC SYSTEM 20 IBM 370 IBM 303X VS
	GRINDER	INTERACTIVE	FORTRAN	DEC SYSTEM 20
KRANZLEY AND COMPANY 1010 SOUTH KINGS HWY. CHERRY HILL, N.J. 08034 (609) 795-1515 A.D. KRANZLEY	PLANET—MODEL	BATCH OR INTERACTIVE	FORTRAN	ANY WITH FORTRAN COMPILER
	PLANET—SYSMODEL	BATCH OR INTERACTIVE	FORTRAN	ANY WITH FORTRAN COMPILER
	PLANET—LOCON	BATCH OR INTERACTIVE	FORTRAN	ANY WITH FORTRAN COMPILER
	PLANET—NETSYN	BATCH OR INTERACTIVE	FORTRAN	ANY WITH FORTRAN COMPILER
STSC INC. 7316 WISCONSIN AVE. BETHESDA, MD. 20014 ROBERT ELLIS (301) 657-8822	ARIES—REGIS	INTERACTIVE	APL	VENDOR-SUPPLIED TIMESHARING (AMDAHL 470/V6)
	ARIES—DEXUS	INTERACTIVE	APL	VENDOR-SUPPLIED TIMESHARING (AMDAHL 470/V6)
	ARIES—QUEUE	INTERACTIVE	APL	VENDOR-SUPPLIED TIMESHARING (AMDAHL 470/V6)
	ARIES—ANALINE	INTERACTIVE	APL	VENDOR-SUPPLIED TIMESHARING (AMDAHL 470/V6)
	ARIES—QTAC	INTERACTIVE	APL	VENDOR-SUPPLIED TIMESHARING (AMDAHL 470/V6)
	ARIES—ODIN	INTERACTIVE	APL	VENDOR-SUPPLIED TIMESHARING (AMDAHL 470/V6)
IBM SYSTEMS COMMUNICATIONS DIVISION	SNAPSHOT	NOT AVAILABLE AT CUSTOMER SITE BUT ACCESSIBLE TO IBM CUSTOMERS AND TECHNICIANS FOR SYSTEMS- AND NETWORK-THROUGHPUT ANALYSES FOR IBM CONFIGURATIONS. CONTACT IBM SERVICE REPRESENTATIVE FOR ADDITIONAL INFORMATION.		
AT&T	NERCE	USED ONLY BY AT&T FOR NETWORK ANALYSIS, INCLUDING EVALUATION OF PRIVATE NETWORKS THAT EMPLOY AT&T FACILITIES AND EQUIPMENT.		

NETWORK TYPES SUPPORTED	IMPLEMENTATION METHOD	INPUTS	OUTPUTS	PRICE
IBM CICS	SIMULATION OF CAPTURED LIVE DATA	TRAFFIC PROFILES TERMINAL CONNECTIONS LINE CONNECTIONS PROTOCOLS OPERATOR CHARACTERISTICS	LINE STATISTICS TERMINAL STATISTICS NETWORK-ACTIVITY ANALYSIS SENSITIVITY ANALYSIS	$185/MONTH
POINT-TO-POINT MULTIPOINT DISTRIBUTED	ANALYSIS	TARIFFS CITY NODES NUMBER OF CIRCUITS STATION LOCATIONS	POINT-TO-POINT PRICING TARIFF COMPARISONS INVENTORY OF AVAILABLE TARIFFS	$10,000–$18,000 PURCHASE
IBM 3600 DISTRIBUTED	SIMULATION HEURISTICS MATHEMATICAL PROGRAMMING	TERMINAL TRAFFIC EQUIPMENT CHARACTERISTICS TERMINAL LOCATIONS MESSAGE PROFILES	NETWORK LAYOUT (MINIMUM COST BASED ON RESPONSE-TIME GOALS)	$30,000–$50,000 PURCHASE
CENTRALIZED DISTRIBUTED WITH CONCENTRATOR LOCATIONS	HEURISTICS	LINE LOADS MESSAGE PROFILES TERMINAL LOCATIONS CONCENTRATOR LOCATIONS	NETWORK CONFIGURATION (LEAST-COST NETWORK FOR A PARTICULAR RESPONSE- TIME GOAL)	$8,000–$25,000 PURCHASE
CENTRALIZED DISTRIBUTED WITH ONE OR TWO STAGES OF LEASED LINES	QUEUING ANALYSIS	MESSAGE LENGTH DISTRIBUTIONS, LINE SPEEDS PROTOCOLS RESPONSE-TIME GOALS TERMINAL TRAFFIC RATES	LINE TRAFFIC TRAFFIC RATE TABLES LINE UTILIZATIONS TERMINAL CONNECTIONS	$10,000–$25,000 PURCHASE
STAR MULTIPOINT DISTRIBUTED	HEURISTICS SIMULATION	TERMINAL LOCATIONS TARIFFS REQUIRED MESSAGE DISTRIBUTIONS PROTOCOLS HARDWARE PARAMETERS	LINE COSTS CONCENTRATOR LOCATIONS MULTIPLEXER LOCATIONS TARIFF ALTERNATIVES NETWORK LOADS RESPONSE TIMES QUEUE ANALYSIS	$25,000 PURCHASE $9,000 RENTAL PLUS TIMESHARING COSTS
HIERARCHICAL DISTRIBUTED	HEURISTICS SIMULATION	TERMINAL LOCATIONS TARIFFS DESIRED MESSAGE DISTRIBUTIONS PROTOCOLS LINE LOADINGS HARDWARE CHARACTERISTICS	LINE COSTS CONCENTRATOR LOCATIONS MULTIPLEXER LOCATIONS TARIFF ALTERNATIVES RESPONSE-TIME ANALYSIS SYSTEM DELAYS GRAPHS AND TABLES	MINIMUM $500/ MONTH PURCHASE AVAILABLE
MULTIPOINT	DISCRETE-EVENT SIMULATION	TRAFFIC PROFILES RESPONSE-TIME OBJECTIVES LINE CONFIGURATIONS NETWORK LOADS	PERCENT TRANSACTIONS DELAYED LINE UTILIZATIONS RESPONSE TIMES CPU BUFFER REQUIREMENTS	$4,900–$5,400 PURCHASE
CENTRALIZED MULTIPOINT	MONTE CARLO SIMULATION	FACILITY CONFIGURATIONS TRANSACTION PROFILES ROUTING CONVENTIONS TRAFFIC PROFILES	FACILITY UTILIZATIONS PROCESSING TIMES QUEUE SIZES DELAY TIMES NETWORK BOTTLENECKS	$11,000 PURCHASE
CENTRALIZED	HEURISTICS	TERMINAL LOCATIONS TERMINAL LOADINGS MULTIPLEXER AND CONCENTRATOR CHARACTERISTICS	CONCENTRATION POINTS TERMINAL-CONCENTRATOR ASSIGNMENTS	$5,900–$6,400 PURCHASE
ALL MAJOR TYPES	HEURISTICS	HUB LOCATIONS TERMINAL LOCATIONS TERMINAL LOADS TRAFFIC RATE TABLES	OPTIMUM NETWORK DESIGN FROM-TO LINKS, MILEAGE LINK COSTS CIRCUIT DETAILS TOTAL NETWORK COST	$5,900–$7,900 PURCHASE
ALL	ANALYSIS	USER-DEFINED NETWORK DESCRIPTIONS	MANAGEMENT REPORTS AND INTERFACES WITH OTHER ARIES PACKAGES	$2,000–$5,000 SETUP PLUS TIMESHARING COSTS
POINT-TO-POINT STAR MULTIPOINT OTHER USER-DEFINED	MATH PROGRAMMING	NODE LOCATIONS LINE CONNECTIONS TARIFFS	OPTIMUM PRICING TARIFF ALTERNATIVES MULTINODE CONNECTIONS	TIMESHARING COSTS
MULTIPOINT	QUEUING ANALYSIS	LINE AND TERMINAL CONNECTIONS	RESPONSE TIME QUEUE STATISTICS	TIMESHARING COSTS
MULTIPOINT	QUEUING ANALYSIS	LINE TYPES TERMINAL TYPES TERMINAL CONNECTIONS	DELAYED TRANSACTIONS LINE UTILIZATIONS RESPONSE TIMES, QUEUE ANALYSIS	TIMESHARING COSTS
MULTIPOINT POINT-TO-POINT	HEURISTICS QUEUING ANALYSIS	PROTOCOLS TERMINAL LOCATIONS LINE TYPES	TRAFFIC VOLUMES	TIMESHARING COSTS
MULTIPOINT DISTRIBUTED HIERARCHICAL	HEURISTICS	TERMINAL LOCATIONS TERMINAL LOADINGS TARIFFS	CONCENTRATION POINTS TERMINAL-CONCENTRATOR ASSIGNMENTS	$2,500/YEAR PLUS TIMESHARING COSTS

1. Structured software. *Components of DMW's network-design and management modules are depicted. A user-interface module selects and defines parameters for the other three modules: line-performance analysis, design for the least-cost configuration, and database manager for maintaining network locations and statistics.*

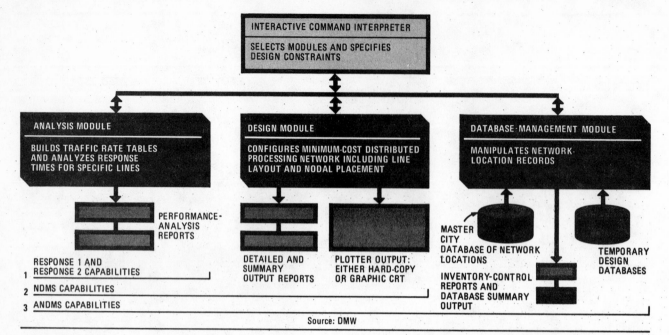

Source: DMW

software tools used to support the design of hierarchical networks, such as IBM's SNA-based or packet-switched configurations. Grinder can handle development studies of corporate and public communications utility networks and can help solve problems related to protocol trade-offs, end-to-end message delay, cost versus performance, node performance requirements, optimized node placements, optimized local-access facilities, alternative network architectures, reliability and throughput analyses, trunk bandwidth requirements, and tariff alternatives.

Some components of Grinder are evolutionary enhancements to similar modules contained in MIND. The Grinder structure is optimized for graphics, and displays network solutions and trade-offs in both tabular and graphic formats. The package is also geared to interactive design, with detailed explanations available at each stage of the dialogue.

Planet

Planet (Programs for Line Analysis and Network Engineering Tasks) is a set of software packages produced by Kranzley and Company. A major component, Model, is a discrete network simulator that provides information on line-loading rules. Inputs include message characteristics, error rates, CPU processing estimates, and response-time constraints. Among the outputs are a detailed analysis of the simulation run, such as message-response times, queuing calculations, and line utilizations.

Another module, Sysmodel, provides an analysis of queuing procedures in the overall system environment. It identifies potential bottlenecks and overload areas in addition to utilization percentages of lines, terminals, and other facilities.

Two other components of the package are Locon and Netsyn. Locon analyzes potential concentrator/multiplexer locations based on given terminal locations. Netsyn (network synthesizer) places terminals on a communications link using cost/response-time constraints. From inputs such as terminal and line characteristics, variable hardware parameters, and traffic and message volume rates and distributions, Netsyn outputs line charges, line loadings, total hardware costs, and total network charges.

Yet another network-design alternative is available from the Scientific Time Sharing Company (now STSC Inc.). Customers use the Aries package by accessing the remote computing vendor's services. The Aries software is not sold and does not run at the user site. In addition to a cost for the software usage, the user pays normal timesharing charges.

Main user interface to the Aries software is via the Regis network database manager, which, in turn, interfaces to the other software modules. Dexus, for example, is one module that offers optimization and pricing information for private line networks configured under a variety of tariffs. Two other modules, Queue and Analine, determine response times and queuing statistics for terminal connections. Qtac is used to compute maximum traffic volumes for specified response-time goals. Different results can be evaluated by changing the type of protocols used. The final module, Odin, is accessed for general network optimization, and it evaluates networks based on cost, tariff, response time, and loading constraints.

Proprietary packages

Another class of packages used in configuring customers' data communications networks is employed by

2. Output sample. *Network Analysis Corporation's TOPO (Topological Optimization) module furnishes reports detailing line and termination costs.*

```
                      CITY      ST -ACEX- VVVV HHHH AB ALMI COST
        FROM NADNY GRTNECK NY   516829 4956 1378 B
          TO NACOM GRTNECK NY   516829 4956 1378 B    0.   50.00
CONCENTRATOR NACOM:
  CIRCUIT NACOM :
    STATION DETAILS
              TERID ------LOCATION------ CITY      ST   COST
              NACOM                      GRTNLCK NY       0.00
              BOSMA                      BOSTON  MA      25.00
              HARCO                      HARTFRD CO      25.00
              PHIPE                      PHILADE PA      25.00
              DETMI                      DETROIT MI      25.00
              PITPE                      PITTSBG PA      25.00
              WILDE                      MILMING DE      25.00
              BALMA                      BALTIMO MD      25.00
              RIDVI                      RICHMON VA      25.00
              NYDNE                      NEWYORK NY      50.00
    INTEREXCHANGE CHANNEL DETAILS
                      CITY      ST -ACEX- VVVV HHHH AB ALMI COST
        FROM BOSMA BOSTON  MA   617723 4422 1249 A
          TO HARCO HARTFRD CO   203522 4687 1373 A   93.  167.36
        FROM HARCO HARTFRD CO   203522 4687 1373 A
          TO NYDNE NEWYORK NY   212425 4997 1406 A   99.  174.08
        FROM NYDNE NEWYORK NY   212425 4997 1406 A
          TO PHIPE PHILADE PA   215375 5258 1612 A  106.  179.16
        FROM PHIPE PHILADE PA   215375 5258 1612 A
          TO BALMA BALTIMO MA   301393 5510 1575 A   81.  153.92
        FROM DETMI DETROIT MI   313965 5536 2828 A
          TO PITPE PITTSBG PA   412452 5566 2246 B  185.  296.30
        FROM PITPE PITTSBG PA   412452 5566 2246 B
          TO BALMA BALTIMO MD   301383 5510 1575 A  213.  314.78
        FROM WILDE WILMING DE   302678 5429 1408 A
          TO BALMA BALTIMO MD   301383 5510 1575 A   59.  129.28
        FROM RIDVI RICHMON VA   804643 5906 1472 A
          TO BALMA BALTIMO MD   301383 5510 1575 A  130.  195.00
        FROM NACOM GRTNECK NY   516829 4956 1378 B
          TO NYDNE NEWYORK NY   212425 4997 1406 A   16.  101.30
        9 DEVICES,     7.350 TRAFFIC UNITS TRANSMITTED,
                       4.080 TRAFFIC UNITS RECEIVED.
        CIRCUIT  DROP-COST LINE-COST    TOTAL
        NACOM    $ 250.00 $ 1711.18 $ 1961.18
```

vendor marketing and technical personnel primarily to optimize alternative designs. Packages such as IBM's Snapshot and AT&T's Nerce fall into this category and are not available to the general public.

Snapshot is a discrete system simulator, which allows IBM network technicians to design and analyze performance of a host processor, a data communications network, or a combination host-network configuration. Although an IBM proprietary package, it is accessible to IBM users.

Input to Snapshot is through a set of processor instructions, or macros, that specify the desired system configuration and design parameters. The interface between the design models and the user is also handled by the processor macros—the Snapshot processor formats the simulation model outputs for easy analysis. Outputs include network layout, message/data input and output rates, line and terminal response times, front-end-processor analysis, CPU response times, and application program response times.

Nerce (Network Response-Time and Configuration Evaluator) is a proprietary package used by AT&T to configure networks of terminals in multipoint environments. Several terminals supported under Nerce are Dataspeed 40s and IBM 3270s using the binary synchronous protocol under Telco tariffs for private lines, DDD (direct distance dialing), and DDS (Dataphone digital service). Nerce, and a related package, Cirgen (circuit generator), are used for both internal and customer network design by Bell system technicians. ∎

Defining requirements for a computer-aided net-design package

Benn R. Konsynski III and William E. Bracker Jr., University of Arizona, Tucson

An easy-to-use definition language facilitates user interface to network-design systems and permits groups of network planners to independently work on design and modeling.

One of the hardest parts of data communications network design is defining network requirements. The network statement language (NSL) facilitates this task by allowing users to state design requirements for data communications networks in the same manner that analysts use a problem statement language, or PSL, to define requirements for general information processing systems. The language provides the user with an interface to the network-design software. Until recently, the lack of efficient definition facilities has inhibited the optimal use of such computer aids.

Communications researchers at the University of Arizona are developing a network-design system (NDS) that formalizes the network-design "life cycle" in support of a computer-aided design process (Fig. 1). NDS embodies a generalized planning, or "decision-support," philosophy that gives the network planner/designer maximum flexibility in creating an optimized network that meets various design criteria and constraints. Using this methodology, the network planner can focus on the design issues and network configurations rather than on the data-management and interface specifications.

The human interface to NDS is, in most cases, an individual or a group of individuals who make up the planning/design team. Their job is to state the network parameters and constraints to NDS using NSL and to interact with the system through the network statement analyzer (NSA), a component that processes interactive queries. Figure 2 depicts the interrelationship among these planning components and the user.

The network statement language is the user's main contact with the set of design models in NDS. The current implementation of NSL has 14 sections, 34 individual statements, and 6 connector words, which, when properly linked, describe their particular sections (Table 1). These let the user describe the physical and logical network components.

There are several software tools for constructing and modifying the network statement language and analyzer. Use of these provides the desired specification language with the flexibility and compatibility necessary for interface with other network and information systems' specification languages. Since the language and reports can be easily modified, the software accommodates language specifications for particular network environments.

The network statement analyzer is the NDS component designed to accept network specifications produced by NSL, obtain and process design inputs, and report requests obtained by the query system. The NSA query processor outputs a menu from which the NDS user selects the supported NSA command types (shown in Table 2).

NSA also performs consistency checks on the network database, such as determining whether all nodes in a proposed network can be reached by all other nodes, verifying that line and terminal speeds match, and checking proper multiplexer/concentrator connections. An NDS user chooses check routines based

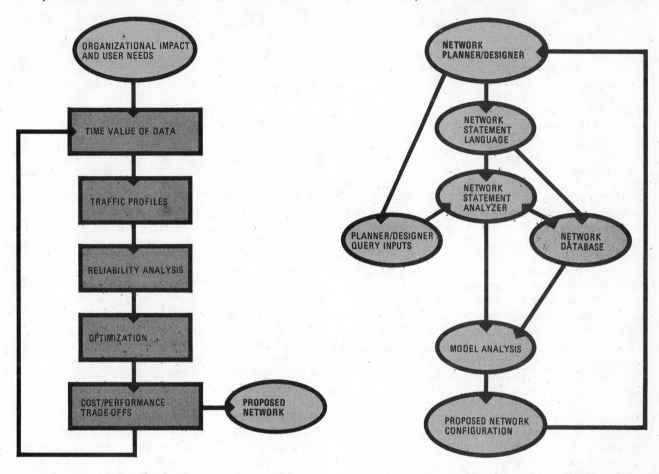

1. Design cycle. *Any data communications problem-solving process, whether automated or manual, must incorporate these basic criteria, values, and influences.*

2. User interaction. *The network statement language (NSL) is only a part of the overall network-design software, but the part that handles most of the user interface.*

on various hardware connections.

NSL and NSA, as Figure 2 depicts, provide the user with an interface to the design software but do not actually perform the network analysis. This is handled by the core software, which is transparent to the user and activated only through one of the previously described components.

Determining design options

The network optimization and design executive (NODE), via the user interfaces, provides a set of models with which the network planner can evaluate various design alternatives. In the current NDS implementation, the planner can select from five design models, depending on the information he desires.

The overall purpose of model implementation and integration is to create a design interface that requires minimum user training and interaction. In addition, it should provide outputs that are easy to interpret. The user need be concerned only with the information that the models provide and not with details on how the results are computed.

The models derive their inputs from two sources: NSL design specifications in the database and NSA-user interactions. The NSL design specifications pro-

duce a set of initial network conditions and assumptions to the design problem, while user interaction with the NSA produces more-specific design constraints and performance criteria.

Figure 3 shows one interactive session between the NDS user and a capacity-assignment model. In this example, the network planner logs into NDS and is presented with a menu of options. He selects the NODE "model's" application and, with another menu prompting, engages the capacity-assignment module. The analysis software then details the sections required, performs a consistency check of that data, and outputs the requested information.

NSL statements

The basic unit of NSL is a word that is recognized as one of three types: reserved words, names, and "noise" words. Reserved words have a particular meaning and must be specified in a formal or synonym form, as listed in Table 1. Names, formed by a given set of rules, are supplied by the user and describe an object or characteristic of the target network. A noise word is one that, in NSL, enhances readability of an NSL statement but is not necessary for NSA to react and process the statement. NSL words are generated using the characters A to Z, the numbers 0 to 9, and the dash (—) in any combination, as long as the word length does not exceed 30 characters.

NSL sections are grouped to form an NSL network problem statement. A section consists of a series of statements. The first statement in a section is the header, which determines the section type. The header is followed by any sequence of valid section statements. Anything printed after a semicolon (;) on a line is treated as an unstored comment and is never added to the NSL database. The statements DESCRIPTION and SEE-MEMO facilitate the definition of comment entries that are added to the NSA database.

Object classifications

An NSL user defines an object, a specific network component, by giving it a unique name (or list of names). Consequently, most allowed NSL sections specify user-defined object types. Once an object has been assigned a name, it may be included in the various NSL relationships.

The physical-organization objects describe the actual linkages and relationships between NSL object types such as the connection of a modem to a terminal, which specifies a physical-network-organization property. Logical-organization objects, on the other hand,

Table 1 NSL reserved words

NSL SECTION TYPES

NODE	HOST
TOPOLOGY	DATABASE
TRAFFIC	MULTIPLEXER
INFORMATION-USER	TERMINAL
TERMINAL-USER	INFORMATION-CENTER
APPLICATION	LINE
REPORT	MODEM

NSL STATEMENT TYPES

TERMINAL	INTELLIGENCE	HOST
MULTIPLEXER	INFORMATION-USER	RESPONSE
TOPOLOGY	TERMINAL-USER	SIZE
HOST	SEE-MEMO	DATABASE
LINK	TRAFFIC	HAPPENS
FAN-IN	FLOW	LOCATIONS
FAN-OUT	KEYING	RELIABILITY
PROTOCOL	PRIORITY	COST
TYPE	GENERATES	SECURITY
MODE	RECEIVES	DESCRIPTION
ERROR	SYNONYMS	
KEYWORDS	APPLICATION	

NSL CONNECTOR WORDS

TO	BY
FOR	VIA
IS	ARE

Table 2 NSA-supported statements

NDS/NSA STATEMENT TYPE	PURPOSE
QUERY	ACTIVATES NSA QUERY PROCESSOR
MODEL	ACTIVATES NDS-SUPPORTED MODELS
CONSISTENCY	CHECKS CONSISTENCY ON THE NETWORK DATABASE
MACRO	ACTIVATES NSL MACRO (INSTRUCTION) PROCESSOR
INVENTORY	GENERATES VARIOUS NETWORK REPORTS

describe the network's nonphysical aspects. For example, the description of an information center is classified as a logical-organization object type because its special identity is not based solely on a single hardware component.

An NSL system-flow object defines the eventual transfer of data from an information source to an information pool. Normally, this flow is described by either a topology object (in the topology section) or via a logical topological description (in the traffic section).

A volume object describes the frequency and amount of data being transferred in a network. These estimates are normally based on statistical analysis or rules of thumb and are usually specified through frequency distributions.

Most objects that describe the network have characteristics which separate them from other objects. Their properties involve a description of a given object (for example, line speed or conditioning) and are specified using constants or probability distributions.

Common statements

The following are NSL statements that can be used in each of the 14 NSL sections to specify particular properties of network components:

Cost. This statement causes a standard cost function to be applied to a section. Cost is normally specified on a per-month basis, but other measures may be applied. The user may also specify a standard cost table, using the cost-table section.

Error. The Error statement allows the user to associate an error rate with a particular network component. Currently, NDS interprets error rates in terms of characters. For example, Error 1000 is interpreted as one error in 1 million characters. Error rates may also be specified using a constant or a probability distribution.

Location. All network components may be associated with a physical location. In the present implementation, a standard vertical-horizontal coordinate system is used to show the relationships.

Reliability. Reliability has two components: mean time between failures (MTBF) and mean time between repair (MTBR). NDS currently allows MTBF to be specified as a reliability measure.

Security. Security levels are specified in a simple hierarchy, with the lowest security level assigned the lowest

3. Interactive conversation. *The printout details a user's conversation with the network-design software. After network definition has been completed, the user logs on to the analyzer modules. In this case, the user responds to a menu selection of active modules and obtains information specifying capacity assignment by link.*

```
NDS--UNIVERSITY OF ARIZONA    VERSION 1.0 8/3/79  10:20

-->NSL=TEST.NSL
-->LISTING-->TEST.LST        (Source/Diagnostics File)
-->DATABASE-->TEST.DB        (META Produced Database)
** NO DIAGNOSTICS **
   SECTIONS PROCESSED:6
   STATEMENTS PROCESSED:55
   OUTPUT FILE AND DATABASE FILE WRITTEN

** NDS/NSL COMPLETE 8/3/79 **

**NDS/NSA VERSION 1.0 8/3/79 **
OPTIONS:
1. EXIT
2. MODELS
3. REPORTS
OPTION--> 2
** NSA MODEL ANALYSIS **
ACTIVE MODELS:
1. CONCENTRATOR LOCATOR
2. CAPACITY ASSIGNMENT
3. TERMINAL LOCATOR
4. SPANNING TREE
MODEL--> 2
** CAPACITY ASSIGNMENT **
REQUIRED SECTIONS:
TOPOLOGY-SECTION
TRAFFIC-SECTION
** ALL REQUIRED SECTIONS CONSISTENT **
ROUTING--> SHORT
CAPACITY-->1000
** MODEL COMPLETE:CAPACITY **
RESULT FILE-->TTY
MODEL:CAPACITY
ROUTING:SHORT
CAPACITY:1000
LINK                CAPACITY(BPS)
====                ============
LINE1               200
LINE2               450
LINE3               110
LINE4               100
LINE5               120
**ALL CONSTRAINTS MET
** NDS/NSA   VERSION 1.0 TERMINATED   8/3/79 **
```

numerical value. An unspecified security value implies the lowest possible level.

A network node is made up of any combination of network subcomponents: terminals, multiplexers, lines, and hosts. Internally, the node components may be connected in any manner. However, the node interacts with other network components according to its definition in the topology section.

Consider the following node section:

NODE-SECTION EXAMPLE-1;
    TERMINALS ARE T-1, T-2, T-3, T-4, T-5, T-6;
    MULTIPLEXER MUX-1, MUX-2, MUX-3, FEP-1;
    HOST IS 370/168-1;

A terminal is characterized by a line speed, protocol type, and transmission mode (duplex, half-duplex, receive only, and so on). In addition, the NDS design system allows a specification of intelligence levels (degree of programmability). Lines have several characteristics of importance in network design, such as speed and conditioning.

The multiplexer section allows the user to describe

three types of multiplexing techniques: true multiplexing, concentration, and front-end processing. Multiplexing and concentration techniques allow linesharing to be performed. Front-end-processing, on the other hand, permits the off-loading of network-dependent functions from the host CPU, typically to an auxiliary specialized communications processor.

Topology section

Another section describes the physical connection of network components—also known as the topology. The topology section defines the concentration and switching points, as well as the general physical form of the network. For example, the network topology shown in Figure 4, that of a distributed configuration, would be described as follows:

TOPOLOGY EXAMPLE-1
    LINK NODE-1 TO NODE-2 VIA LINE-2;
    LINK NODE-1 TO NODE-4 VIA LINE-3;
    LINK NODE-2 TO NODE-4 VIA LINE-5;
    LINK NODE-3 TO NODE-4 VIA LINE-4;
    LINK NODE-1 TO NODE-3 VIA LINE-1;

The network-design system, unless otherwise stated, assumes that traffic is bidirectional, as specified by the topology section. In addition, it performs consistency checks to ensure that each network component is connected either directly or indirectly to all other network components.

A host, assumed to contain one or more CPUs and associated peripherals, is defined to be a major source of computer processing power. Of prime importance are the application programs available on a particular host and the database(s) associated with the host.

NDS allows only two parameters associated with a database: the application that requires the database and its peripheral storage size in bytes (characters). This area (database definition) is still under development. A model is being constructed for analysis of object distribution (data, directories, processes, and so on) in distributed networks.

An application can reside in either a host or a front-end processor, as specified within the multiplexer section. Three parameters specify an application:
1. Response, which is the time (in seconds) it takes the application to respond to a query
2. Size, which denotes the application's maximum core size (in bytes)
3. Database, which refers to the database(s) required by the application for execution

NDS specifies modems similarly to the way it handles multiplexers. Modems, used to interface the digital world with the analog world, normally employ several different keying and transmission techniques. The user may specify these, in addition to modem turnaround properties and speed.

Another section of NDS deals with information flow. An information-center section, or IC, groups a set of network users, who may access the network directly (via terminals) or indirectly as consumers and producers of various reports. The main function of an information center is to allow NDS to place terminals and other network-access devices at strategic locations.

NDS's information-user section describes a person who requires or generates information in some organization, but who may not necessarily interact directly with the network. The actual use of a terminal for network access is described within another part, the terminal-interaction section, either as a constant or as a probability distribution over some time period. While a topology section defines the physical connections of network nodes, a traffic section provides the message rates between all node pairs. Traffic may be specified as simplex or duplex, depending on the existing message profiles.

Sample definition

The following example illustrates how a network planner connects three terminals to a remote host via a multiplexer / demultiplexer arrangement, as shown in Figure 5. The terminals (T-1, T-2, T-3) are attached to the multiplexer (MUX-1) through short-run cables (D-1, D-2, D-3). On the host computer side, the multiplexer (MUX-2) is linked to the front-end processor by short-run cable lines (DL-4, DL-5, DL-6). The high-speed data line, LINE-1, connects the two multiplexers through modems, MODEM-1 and MODEM-2. The front-end processor (FEP-1) contains an application program that handles screen formatting and interface with a small database.

By a predetermined convention, the planner of this elementary network decides to call T-1, T-2, T-3, MUX-1, and MODEM-1 by the name NODE-1, while calling MODEM-2, MUX-2, FEP-1, and HOST-1 by the name NODE-2. The user will first specify the topology of this simple network as follows:

```
TOPOLOGY-SECTION TOP-1;
    LINK MUX-1 TO MODEM-1 VIA DL-2;
    LINK MODEM-1 TO MODEM-2 VIA LINE-1;
    LINK MODEM-2 TO MUX-2 VIA DL-3;
    LINK MUX-2 TO FEP-1 VIA DL-4;
    LINK MUX-2 TO FEP-1 VIA DL-5;
    LINK MUX-2 TO FEP-1 VIA DL-6;
    LINK FEP-1 TO HOST-1 VIA DIO;
```

Next, the node compositions are specified:

```
NODE-SECTION NODE-1;
    TERMINALS ARE T-1, T-2, T-3;
    MULTIPLEXER IS MUX-1;
    MODEM IS MODEM-1;
NODE-SECTION NODE-2;
    MODEM IS MODEM-2;
    MULTIPLEXERS ARE MUX-2, FEP-1;
    HOST IS HOST-1;
```

To complete the network specification, the user must then define component parts such as multiplexers, modems, facilities, and applications.

```
MULTIPLEXER-SECTION FEP-1;
    DESCRIPTION;
```

```
        ACTUALLY, THIS IS A FRONT-END PROCESSOR
        LINKED TO A HOST PROCESSOR VIA A DIO CHAN-
        NEL. THE FEP ALSO CONTAINS A SMALL SCREEN-
        FORMATTING APPLICATION PROGRAM AND ASSO-
        CIATED DATABASE;
    COST IS 200 PER MONTH;
    LOCATION IS LOC-3;
    FAN-IN IS 6;
    PROTOCOL IS DIO;
    RELIABILITY IS 200 HOURS;
    ERROR IS 10000;
    APPLICATION IS SCREEN-FORMAT;
APPLICATION-SECTION SCREEN-FORMAT;
    DESCRIPTION;
        THIS APPLICATION RESIDES IN THE FEP AND IS
        SUPPORTED BY A SMALL DATABASE;
    RESIDES IN FEP-1;
    RESPONSE-TIME IS BINOMIAL;
    REQUIRES 200 INTERFACE DATABASE-1;
MODEM-SECTION MOD-1, MOD-2;
    KEYING IS FSK;
    TURNAROUND IS 20;
    COST IS 20 PER MONTH;
    MODE IS HDUPLEX;
    RELIABILITY IS 400;
    SPEED IS 19200;
LINE-SECTION D-1, D-2, D-3;
SPEED IS 300;
MODE IS HDUPLEX;
ERROR IS POISSON;
RELIABILITY IS 1000;
SECURITY IS 0;
TYPE IS PRIVATE-COAXIAL;
LINE-SECTION LINE-1;
    DESCRIPTION;
        9600 BPS LINE CONNECTING TERMINALS T-1 — T-3
        TO FEP-1 VIA MULTIPLEXERS;
    MODE IS DUPLEX;
    COST IS 200 PER MONTH;
    ERROR IS POISSON;
    RELIABILITY IS 400;
```

4. Sample network. *In the definition process, all network entities and facilities are named. The nodes in this configuration and their interconnections make up the topology.*

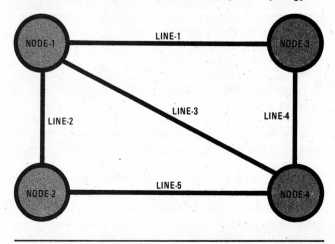

5. Naming components. *Each network component and the composition of nodes must be defined and specified in the design database before the analysis is performed. In this simple configuration, a name is assigned to each terminal (T), data link (DL), multiplexer (MUX), modem, front-end processor (FEP), and host.*

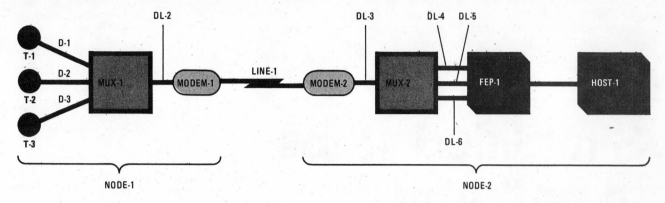

SECURITY IS 0;
TYPE IS 3002 CONDITIONING C2;

After specifying the physical network configuration, the planner describes the various logical properties of the network. These include descriptions of the terminal interactions produced by the various system users.

In our sample case, assume that there are two service managers who require daily data reports and a regional manager who requires a weekly report. Service manager number 1 interacts directly with the system via terminals T-1 and T-2, while the second service manager interfaces with a terminal user to produce the necessary reports. The appropriate sections, based on these requirements, are generated as follows:

INFORMATION-CENTER-SECTION INFO-CENTER-1;
    INFORMATION-USER REGIONAL-MANAGER, SERVICE-MANAGER-1, SRV-MGR-2;
    TERMINAL-USER TERMINAL-USER-1, TERMINAL-USER-2;
    LOCATION IS LOC-1;
    SECURITY IS 0;
INFORMATION-USER-SECTION SRV-MGR-2
    PRIORITY IS 1;
    RECEIVES DAILY-STATUS-REPORT-1 INTERFACE TU-1, TU-2;
    GENERATES WEEKLY-STATUS-REPORT-1 INTERFACE REGIONAL-MANAGER-1;
    SECURITY IS 0;
    LOCATION IS LOC-2;
TERMINAL-USER-SECTION TU-1, TU-2;
    TERMINALS ARE T-1, T-2;
    SECURITY IS 0;
    LOCATION IS LOC-3;
TERMINAL-USER-SECTION SERVICE-MANAGER-1;
    ERROR IS UNIFORM;
    GENERATES DAILY-STATUS-REPORT-2 INTERFACE T-1, T-2, T-3;
    SECURITY IS 0;
    LOCATION IS LOC-4;

After NDS has established the various information

centers, the users can describe required reports that specify network use over a period of time. For this example, we are concerned with three reports: daily-status-report-1, daily-status-report-2, and weekly-status-report-1. These are described in NSL as follows:

REPORT-SECTION WEEKLY-STATUS-REPORT;
    HAPPENS 1 PER WEEK;
    APPLICATION IS REPORT-DOCUMENTER;
    SIZE IS 20000;
REPORT-SECTION DAILY-STATUS-REPORT-1,
    DAILY-STATUS-REPORT-2;
    HAPPENS 1 PER DAY;
    SIZE IS 10000;
    APPLICATION.IS REPORT-DOCUMENTER;

Once the users determine the reports needed and their frequencies, they specify the application programs and databases that support these reports, which end with the host-computer specifications.

APPLICATION-SECTION REPORT-DOCUMENTER;
    HOST IS HOST-1;
    RESPONSE-TIME IS 10;
    SIZE 64000;
    DATABASE REPORT-SUPPORT-1;
DATABASE-SECTION REPORT-SUPPORT-1;
    APPLICATION IS REPORT-DOCUMENTER;
    SIZE IS 100000;
HOST-SECTION HOST-1;
    APPLICATION IS REPORT-DOCUMENTER;
    LOCATION IS LOC-1;

This network, although a relatively simple one, has now been defined using the network statement language. This represents the bulk of user interaction with the design software. Any specification may be easily changed by the user's calling up and modifying the appropriate subsection. The network statement analyzer will then "digest" these specifications and generate database files for their storage and retrieval. The user may, at that point, invoke the required analysis or modeling modules, using the query instructions. ∎

Simplified steps to optimize data networks

Robert L. Ellis, The Aries Group, Rockville, Md.

**With these basic algorithms, even the nonspecialist
can undertake an initial data network design study.
And the programming language APL facilitates the task.**

Network managers constantly grapple with the problem of choosing the more economical alternative for connecting terminals to a main computer—multiplexers or multipoint lines. This decision has become even more difficult of late, with the arrival of distributed data processing. Now managers must contend with multiple host computers and multiple user applications. What is more, they may have to fuse several independent networks, often with incompatible hardware, into a single multipurpose network.

To find better and more affordable ways to enable remote users to access a computer, network managers, over the years, have had to turn to data network consultants, who have developed complex network-design algorithms. Fortunately, these algorithms have been simplified so that even nonspecialists can apply them in a first-pass design. This means that today's network manager can evaluate the initial design feasibility merely by learning the algorithms presented in this article. And by using them with the programming language APL, he can undertake an even more in-depth study. As a bonus, the techniques can be applied in part to voice networks that, because of the development of voice- and data-handling private branch exchanges, behave like data networks.

Data network designers have discovered several design options for cutting costs and several optimizing methods for evaluating the cost-effectiveness of each. For example, to do one calculation, the clustering algorithm, compute the cost of both the current network and the network with certain design changes. If user locations A, B, C, and D are connected to the central processing unit at point X by leased lines, a clustering device (such as a multiplexer, concentrator, or remote front-end processor) will be cost-effective only if the cost of the network with the device is less than the cost without it. Clearly, the cost of the device must include any extra equipment such as high-speed modems and demultiplexers.

One technique for minimizing costs while connecting all users is to build a minimum-spanning tree network (a tree architecture connecting all nodes using as few branches as possible). There are several algorithms for building this configuration, and the traditional one is shown in Table 1.

By using a minimum-spanning tree to connect several points on a single line, the analyst assumes that a single line will accommodate the traffic from these points while maintaining performance standards. To determine whether a line can service this traffic within a specified response time, calculate the response time using the equation

$$R = Q_{IN} + S_{IN} + CPU + Q_{OUT} + S_{OUT}$$

where R = Response time
Q_{IN} = Inbound (to the host) wait time
S_{IN} = Inbound line transmission time (service time)
CPU = Processing time at the CPU and front-end processor
Q_{OUT} = Outbound (from the host) wait time
S_{OUT} = Outbound line transmission time (service time)

112

Table 1 Minimum-spanning tree

1. CHOOSE THE POINT (D) FARTHEST FROM THE CPU (FIG. 1A).

2. CALCULATE THE COST FROM D TO ALL OTHER POINTS.

3. CONNECT D TO THE POINT THAT IS CLOSEST TO IT IN TERMS OF COST (ASSUME C).

4. CALCULATE THE COST FROM C TO ALL OTHER POINTS.

5. SELECT THAT POINT CLOSEST TO C IN TERMS OF COST.

6. CHECK THAT THE SELECTED POINT IS NOT ALREADY CONNECTED TO THE LINE. (IF SO, THE LINE HAS LOOPED BACK ON ITSELF.)

7. IF THE LINE HAS NOT LOOPED BACK ON ITSELF, CONNECT C TO THIS POINT, REPLACE C WITH THE NEW POINT, AND RETURN TO STEP 4.

8. IF THE LINE HAS LOOPED BACK ON ITSELF, DEFINE THIS LINE SEGMENT AS A CLUSTER, SAVE IT FOR LATER, PICK AN UNCONNECTED POINT, AND RETURN TO STEP 4.

9. WHEN ALL POINTS HAVE BEEN CONNECTED, MERGE THE LINE CLUSTERS BY CALCULATING THE COST FROM EACH POINT IN ONE CLUSTER TO EACH POINT IN THE OTHER CLUSTER. USE THE LEAST-COST LINK TO CONNECT THE TWO CLUSTERS.

10. CONTINUE UNTIL ALL LINE CLUSTERS HAVE BEEN MERGED INTO A SINGLE LINE (FIG. 1B).

Of these terms, only Q_{IN} and Q_{OUT} are hard to calculate and require a knowledge of queuing theory, although some general information about them is usually available. CPU is typically a fixed value outside the network designer's control and can be obtained from the data processing staff. S_{IN} and S_{OUT} are relatively easy to compute by calculating

$$S = \frac{(Characters/message) \times (Bits/character)}{Line\ speed\ in\ bit/s}$$

$$= Transmit\ time\ in\ seconds$$

For example, a calculation of the line transmission time over a 2.4-kbit/s line of a 300-character message using 10-bit code shows that

$$S = \frac{300 \times 10}{2,400} = \frac{3,000}{2,400} = 1.25\ seconds$$

If the inbound and outbound messages are each 300 characters and the CPU and front-end processor use 1 second to process a request, the response time in the best possible case cannot be less than

$$R = Q_{IN} + S_{IN} + CPU + Q_{OUT} + S_{OUT}$$

$$= 0 + 1.25 + 1.0 + 0 + 1.25\ seconds$$
$$= 3.5\ seconds$$

This example is the best case, because it is assumed that the inbound and outbound wait times are zero. Also, S_{IN} and S_{OUT} include only transmit time and make no allowance for modem delays, error retransmissions, propagation delays, or message blocking. More elaborate equations to calculate service time with greater precision are widely available.

However, as a best case, the quick calculation of the transmit time for a round-trip transaction can save many a network designer from embarrassment. If a line cannot meet the designer's response-time goal in the best case, it clearly will not meet this goal in the real world where line errors, polling, queuing, and other delays occur.

Complex clustering algorithms

In the previous example, it is assumed that one device (multiplexer, concentrator, or front-end processor) can handle all the remote network locations. If the user has a large network, the optimizing algorithm has more implications. It aids the network designer in deciding how many multiplexing devices to place in the network, where to place them, and which part of the network each device will serve, as well as how to connect the terminals to each multiplexing device and how to interconnect the devices.

There are three techniques for optimizing large networks using multiplexers. The first is known as the "add" algorithm. Its operation is straightforward, although tedious. Simply connect all terminals to the CPU by point-to-point private lines. Then, from a list of candidate sites for the multiplexers and a description of the line tariffs, and taking into account the cost and limitations (port and traffic capacities) of the multiplexer, suppose a device at each candidate site. Assign the most cost-effective terminals (relative to those still assigned to the CPU) to this multiplexer (use the simple clustering algorithm) and calculate the cost saving. After evaluating all candidate sites, select the site that yields the greatest overall cost saving. Then remove from the CPU the original cost-effective terminals and assign them to this site. Continue this procedure, eliminating one multiplexer at a time, until the greatest cost saving becomes negative. When the calculated saving

Minimum-spanning tree. Network cost can be optimized by building a network in which all nodes are connected with as few branches as possible.

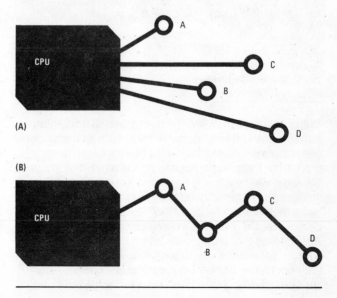

(A)

(B)

Table 2　The Esau-Williams algorithm

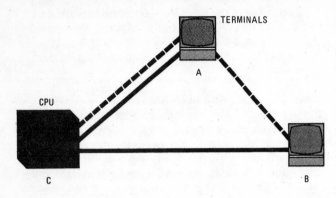

TERMINALS

A

CPU

C   B

1. COMPUTE THE COST OF THE RADIANT NETWORK (LOCATIONS TO CPU: A TO C, B TO C).

2. COMPUTE THE COST OF LINKING ANY NETWORK LOCATION TO ANY OTHER NETWORK POINT (A TO C, B TO A).

3. USING THE RESULTS FROM STEPS 1 AND 2, COMPUTE THE COST SAVING OF LINKING TWO NETWORK POINTS THROUGH AN INTERMEDIATE POINT (A) OVER USING TWO POINT-TO-POINT LINES.

   COST SAVING = [(AC) + (BC)] − [(AC) + (BA)]

   COST SAVING = (BC) − (BA)　　　(AC CANCELS OUT)

4. FIND THAT PAIR OF NETWORK POINTS WITH THE GREATEST COST SAVING.

5. IF CONNECTING THESE TWO POINTS DOES NOT VIOLATE ANY NETWORK CONSTRAINT, ACCEPT THIS PAIR OF POINTS AS A NETWORK LINK.

6. REMOVE THE POINT-TO-POINT LINES AND REVISE THE COST SAVING TABLE.

7. RETURN TO STEP 4 TO CONSIDER A NEW NETWORK LINK.

8. CONTINUE UNTIL EITHER ALL POINT-TO-POINT CIRCUITS ARE GONE OR NO POSITIVE COST SAVING REMAINS.

SIMPLIFICATIONS:

ASSUME COST IS DIRECTLY PROPORTIONAL TO DISTANCE, AND COMPUTE SAVING IN DISTANCE.

ASSUME THAT INTRASTATE POINTS CAN BE SERVED BY THE INTERSTATE CARRIER.

ASSUME THAT FIXED TERMINATION CHARGES CANNOT BE OPTIMIZED.

ASSUME THAT THE LAST POINT CONNECTED ON ANY LINE IS THE LEAST-EXPENSIVE CONNECTION FOR THAT LINE TO THE HOST.

---

the line tariffs. Remove a device and recalculate the network's cost. After evaluating the cost consequences of removing a multiplexer at each candidate site, eliminate the multiplexer that yields the greatest reduction in total cost when removed, and reassign its terminals to the other devices. Continue removing one multiplexer at a time, until the removal of any multiplexer causes the network's cost to increase.

Finally, there is the "center-of-gravity" algorithm. Start this method by determining all possible ways of placing the maximum allowable number of multiplexers among the candidate sites. Build a table of distances from each terminal to each candidate site for a multiplexer. Then, from the appropriate tariffs, compute the line cost of connecting each terminal to a multiplexing device by a point-to-point private line. Assign every terminal to the most cost-effective multiplexer, for all possible configurations, and select the fewest possible ways of siting N multiplexers among M candidate sites. Then connect the sited multiplexers either to the central processing unit or to each other.

The "center-of-gravity" algorithm is most appropriate for optimizing networks in which the multiplexers have a great deal of intelligence and are more akin to remote processors, especially if they communicate with each other directly. The "add" algorithm is better for those networks with very few multiplexers. The "drop" algorithm is best suited to a network that has many multiplexers.

Esau and Williams' formula

Unfortunately, it is a very rare network that can connect all its terminals by one multipoint line (party-line method). In large networks, this type of connection is not feasible except where the host broadcasts to its terminals. The single-line design, although clearly the least costly way to connect the terminals, will nearly always violate either the maximum number of drops allowed by the front end on a single multipoint line (the addressing limit, usually 16 or 32 drops) or the maximum allowable traffic volume as determined by a response-time analysis. Thus, the network manager must first check that no constraints are violated before adding a new terminal to a line.

The traditional algorithm for such a large network layout (50 or more sites) is known as the Esau-Williams algorithm. It calculates the cost saving that results from linking each point in the network to the CPU through its most cost-effective intermediate point, then connects points to each other, beginning with the most remote points.

This algorithm begins with all locations connected to the CPU, each with its own point-to-point private line (a radiant or star design), considers all possible cost-saving pairs, and defines that pair with the greatest cost saving as a network link, provided no constraint (traffic volume or number of drops or total mileage) is violated.

When all positive cost-saving pairs have been exhausted, the network has reached a near-optimum design. The example in Table 2 shows how a simplified version of this algorithm enables an excellent first-pass

---

in line costs is cancelled by the calculated equipment costs, recalculate the network costs with all the selected multiplexers in place and shift terminals among them to correct errors caused by the algorithm's "greediness."

The second technique for optimizing large networks using multiplexers is called the "drop" algorithm. To begin, site a multiplexer in each candidate city. (If more than one type of multiplexer is to be used, determine which type is most cost-effective at each site.) Then, connect all terminals to the most cost-effective multiplexer based on a description of the device cost and

Table 3 Connecting network nodes

1. DETERMINE THE COST PER TRANSACTION OVER EACH LINK (FIG. 3).

2. FIND THE LINK WITH THE HIGHEST COST PER TRANSACTION (ASSUME THIS LINK IS C TO D).

3. REMOVE THIS LINK FROM THE NETWORK AND DETERMINE THE MOST COST-EFFECTIVE ALTERNATIVE ROUTE FOR TRANSACTIONS (ASSUME THE ALTERNATIVE ROUTE FOR C TO D IS C TO B AND B TO D).

4. ADD THE REROUTED TRANSACTIONS TO BOTH LINKS OF THE ALTERNATIVE ROUTE.

5. ADD IN SWITCHING DELAYS AT THE INTERMEDIATE CPU AND RECOMPUTE THE PERFORMANCE OF BOTH LINKS OF THE ALTERNATIVE ROUTE.

6. DETERMINE WHETHER THIS PERFORMANCE MEETS THE NETWORK-DESIGN GOAL. IF NOT, ADD MORE BANDWIDTH TO ACCOMMODATE THE EXTRA TRANSACTIONS.

7. RECALCULATE THE NETWORK'S COST, AS MODIFIED. IF THE COST HAS DECREASED, ACCEPT THIS CHANGE AND RETURN TO STEP 1.

8. IF THE COST HAS NOT DECREASED, SELECT THE LINK WITH THE NEXT-HIGHEST COST PER TRANSACTION AND RETURN TO STEP 2.

9. CONTINUE UNTIL THE NETWORK REDUCES TO A STAR OR UNTIL YOU ARE ATTEMPTING TO REMOVE THE MOST COST-EFFECTIVE NETWORK LINK.

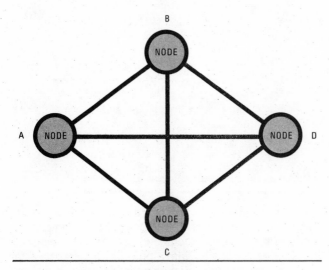

network design of multipoint lines.

If the multiplexing devices sited by the clustering algorithms are capable of communicating directly with each other, behaving more like network nodes or remote processors, the network planner must decide how to interconnect them.

The cluster-interconnection algorithm
The process of connecting the clusters is sometimes called "backbone design." If the major devices do not communicate directly with each other, but only through a master node, the backbone design is simply the minimum-spanning tree (Fig. 1B). Otherwise, the designer must use the cluster-interconnection algorithm.

This algorithm, appropriate only for complex multi-node networks, begins with a fully connected network (one link connecting all the major multiplexing devices). Links are removed one at a time until the design cost cannot be reduced any further. Table 3 presents this algorithm in detail.

Optimization pitfalls
The algorithms presented here, although simple in theory, are tedious and time-consuming if attempted by hand. They are fortunately perfectly suited for a computerized effort. However, in implementing these algorithms with whatever method chosen, the network designer should be aware of certain pitfalls. First, distance optimization is not cost optimization. So, optimizing a network's distance does not necessarily optimize its cost, especially given present-day multitiered tariffs. Under these tariffs, the cost of a line depends not only on distance but also on a city's class. (For example, under AT&T's MPL rate structure—part of the Federal Communications Commission general AT&T tariff 260—400 U.S. cities are classified as Category A. The remaining 23,000 U.S. cities come under Category B. The lines connecting Category A cities have the most favorable rates.)

Another consideration is that many communications services are not universal. Cost-effective or efficient services such as AT&T's dataphone digital service or other common-carrier offerings may not be available at all network sites. The network designer therefore may need to connect the unserviced sites to the network core by relatively expensive services.

There are many other pitfalls. For example, tariffs are volatile. Today's cost-effective network may become suddenly expensive to operate if a new tariff is filed by a communications vendor. Also, communications vendors are constantly expanding their services and modifying the list of service areas. Therefore, software to design data networks must be flexible and easy to maintain. It should conform to generally accepted good-programming practices, such as structured organization, adequate documentation, and top-down design. (Top-down design means building a program by first writing the main program, then interfacing that with the subroutine called directly by the main program. Likewise, the next-lower-level subroutines are written and interfaced until the program is complete. The advantage of top-down design is the ability to pinpoint errors at a specific level of subroutine.)

Large network designs consume large amounts of computer resources. The complexity of a network design does not increase linearly with the number or network locations, N. It increases factorially ($N!$, the worst case) or with the square (N^2, a better case). Trade-off tables and distance tables may quickly become very large and soon overwhelm the computer's core memory, forcing the network designer to store these tables in peripheral files.

Efficient data manipulation is more important than algorithmic elegance. The distinguishing feature of

APL: A natural language for net design

The APL programming language is based on a special algebraic system for writing equations and algorithms. In APL, special symbols represent the common arithmetic operations (see table). These special symbols invoke machine-language macros that handle any looping required at the object-code level.

APL is an array-oriented language allowing the user to manipulate matrices and higher-order arrays without using program loops. Data can be easily retrieved from such arrays by using either Boolean operations or direct indexing. For example, to determine the minimum distance between a city whose V and H coordinates are in A to a number of cities whose V and H coordinates are in B, let A be a two-element vector containing the V and H coordinates of the first city. Similarly, let B be a two-column matrix containing the V and H coordinates of the other cities. The V/H distance formula is

$$D = \sqrt{\frac{(V_1 - V_2)^2 + (H_1 - H_2)^2}{10}}$$

where the answer is rounded to the next-higher mile.

This equation is easily written in APL as

$$D \leftarrow \lceil((((A[1] - B[;1]) * 2) + ((A[2] - B[;2]) * 2)) + 10) * 0.5$$

When it is calculated, D will contain a vector of distances from A to all cities in B, computed all at once, without a loop. The minimum of these distances can be found by

$$M \leftarrow \lceil/D \text{ (search for the minimum within D)}$$

The index of the city with this minimum distance is

$$I \leftarrow D\iota M$$

The following example shows how APL can be used for network cost calculations. Let C be a vector indicating with 1s those cities in category A and with 2s those cities in category B. Assume that the tariff is $1.80 per mile to connect the first city to a category A city and $3.30 per mile to connect it to a category B city. Therefore

$$C \leftrightarrow 1\ 2\ 1\ 2\ 1 \text{ AND } D \leftrightarrow 10\ 20\ 30\ 10\ 20$$

Thus

$$COST \leftarrow D \times (1.80\ 3.30)\ [C]$$

or

$$COST \leftarrow 10\ 20\ 30\ 10\ 20 \times 1.80\ 3.30\ 1.80\ 3.30\ 1.80$$

or

$$COST \leftrightarrow 18\ 66\ 54\ 33\ 36$$

As an additional benefit, APL does not encumber the programmer with dimension and data-declaration statements and does not care if the programmer is trying to put bits in an array that once held floating-point numbers. Originally conceived as a more rational algebraic notation, APL makes it easy to program the complex queuing-theory equations, especially those involving a lengthy series, and often without a program loop.

APL SYMBOL	ALGEBRAIC EQUIVALENT
A*B	A TO THE POWER B, (A^B)
A⌈B	THE GREATER OF A OR B
A⌊B	THE LESSER OF A OR B
ιA	COUNT FROM 1 TO A
A[⍒A]	SORT A IN DESCENDING ORDER
AιB	FIND WHERE IN THE VECTOR A THE VALUES OF B OCCUR
3 3ρA	MAKE A 3 BY 3 MATRIX FROM A
*B	e TO THE POWER B
⌈B	ROUND B TO THE NEXT HIGHER INTEGER
⌊B	ROUND B TO THE NEXT LOWER INTEGER
A=B	DOES A EQUAL B?
A←B	PUT B INTO A
A[B]	INDEX A BY B

successful software packages for network design is not their optimizing algorithms, which are well-known and in the public domain, but the amount of data they require and their effectiveness in handling it. Large tables stored in core memory not only bog down computation but also force extra programming effort to move and process the additional data.

Control information is as important as the data. A well-thought-out network-design program uses pointers (addressing information to data) and data-table abstracts for tracking data rather than employing the full data tables. To prevent program disasters, the network designer must pay attention to this control information and closely monitor the optimization process.

The computer implementation of the Esau-Williams and other network-design algorithms is best done in a symbolic language known as APL (see "APL: A natural

language for net design"). APL's structure makes it especially suitable for network design. For example, since APL radically reduces the number of source-code statements needed to write a program, it is much easier to code software to design complex networks because the user can manipulate data wholesale. The APL language forces the analyst to solve problems globally, without looping and without bogging down in the minutiae of program bookkeeping.

Implementation of a special language

Thus, APL implementation of the Esau-Williams algorithm reduces the number of design trade-offs in two ways. In the first reduction, all points in the same rate center (an area under one rate of cost) are collected for finding cost trade-offs. In APL, this is done in four steps. Here, *A* is a matrix with rate-center identifiers in the first column and data such as the number of devices and messages in the other columns. The first step separates the rate-center identifiers:

$$B \leftarrow A[;1]$$

Then the user brings together all data for the same rate center:

$$A \leftarrow A[\Delta B;]$$

The third step finds the beginning of each rate center's data:

$$C \leftarrow 1,(1 \downarrow A[;1]) \neq {}^{-}1 \downarrow A[;1]$$

And finally, the program adds up the data for each rate center and creates a new matrix:

$$D \leftarrow (C/A[;1]), C \ \underline{SPLRED} \ O \ 1 \downarrow A$$

D now contains the data in A summarized by rate center and a rate-center identifier in the first column.

In the last step, *SPLRED* is an APL utility, "substring plus reduction," that adds up the data in specified slices of an array. Thus, if C is a vector of binary 1s and 0s, with the 1s indicating the beginning of each slice, and A is the matrix of data, this is written as

$$R \leftarrow (1 \ \phi \ C) \neq + \ \backslash \ A \quad R \leftarrow R - ((\rho \rho R) \uparrow {}^{-}1) \downarrow 0,[1]R$$

The second reduction assumes that the cost to go from city X to Y is nearly always the same as the cost to go from Y to X. This means that only the lower left triangle of the trade-off matrix is used. Thus, if a network consists of 1,000 points in 200 rate centers, the traditional trade-off matrix will contain 1,000 x 1,000 elements, or 1,000,000 cells; if the points in the network are gathered by rate centers, the matrix will contain 200 x 200, or 40,000, cells. But when using the second reduction method, the network can be 200 x 100, or 20,000, cells. The extra bookkeeping needed for tracking data for individual points is well worth reducing the size of the matrix by a factor of 50. Not only is core memory better utilized, but the optimizing algorithm is manipulating much less data, yielding a significant cost saving.

Coming together

After many years of being separate disciplines, the data and voice network-design worlds are converging. In fact, many approaches for designing and optimizing data networks can be applied to voice networks.

The design of voice networks has traditionally focused on the optimum mix of toll services such as direct distance dialing (DDD), wide-area services such as WATS, foreign exchange services, and tie lines. The voice network designer has a choice of two ways of making the best use of these services. The first is off-net optimization, or connecting network users to the places they are calling in the most cost-effective manner. This means determining the best mix of DDD, WATS, and FX services.

The second technique is on-net optimization, or connecting network users to the network and to each other cost-effectively. For on-net optimization, the voice net-

work designer will use primarily tie lines but will also use the other three services in cases where tie lines are not cost-justified.

Since a voice network dispatches many callers to many different places and not to a central facility that handles all communications between a central host and its terminals, it cannot be modeled as a single-server queue, as can a data network. Instead, it requires special multiserver queuing equations such as the classic Erlang equations. [For the actual equations, see *Telecommunications Switching Principles* by M. T. Hills, MIT Press, Cambridge, Mass., 1979, p. 90.] Despite this difference, certain voice-networking problems are very much like data-networking problems. In fact, the only data-network-design method that does not help in designing voice networks is the party-line method. But until voice-networking technology (possibly digitized voice) allows a single line (or server) to handle simultaneously more than one telephone call, clustering methods will be the primary data-network-design aid of use in voice networks.

There are changes in the wind, however. Recently, the largest private branch exchanges (PBXs) have themselves become computers or computerized branch exchanges (CBXs). With a computer to control the calls placed by the network's users, the voice network designer, or traffic engineer, can now impose some very stringent controls. These include the ability to perform call-monitoring, route selection, and various bookkeeping functions. The designer can record an extension's placing a call and then bill the call back to an internal department; limit access to the DDD system; and insert queuing delays when necessary.

This means that when the traffic engineer connects two or more CBXs (a tandem tie-line network), he is, in fact, operating his own telephone company, complete with central offices and intercity long lines. This is similar to the chore performed by the data network designer who has just assembled his own packet-switching network, complete with wideband connecting lines, and is operating his own telephone utility; his network design will not differ much at the conceptual level from that of the traffic engineer.

With traffic engineers and data network designers building private networks that mirror the telephone companies' public networks, the future course of telecommunications may not be that difficult to predict. Since telephone company electric switching systems and intercity long lines can already accommodate voice and data together, it will not be long before the traffic engineers have CBXs that can do the same. In fact, recent product announcements by Datapoint Corporation and Rolm Corporation reinforce this idea. Since most large organizations generally spend far more on voice than on data, it is likely that the traffic engineer will acquire a super-CBX to piggy-back data onto the voice network before the data communications manager acquires voice digitizers to mesh voice and data. In any event, voice and data will become complementary applications in a unified telecommunications network, which will be designed using many optimizing methods now used for data networks. ∎

Krishna S. Sharma, Royal Bank of Canada, Toronto, Ont.,
and Robert L. Ellis, The Aries Group, Rockville, Md.,

Freeing inundated managers to run their networks

Data communications managers can be relieved of their toughest job—configuring the most economical setup— and return to directing operations.

ata communications technology is becoming extremely complex, and an ever-increasing number of vendors is offering a wide choice of terminals, protocols, communications services, and architectures. It is no small wonder that many data communications managers feel overwhelmed. This feeling becomes one of hopelessness when business needs require upgrading or configuring a network using state-of-the-art features. How is the data communications manager to make a wise choice among the many options available—such as network structures, tariffs, response times—to plan and implement an effective network? Can he do this work on his own, or should he depend upon hardware vendors, communications carriers, and consultants?

If he is to remain in control of the network-design process, the data communications manager should deal with these five considerations:

1. Determine the most cost-effective configuration of equipment and communications lines that will meet users' needs.

2. Determine the relative strengths and weaknesses of the equipment to be used on the basis of

—savings in communications costs

—equipment reliability, capability, functionality, and special features

—financing terms

—implementation ease

3. Recommend which equipment should be used and a timetable for installing it.

4. Monitor and supervise the actual installation and maintenance of the new network.

5. Monitor the trends in data communications to determine which new state-of-the-art equipment, protocols, and architectures could be used successfully.

Only the first consideration actually involves the network configuration; the other four challenge the data communications manager's talents as a manager—as the person tempering the proposals of vendors to the needs of his organization. However, the first problem often consumes most of the manager's time because it is the most difficult one to do—as well as the problem he is probably least trained to handle. He often finds himself either spending all his time connecting multicolored pins on a map—or operating completely at the mercy of his vendors or the consultants he calls in to arbitrate their proposals. In the first case, he has become so involved with actual network configuration, he has no time left for the other four parts of his job. In the second case, he has turned over his responsibility for the first problem to others, who, as outsiders, do not necessarily have the interests of his organization foremost in any proposal they make.

How does the data communications manager regain control over the mysterious first problem? Not by becoming a queuing theory guru or an ace programmer, but by using a computerized network-design tool such as the Aries Group's optimizer for the design of information networks (ODIN). Such tools make the process of network design understandable to the typical data communications manager, and not an esoteric endeavor shrouded in nearly religious mystery, requiring the special talents of one initiated in the secrets of the network-design brotherhood.

As an example of a network-design-tool application, let us consider the Royal Bank of Canada. It is Canada's largest bank and the fourth largest in North America, having 1,440 branches. Banking regulations do not restrict branch banking in Canada. The industry consists of only 58 chartered banks, the five largest of which operate coast-to-coast. There are also several hundred trust companies (equivalent to U.S. savings

1. The way it was. *The earlier network used nonintelligent terminals and was designed, implemented, and maintained by three different service bureaus.*

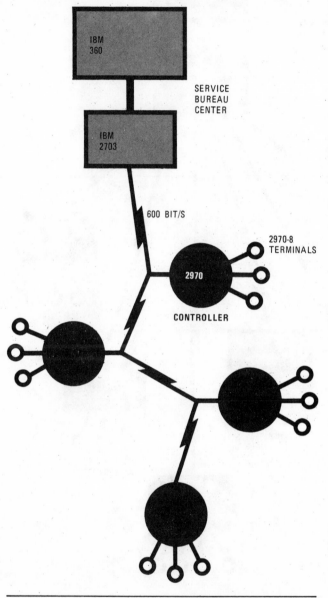

Figure 1 is representative of the Royal Bank network from 1970 to 1976. It was configured by the service bureaus, which had responsibility for maintaining the network after installation and acquiring new equipment and private lines as needed to accommodate growth. Both the network and the service bureaus performed well during the six years they were in operation.

In 1976 the Royal Bank faced a major network-design problem when it made a twofold decision: to take advantage of IBM's then newly introduced systems network architecture (SNA) in its Ontario On-Line Banking Network, and to gain direct managerial and operational control over the network, bringing a significant bank resource in-house. The envisioned network concept is illustrated in Figure 2, in simplified form. Note the equipment from three different vendors with three different protocols: asynchronous, binary synchronous (BSC), and synchronous data link control (SDLC). Not shown are IBM 5955 controllers, which are currently supplementing the 3601s.

The concept of a multipoint line using the IBM 3600 equipment is illustrated in Figure 3. The line protocol is SDLC, typically at 1.2 or 2.4 kbit/s. The bank's design called for each 3601 controller to handle one local loop and up to four remote loops. Each loop, local or remote, can support up to five workstations or two automated teller machines (ATMs). Each workstation comprises an IBM 3604 teller terminal and an IBM 3611 passbook printer; the ATM is an IBM 3624. Remote loops are linked to their controllers by 1.2-kbit/s lines.

Seeking design help

The decision to upgrade and convert the previously configured service-bureau networks necessitated planning, configuring, and optimizing a new combined intelligent (IBM 3600) and nonintelligent (IBM 2970) terminal network—a mammoth job requiring months of manual effort of highly trained people. To make this task at all approachable, the bank asked the hardware vendor to provide networking guidelines for configuring its equipment. For example, the rules of thumb for designing the IBM 2970 terminal into a network were:

- Five controllers average per controller-host line
- Eight terminals average per controller-host line
- Twelve terminals maximum per controller-host line.

These guidelines effectively reduced a response-time goal—95 percent of the transactions to be handled in five seconds—into a device constraint that assumed only one type of transaction (the average transaction) occurs, each controller generated the same number of transactions, and each controller had the same number of terminals. Thus the rules of thumb assumed that the intra-controller and the inter-controller variances in the network's transactions were zero—yielding somewhat optimistic designs for those networks with a broad mix of transaction sizes.

However, the rules of thumb did enable the bank's network designers to define a tentative network layout (equipment-to-line assignments) optimized somewhat on the basis of response time. This network layout was then submitted to the common carriers to optimize the leased-line costs. The result was next incorporated

and loan banks) and credit unions. Thus the Canadian banking industry is extremely competitive, not only in the interest rates and banking services offered to its consumers, but also in conveniences requiring complex data networks to support.

For the Royal Bank, 1,350 of its branches are on-line. Their 4,000 terminals are served by three on-line processing centers. A network of leased lines supports these terminals, and the bank's data communications outlay is in excess of $10 million.

In the early 1970s, the network consisted entirely of nonintelligent terminals (IBM 2970 Model 8 banking terminals, and similar devices from other vendors) served by three different service bureaus. Each service bureau operated in its own hardware and communications-software environment.

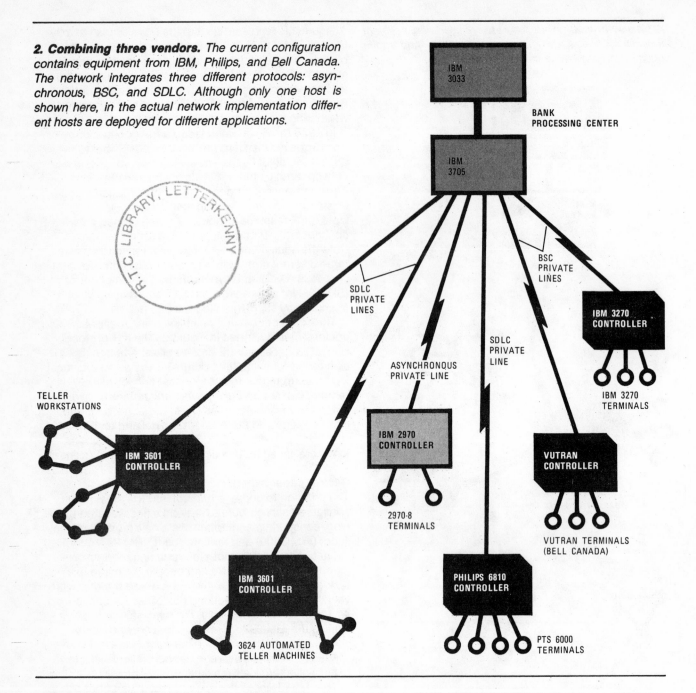

2. Combining three vendors. *The current configuration contains equipment from IBM, Philips, and Bell Canada. The network integrates three different protocols: asynchronous, BSC, and SDLC. Although only one host is shown here, in the actual network implementation different hosts are deployed for different applications.*

IBM 3033

BANK PROCESSING CENTER

IBM 3705

SDLC PRIVATE LINES

BSC PRIVATE LINES

IBM 3270 CONTROLLER

IBM 3270 TERMINALS

ASYNCHRONOUS PRIVATE LINE

SDLC PRIVATE LINE

TELLER WORKSTATIONS

IBM 3601 CONTROLLER

IBM 2970 CONTROLLER

2970-8 TERMINALS

VUTRAN CONTROLLER

VUTRAN TERMINALS (BELL CANADA)

IBM 3601 CONTROLLER

3624 AUTOMATED TELLER MACHINES

PHILIPS 6810 CONTROLLER

PTS 6000 TERMINALS

into an overall equipment/leased-line design. This design was recognizably neither as rigorous nor as optimized as it could have been theoretically. However, it was the best possible under the circumstances.

This project made the bank realize the complexity of designing new networks. In planning the evaluation of the SNA option—initially for Ontario and finally for the entire network—the designers were resolved to keep the design process under control, to design the network more thoroughly and cost-effectively, and to make the wisest choices among the various vendors. These choices included financial-terminal vendors such as IBM and Philips, and such common-carrier service providers as Canadian National Canadian Pacific (CNCP) and Trans Canada Telephone System (TCTS). Use of leased-line networks versus packet-switching

networks, for example, had to be weighed.

In the planning process, these objectives became clear:

■ Cost-effective high-performance network configuration. Given the intensely competitive nature of the Canadian banking industry and the strong impetus to service, banking networks must not only be cost-effective, but also offer a very high level of performance to their customers.

■ Timely and accurate network planning that could address questions relating to network cost, flexibility, and growth, and to the functionality and technical features of the equipment under consideration.

■ To show the effect of changes in line speed, traffic growth, and protocol on response time and network cost, by "what if" analyses. Since many equipment

3. Controlling the multipoint line. *Detailed here is how the IBM 3600 equipment is typically configured. The multipoint polled line operates under the SDLC protocol.*

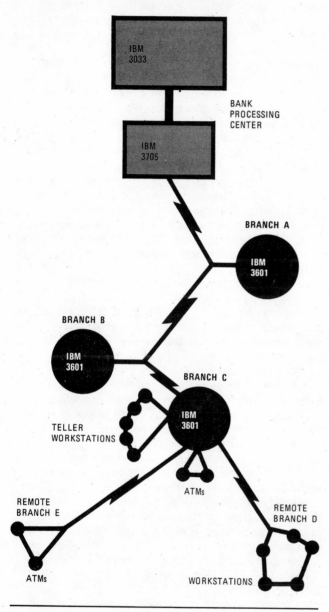

options and protocols were feasible, and these options could be combined in a variety of ways, a well-considered set of "what if" analyses would limit the choices to a defined few for detailed study.

■ Ability to evaluate and compare the costs of various vendors' distributed networks, as well as to analyze various common-carrier services available. Though several hardware vendors were under consideration originally, a number were eliminated quite early. Either their equipment was not compatible with the bank's on-line CPUs, host software, teleprocessing software, network architecture, or line protocol; or they did not offer local support at all 1,350 on-line network points. Unlike the U.S. where banks operate on-line networks in very limited areas and therefore do not take comparatively big risks when using unfamiliar vendors, in Can-

ada a banking network's lack of local support and service at every user point is a significant risk.

■ Increasing the network-design group's productivity by reducing its manual efforts and enriching its skills. Manually designing large-scale networks is an extremely tedious, error-prone, and time-consuming process that does not truly challenge the talents of those designing them. A network-design aid to handle the detailed calculations needed to compute response times and to optimize a network's layout lets the designers concentrate on more-management-oriented design issues and not the details.

Design trade-offs
Intrinsic to the objectives of this planning process is the ability to trade communications line costs off against hardware costs. For example, a knowledgeable data communications manager, by increasing the hardware placed in his network, may be able to reduce its line costs dramatically and realize significant savings in the overall costs of the network. Conversely, by using more lines, he may reduce the amount or complexity of the hardware used in the network. However, a not-so-knowledgeable manager might end up increasing line costs if the additional hardware does not cluster traffic onto more cost-effective lines, thereby increasing the overall cost.

In addition, more complex hardware requires more complex software in the host and communications processor; more sophisticated line protocols, to make effective use of the network's lines; more talented people to operate and maintain the network and its components; and extra resources to ensure network reliability. Though the data communications manager can achieve most of these objectives by using the results from vendor-provided planning tools—either from the common carrier or the terminal vendor—the burden is really on the data communications manager to optimize the network on his own if he is to remain truly in control of his network.

The bank's network designers used ODIN to solve the following problems in their new SNA network:

1. Circuit optimization. Given a list of controller sites and the host location, determine the optimum circuit routing using the best mix of analog and digital services. The original IBM 2970 network, as well as the IBM 3600 hardware that was added later, can support multipoint polled lines. Determining the optimum circuit routing to connect a number of controllers is a basic task required in any network-optimizing aid. This task is particularly complicated in Canada since digital private lines are priced at a much lower rate than analog lines. This rate is made possible because digital lines are cheaper and easier to operate and maintain, and are easier to share via multiplexers. There is thus a strong economic incentive to interconnect cities that have only analog service by analog-extension channels to digital homing cities. To determine the best routing for a circuit connecting controllers in a mix of digital-homing and analog-termination cities can be a difficult task, since one must decide not only the best circuit routing but also the most cost-effective combination

of analog and digital facilities.

2. Response-time analysis. Given a description of the network's transaction types and operation (such as SDLC) as well as the transaction traffic at each controller (IBM 3601 or Philips 6810) on a line, determine the response time and line utilization. Knowing how many transactions of each type that occur at each station on a multipoint polled line, one can determine, using well-known queuing equations, the response time that can be expected at various confidence levels. Though well known, these queuing equations are extremely tedious and require painstaking accuracy to yield meaningful results. This task is basic in any network-optimizing aid. The inverse problem is to determine the maximum transactions a line can handle within a specified response-time goal (such as 95 percent within five seconds) as the number of points on a multipoint line is increased. This is an exceedingly difficult task, requiring a computer either to simulate the line and its transactions or to use the complex numerical analytical techniques needed to invert the queuing equations. However, a network-design aid that solves this problem is able to use the actual distribution of transactions in a network rather than rules of thumb in its optimization, and thus will yield a design more in tune with the realities of the network.

3. Lower-order network design. Given the locations of branches and their associated workstations, and the transaction traffic at each workstation, determine the most cost-effective branch sites for controllers (IBM 3601 and Philips 6810) to serve the workstations. This process not only has to be sensitive to the significant cost-savings realizable by mixing analog and digital services in Canada, but also has to take into account the specified controller constraints in terms of the number of loops, workstations, and the maximum allowable traffic.

4. Higher-order network design. Given the controller locations and transaction traffic, determine the most cost-effective mix of multipoint polled lines to serve these controllers within a specified response-time goal. This problem combines problems 1 and 2, taking the amorphous collection of controllers positioned previously (problem 3) and assigning them each to the multipoint line that yields the greatest overall network savings. This problem is also complicated in Canada by the cost-saving opportunities gained by mixing analog and digital services. Thus what may seem to the network designer to be one physical circuit actually consists of several separately identified segments, depending on which are analog extensions, which others are intercity digital channels, and which segments are totally analog channels. Though this optimizing process is much more complicated than in the U.S., failing to mix analog and digital services can cost the data communications manager a great deal in higher line charges.

Solving the problems
Using a computerized network-design aid to evaluate its SNA network, the bank significantly improved its ability to address the four problems:

Example, Problem 1. Circuit optimization.
Given four IBM 3601 controllers located in three analog cities in Ontario (Strathroy, Lambeth, Thamesford) and one digital city (Kitchener), and the host located in Toronto (a digital city), determine the least-cost mix of digital and analog services, and the minimum cost routing.

Solution: Optimum design is shown in Figure 4. Note that this optimum configuration consists of one analog segment and one digital segment connecting the five Ontario cities. Although London, Ont., is not one of the five, it is used as a digital homing point for Strathroy, Lambeth, and Thamesford. It enables those three analog cities to share, cost-effectively, a 50-mile digital link to Kitchener. As both a digital homing point and an analog point, London is assessed for both types of terminations. The design cost $15 in computer time in running one 10-minute terminal session, as compared with the one hour of a network analyst's manual effort, primarily using maps. The optimized design was $111 a month, or 7 percent lower in line charges than the manual design.

Example, Problem 2. Response-time analysis.
Given a point-to-point, asynchronous, half-duplex private line connected to an IBM 2972 controller, operating at 600 bit/s, and handling 550 peak-hour inquiries of 25 characters and 1,100 replies of 45 characters, determine the line utilization and the response time at various confidence levels.

Solution: Using a computerized network-design aid, a 15-minute terminal session was needed costing $40 in computer time. The results: The line utilization is 33.8 percent and has a mean response time of 2.8 seconds. At a 95 percent confidence level, response time is about 5.1 seconds. Manually, a network analyst needed 6 hours to calculate the mean response time and the distribution of response time. By having a computerized response-time-analysis tool, many "what if" scenarios can be tried to learn the effect of changes in line speed, line protocol, modems, or traffic volume on a multipoint line.

Example, Problem 3. Lower-order network design.
Given 256 IBM 3600 financial workstations in 92 branches in 45 cities in Ontario, and a list of 12 candidate sites (cities with digital service), determine the best locations for placing IBM 3601 controllers. Each controller costs $1,095 and serves a maximum of five branches (loops) and 18 workstations. Use the best mix of analog and digital services.

Solution: This problem is an extremely difficult one that previously took a network analyst over two weeks to do manually. Not only must one determine where the IBM 3601 controllers will be cost-effective against leased lines but also when digital services are cost-effective against analog services. The optimized design required one day to gather data about the 256 workstations and to limit the possible sites to 12. The optimization was done in a one-hour terminal session costing $325, and positioned 17 IBM 3601 controllers. This configuration cost over $8,500 a month less than the manual one, or a 16 percent saving.

Example, Problem 4. Higher-order network design.

4. Optimizing cost-effectively. *The optimum circuit to connect these three analog, one digital, and the host cities uses a digital homing point in London.*

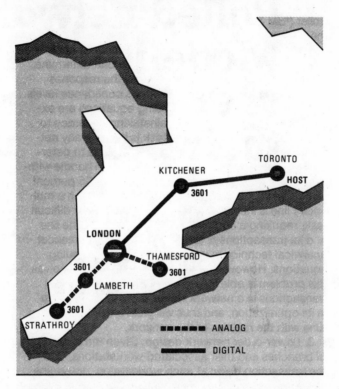

ANALOG
DIGITAL

Given 14 IBM 3601 controllers in 10 cities in Ontario and the host in Toronto, determine the most cost-effective mix of multipoint, analog/digital lines to connect them. Assume a multipoint line can support no more than three controllers with 54 workstations and still meet the network's response-time goal.

Solution: This problem is somewhat less difficult than Problem 3 since the network being optimized has only 14 terminations compared to 92. However, it still took a network analyst one week to do the optimizing job manually, again complicated by the cost trade-off between analog and digital services. A one-hour terminal session, which required an hour of preparation and cost $150, yielded an optimized configuration consisting of five multipoint lines costing $500 a month less than the manual design.

As a result of using a computerized network-design tool to evaluate the SNA option, the Royal Bank achieved all of its network planning objectives well within deadline. The total savings over three years in equipment and data communications costs reached $600,000, with $22,000 in computer running expenses and $28,000 in incidental software and terminal expenses. This amounts to a cash return on investment of $600,00 ÷ ($22,000 + $28,000) = 1,200 percent before adjustment for the time value of money. Nearly two man-years of systems analysis effort was freed from purely network reconfiguration efforts to tackle the other four more professionally rewarding aspects of the network-design process; the data communications manager can focus on the short-, medium-, and long-term planning process of his network. ∎

Narayan Subramanian and David A. Rubin,
Contel Information Systems Inc., Great Neck, N. Y.

Polled networks: Modeling helps the user evaluate their performance

Both analysis and simulation techniques must work together as a hybrid to gain insight into critical design areas.

The design of data communications networks poses many challenging problems. One of the most significant of these to the systems analyst is the performance evaluation of an existing or planned network. Unfortunately, collection and analysis of performance data can only provide insight into the operation of an existing network. To assess the performance of one that is planned, predictive techniques are necessary. Modeling, however difficult, is the general technique needed to predict network performance and to gain insight about its critical components.

There are two modeling techniques available to the network designer, but both have severe drawbacks as standalone procedures. For example, analytical queueing models of polling methods are extremely complex and can be made tractable only if many simplifying assumptions about the network are made. This frequently—and often unpredictably—results in inaccuracies in the response times obtained and/or restricts the applicability of the model to certain traffic levels. Consequently, these models should not be relied on unless the designer is only interested in gross answers.

Pure simulation models, while more accurate than analytical queueing models, are cumbersome and costly to run. Fortunately, a hybrid technique in which the analysis is embedded within the simulation yields a flexible model that provides accurate results. For Contel Information Systems (formerly Network Analysis Corporation), this hybrid approach is the method of choice for the analysis of most practical data communications networks. The input to the hybrid model can be detailed empirical data, if it is available, or it can be defined approximately by statistics furnished either by the user or Contel.

There is one more advantage to the hybrid model: It is a general-purpose design package. Thus a major limitation of specially developed analytic or simulation models—development cost—is overcome. In effect, the cost has been distributed among many different users—a classic example of cost reduction through resource sharing.

To understand this hybrid modeling concept and decide if it should be applied to a specific data communications network, the details of both pure analytic and simulation models must be understood. Since a model is a representation of a real system that embodies the functional capabilities of that system, it must be capable of accepting inputs and generating outputs that are consistent with the transformations made by the real system. This definition of a model and its function is the basis for an intelligent comparison of the two model classes.

An analytical model is a mathematical representation of the system that relates system output to input via a functional relationship. In other words, there are dependent and independent variables much as in calculus. Ideally, the function is an explicit relationship that yields a solution for the dependent variables by simple substitution for the independent variables.

In more complex models, the functional relationship requires iterative numerical solutions. For example, the network consisting of messages arriving at a terminal for processing can be modeled analytically by what is known as a single-server queue. By describing the arrival and service processes mathematically, and making simplifying assumptions regarding these processes, it is possible to functionally relate the performance measures such as queue length and waiting times to the statistics of the processes.

In contrast to the equations that represent an analytic model, a simulation model is a computer program. Its instructions enable a computer to accept inputs and transform them into outputs just as it is done in a real network. Clearly, it is possible to have a hybrid model in which the analytic model's functional equations are embedded within the simulation program (software). In any case, both the analytical and simulation approaches to modeling require a detailed, precise understanding of what goes on in the data communications network. Having this understanding in itself is a major payoff of any modeling activity.

It should be clear at this point that the two modeling approaches are not competitive but are complementary. Analytical models generally make several simplifying assumptions to make their mathematics tractable. They provide results that can be evaluated easily and cheaply. They are generally applicable in the stage of strategic network planning when tradeoffs have to be made at a high level without attention to the details of each of the many candidate networks.

Simulation models, on the other hand, can reflect the working of a network to any desired level of detail. But the time and cost of development and program runs are directly proportional to the level of detail incorporated. Thus they can be expensive. Simulation is generally used when a candidate has been selected (using the analytical approach) and more precise answers are sought regarding the selected network.

Further comparison of the two approaches is best accomplished with reference to a specific data communications network. This will be done in the context of a specific design problem related to the response time and throughput performance of a centralized teleprocessing network with polling.

Master and slaves

Analytical and simulation modeling techniques apply to classical data network configurations—for example, a set of N terminals connected to a central computer (CPU) via a multidrop line (Fig. 1). The CPU and the terminals have a master-slave relationship. This means that the transmissions from the terminals are controlled by the CPU with some kind of polling technique.

Since there are many variations of polling, evaluating the performance of the data network for a polling discipline offered by a particular vendor is the task of the network designer. The designer uses modeling as a means to predict network performance and answer a variety of questions. For example, it is important to determine how network response time varies as a function of the terminal load and the number of terminals. And it is similarly critical to determine how the response time is affected by a specific polling approach, such as giving priority to outbound traffic (CPU to terminal) over inbound traffic.

There is a multiplicity of design tools—analytical, simulation, and hybrid—to help network designers answer these and other questions.

Consider the question of response time. In order to analytically predict the response time and the subsequent throughput of a polled network, the designer can resort to queueing models. One such general queueing model is shown in Figure 2. In this model, queues are served in cyclic order with specific "walk"

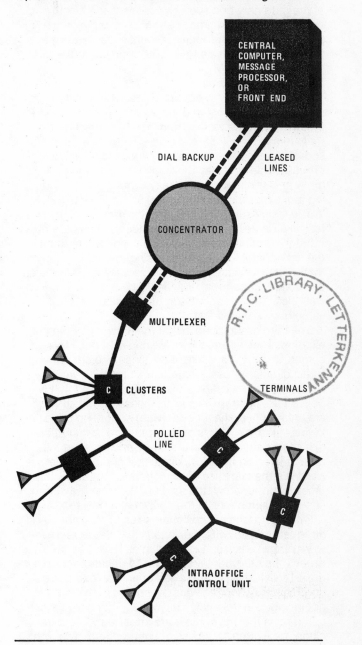

1. Standard form. *Contel's hybrid model for analyzing data communications networks is applicable to a variety of polled networks such as the centralized configuration.*

times. The walk time is the time to switch the network's service from one queue to another. It includes the overhead time attributable to polling messages, propagation delay, and modem synchronization.

Message servers

In the queueing model, messages arrive at a terminal according to a random process. This process may in turn be terminated according to a random process. This process may be terminal dependent, but, in any case, messages are queued up for transmission. The message server in this case is the transmission medium. It is made available to each queue periodically, as defined by the network's polling protocol.

125

The polling protocol also defines the amount of service received when the server arrives at a queue. This is known as chaining. Other important characteristics of the data network, such as poll-message length and modem turnaround time, are modeled in the network switchover time. Outbound response messages may be included as arrivals to an output queue at the CPU.

Problems, problems

The major difficulty in obtaining meaningful data from a queueing model is the complex relationship among the queues at the various terminals. An exact model for N terminals will therefore have to solve what is known among experts as an N-dimensional queueing process. This is, to say the least, a formidable task. A more or less exact solution may be had only after making four simplifying assumptions about the network.

The first assumption is that traffic arriving at the N terminals is described by independent, identically distributed, random variables. If this assumption about the network terminal statistics is not made, the network mathematics is intractable. It is also assumed that walk times are independent, identically distributed, random variables. This second assumption is made for the same reason as the first.

The third assumption is that the network's communications lines operate in a half-duplex mode. This, of course, is a great simplification, since one out of two traffic directions is eliminated and it must be valid for the network in question. Finally, it is assumed that a polled terminal transmits all its messages until its buffers are empty (exhaustive service) according to first-in-first-out rules. This is often a practical assumption.

If all four assumptions are made and apply to the data network in question, elegant, if complex, analysis can yield the statistics of the queue length and waiting times. Unfortunately, the network designer may often find the assumptions in the analytical model too severe.

Simply put, the approximations used may not be adequate to deal with the various features in real network operations, such as full-duplex lines. The approach the designer takes now is to decide to build a more realistic model and attempt an approximate solution. This may happen whenever some of the features not included in the analytical model—but which are common in real networks—are important. These include, for example, the use of buffered terminals with cluster controllers and correlated arrivals. When arrivals are correlated, terminal outputs are caused by inputs.

There are other practical network features that today's purely analytical models cannot handle. These include, for example, how often terminals are polled (for load balancing). There is also the problem of asymmetric arrival rates, although recent work—which has not been fully evaluated—seems to extend the analysis procedures to allow different arrival times at the terminals. Lastly, there are the problems of full-duplex traffic and the handling of data networks with different message priorities.

Of course, networks are analyzed and built even though the listed complications cannot be taken into account accurately. To do this, many approximate

methods have been developed and documented. They generally are attempts at solving specific variations for specific polled networks.

Fundamental limitations

These particular analytical models are valuable in providing initial insight and understanding for both the network analyzed and similar networks. But the user of the model must fully understand and appreciate its assumptions and limitations in order to avoid making wrong inferences. For example, in one data network there may be an approximation that assumes low line use and a low ratio of polling time to message transmission time. This approximation model will be inapplicable to the common situation where terminals are polled for short inquiry messages that are followed by brief responses.

There are even more fundamental limitations to models. It is no easy task, and is a major limitation of the analytical model, that a designer who wants to adapt a model to a slightly different situation (comparison of bisync to SDLC, for example) must fully understand the mathematical analysis and be capable of modifying

---

2. Lots of queues. *A polled system may be modeled as a queue that allows the network's response time and throughput to be predicted in advance.*

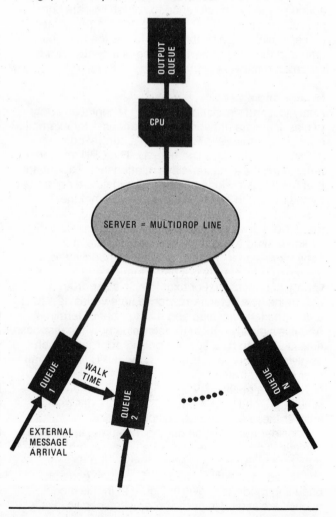

3. Typical output. *Contel's multipoint line simulation program provides overall response times by terminal and transaction type and furnishes device time delay.*

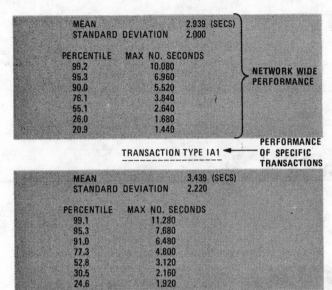

```
******TERMINAL RESPONSE TIME STATISTICS******
```

MEAN	2.939 (SECS)	
STANDARD DEVIATION	2.000	

PERCENTILE	MAX NO. SECONDS	
99.2	10.080	NETWORK WIDE
95.3	6.960	PERFORMANCE
90.0	5.520	
76.1	3.840	
55.1	2.640	
26.0	1.680	
20.9	1.440	

TRANSACTION TYPE IA1 ← PERFORMANCE OF SPECIFIC TRANSACTIONS

MEAN	3.439 (SECS)	
STANDARD DEVIATION	2.220	

PERCENTILE	MAX NO. SECONDS
99.1	11.280
95.3	7.680
91.0	6.480
77.3	4.800
52.8	3.120
30.5	2.160
24.6	1.920

TRANSACTION TYPE IA2

MEAN	1.674 (SECS)	
STANDARD DEVIATION	0.887	

PERCENTILE	MAX NO. SECONDS
100.00	4.800
97.0	3.600
90.9	3.120
78.8	2.160
57.6	1.440
36.4	1.200
21.2	0.960

CLUS	TERMINAL/TYPE	MEAN	STANDARD DEVIATION	
C1	1 - T1	3.434	2.824	
	2 - T2	2.597	1.855	
	3 - T3	2.857	1.918	
	4 - T4	2.954	2.767	
	5 - T4	2.798	1.854	← SPECIFIC
	6 - T5	1.887	1.803	TERMINAL
	7 - T5	1.697	1.257	RESULTS
C2	8 - T5	2.709	1.181	
	9 - T5	2.989	1.215	
	10 - T5	2.847	1.189	
	11 - T6	3.179	2.017	
	12 - T7	4.442	1.982	
	13 - T7	3.800	1.799	
	14 - T7	3.940	2.677	

it to the new situation. No casual set of changes will do the job here.

It is evident that an analytical model requires a sophisticated user who is competent in mathematics. Moreover, the model must be employed judiciously. When adapted by this discriminating user, the analytic model can provide preliminary insights. But it can seldom yield numerical values of sufficient accuracy for a network's operational design.

To obtain a more realistic model capable of providing accurate numerical answers, simulation is the method of choice. The attempt to produce a better analytic model leads to mathematical complications. In fact, a level of complexity is soon reached at which a simple simulation model begins to seem the easiest way of finding, for example, permissible line loadings— a common need in preliminary network design.

A possible solution

The multipoint line simulation system (MLSS) is an example of a simulation tool for the design of multipoint lines. It is offered separately or embedded as one of the modules in Contel's proprietary network analysis package known as Mind.

With MLSS, the user enters a model of his network traffic load and obtains an analysis of waiting times and response times in various parts of the network. The model may be tailored to the user's individual network by entering specific parameter values.

Often these parameters are unavailable or unknown for specific networks. The simulation tool is set up to take care of this problem. The user simply relies on the set of parameter defaults provided to him by the simulation. This set of defaults not only simulates a line operating under the different line protocols that are the most commonly used, but is also representative of many other available protocols.

Thus a simulation tool is by no means limited to bisync or SDLC-like protocols. Additionally, operation of most terminal-oriented networks under full-duplex protocols such as SDLC can be closely—although not exactly—modeled. This can result in a final design network with lower costs and higher throughput than would otherwise be possible.

Multiple modeling

The focus of MLSS is on modeling the multipoint line. To do this, many variables are modeled directly. Polling (the determination of whether or not a terminal is ready to send input), selection (the determination of whether or not a terminal is ready to receive output), positive and negative acknowledgments, error occurence and recovery, and hardware delays in all devices (terminal, modem, terminal controller, concentrator) are examples of these variables. The output of the simulation tool provides response times on either an overall basis or by terminal type and by transaction type. It also indicates the delay at the various devices. A typical printout is shown in Figure 3.

More is not better

Experience with the simulation of complex data communications networks has led simulation vendors to the conclusion that more harm than good is usually done by attempting to model and simulate the entire network in detail. MLSS, therefore, does not attempt a pure simulation. It uses a hybrid approach in which a simplified analytical model of the operation of the communications processor and the central processor is embedded in the simulation. This allows the designer, for example, to examine the response time issue in the context of a complete network, without so many complications that no sense can be made of the results. ∎

Network efficiency takes more than speed alone

Phillip G. Elam, Cincom Systems Inc., Cincinnati, Ohio

Gauging data retrieval performance shows whether you're getting the information you want, when you want it; it also aids in making prudent changes to improve network efficiency

Network retrieval efficiency should be the goal of every data communications manager, and one of the best ways to ensure a smooth-running, cost-effective network is by carefully examining database response and such related areas as formats and file completeness.

There are many factors that can be used to gauge database response, but from the user's standpoint, these are the key considerations:
- Recall. Ability of the user to access data needed to satisfy some information request.
- Precision. The network's ability to deliver data relevant to a particular user need.
- Response time. The time from when the user presses "enter" key to when a response image appears on CRT screen or printer.
- Form of output. Format in which information is displayed on CRT screen or printer.
- Information coverage. Containment of all files in database relevant to a particular user's information needs.
- User effort. Activity that must be initiated by a user to satisfy an information request.

All on-line system (the database, attached remote terminals, and network) users have at least one fundamental requirement: retrieval of data that will contribute to the satisfaction of an information request.

In most situations, the user wants and expects the network to return relevant data. And evaluation of the network should be based on how well it does that. It is possible to quantitatively express the degree of success achieved in retrieving relevant data by determining its recall ratio. The formula for determining recall ratio:

$$\frac{\text{Relevant items retrieved}}{\text{Relevant items in database}} \times 100 = \text{Recall ratio}$$

For instance, say that for a particular request there are only 10 relevant data items in the database. A user initiates a search strategy using normal system procedures and retrieves seven of the 10 data items, for a 70 percent (seven divided by 10) recall ratio.

Although recall ratio is an important measure of search success, it is meaningless by itself. Users can always get 100 percent recall for any search strategy in any network if they are prepared to search broadly enough—retrieving a sufficiently large portion of total database files. But an information retrieval system is essentially a filter and should pass only what is needed. Therefore, the recall ratio expresses the ability of the network to let through only that data which users have requested. However, a companion measurement is needed that also expresses the ability of the network to hold back any unwanted information. One such

1. Precision. *The degree to which databases are capable of responding to terminal operator requests by separating relevant data from irrelevant data is called precision.*

measure, and there are many, is the "precision ratio," which is expressed:

$$\frac{\text{Relevant items retrieved}}{\text{Total items retrieved}} \times 100 = \text{Precision ratio}$$

Employing the hypothetical search mentioned above, further investigation might reveal that the system retrieves a total of 50 data items—seven of which are relevant and 43 that are not, for a precision ratio of 14 percent. In other words, the search has operated at 70 percent recall and at 14 percent precision. Together, these two measures indicate a network's filtering capacity as well as its effectiveness. But neither one can stand alone.

A precision ratio measures the efficiency of the network to achieve a particular recall ratio. Clearly, achievement of 70 percent recall with a precision of seven relevant items out of 14 (50 percent) indicates greater efficiency than the attainment of the same recall with a precision of seven relevant items out of 50 (14 percent). In a sense, the precision ratio may be regarded as a measure of the effort required by users to achieve a particular recall ratio. User efforts are expended—after the search results have been delivered by the network—by separating the relevant items that were retrieved from the irrelevant items.

Separating items

Obviously, it takes longer to separate seven relevant items from 93 irrelevant ones (7 percent precision) than it does to separate seven relevant items from 43 irrelevant ones (14 percent precision). And the latter

requires more effort than separating seven relevant items from an equal number of irrelevant ones (50 percent precision). Viewed this way, the precision ratio is clearly a valid measure of search efficiency.

Recall and precision most often tend to vary inversely in searching. That is, whatever is done to improve recall (by broadening a search) generally reduces precision; and whatever is done to improve precision (by searching more stringently) tends to reduce recall. In fact, in conducting one search or a group of searches at varying strategy levels—from very broad to very precise—it is possible to derive a series of performance points that allows plotting a performance curve.

Different users will, of course, have different recall and precision requirements. For instance, a user looking for a specific customer order will receive high precision. Another user, however, looking for all customer orders on which a certain inventory item is specified, will have a low precision, but high recall requirement.

Keep response time in perspective

Response time is obviously important to information retrieval system users. However, it must be kept in perspective. In fact, the impetus for boosting response time in a company is more likely to come from vendors—who want to sell new equipment—than it is from the people who actually use the terminals. Response times of 3, 5, and even 7 seconds may be slow in comparison with those of an airline's flight reservation system, for example, but they may be perfectly acceptable to users in your company.

Certainly, most users are working against deadlines beyond which receipt of an on-line response will be of little or no value. Nevertheless, response time is less important than either recall or precision. If response time were the major user requirement, users would therefore be happy with immediate access to 100 percent irrelevant information, which, of course, is absurd.

Only recently have organizations become sophisticated enough to realize that adding faster hardware is only an expensive, temporary solution to speeding up unacceptable response times. However, response-time problems often can be alleviated by reexamining the purpose of the search and evaluating its validity in the user's current operating environment.

The performance criteria of coverage and form of output are much the same for on-line and off-line systems. Because many on-line systems are likely to be used frequently for low-recall, high-precision searches, coverage comprehensiveness may not be a very important requirement for many on-line databases. Indeed, there may be a strong case for making available only on-line selective databases of high-value and reasonably current data. If a selected portion of a huge database is available on line, it should still be possible for the searcher with a high-recall requirement to develop a subset strategy at the terminal and then to request that this strategy be used in an off-line search of the entire database.

For some users, however, information coverage can be considered the most critical performance benchmark. Coverage comprehensiveness in a specific application area is only of real concern to users who need genuinely high recall. In a sense, then, coverage is an extension of recall beyond local application files to the entire database.

How much did you get?
The user who needs high recall may legitimately say, "You estimate that you have given me 95 percent of the relevant data in the database, but does this represent 95 percent, 50 percent, or only 10 percent of the data on the subject?" These are legitimate questions because they deal with the extent of database coverage. Users with low recall requirements, on the other hand, are not too concerned about coverage. They simply want a representative sampling and do not really care whether it contains all relevant data items or only 17 percent of them.

These performance criteria are not unique to interactive network environments. In fact, they are pertinent to all retrieval-system types. Consequently, it would be inappropriate to ignore batch systems—especially because so many interactive networks evolved from the batch mode.

The user judges the system primarily on whether the retrieved items can contribute to the satisfaction of an information need. However, high recall is likely to be less important to many on-line terminal operations than to the majority of off-line, batch-processing operations. Because of comparatively long turnaround delays, most batch-system users tend to prefer comprehensive searches.

Interactive system users whose data needs require the identification of specific files or items will generally want on-line facilities. However, the users should obviously allow for the possibility that they might want to conduct highly complex searches that would be diffi-

2. Response time. How fast on-line systems respond to data requests is important in retrieval applications. However, its significance must be kept in perspective.

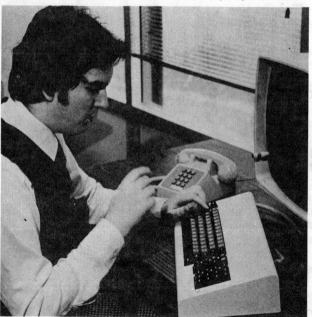

cult, if not impossible, to execute by a conventional manual search in an assortment of printed publications or reports.

Precision tolerance
In addition, a network's response format is important because it has an impact on the precision tolerance level—which is how precisely a network must retrieve data for a user. Users are likely to tolerate lower precision in delivered information if it appears in a format that facilitates rapid scanning and allows irrelevant data to be discarded easily.

The form in which data is presented at the on-line terminal is likely to be important to the user, because of the need not only to rapidly assess the relevance of retrieved items but to modify each strategy if it appears to be missing the mark. The more information presented to users, the more accurately they will judge the potential relevance of items presented. Fortunately, some on-line systems provide more than one output option. For example, they might provide the user with the ability to specify what portions of a record are to be displayed or printed and in what order. Some give various sorting options, others allow ranking of output, and a few include a highlighting feature. These forms provide the user with more latitude in using the retrieved data. Thus it should be easier for users to satisfy their information needs.

It is unrealistic to assume that on-line systems will never be used for searches where high recall is required—or that they are inappropriate for this type of requirement. On-line systems are likely to be used for many searches in which high recall is not needed as much as fast response. These are situations in which the batch system would probably not be used. For those on-line searches where the user is not looking for all relevant data items, absolute recall is practically meaningless. However, it is unrealistic to assume that on-line systems will never be used for searches in which high recall is required—or that they are inappropriate for this use.

Users will stop searching when they have found enough relevant data items to satisfy their needs. For these occasions, search efficiency may be measured in terms of the amount of effort required to find relevant items. Therefore, search effort is likely to rate equally with search time.

An absolute recall substitute
A possible substitute for absolute recall in this type of situation is "relative recall"—a measure of the number of relevant items retrieved as a proportion of the number the user would like to have. Thus, if a user wants five relevant items, but retrieves two, the relative recall is 40 percent. This measure, however, is artificial because it is unlikely that the typical user will demand a particular number of relative items from a network.

Remember, the precision ratio of a search is one measure of the effort required to obtain a particular recall ratio. In a batch processing system, it is a measure of the effort expended by users once their search results are delivered to separate relevant from irrelevant items. Here, precision ratio is a less useful function and can actually detract from search value. A performance measure should penalize a system for retrieving irrelevant data, and this is exactly what the precision ratio is designed to do.

The on-line system, on the other hand, allows the user to initiate various search strategies and evaluate the data items that are retrieved. In this situation, at certain points, irrelevant data items may be almost as useful as relevant ones. They may indicate defective strategies, and refinement then can be implemented. Searching strategy mistakes are less costly in the on-line system because they can be rapidly and easily rectified. It is for this reason that precision ratio may be a less useful measure in on-line, as opposed to batch system, performance evaluation.

Unit cost as a performance measure

Usually, as users try various approaches on the terminal, their search strategies will improve in that more relevant items will be retrieved—increasing precision. The fewer mistakes made, or the quicker mistakes can be corrected, the faster the user can discover relevant data and complete a search. In fact, on-line-search efficiency is probably best measured in terms of the time it takes to find 'X' relevant items.

A useful measure of search efficiency, for use in conjunction with recall in certain areas, is the unit cost (in time) per relevant data item retrieved. Suppose searcher A spends 16 minutes at the terminal and finds eight relevant data items. The unit cost is 6 minutes divided by 8 minutes, or .75 minutes per relevant data item. Searcher B, on the other hand, retrieves four relevant data items after spending 10 minutes at the terminal. Unit cost for this search is 10.4 minutes, or 2.5 minutes per relevant data item. A side-by-side comparison could be set up like this:

Searcher	A	B
Search time	6 minutes	10 minutes
Items retrieved	8 items	4 items
Efficiency factor (Unit cost in time)	.75 minutes	2.5 minutes

Clearly, searcher A is more efficient than searcher B. This does not necessarily imply that searcher A is more satisfied with the results than searcher B. Nor does the result indicate why searcher A was more efficient than searcher B, although it is probably for one of the following reasons:

■ Searcher A is better or more experienced than searcher B.
■ The network was better able to cope with A's search than with B's.
■ B's search strategy was more difficult.
■ Searcher A was luckier than searcher B in finding a good strategy right away.

The precision ratio, in an off-line system, is the only reasonable measure of search efficiency in terms of cost to searcher for obtaining a particular recall level. It is really a measure of how long it takes after the search is completed to separate the relevant from the irrelevant. But generally speaking, there is no direct measure of search time and search efficiency in an off-line situation.

Direct-search-time measure

In the on-line search, however, it is possible to measure search time directly and relate this time to a particular achievement level—namely, the number of relevant data items discovered.

Unit cost, like precision ratio, is a measure of the effort required to achieve a particular recall level. But other aspects of user effort will affect on-line-system performance, and these must be considered, too. For example, how much effort is required to learn to use the system? This is likely to depend on whether it is a converted non-communications batch system designed primarily for use by information specialists. The more the network is dependent on a carefully controlled vocabulary and complex sets of protocols, the more difficult it will be to learn how to use it effectively. A natural language syntax is likely to be easier to learn because it is not dependent upon protocols, and the language required in search strategies may be closer to the language of the practitioner than a controlled vocabulary would be. Moreover, a network that can be queried in English-sentence form requires less effort from the user than one that can be queried only by precise Boolean search logic.

The way users are trained to operate the system is also important. Many so-called user manuals are poorly written, lack adequate illustrations and examples, and frighten potential users by their sheer bulk. Although

3. Format. *How precisely an on-line system must retrieve data pertaining to a specific user request is affected by the method of displaying that information on a CRT.*

a complete user manual is necessary for reference purposes, once users have tried the terminal a few times, they will quickly learn by experience. A hands-on technique conducted by an experienced searcher is likely to be more effective than a printed manual. However, the search programs themselves should be instructive and guide the user in the construction of appropriate strategies.

Search effort vs. user tolerance

Besides the effort involved in learning the system, users should be concerned with the effort level needed to conduct a search. If the effort exceeds the prospective seacher's tolerance, the system will probably be abandoned and an alternative information source sought. Well-designed on-line systems minimize user effort by compensating for common errors. For instance, a network could contain a list of frequently misspelled words and automatically substitute the correct word when necessary. Or when ordering a commodity of some kind, say, butter, the system could automatically check to make sure the right unit of measure (in this case pound) is noted, and corrected if wrong. Also, the network should require a minimum amount of keying and provide assistance and guidance—such as automatic queuing—in the creation of search strategies suitable to the needs of the user.

Response time in a communications system takes a somewhat different connotation than it does in other data processing systems. Typically, there may be a delay of several days between the time a user submits a request to a batch system and the time a satisfactory response is received. The only comparable delay associated with an on-line system is that which might occur while a potential user waits for a particular database to become available. Few, if any, on-line databases are available constantly. Some are available for several hours a day, while others may only be on line for a designated period each week. Thus a user may have to wait several days to consult certain databases, although most organizations make the database available if an emergency arises.

When the on-line system is available, there is usually no significant delay for the user. However, the time it takes for the system to respond to a user request should also be considered. Typically, this is in the range of from 2 to 10 seconds, but can be increased considerably under such conditions as serial operations and system overload.

Most information specialists say that response time depends on a number of factors: computer speed, amount of core storage available, operating system, number and type of users on line at a particular time, local vs. remote terminals, terminal type, line speed, job mix, operating system, priority given to the user, and on-line program efficiency. If response time must exceed 3–4 seconds, in the case of a complex command, the user should be informed in advance or at the terminal itself.

As already mentioned in terms of unit cost per relevant data item retrieved, time spent at a terminal while conducting a search is another major time factor. The

4. Ease of instruction. *It should be possible to teach simple searches in words that are readily familiar to the user—as opposed to difficult-to-learn machine languages.*

only additional time factor of possible concern is the elapsed time between conducting an exploratory on-line search, requesting an off-line printout of the search results, and obtaining these off-line results from the network—probably through the mail if a printer is not locally available.

Consider novelty ratio

One final performance measure worth mentioning is the "novelty ratio," which measures the proportion of retrieved relevant data items that are new to the user (brought to his or her attention for the first time by the search). For example, if a search retrieves 15 relevant items—10 new ones and five familiar ones—the novelty ratio of the search is 66 percent. When applied to retrospective search systems, the novelty ratio measures a user characteristic, rather than an on-line-system characteristic. That is, the novelty ratio is a measure of the user's previous knowledge of the search topic. Here's the equation:

$$\frac{\text{Number of new items}}{\text{Number of items retrieved}} \times 100 = \text{Novelty ratio}$$

However, the novelty ratio is a useful measure of the user's awareness of what's contained in the database or information system. Presumably this is useful if the system is expected to bring relevant items to a user's attention before they are discovered at another source. In addition, it is a way of measuring how well user's know what is contained in the database or determining the lag time between data creation and its ultimate appearance in the database.

In interactive, on-line environments where many users may be accessing the same data frequently, and perhaps simultaneously, it is important that data be entered and updated in the database as rapidly as possible in order to permit management to make timely and correct decisions. ∎

Tuning databases enriches network performance

Stephen D. Blazier, Bell Telephone Laboratories, Piscataway, N.J.

Reorganizing data files that reflect actual use cuts time spent looking for and transferring data, improves response time, and reduces user costs.

When a computer wastes time just finding and transferring data, response time decreases, users become irate, and company efficiency goes down. But a properly organized, or well-tuned, database reduces total computer time and increases programmers' productivity, saving millions of dollars. A database is considered tuned when it minimizes the amount of time the computer spends looking for and transferring data. It does this by rearranging data files to reflect actual use.

Such fine tuning is even more important for distributed database transactions. Retrieving information from distributed databases involves more overhead and cost and a greater probability of response-time problems than centralized databases because the data is distributed among several computers. Therefore, the machines must interact to find and access information. This makes it essential to perform each aspect of data retrieval as efficiently as possible, minimizing the number of transfers.

Further, as data needs have become more complex, so has the need for a well-tuned database. Tuning a database depends on a combination of disciplines—particularly, data communications and database management—and the cooperation of systems analysts, users, and data communications personnel. To a high degree, database management focuses on reorganizing data files to reduce the number of information transfers required to retrieve a piece of data.

Until recently, there were few data-management tools. Data was commonly organized into contiguous groups called records. The set of all records was called a data file. Relationships were maintained by storing the data in specific sections, or fields, within the record. For example, a field might contain the name of an employee or a department number.

The records often were ordered according to the contents of one of the fields. This ordering was usually maintained physically, and only one such ordering was allowed. Once a record was obtained, the particular fields desired could be found at specific positions within the record. When modifying one field, care had to be exercised that other fields were not accidentally destroyed. Copies were frequently made of the records to reduce the possibility of accidental loss of data. When an accident did occur, special-purpose programs were written to try to recover the data. Often, only one program at a time was allowed to update the records. Over all, the process was tedious and expensive.

As more applications for data management were developed, programs for database management were developed as well. These tools allow the application programmer to view data differently from the way it is physically stored. For example, database-management programs might allow the application programmer to treat a group of fields as being contiguous while in reality the fields are stored on completely separate devices. This makes it much easier for the programmer to request data that matches complicated relations. It also allows the programmer to ignore data that is not of interest and protects data from careless mistakes. The programs also provide tools that recover data lost because of a hardware failure. In general, data man-

Structuring databases

A hierarchical file has a multilevel tree structure containing relationships between items at different levels. One item at a given level may be related to one or more at the next lower level. An example of a hierarchical structure is a corporation's organization chart. The president is at the top of the hierarchy. Immediately below the president are the vice presidents. Other more junior executives may appear in the hierarchy. At any given level in the hierarchy all of the executives have equal rank. Every executive but the president reports to one other executive at the immediately higher level.

In a network structure, any item can be linked to others of a given type. There is no concept of level in a network structure, but relationships can be represented by linking one item to any number of descendants or to immediate ancestors. In contrast, the maximum number of immediate ancestors allowed in a hierarchical structure is one. In a network structure two relations could be maintained about goods sold to customers: For billing information, a record could be kept of what products are bought by each customer. And for warranty information, a separate record could show which customers purchased a specific product.

In a relational database, data is structured in two-dimensional tables with linkages, called joins, between related rows or columns of the tables.

An example of a relational structure might be defined for an employee's record. The record could contain name, social-security number, identification number, department number, supervisor's name, salary, and years of service. The relational structure would allow easy extraction of all records meeting a complex set of criteria. For example, a single command would find all employees in specific departments with under 10 years of service who earn more than a certain salary. Relational data structures provide great flexibility, but most implementations are too slow. With improvements in speed they will become more widespread.

agement has become much easier since the development of data-management programs, and application programmers have become more productive.

Database-management programs come in various forms. They are usually categorized by the format in which the data is presented to the application programmer. The three major forms of database storage are hierarchical, network, and relational (see "Structuring databases").

A hierarchical structure relates one item to many others at levels beneath it. Many levels can exist. A network structure relates one item to many items of a given type. Many relations can be defined that allow bidirectional information to be represented. There are no levels as there are in hierarchical structures. A relational structure allows many items to be related to

many others at the same time. The existence of a record in the database defines relations among all of the fields within the record.

Of the three, the hierarchical database-management program is most widely used. Like the others, it stores data differently from the way application programmers view it. Application programmers are provided with a more convenient representation. But this poses a problem: Because application programmers need not be aware of the physical structure, the database may not be used efficiently. And to require them to know how requests to the database manager are physically carried out would remove the database-management program's advantage. So to solve the problem, database designers and systems analysts have begun to match the physical structure with the format and processing requirements of the application programmers. This physical structure is tuned, then, to optimize network data-retrieval efficiency.

Finding the data

The following example of a large and diverse database application will help to show how a hierarchical program is tuned. The Trunks Integrated Records Keeping System (TIRKS) was developed by Bell Telephone Laboratories for use by the operating telephone companies. TIRKS helps the operating companies to meet circuit-requirement forecasts, track circuit orders, design the circuits, select and assign circuit components, maintain inventory records, and distribute work orders.

TIRKS needs an enormous amount of data to keep track of these circuits. At a typical operating company, TIRKS is responsible for more than 25 billion pieces or "bits" of data covering equipment and circuits, stored in more than 100 databases. TIRKS users retrieve information from the databases 100,000 times a day.

As with any large multifunctional database, users must be able to easily retrieve, add to, change, and manipulate the data. They also want the computer to respond as quickly as possible. Yet a good part of computer response time is devoted simply to finding some particular piece of data.

The computer spends much more time searching the databases and storing data than it does moving, comparing, and otherwise manipulating the data logically within its working memory. The reason for this is that the manipulated data is handled by the relatively fast main memory. But databases are usually stored more cheaply on electromechanically driven, relatively slow, disk memories (see "The disk pack"), then brought to primary storage for manipulation, a few segments at a time.

Even a small change in the way searching is done can significantly decrease a user's access time. For example, a database manager might take three-hundredths of a second to find and transfer two numbers to the main memory—a long time compared to the millionth of a second necessary to add the numbers together. Although most operations involve much more than just one simple arithmetic manipulation, similar relationships exist. A database application like TIRKS spends, on the average, about five times longer looking

The disk pack

Electromechanically driven magnetic disk packs are one of the most common means of storing data outside the computer's own primary memory. They function as direct-access storage devices, meaning that a piece of data stored in the middle of a disk can be fetched directly instead of having to be sought sequentially—a time saving feature. The organization of data in a disk memory affects the information-retrieval efficiency of a computer.

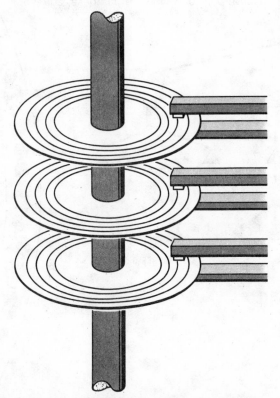

A disk pack consists of about 15 platters arranged in a stack with a gap between each platter, as in the drawing. A single platter is analogous in operation to a phonograph record, although the data pickup is magnetic rather than via direct contact. Data is stored on both surfaces of a platter in concentric circles called tracks. There are about 500 tracks on each platter surface (about 15 inches in diameter). In the TIRKS system, a track will often hold about four data-storage blocks. A data block contains about 40,000 bits. Data stored sequentially on each track is addressed by specifying the disk pack, track, and position on the track. Disk arms, each one analogous to the tone arm of a phonograph, read and write data onto the platters. Separate disk arms exist for each surface of each platter in a disk pack, and the arms move in concert.

When data must be read from a disk, the disk arms are first simultaneously moved in or out to the correct track and positioned near the surface of each platter. Then the arm over the desired surface is connected electronically.

The delay incurred in getting to a peice of data depends, primarily, on how long it takes to position the disk arm over the desired track, and, secondarily, on how long it takes the data on the track to rotate into position beneath the disk arm. These delays are typically 0.025 and 0.008 second, respectively.

Delays can be minimized if information is organized so that data required for a new opeation is stored on a track somewhere above or below the data just accessed—that is, in the same vertical "cylinder." In that case, no further disk-arm movement is required to get to the data; the electronic connection is simply switched to the arm on the next track to be read. If the needed data is on the same track and immediately after the last-used data, even less delay is incurred.

for and transferring data than it spends manipulating data—assuming the databases are well "tuned." It can spend as much as 15 times longer looking for data if the databases have not been tuned.

Is this difference actually significant when measured by company time and money? In one case, tuning changes made to all of one operating company's databases reduced the average processing time by 67 percent. These changes also saved the operating company well over a million dollars that could otherwise have gone toward new hardware to improve performance. In another case, tuning the databases reduced the program running time from 20 minutes to 15 seconds.

One program, run frequently at each TIRKS installation, used to require approximately 50 transfers from one database each time a new item was added to a list. A reorganization of the database reduced the number of transfers to two. As a result, the program running time was cut from several hours to just minutes.

Such reductions hit at the heart of database tuning: namely, to cut the amount of time that is spent transferring data. To better understand how such databases are tuned, it is also necessary to understand how a database is structured and how a user actually retrieves data from it.

Accessing the database

A database consists of a number of information segments stored in a memory such as a disk. Each information segment resides alongside other segments in one of many "blocks" of storage space on the disk.

Information segments in a block can be related in one of two ways: either they are adjacent physically or one segment contains a "pointer" to another non-adjacent but related segment. (A pointer is a piece of data that specifies the location of a segment.) When the computer needs a particular segment of information, it uses adjacency and pointers to locate the segment, instead of having to search each of the many blocks of a database from beginning to end.

Although adjacent segments guarantee fast access from one segment to the next, it is sometimes impossible to maintain all segment relationships by adjacency, especially in a complex database setup like TIRKS.

Storing databases

Data segments are physically stored sequentially on the various concentric tracks of a disk. But a database whose logical structure (the way the user views the data) is hierarchical takes different information segments and relates them logically in a tree structure, rather than a linear structure.

A typical hierarchical structure is shown by the "polygon trees" in the drawings. Each shape represents an information segment, with the relationships between segments shown by connecting lines.

information from the polygon trees can be stored sequentially in a data-storage block. Information segments are entered one by one, reading down each subtree hierarchy from left to right. Although the physical structure of the polygons is now that of a one-dimensional array, software "pointers" in the segments maintain the tree structure. The pointer is a piece of information that identifies where a related segment can be found in the database. It does so by specifying a relative position within the database, corresponding to

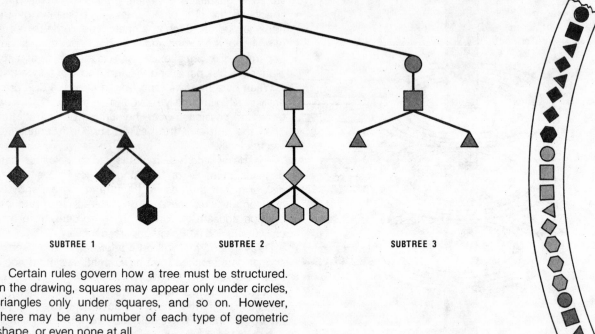

SUBTREE 1   SUBTREE 2   SUBTREE 3

Certain rules govern how a tree must be structured. In the drawing, squares may appear only under circles, triangles only under squares, and so on. However, there may be any number of each type of geometric shape, or even none at all.

A hierarchy of shapes can be created to represent information about various pieces of telephone equipment and their functions in several locations. A circle represents information about each location. One or more squares under each circle can identify pieces of equipment at each location. Finally, a piece of equipment may perform more than one function, and triangles represent those functions. Polygon subtree 1 shows this structure for one such location. Subtrees 2 and 3 may contain analogous information about other locations, or different kinds of information altogether.

The ribbon of shapes to the right shows one way this

an "address" on the disk that contains the database.

If this structure proves inefficient, the database can be "tuned" by reordering the information segments and establishing new pointers. For instance, if the equipment-function information in this example is rarely accessed, it may be more efficient to move all such information—that is, all triangles, regardless of which subtree they come from—to a separate storage area or track in the database.

After all, only one segment can follow another. So, if a segment is related logically to two or more others, it can follow at most one of these and must use pointers to refer to the others (see "Storing databases").

To locate a particular segment, the computer determines which block of storage space most probably contains the segment, then transfers (in reality, copies) that block to primary storage. If the requested segment is not in the block, a pointer will specify which new block, if any, the computer should transfer into primary storage and search. If the desired segment is not in this new block, another pointer will specify which block

should be searched next. After transferring and examining each block in turn, the computer will either find the information segment or report that such information does not exist. A well-tuned database aids in the transfer of a minimum number of blocks to access a piece of information.

It is frequently necessary for a database manager to access several related segments of information at one time. If all the segments are located in the same block, a minimal number of transfers will be needed. Unfortunately, block size is limited by constraints of the storage medium used, such as the type of disk.

Thus, it is rarely possible to put the many segments needed for an operation into just one block.

The best alternative, then, is to structure the databases so that the segments used together most frequently are contained in the smallest number of blocks. Although some requests for information that occur infrequently may require several blocks to be transferred and searched, those requests that occur most often should require only a small number of transfers.

Organizing a database in this way is no simple matter. Databases may consist of billions of pieces of information. In tuning databases, it is impractical to examine all paths that connect segments of information and all operations performed on these segments. Instead, systems analysts use computer programs and models—the tools of database tuning—to identify databases associated with any network performance problem. These databases may be selected for tuning if they meet two criteria: they are poorly organized and the data blocks within them are frequently accessed.

Selecting databases to tune

Several monitoring techniques exist to help users and analysts recognize poorly organized databases and spot the possible problems. For example, one tuning program determines the average number of blocks that must be transferred to find all the segments in a database. This program must take into account records split across more than one block and blocks shared by more than one segment that must therefore be counted twice. This determination can be done for the database as a whole or for any portion of it.

Another way of recognizing a poorly organized database is to examine how much free space is in each block. Too much free space indicates wasted memory, but too little makes it costly to modify the database. Databases should ideally be organized so that any changes made to them through normal use preserve their efficiency. This is most easily done by leaving free space in each block for new segments to be added.

Other programs identify frequently accessed blocks by monitoring the many thousands of database transactions each day. Still others identify the databases and blocks that are changed most often and are therefore most likely to become disorganized.

Further database-tuning tools take the form of models of hardware and software behavior that should be created as database applications are developed. These models provide guidelines to allow database designers and systems analysts to identify which databases to tune first (based on need for tuning and resulting cost benefit), to suggest the best way to restructure the databases, and to predict the effects of their proposed changes. These models incorporate knowledge about how the databases are used, the ways that use may change, how use affects response time, and what computer resources are required to access them.

Tuning databases

One method of altering physical structure to improve database performance is shown in Figure 1. Before tuning, the large gray segment in block 1 occupies so

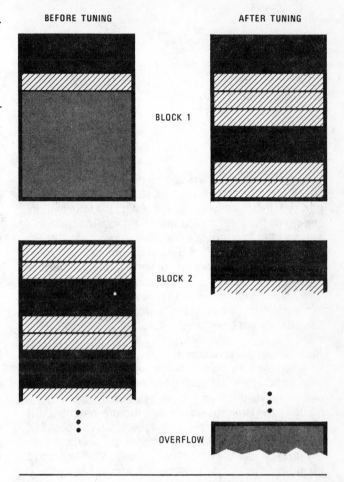

1. Restructuring a database. *If the frequently accessed database segments are condensed into the fewest blocks, access time will be improved.*

BEFORE TUNING   AFTER TUNING

BLOCK 1

BLOCK 2

OVERFLOW

much space that the next two striped segments, both containing information related to that stored in the blue segment above them, cannot fit into the same block. Yet the gray segment is used much less frequently than the blue and striped segments in the first two blocks.

Clearly there is little advantage to having the gray segment in the first block, where it only serves to increase the number of transfers and hence the access time to those frequently needed segments in other blocks following it. Yet such configurations are common wherever a database contains large, infrequently used segments.

Systems analysts tuning this database would most likely move the gray segment to a separate block at the end of the database. Then, with frequently used segments condensed together into fewer blocks, access time would be measurably improved. This is a complex procedure, since databases may contain hundreds of thousands of blocks.

Systems analysts employ models to predict the amount of disk-storage space to set aside when they restructure a database, and how to distribute this space. This includes both the space for existing segments and some empty space between segments to accommodate growth.

Once systems analysts agree on a solution, databases that are performing inefficiently must be reorganized. Programmers first extract all the information segments from each database, then replace them in a more effective sequence within the blocks, establishing new pointers throughout the database.

The systems analysts continue to monitor database system performance after the databases are tuned to make sure that the desired improvements indeed result. In the majority of cases, the performance problem is solved with just one tuning effort.

Monitoring performance

The database-management system must not only be monitored after a database has been tuned, but periodically while it is being used. If updates are being made to the database, then its structure is continually changing. Periodic monitoring for excessive accesses and long transfer times is necessary to discover when a database has become disorganized to the point that tuning is called for. In most organizations, the individuals responsible for monitoring are not users of the database management system. Since they do not experience the performance of the system first-hand, they are often unaware of performance problems.

Detailed monitoring consumes both computer resources and personnel time. This prompted systems analysts concerned with the TIRKS application to develop a general-purpose tool that automatically performs continuous database monitoring. The tool indicates when response time has deteriorated to a level that warrants further investigation, and then alerts the personnel responsible for monitoring.

Although the monitor operates continuously while the database-management program is active, it consumes very few computer resources because it monitors only a few crucial activities. And systems analysts need not waste their time performing detailed monitoring. Instead they are alerted to a problem as soon as the users experience it. Extensions to this software tool that are being developed will prompt it to initiate more detailed analyses automatically. Similar tools can be developed for the various commercially available database-management systems.

The entire process of database tuning, then, consists of understanding certain complex factors and their relationships, and then restructuring the databases according to their actual use. This tuning process is time-consuming and requires significant use of computer resources. But the results are well worth the effort. Improved database structures have already reduced TIRKS computer and user costs, while significantly increasing user productivity and satisfaction.

Databases are a major reason for the existence of networks today. Database-management systems are making it much easier to develop applications that control large and complex sets of data. They present a view of the data that makes it easier for application programmers to be productive. Finally, monitoring network performance and analyzing database behavior contribute to rapid, efficient information retrieval while preserving application-programming productivity. ∎

The TP monitor: know what's important to ask before buying

David Brownlee, Altergo Software Inc., Wellesley, Mass.

Before the decision to go on line is made, system designers must understand the TP monitor function and be sure it supports network objectives

On-line networks, whether local or widely dispersed, cannot function efficiently without a teleprocessing (TP) monitor for controlling the mainframe computer. But before committing yourself to a particular monitor, there are a number of questions that need to be asked and answered.

A TP monitor checklist of 22 questions, along with explanations of their importance (in italic), starts on the facing page. The questions are formulated to evaluate points that pertain to most users' operational environments as well as current and projected network requirements. Providing precise answers to these questions will greatly help to avoid false starts and narrow the field of equipment and software possibilities and, hence, suppliers. In addition to providing a clear picture of user needs, the answers to these questions will help save a lot of time by reducing the number of products that have to be examined—from dozens to no more than three.

It is helpful to assign varying values to each question according to its importance to your installation and objectives. For instance, each question could be assigned a value on a scale from 10 to 50—with the answers being given a score up to the highest value assigned to the question. Each score would depend on a vendor's answer to the question.

Although that is a simple method, it effectively narrows the field of choice. Moreover, if the questions and weighting factors are sent to prospective suppliers, many of them will be able to eliminate themselves before wasting their own, as well as your, time.

In asking these questions, and adding others as individual situations require, it is essential that answers be considered in light of TP monitor objectives—based on user needs—which the on-line-network designer enumerates. The importance of asking the right questions becomes apparent when considering the enormous impact a TP monitor can have on the cost and success or failure of a network.

Essentially, the function of the TP monitor is to keep data flowing in an orderly fashion (DATA COMMUNICATIONS, July 1978, p. 67). To accomplish this, the monitor performs task scheduling, application control, resource allocation, network control, start-up and recovery, and error and failure processing.

TP monitors can be imbedded in special operating systems, be part of a database management system package, or be a stand-alone package provided by a computer vendor or by many of the growing number of independent software houses.

The major objectives of on-line network software:
- Save money compared with the clerical or

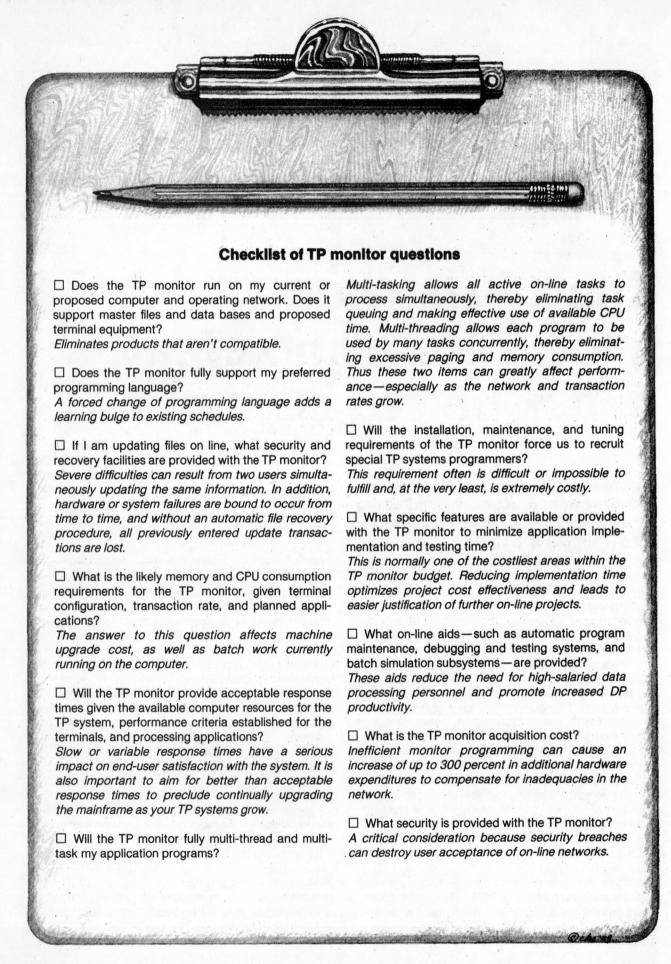

Checklist of TP monitor questions

☐ Does the TP monitor run on my current or proposed computer and operating network. Does it support master files and data bases and proposed terminal equipment?
Eliminates products that aren't compatible.

☐ Does the TP monitor fully support my preferred programming language?
A forced change of programming language adds a learning bulge to existing schedules.

☐ If I am updating files on line, what security and recovery facilities are provided with the TP monitor?
Severe difficulties can result from two users simultaneously updating the same information. In addition, hardware or system failures are bound to occur from time to time, and without an automatic file recovery procedure, all previously entered update transactions are lost.

☐ What is the likely memory and CPU consumption requirements for the TP monitor, given terminal configuration, transaction rate, and planned applications?
The answer to this question affects machine upgrade cost, as well as batch work currently running on the computer.

☐ Will the TP monitor provide acceptable response times given the available computer resources for the TP system, performance criteria established for the terminals, and processing applications?
Slow or variable response times have a serious impact on end-user satisfaction with the system. It is also important to aim for better than acceptable response times to preclude continually upgrading the mainframe as your TP systems grow.

☐ Will the TP monitor fully multi-thread and multi-task my application programs?

Multi-tasking allows all active on-line tasks to process simultaneously, thereby eliminating task queuing and making effective use of available CPU time. Multi-threading allows each program to be used by many tasks concurrently, thereby eliminating excessive paging and memory consumption. Thus these two items can greatly affect performance—especially as the network and transaction rates grow.

☐ Will the installation, maintenance, and tuning requirements of the TP monitor force us to recruit special TP systems programmers?
This requirement often is difficult or impossible to fulfill and, at the very least, is extremely costly.

☐ What specific features are available or provided with the TP monitor to minimize application implementation and testing time?
This is normally one of the costliest areas within the TP monitor budget. Reducing implementation time optimizes project cost effectiveness and leads to easier justification of further on-line projects.

☐ What on-line aids—such as automatic program maintenance, debugging and testing systems, and batch simulation subsystems—are provided?
These aids reduce the need for high-salaried data processing personnel and promote increased DP productivity.

☐ What is the TP monitor acquisition cost?
Inefficient monitor programming can cause an increase of up to 300 percent in additional hardware expenditures to compensate for inadequacies in the network.

☐ What security is provided with the TP monitor?
A critical consideration because security breaches can destroy user acceptance of on-line networks.

1 Large-user network costs

Don't underestimate expenditures. The graph illustrates real costs—on a percentage basis—incurred by large TP users when they go on line. The actual dollar amount obviously varies considerably from user to user. Experience shows that these costs are invariably higher than the user predicts at the beginning of the project.

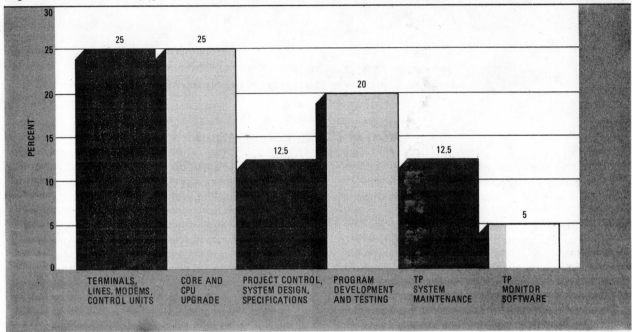

batch-oriented system that is about to be replaced.
■ Perform at least some business functions more accurately and faster—thereby enabling management to make better decisions and improve company service and competitive position.
■ Boost productivity of on-line networks.
■ Gain access to information or functions not previously available.

A comprehensive plan
There are likely to be a number of other objectives, depending on individual needs. The ones listed above represent a general overview.

Once a potential user defines network objectives, including the specific applications for which TP plans will be initially justified, there are still many important areas to cover before launching a full-scale project. These include:
■ Determining the type of terminal equipment best suited to network needs.
■ Determining, for remote locations, adequate line speeds and the correct modems, lines, control units, and front-end processing equipment.
■ Determining if the mainframe computer is capable of processing additional on-line applications, and if not, what hardware upgrades will be necessary.
■ Determining if the data processing group is large enough and sufficiently experienced to implement the system design, programming, testing, implementation, maintenance, and user training for the new network.
■ Determining cost.

Choosing mainframe TP monitor software for controlling on-line networks is harder than selecting the

necessary terminal and communications equipment—which is readily available in a number of models, capabilities, and prices. (One exception: IBM mainframe computers, for which there is a wide variety of software available from hardware and independent software companies.)

However, the choice of teleprocessing monitor software usually determines the ultimate success or failure of a project. Unfortunately, in the majority of cases, the time devoted to the selection of hardware, equipment, and project design—all of which, of course, are important factors—overshadows the choice of TP software.

Take time to evaluate
Apparently the main reason why thorough software evaluations are often not conducted is that users feel they lack the technical expertise to make the proper analyses; or the time, money, and personnel requirements to make a comprehensive study are greater than users believe practical. Improper TP software can lead to decreased network efficiency. For example, high computer overhead will cause expensive mainframe upgrade, and the selected TP monitor may not be able to perform all project requirements. In addition, terminal response times will suffer, project implementation may be delayed, and the monitor may not be able to support terminal equipment, network architecture, files, or databases.

Indeed, the teleprocessing world is filled with case histories documenting these and other problems. As a result, the final network often includes many compromise solutions that exceed the original budget and

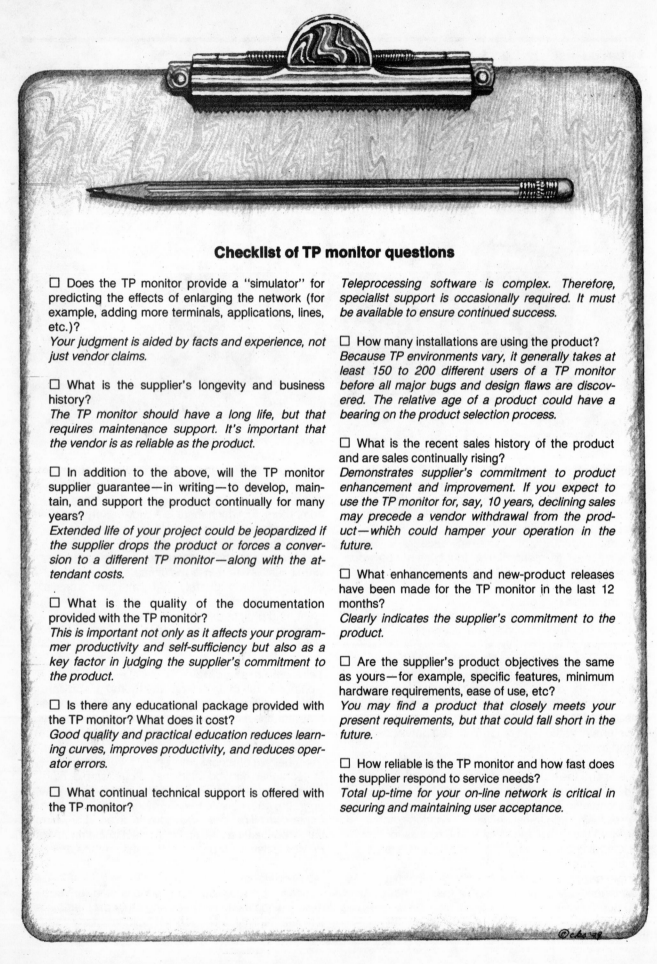

Checklist of TP monitor questions

☐ Does the TP monitor provide a "simulator" for predicting the effects of enlarging the network (for example, adding more terminals, applications, lines, etc.)?
Your judgment is aided by facts and experience, not just vendor claims.

☐ What is the supplier's longevity and business history?
The TP monitor should have a long life, but that requires maintenance support. It's important that the vendor is as reliable as the product.

☐ In addition to the above, will the TP monitor supplier guarantee—in writing—to develop, maintain, and support the product continually for many years?
Extended life of your project could be jeopardized if the supplier drops the product or forces a conversion to a different TP monitor—along with the attendant costs.

☐ What is the quality of the documentation provided with the TP monitor?
This is important not only as it affects your programmer productivity and self-sufficiency but also as a key factor in judging the supplier's commitment to the product.

☐ Is there any educational package provided with the TP monitor? What does it cost?
Good quality and practical education reduces learning curves, improves productivity, and reduces operator errors.

☐ What continual technical support is offered with the TP monitor?

Teleprocessing software is complex. Therefore, specialist support is occasionally required. It must be available to ensure continued success.

☐ How many installations are using the product?
Because TP environments vary, it generally takes at least 150 to 200 different users of a TP monitor before all major bugs and design flaws are discovered. The relative age of a product could have a bearing on the product selection process.

☐ What is the recent sales history of the product and are sales continually rising?
Demonstrates supplier's commitment to product enhancement and improvement. If you expect to use the TP monitor for, say, 10 years, declining sales may precede a vendor withdrawal from the product—which could hamper your operation in the future.

☐ What enhancements and new-product releases have been made for the TP monitor in the last 12 months?
Clearly indicates the supplier's commitment to the product.

☐ Are the supplier's product objectives the same as yours—for example, specific features, minimum hardware requirements, ease of use, etc?
You may find a product that closely meets your present requirements, but that could fall short in the future.

☐ How reliable is the TP monitor and how fast does the supplier respond to service needs?
Total up-time for your on-line network is critical in securing and maintaining user acceptance.

2 Small-user network costs

Expenditures are relative. As with the large user, small-user network costs will vary from company to company. In addition, the small users' six cost areas will differ relative to those of a large user. A small, local network, for instance, does not require long lines, modems, multiple control units, and layers of project-control personnel.

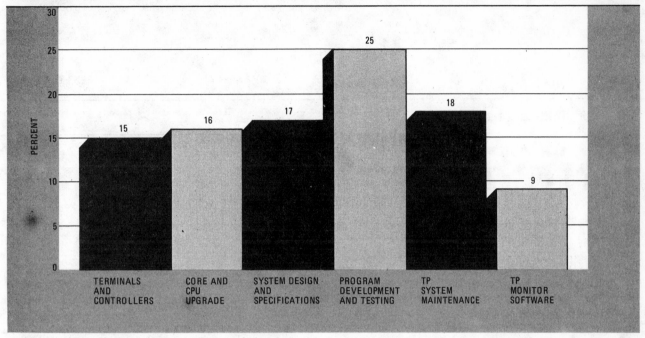

timetable by such a wide margin that justification for the on-line network is lost. Therefore, because of a TP monitor's impact on a project's success, the wherewithal and time must be found to conduct the proper analyses.

Take cost, for instance. Figures 1 and 2 illustrate real costs—on a percentage basis—incurred by very small and relatively large TP users when they go on line. The actual dollar amount obviously varies considerably from user to user, but the graphs serve to illustrate relative costs, which are invariably higher than the user predicts at the beginning of the project.

Choosing the correct TP monitor software, then, is the best way to avoid disaster. Moreover, it avoids a loss of data processing department credibility, a situation that could cause management to view future projects with skepticism.

Finishing the job

After TP monitor selection, the next task is implementation. The steps involved are planning, personnel training, system design and testing, program development and testing, and live production.

To assure success, the TP monitor should be implemented well in advance of TP hardware installation. That will undoubtedly be required to use and test the initial on-line programs. Usually, the teleprocessing monitor has a batch-simulation testing system, so that testing can be done well in advance of terminal installation.

A user must insist that the vendor completely train user personnel in applications and systems programming immediately following TP monitor implementation.

Training flattens the users' learning-time curve and enables the network to achieve maximum productivity quicker.

It is important that data processing department personnel are aware of the major functions and the architecture of the selected TP monitor. This will enable the equipment user to take advantage of software opportunities that could reduce program development time and boost overall network efficiency.

Security breaches

Appropriately designed TP monitors can provide protection against security breaches. Of course, there are likely to be many users and many varied applications running concurrently in the same region or partition of the computer. As a result, the potential for security violations and operational inefficiencies is always present, and thus it is advisable to query the vendor about other standards and procedures that may further ensure security.

Of course, for any network to operate efficiently requires adequate testing, which also applies to the TP monitor. Testing time is somewhat reduced by the availability of sophisticated system testing programs in today's TP monitors. To make certain that the network runs smoothly on the first day of operation, have both your technical staff and technical representatives for the vendor present.

A successful on-line network creates enthusiasm, growth, and cost benefits throughout an organization, but a failure creates despair that can haunt a company—especially its data processing section—for many years. ∎

Performance: the battle of needs vs desires

Gary Audin, Logica Inc., New York City

When balancing the efficiency of any particular circumstance of programming reality, what is wanted weighs against what is possible

Everyone wants to know a system's capacity in quantifiable terms: what is the capacity in transactions/second, characters/second, processing time, etc? Once an answer is created (not necessarily calculated) another series of questions arises:
- How can the variables be changed to increase throughput?
- How can the variables be changed to reduce response time?
- What is the system's peak by transaction type?
- When does the system start to increase response time?

There are many other variations of these and other questions—all of which may have more than one answer depending upon the variables that are changed.

Before any attempt can be made to answer the questions, a uniform set of definitions must be created which is independent of the communications applications, e.g. message switching, RJE, data collection, inquiry/response. A transaction (message unit or entity) is defined here as a single logical unit of information which is received, processed, and delivered by a computer. A transaction may be a line of text from a teletypewriter, a CRT screen, or a block of characters from another computer. A message to be switched is a single transaction.

The most commonly mentioned parameters for defining capacity, and used to determine performance, are response time (in seconds) and throughput (transactions/second or sometimes characters/second). Response time is the interval between the initiation of transaction transmission (pushing the transmit key) and the delivery of the response (first chracter) to the destination. Throughput is the count of the number of transactions completely serviced in a unit of time. This is a measure of the work performed by a system.

These measurements are affected by the computer hardware, software, and network. Those variables which relate to CPUs, peripherals, and software and their interaction and interference are within the scope of this discussion. The variables which are found in the network will not be discussed in this article.

There are many variables to be considered which affect the capacity of a computer software system. They can be generally listed as follows:
- disk accesses per second available;
- core space available;
- CPU speed;
- CPU instruction set;
- communications equipment (multiplexer or front-end usage and design);
- input/output channel utilization;

- application program design;
- database design; and
- queuing methodology (core or disk).

All of these play varying roles (Fig. 1) in enhancing or reducing the performance of a data communications software system. Some are not even worth considering if their utilization is low (less than 50 percent), but some of these become very important as their utilization exceeds 70 percent.

When a transaction is received by a computer, the variables which hinder throughput may not be found in each stage of a data communications processing system, but they may also be repeated more than once (Fig. 2). Each variable is a tunable element which can be associated with multiple stages. Core space for data communications buffers is a separate problem from core space for application program work areas. Two distinct sets of core space are in use and their size, distribution and activity level (how often they are used and held) vary independently. Each variable will become important as its use goes past 50 percent; therefore, there is not a fixed priority list of variables that should be reviewed. Experience has shown that of all the variables: disk accesses per second; core space available, and CPU utilization are the most commonly consumed resources. They are listed in the order in which most data communications software systems encounter them as problems.

CPU capacity

The ability of a CPU to perform useful work depends greatly upon how much the CPU, with associated software, must do to move a transaction through to the completion of processing. A fine example of this is the amount of work done by a CPU with a hardwired, unbuffered data communications multiplexer. This piece of hardware interfaces modems to a computer channel. The CPU is interrupted for every character sent or received and must fill or empty buffers (which contain the transaction) on a character-by-character basis. This interrupt triggers a program which inspects the character for control and error detection purposes and builds a transaction in a buffer (a section of core memory assigned to a line). The computer time used for a received character may be 50 to 100 microseconds per character, and 35 to 70 microseconds for every character transmitted. Once a completed transaction is received, computer time is consumed while the transaction moves from the buffer to disk and while an acknowledgement is sent back to the terminal.

A buffered multiplexer or front-end does not bother the CPU until a buffer is filled or a complete transaction is received. A comparison of the two data communications interfaces for the receipt of a 200-character transaction looks like this:

Character multiplexer
200 characters per transaction x 75 microseconds per character + 500 microseconds per transaction = 15,500 microseconds per transaction.

Buffered multiplexer or front-end
500 microseconds per transaction.

1 Demand vs capacity

Capacity demands. *In order to achieve a balanced result in software system performance, each area must be given a proportionate share of the total system's capacity.*

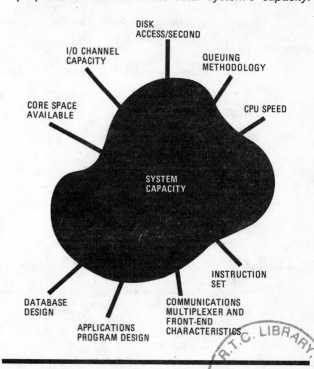

The character multiplexer consumes almost 32 times more CPU time than the buffered multiplexer of front-end. This figure will vary depending upon the CPU speed, instruction set, and the size of the buffer—with the character multiplexer using 20 to 40 times more CPU time. The buffered devices can hold a whole transaction; therefore multiplexers which have buffers that are very small, e.g. two to four characters, are not much better than a single character buffered device. The choice of equipment is obvious, but is not that simple. A whole range of capabilities which vary the CPU time used include:
- character recognition capability;
- error detection;
- block checksum calculation;
- protocol operation; and
- buffer size relative to transaction size.

Effect of software on the CPU

The collection of capacity-data for a network is much easier than for a computer system. There are many interrelationships which make the prediction on computer-system capacity difficult. It is, therefore, only possible to set ranges for the variables rather than determining any absolute limits.

All work performed by a computer is done as a series of instructions organized in groups that handle specific tasks (programs). It would seem that the CPU time consumed can be calculated by multiplying the instruction time by the number of executions and adding them together. This proves difficult to determine since the

2 Performance variables

Change factors. At each stage of a piece of data's progress through the central processing unit, hardware and software variables determine how quickly and effi- ciently the information will be processed. The user must weigh all of the variable factors that exist in the system (hardware and software) to maximize throughput.

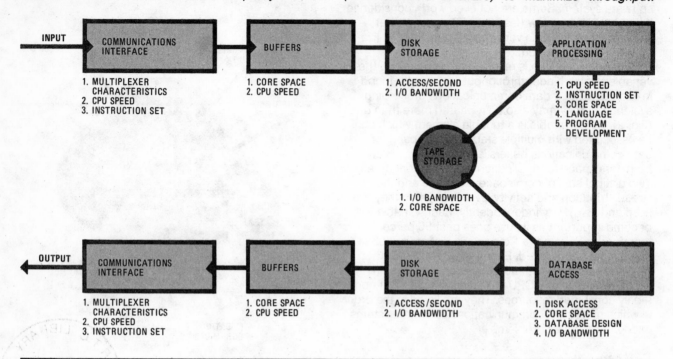

user must know the exact set of instructions used. Usually an estimated "average" instruction time is used, but it is only useful as an approximation.

Therefore, using an "average" instruction time to determine how much CPU time an application program will consume will yield a good estimate. However, if the total estimated CPU time for all programs (operating system, access methods, database management system applications, etc.) reaches more than 80 percent of capacity, then it is reasonably safe to assume the programs are causing system saturation.

The simple calculation of the total execution time will generally produce an estimate of the fastest time possible. There are several reasons why a program will take longer:

■ Every time a program needs to use a busy peripheral, it must wait.

■ An application may be written as several programs which are brought into memory individually. This helps reduce core requirements, but increases the operating system overhead and CPU time.

■ The application may be written in re-entrant code (the program is re-usable by several transactions concurrently) which also increases overhead while reducing transaction response time.

The design of application programs therefore is a trade-off of speed of execution versus response time, overhead, and core utilization. Each system designer will have to negotiate a different set of these variables in response to requirements.

Languages also become an important consideration.

The higher the level, the easier to develop and maintain a program. However, these languages usually produce programs which take longer to execute (more instructions are produced) and consume greater core space. Programs written in languages closer to the computer's fundamental instruction language are generally shorter (less core space used) and faster to execute. These programs, however, require programmer talents which are scarcer, and the programs themselves are more difficult to charge and maintain. Again another trade-off; here it's between system productivity and system development and maintenance.

The allocation of core space

As mentioned, buffers and programs seriously affect how much core is being used. The use of buffers to support the input/output of a transaction to/from data communications interfaces, disks and magnetic tapes will vary with:

■ the number of devices (lines) operating concurrently;

■ the speed of the devices (lines); and

■ block (transaction) length.

The trade-offs for core space in data communications revolve around providing big enough buffers in enough quantity so the CPU does not get interrupted too often. But if the lines are slow, much of the core will be under-utilized (a 100-character buffer takes 10 seconds to fill on a 10-character-per-second line). Also, response time may be increased if it takes a while to determine that a complete transaction has been received—especially when it does not fill a buffer. Enough buffers must be provided so that once input from a terminal is started, there will be guaranteed space available to receive it. If, however, these data communications buffers must be emptied into disk buffers and the disk is momentarily falling behind in accesses, then an extra set of buffers must be provided to continue storing the transaction. The need for buffer space, therefore, increases as the disk-access rate starts approaching its maximum speed.

The storage of applications also uses work areas that are like buffers. The larger the number of applications which can concurrently exist in memory, the faster the average response time. However, if applications are written as large programs or if the space available is not large, then the response is much longer. If the applications are written as smaller programs, then more can operate simultaneously, but more disk accesses will be consumed in bringing in the additional programs to finish the applications processing. The best of all models would be to have enough space for all applications to reside in core memory. However, this is not possible in most cases. Therefore, the number of core-resident programs is limited and the response time for applications resident on the disk will be greater.

Data communications systems use disks very heavily for storing:

(A) transactions in queue;
(B) applications programs;
(C) databases;
(D) information for recovery/restart; and
(E) copies of the operating system, database management system access methods, etc.

Disks are basic workhorses, but they are limited in the number of accesses per second they can deliver. The use of these accesses cannot exceed a maximum, e.g. 50 per second, therefore:

$$A + B + C + D + E = 50$$

where the sum of all uses is limited to 50. If the database needs more accesses to complete its work, then some other function (usually queuing) must reduce its accesses. This facility is usually consumed first, before CPU utilization or core space.

There are methods which can increase the number of accesses per second available. Fixed head disks, although smaller, produce rates 4 to 16 times faster than moving head disks. The five aforementioned storage functions can be divided between the two types of disks. Transaction queues, copies of application programs, and, possibly, the recovery information are candidates for a fixed head disk. The lower activity functions, which also require considerable storage space (10 to 100 times more than the first three functions) can be economically stored on moving head disks.

If only a moving head disk is available, then the functions and their storage areas should be distributed on the disk by activity. The most active function, queuing, should be placed to minimize head movement with the less active functions stored on either side (with the least active on the outer edges).

This technique reduces the amount of time consumed to move the head to the proper track. It can increase the number of accesses/second available by as much as 100 per cent.

Although a disk is used to hold transactions in queue, it is not necessary to always follow this practice. The advantages of disk-queuing compared to core-queuing are the large storage area available and the recoverability of a transaction in process when a system fails. Anything in core after a failure can be assumed to be lost. In an inquiry situation, this is allowable because a terminal operator can always re-enter without causing a problem. Core-queuing is not acceptable if a database update is in progress or if the transaction has been acknowledged and the operator assumes it is safely stored. Core-queuing simply relieves the disk, but requires considerably more core space. The CPU time consumed is not significantly changed, The response time achieved when using core-queuing, however, is much faster.

A potential bottleneck

The data communications multiplexer, disks, and magnetic tapes units use the I/O channels quite heavily. It may not be possible to realize the bandwidth (bytes or words per second) described in the computer's specifications. Depending upon the system construction, there will be varying degrees of interference between the I/O channels and the operation of the CPU. The cycle-stealing design of most direct memory access (DMA) devices will reduce the effective instruction rate (increase instruction execution time). Disks are usually DMA devices. As the disk access rate increases, with a corresponding increase in total character (byte) transmission, the CPU time available decreases rapidly. It is impossible, in most cases, to have 100 percent CPU time available while the I/O channels are in heavy use.

The data communications interface and magnetic tape drive may be DMA devices, but in a majority of medium and small systems they operate on a character-by-character basis. This consumes considerable CPU time for each character that is moved. If the total line speed and the number of tape reads and writes are low, then there is little to be concerned about. However, several voice-grade lines and dozens of tape accesses/second can significantly reduce the available CPU time.

There are many minicomputers on the market which use a common buss structure to connect the CPU, core memory, and peripherals. It looks good on paper, has a clean design, and works well in low I/O oriented systems. However, the use of core memory by the CPU requires a buss access, so does any access to/from perpherals. Therefore, the more peripheral transfers, the fewer CPU to memory transfer that are available.

Since a peripheral cannot stop in the middle of a transfer, it has a higher priority for a buss access. This leaves the CPU well down in priority. It is possible to create situations where only 50 percent of the CPU time is available because of I/O transfers. Some very high speed disks are so fast that the manufacturers have created bigger minis to support them with special busses which do not interfere with the CPU. However, all the other devices still interfere on the slower buss. CPU time and I/O bandwidth are not mutually exclusive. They cannot be read from a manufacturer's specification and then treated separately. Unfortunately, many manufaturers do not have good models which can determine the system performance when high I/O activity is involved. The user should play it safe and create a design with lots of extra I/O capacity.

Databases influence performance

Database designers can (and often do) construct their structures independent of the data communications environment. This, however, is not effective if the system capacity is to be maximized because databases:
- consume CPU time;
- use many disk accesses;
- require buffers for transfer; and
- consume I/O bandwidth.

Since all these resources are fixed, any consumption reduces their availability to other functions. The structure of a database should be developed to provide easy access to data, the ability to change data, be easily maintainable, and reduce or eliminate multiple copies of data. The goals may, however, conflict with the achievable performance, especially in the consumption of disk accesses. Two different structures may require 2 and 1.5 disk acccesses per request, respectively. These figures do not seem large, but there is a 25 percent difference. Ten requests per second means a difference of five accesses. For a disk capacity of 50 accesses per second, this is a 10 percent difference in consumption fo the whole system. The database designer may have to compromise some of his goals. It does not pay to respond to 10 requests per second if so many disk accesses are consumed that the rest of the system can produce only eight requests per second.

The use of hardware resources in a data communications environment depends heavily on how the software manipulates the available resources. The use of the resources is a multi-dimensional problem where no answer is perfect, but is a compromise. A data communications software system must be tuned in response to the environment. The environment has an annoying way of changing. A successful system is sure to attract more users and uses, more than planned. Going through an exercise to tune the resources is never the end. The tuning exercise may have to be performed every six months and every time a new application is added.

All of this tuning, however, is useless unless adequate statistical information about the actual resource utilization is available. Software and hardware activity monitors and periodic performance evaluation are mandatory. The actual execution time of a program may vary ±25 percent when compared to the calculated time. The published instruction execution times are often conservative, i.e. longer than what can be achieved. The timing and resources reallocation of a software system is never finished. ■

Joe M. Wiley, Tennessee Valley Authority, Chattanooga, Tenn.

Achilles' heels of modern networking: A user's lament

A great deal has been accomplished in the science of networking, but in pushing the frontier, have we forgotten some problems?

It would be interesting to know just what percent of the world's private data networks are implemented with advanced networking concepts. Judging from the extensive literature and articles on local networks, hybrid circuit- and packet-switched networks, electronic mail, system network architecture (SNA), and the like, the network manager who hasn't implemented such things probably feels old fashioned.

If the facts were known, though, probably something less than 10 percent of networks are actually employing new networking techniques, while 90 percent are still studying and considering them.

It is probably just as well that the bulk of users have not yet signed up for advanced networks, since the proponents of these schemes usually neglect to mention the pitfalls associated with them. (That is to be expected, as sales people don't dwell on such things that may not apply in every case.) Advanced networks' flaws are often so obvious that they can be readily detected, but there are several subtle problems that are of equal concern. Such subtle problems are not significant in small networks, but they escalate rapidly as network complexity increases.

Before considering the Achilles' heels of today's advanced networks, let's consider what ingredients make up such networks. One is switching, whether it be circuit, packet, or message. Another is connectivity. In an advanced network the connections during one instant can be quite different from the connections at another time. That is, session paths can be, and usually are, altered from session to session.

Switching of messages or sessions is usually not required on a star network that employs a single host processor. The minimum network exists—the first stage if you will—when two co-located hosts are involved with a front-end processor that switches be-

tween the hosts and terminals on a session-by-session basis.

The second stage is representative of networking by the connection of a terminal to one of several remotely located hosts. The third stage, and beyond, is realized by the implementation of distributed data processing, especially when remote processors are communicating. As the distributed mix becomes more diverse, in the sense of terminals and session-to-session possibilities, the network moves beyond stage three toward actual complex networking.

Complex networking exists in cases involving a large number of processors serving hundreds of users with hundreds of terminals. Any terminal and its user in a complex network should have the ability to connect to any processor and any processor should have the ability to connect to any other processor.

The potential for networking problems may be more prevalent than at first assumed, and, as mentioned, exists at every stage of complexity. For instance, any company with communicating word processing, facsimile, or electronic mail has networking. A firm with several hosts and terminals needing to connect to any one host has networking. Any organization implementing SNA or any of the other proprietary computer communications architectures is getting into it. Regardless of the complexity, they have or will have several problems in common. These problems, or pitfalls, are the Achilles' heels of networking.

One of the first "heels," and sometimes the most troublesome, is control. The difficulties associated with control are certainly the most subtle, least obvious, and yet probably the biggest potential problems in the science of data communications networking. Looked at more realistically than usual, control problems are insidious because they usually wait to show themselves

1. Simple. *This not uncommon network configuration is by most accounts quite simple. The user terminal has a direct link with host A and secondary path to host B.* *Merely adding one more terminal at E, however, requires costly software additions or modifications at every host and every front-end processor on the network.*

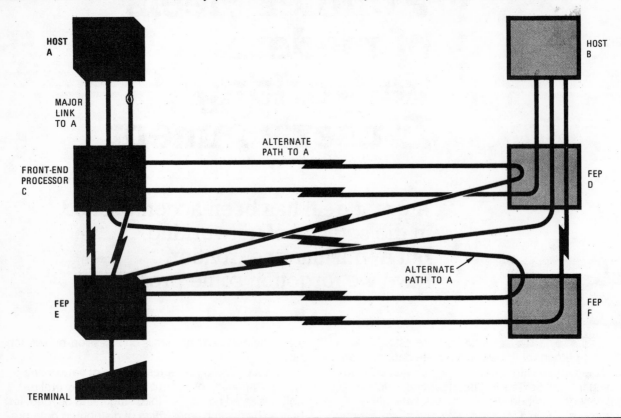

until long after a new network has been installed.

Take SNA-type networking as an example. SNA here is generic and meant to cover the communications architecture and networking concepts offered by several front-end and mainframe vendors besides IBM.

With SNA-type networks, control problems are mostly, but not exclusively, associated with centrally controlled networks and master-slave protocols. Let's start with a reasonably simple example, shown in Figure 1.

Considerable additions

If the terminal is "owned" by host A, but can access B, then it is in A's domain and in B's cross-domain. The networking controls reside in six hosts and front-end processors (A, B, C, D, E, and F). There are transmission groups, cross-domain resource tables, logical paths, alternate paths, adjacent subareas, and destination tables within this simple network. Consider what happens when another terminal is added to front-end processor (FEP) E. New sysgens (systems generators) are required for two FEPs (C and E) and for host A. The other devices (B, D, and F) also need table updates. In this simple case, the sysgen workload on system programmers is enormous.

Let's consider just the path tables for a moment. There are primary paths, alternate paths, explicit routes, and virtual routes. Figure 2 shows the four paths possible from one subarea to another. Remember that these must be in the tables of each device involved,

and there are six subareas alone in Figure 2. Imagine the possible paths and the control problems as network changes occur.

So far, we have only changed tables in the access method and front-end software. There are, however, still more sysgens needed. Suppose the hosts run CICS (customer information control system) or one of its counterparts. In that case, the two application programs in the hosts require sysgens in order to add a terminal.

Now consider two or more front ends on each host, and add a transmission group between each front end. The picture of the control problem should be forming by now. As growth occurs, the sysgen tasks increase by a factorial. It would not take much growth to reach a point at which there is no way to hire enough system programmers to keep up.

Sysgens obsolete

But this is not the end of the control problem. Another aspect is security. For this control problem, let's use an example not related to SNA. Assume a 100-station word processing network. Each processor has disk storage. Any processor may need to access any of the other 99, but is only allowed certain files. Thus each processor must have controls to define which other devices can access which files. Suppose this is all set up and we add one more word processor. This means that 100 other systems have to be updated.

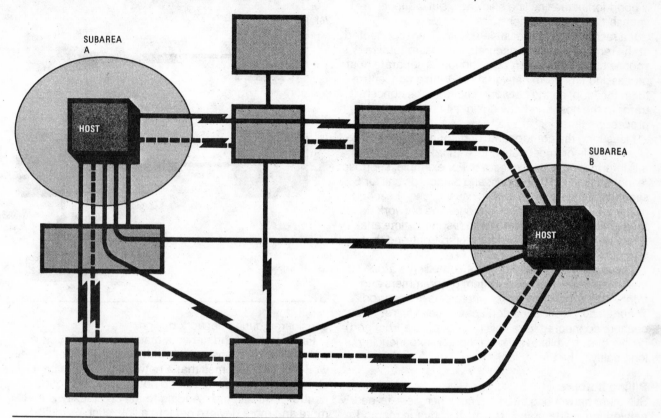

2. Path-a-logical. *To best illustrate the problems of network control, consider this simple link analysis of two subareas. The solid, thinner lines represent primary routes* *between the subareas. The dashed lines define virtual routes. The boxes can be any intermediate device. Thick solid lines are hard-wired path alternatives.*

SUBAREA A

HOST

SUBAREA B

HOST

Still other control problems are caused by such things as fault isolation, billing, moving equipment, changing staff, and so on.

Is there a solution to the control mess? Yes, but it is one of those things easier said than done. What is needed is an automated system for updating the controls. An entire network must be updated by one control-console entry. The updating must be "hot," or online; that is, on the fly and non-interfering with processing. It should be clear than that sysgens are obsolete and have no place in modern networks.

Bottlenecks

Another Achilles' heel is the problem caused by multiplexers, concentrators, and switches. For simplicity, these devices are referred to as line continuity breaks, or LCBs. They are, of course, essential to the cost reduction of a network, but they do cause a problem in that they break the continuity of a circuit. If a host is at point A and a terminal at point B—as shown in Figure 3—with nothing in between, then one uninterrupted circuit connects the two. A point-to-point line such as this is easy to diagnose. But if a concentrator is inserted at some point C between A and B—shown in Figure 3B—then the fault-isolation picture changes dramatically. Instead of one circuit, there are now two: one from A to C and a second from C to B.

If a failure occurs somewhere on link A-B, a network-control center at A has no easy way to diagnose the

C-B link. In many cases, the A-C portion may even be at a different speed. Because data in line C-B is digitized at the concentrator, buffered, maybe stored, and ultimately blended with other data on its way to A, the data from terminal B loses its identity and separateness as it passes point C.

Impossible

Suppose an operator at a terminal places the station's modem in a loopback mode and a failure is indicated. Where is the failure? Without more people or equipment, a diagnosis cannot be made.

Several modem makers propose an answer to this Achilles' heel by offering modem control systems (sometimes called diagnostic modems or network control system). But a buyer must beware; some of the systems offered will not pass data around an LCB. A network control center's main tool is a digital line monitor, such as an Intershake or a Datascope. Unfortunately, these become virtually useless on circuits containing a concentrator. The data on the trunk between the central site and the concentrator are in a form that a digital-line monitor cannot decode. Further, it cannot access the portion of the circuit upstream from the concentrator. A multiplexer is not quite as bad if the data is demultiplexed at the central site. At least, if data flows at all, something can be checked.

There is another problem with a concentrator: checking response time. Many concentrators now perform local polling of interactive terminals. In these cases, the front-end acknowledges (ACKs) the host poll. Thus no polling messages go across trunks. This is good for increasing line efficiency, but it affects response-time measurements.

If a response-time measuring device were connected at the terminal, it would accurately measure total response time. What it can't do, though, is separate host processing time from network time. With a concentrator in the loop, all the network time from the concentrator to the host and back again gets put into host processing time.

Measuring the components of response time is nearly impossible on most networks with front ends. Yet this information is badly needed. For example, suppose response time is 10 seconds, and standards call for 5 seconds. If the network itself is causing only 1 second of the total 10, then action to reduce the network delay time is wasted. The problem with response-time analyzers on the market is that they lump front-end time into host processing time.

I have seen (and have been in) some fierce arguments between operating-system programmers and front-end programmers over where delays occurred. Theoretically, front ends don't cause delays. Yet when channel-connected terminals (that bypass a front end) go like blazes while every other node is experiencing long delays, the theory looks pale.

Billing bothers

Still other networking pitfalls occur when peer-to-peer networking is attempted. The most common method for billing network users is a formula based on host usage. Sometimes a connect-time factor is added as well. That is satisfactory for a master-slave concept using a star network with a single central computer. But as an organization moves toward peer-to-peer processing, trouble begins.

This includes sessions between any devices where one is not a central computer. Examples are minicomputer to mainframe, facsimile, word processing, and any distributed processing scheme where the processors exchange information. If billing is based on central CPU usage, and a peer-to-peer session doesn't connect to a central CPU, then somebody is getting free service and somebody is paying extra.

Some organizations use accounting systems where the user pays for terminals, lines, modems, and circuits. But this doesn't solve the problem of common equipment—trunks, switches, multiplexers, and concentrators. So, as advanced networking systems are implemented, new billing methods are needed.

Isolating faults

With packet switching, accounting is straightforward. The method is to count packets used. In contrast, circuit switching has no way to count data volume. It can only measure connect time. Bear in mind, however, that packet and hybrid switching networks create some unique billing problems of their own. Obviously, solutions have to be worked out on a case-by-case basis. The point is that customer billing methods should be

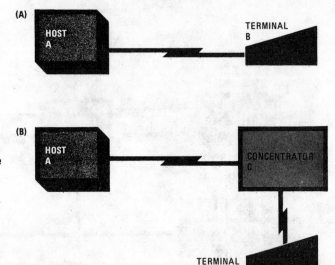

3. Interlopers. Devices such as concentrators, multiplexers, and switches, while essential to networking, create significant problems in several areas.

considered during network design.

Fault isolation and network maintenance become a complex and expensive task with peer-to-peer networking. This assumes that a network ceases to be a star; that is, links exist that do not flow through one central control center. Adding to the complexity is that more and more devices get into a link, such as multiplexers, switches, or cross-domain front ends. Each device adds delay and finger-pointing possibilities.

Obviously, any organization that has advanced networks on any but the smallest scale must assume responsibility for fault isolation. Actual repair could be realized with contract service or in-house maintenance. In either case, though, careful design must take place to ensure a fault-isolation method is built in. The most desirable is a self-diagnosing "alerting" system.

Case-by-case solutions

Response-time measurement on a peer-to-peer network becomes tedious. The cheapest and handiest tool is a stopwatch. Yet a stopwatch provides no diagnostic features for the network operator. If a long delay occurs, where was it held up? Tracing and timing a message along a multiple-link path could involve many people and require complex equipment.

It would be nice to offer some solutions here, but again, since each case is so vastly different, they have to be designed on a case-by-case basis. If the network designer does not build in some diagnostic aids, he could have a network with no way to test it, except by trial and error—which may be the best or only available method. Hardly a sophisticated solution.

Despite these problems, sophisticated networking continues to grow around the world. A swift addressing of the problems detailed here, however, would shift the balance of new versus old networking and close the gap between the promised and the possible. ∎

Ray Sarch, Data Communications

Protocol conversion— Product of profusion

Until data communications vendors agree on protocol standards, the proliferation of conversion products interfacing their devices will continue.

The data communications user who finds that he cannot satisfy his network needs with one vendor's products soon realizes that he is creating unforeseen problems. He discovers that the multivendor approach is growing into a multiprotocol nightmare. Hardware and software from different suppliers are often incompatible: Vendor A's devices do not communicate with vendor B's. This is why protocol conversion was born.

Standards bodies, notably the International Organization for Standardization (ISO), are addressing the compatibility problem. The ISO has proposed an open systems interconnection (OSI) reference model as a basis for interconnecting heterogeneous "systems." The multilayered approach seems feasible, but the completed standard is many years away [Ref. 1].

Fortunately, today's multivendor user does not have to wait for the OSI or other protocol standards to arrive. The protocol-conversion industry is dedicated to the proposition that all protocols can be made "equal." And the user may choose from among a growing number of hardware and software products and techniques. These range from microprocessor-based printed-circuit (PC) boards dedicated to one conversion function—such as making an ASCII-coded terminal's asynchronous output look like an IBM 3270's binary-synchronous-communications (BSC or bisync) signal—to minicomputer-size "boxes" designed to convert between many protocols.

Protocol conversion is also an integral function of many front-end (communications) processors (FEPs). Here, the FEP converts the transmission of many different devices into the protocol that the host computer expects. It then reverses the function and converts the host's output protocol to that of each of the remote devices. The front-end processor's technique usually

involves a combination of microprocessor hardware and some software.

The prevalence of IBM terminals and computers has led to the proliferation of devices that convert not only between the previously mentioned ASCII and 3270 BSC but also to 2780/3780 remote-job-entry (RJE) protocols and to IBM's systems network architec-

1. Converting protocols. *A typical protocol converter may act as a controller while converting the data stream from each interfaced device to the host's protocol. In this application, the converters also switch any terminal to access either the host or the minicomputer and act as communicating multiplexers between two separate sites.*

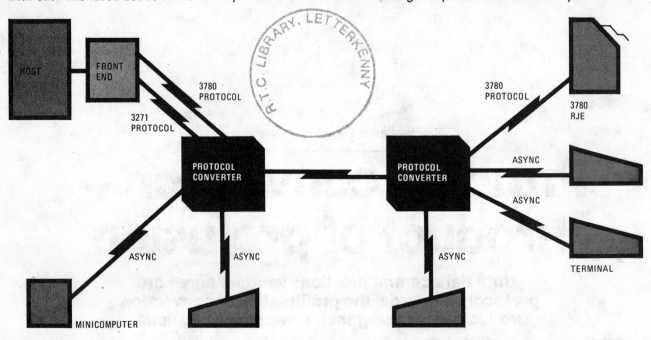

ture/synchronous data link control (SNA/SDLC). Conversion to X.25 is also becoming readily available. What the ASCII terminal user gains is access to a range of applications considerably wider than what is normally available to him. While retaining the use of TWX and Telex services, the teletype machine user can access network communications services and computer databases via the conversion interface.

The BSC terminal user gains — besides wider access — the ability to access the latest networks without incurring the expense of replacing terminals. However, just as a chain is only as strong as its weakest link, the user's operation remains limited by the capacity and functions of the basic terminal.

Figure 1 illustrates the network application of one protocol-conversion device, that of Industrial Computer Controls Inc. (ICCI), Cambridge, Mass. Combined with the switching capabilities of ICCI's CA 12 converter, any terminal can communicate with the minicomputer or the host computer. Here, the CA 12s also multiplex data, communicating with each other in a bit-oriented protocol. The conversions are performed by software modules for asynchronous and BSC protocols and for such codes as EBCDIC, ASCII, and Baudot.

The growing popularity of communicating word processors (CWPs) has exposed another not-yet-standardized area. Each CWP vendor has apparently come up with its own protocol, creating problems for the user implementing a multivendor CWP network. Here again, protocol conversion is fortunately available.

But the compatibility problem is complicated by the special control functions peculiar to word processing — such as centering, inserting, deleting, and moving text. The conversion process maps one CWP's representa-

tion of a control function into the equivalent or nearly equivalent function of the counterpart CWP. In this fashion, when an operator of an inputting CWP keys in, say, a centering command, this command is converted to the corresponding command of the receiving word processor.

Converting the difference
In general, the parameters for conversion of each protocol are essentially the transmission code, data rate, and data characteristics. The conversion process handles such data characteristics as error-checking characters and bit timing — besides the assigned control functions as used with the CWPs. Again, the mapping procedure transforms the data of one protocol to the equivalent representation of another. The combined conversion implementation of all three parameters — code, rate, and characteristics — is called emulation.

The architecture of conversion/emulation may be represented by a series of levels, similar to the ISO's open systems interconnection and to IBM's systems network architecture [Refs. 1,2]. The lowest level is the physical or electrical interface. The next level governs code conversion, often accomplished by large-scale integrated (LSI) semiconductor chips.

On the next-higher level, the conversion process maps one protocol into that of another. Thus, this level assures that the data stream from a sending device is translated properly to appear coherent to the destination device. Examples of this conversion include binary synchronous communications to high-level data link control (HDLC) and asynchronous to synchronous, such as TTY to BSC.

Even with a successful protocol-conversion process,

true emulation can succeed only if all the specification differences between the sending and receiving devices are accounted for. These differences usually consist of data-record sizes and data-blocking characteristics and are handled on the device-emulation level.

A common record size is the 80-character capacity of a punched card. The conversion process would buffer these 80-character records and feed the receiving device its expected block size. The blocking-characteristic conversion is needed to meet a display terminal's requirement for 1,920-character blocks, conforming to the available buffer size.

When necessary, the conversion process reformats the transmitted data to emulate what the receiving device is expecting. For example, if the receiving device is looking for 80-character records ("card images"), the conversion process reformats the sending device's output to conform to this specification.

What may be considered the conversion architecture's top level interprets device characteristics such as control codes—similar to the earlier communicating-word-processor application. This may be called the function-transformation level, where the commands and control codes of one device are mapped into the corresponding commands and control codes of the counterpart device.

Virtual protocol

Another means of classifying protocol-conversion architecture is by data rate. Up to about 9.6 kbit/s, a combination of microprocessor hardware and software operates quite efficiently with an internal "virtual" protocol—called the "right approach" by one industry expert. In this implementation, the conversion process transforms each incoming protocol to its own protocol, then reconverts the data stream to the protocol desired by the receiving device.

This approach pays off in applications that have many varying incoming and outgoing protocols. Each conversion is reduced thereby to three steps: receive the transmitted protocol; convert to the virtual protocol; convert to the desired protocol. The alternative to this technique would require a separate program for each combination of protocol-conversion pairs—a much more complicated and costly undertaking.

Typifying the virtual approach is the 25X series of communications processors from the Icot Corporation of Mountain View, Calif. Its 257 unit, for example, supports up to 13 synchronous and up to 39 synchronous and asynchronous lines. Each line is under microprocessor control and has 12K of programmable read-only memory (PROM) in which the conversion program is stored. In addition, each line's data is buffered in a 2K random-access memory (RAM). Input/output queuing—at line speeds up to 9.6 kbit/s—is conducted in a 48K shared RAM buffer storage area (called the common memory module).

Easier in hardware

Other practitioners of the virtual-protocol technique are ICCI and Racal-Telesystems of Chicago (for CWPs). To do the equivalent conversion entirely in software is

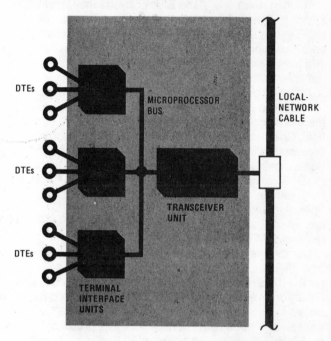

2. Local bus. *The local network's bus interface unit consists of two basic components: the terminal interface unit and the transceiver (cable-interface) unit.*

possible. But to emulate just one terminal type would require about 16K of storage, according to one industry authority. And to cover all 3270 options, supporting an asynchronous CRT on a 3270 line, would require about 100K, he says.

When the desired data rates are in the megabit-per-second range, a different protocol-conversion technique is often used. As typified in the bus interface unit (BIU) implemented in certain Ethernet-like local networks, this technique calls for its own architecture [Ref. 3]. The BIU is designed with multimicroprocessors to interface a number of terminal and computer devices—via 110 to 9.6K bit/s ports—to the network's 1- to 20-Mbit/s rate. The access method considered here is carrier sense multiple access with collision detection (CSMA/CD).

Inside the interface

The BIU has two basic components: the terminal interface unit (TIU) and the transceiver unit (TRU) (Fig. 2). The TIU services the ports and their data terminal equipment (DTE). In an Ethernet-like environment, each TIU—with its own microprocessor—handles two to eight full-duplex ports; with a BIU including up to four TIUs, each BIU can handle 32 DTEs. The TRU connects the TIUs to the network, using CSMA/CD on the cable side. Depending on the BIU design, the TRU is either equipped with a microprocessor for handling link-level protocols or leaves this operation to the TIUs while it performs physical-level functions.

When one DTE communicates over a local network with another DTE—be they terminals or hosts—the sending BIU forms the data into packets to conform to the network requirements. The receiving BIU strips the packet envelope from the data stream and restores the transmission to its original form. If the two DTEs are not normally compatible (operating with different protocols), then one of the BIUs converts the data in addition. If the transmission is between a terminal and a CPU, the conversion would usually be at the terminal end; if between terminals or between hosts, the user and network management would agree beforehand to the conversion site.

Although protocol conversion via software is often too costly in programming efforts and storage space, there are circumstances for which this method is practical. One such case involves IBM's 3705 communications controller. Comm-Pro Associates of Manhattan Beach, Calif., provides software packages that enable the 3705 to interface to non-IBM devices and services. For example, with a recent Comm-Pro release, DTEs operating under IBM's SNA can access X.25-based packet-switching networks. The conversion package requires 26K of storage in the 3705.

Cambridge Telecommunications, Burlington, Mass., also offers a protocol-conversion software package for the 3705. Called DMEP, for data-network modified emulator program, it enables IBM 360 and 370 computers to access—through their DMEP-loaded 3705 front ends—public packet networks. The protocol conversion is performed between 3270 and X.25, allowing a terminal operating with a 3270 controller to access a CPU through a packet-switching network [Ref. 4]. The same company also offers the program in a separate "box," the TP3010 (formerly CTX 9101) network interface processor.

Communications processors (CPs) competing with the 3705, made by such companies as NCR Comten Inc., Computer Communications Inc., and Memorex Corporation, depend on microprocessor-based architectures to achieve protocol conversion. As a front-end processor, the CP handles a variety of terminal types, speeds, and codes. For each type to communicate with the others requires CP conversions, which are made possible by a combination of line-interface devices and software [Ref. 5].

Converting up front

Comten, for example, does conversions in its modem interface module (MIM). A MIM can be microcoded or fully programmable, depending on the application. A software-controlled MIM, such as the data link control (DLC) interface, has its microprocessor program loaded at initial-program-load (IPL) time with the rest of the CP. It accommodates protocols from start-stop asynchronous to BSC and HDLC—depending on the program loaded.

Minicomputer manufacturers are also concerned with protocol conversion. Computer Automation of Irvine, Calif., for example, provides a microprocessor-driven front end, called a microbooster, for each protocol to be accessed. Among the protocols supported and converted between interactive devices on its system-for-access (SyFA) network are start-stop, BSC, SDLC, and X.25.

Another minicomputer vendor, Data General Corpo-

ration of Westboro, Mass., provides an architecture for its Eclipse computers that enables extensive protocol conversion. Called the Xodiac network-management system, the architecture permits a terminal, such as a TTY, ASCII, 2780/3780 RJE, or 3270, to log onto Xodiac, be "converted" to a "virtual" terminal type, and gain access to an Eclipse computer. The minicomputer may, in turn, access an SNA or an X.25 network.

One vendor, Systems Strategies Inc. (SSI) of New York City, has a 17K to 18K software package that provides both SNA and Telenet's X.25 protocol interfaces for Data General minicomputers. Since there are so many X.25 versions, SSI says that no general protocol conversion to the packet-switching-interface standard is possible. SSI also observes that SNA appears to have been made complicated intentionally to discourage non-IBM interfacing.

Networks doing it themselves

The increasing importance of public packet data networks (PDNs) to the implementation of information exchanges between a variety of users has compelled the PDNs to acquire their own extensive protocol-conversion capabilities. Tymnet claims that it can access just about any device—by converting the device's protocol to X.25 interfacing—through its internally switched interface system (ISIS) architecture.

Also, GTE Telenet recently broadened its terminal support to include not only low-speed asynchronous types, but also the 2780/3780 RJE BSC terminals [Ref. 6]. Together with the Trans-Canada Telephone System and Japan's Kokusai Denshin Denwa, Telenet has come up with a set of software modules to map the RJE BSC protocol into X.25. This software interface is called a BPAD, or binary synchronous packet assembler/disassembler.

Where the BPAD is implemented depends on the terminal's line interface. A BSC interface, requiring no terminal software changes, calls for the BPAD implementation in the network's entry node. If the terminal has an X.25 interface and the device's "intelligence"

---

3. Confirming data entry. *A directly connected dumb terminal (A) receives validation within a millisecond. Through a PDN (B), the delay is about 0.25 second.*

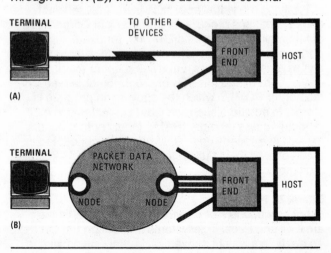

Protocol conversion offerings

Air Land Systems Corporation, Fairfax, Va.: ASCII TTY, 3270 and 2780/3780 BSC. SDLC/HDLC targeted for this year.

Cambridge Telecommunications Inc., Burlington, Mass.: Hardware and software package for 3270 BSC and X.25.

Comm-Pro Associates, Manhattan Beach, Calif.: Software packages for the IBM 3705, including SNA to X.25.

Computer Communications Inc., Torrance, Calif.: Communications processors with ASCII, 3270 and 2780/3780 BSC, SDLC, X.25, and others.

Data Stream Communications Inc., Santa Clara, Calif.: ASCII and TTY asynchronous, 3270 BSC.

DP Communications Corporation, New York, N.Y.: ASCII, 3270 and 2780/3780 BSC, HDLC.

Expandor Inc., Pittsburgh, Pa.: ASCII, 2780/3780 BSC, and others.

Icot Corporation, Mountain View, Calif.: Wide range of protocols via multimicroprocessors, including ASCII TTY, 3270 BSC and SDLC, and X.25/HDLC.

Industrial Computer Controls Inc., Cambridge, Mass.: ASCII, 3270 and 2780/3780 BSC, others.

Innovative Electronics Inc., Miami Lakes, Fla.: Wide range of protocols, including ASCII TTY, 3270 and 2780/3780 BSC, SDLC/HDLC.

InteCom Inc., Dallas, Tex.: ASCII TTY and 3270 BSC. Working on CWP protocols.

Kaufman Research Manufacturing Inc., Los Altos Hills, Calif.: Multimicroprocessors for ASCII TTY, 3270 BSC, SNA/SDLC, and others.

KMW Systems Corporation, Austin, Tex.: ASCII, 2780/3780 BSC.

Local Data Company, Torrance, Calif.: ASCII, 2780/3780 BSC.

Memorex Corporation, Cupertino, Calif.: Communications processors with ASCII, 3270 BSC, X.25, and others.

NCR-Comten Inc., St. Paul, Minn.: Communications processors with ASCII, 3270 and 2780/3780 BSC, SDLC, HDLC/X.25, and others.

Perle Systems Ltd., Willowdale, Ontario, Canada: ASCII, 3270 BSC.

Protocol Computers Inc., Woodland Hills, Calif.: ASCII, SNA/SDLC.

Racal-Telesystems Inc., Chicago, Ill.: Hardware converts between otherwise incompatible CWPs.

and capacity permit the loading, the BPAD can be implemented in the terminal. Depending on the device's architecture and the programmer's skill, the BPAD software takes about 16K of storage.

One problem not yet fully solved is "echoing" when a dumb terminal accesses a packet data network. Normally, when such a terminal operates locally with its CPU (Fig. 3A), the keyed-in data is validated by the computer and appears on the terminal's CRT within a millisecond. But when the terminal gains access to its CPU through a PDN (Fig. 3B), the screen data is delayed about 0.25 second—sufficient to disorient the operator. If the echoing function is left to the PDN's entry node, thus gaining the equivalent of local operation, not all function keys echo correctly. This problem cannot be solved until node processors gain vastly improved intelligence.

Although the bus interface unit is the common protocol-conversion device in local networks, some industry experts see another device as vital to the future of these networks: the computerized private branch exchange (CBX). The CBX is seen as the gateway device to interconnect local networks and to connect them to long-haul communications networks, thus greatly facilitating distributed data processing.

But before the CBX can act as a gateway, it must gain a protocol-conversion capability. This capability should encompass not only the two local-network standards now under consideration (CSMA/CD and token passing) but also packet- and circuit-switching standards (such as X.75 and X.21).

A small step toward this goal was recently announced and emphasizes the CBX's protocol-conversion potential rather than its application to local networks. Dallas-based InteCom enhanced its integrated business exchange (IBX) device to convert between ASCII and 3270 protocols (See Dataletter, DATA COMMUNICATIONS, May, p. 15).

Before such a device can function as a gateway, certain nontechnical issues must be settled. First among them is that CBX and local-network vendors are presently competing for the automated-office market. The application of the CBX to local-network gateways would require a high degree of cooperation between current competitors. But if local networks are to reach their potential as a true component in a distributed data processing network, the CBX must gain the broader protocol-conversion function.

The panel, "Protocol conversion offerings," gives a sampling of available conversion sources and specifies the protocols that each company's products convert. For a more complete listing of vendors, refer to the current *Data Communications Buyers' Guide* under Support Equipment, Protocol Converters.

References

1. Harold C. Folts, "Coming of age: A long-awaited standard for heterogeneous nets," DATA COMMUNICATIONS, January 1981.
2. David P. Misunas and Robert G. Jacobsen, "Protocol converters expanding network horizons," DATA COMMUNICATIONS, October 1979.
3. Tsvi Lissack et al., "Impact of microprocessor architectures on performance of local network interface adaptors," Network Analysis Corporation, June 1981.
4. Gregory Burch and Rubin Gruber, "Packet-switching networks seek bigger public role," DATA COMMUNICATIONS, September 1977.
5. Ray Sarch, "Communications processors—Trends and trade-offs," DATA COMMUNICATIONS, January 1979.
6. Sheldon Fox et al., "A synchronous ticket to packet networks," DATA COMMUNICATIONS, August 1980.

Understanding the fundamentals of line equalization

William J. Barksdale, Universal Data Systems, Huntsville, Ala.

Here is an introduction to equalization at a level that is suitable for the increasing number of technical management personnel involved in networking

Although automatic equalization has now been used in data communications for about 15 years, it is still considered something of a "black art" by many in the industry. This is due to the wide range of engineering disciplines involved in the design and implementation of these complex digital systems, and also to the relatively small number of industries directly involved in their manufacture.

For today's user, the importance of digital transmission is rapidly increasing because of the explosive increase in the amount of information transmitted in digital form. For example, speech can be digitized and coded for error control, security, bandwidth reduction, or integration with other digital traffic. Also, a good deal of data transmission requires significant signal processing, and it is natural to perform this function digitally whenever practical. The flexibility and the cost effectiveness of digital signal processing has resulted in the widespread use of digital filters, including digital equalizers.

Equalizer hardware has followed the general trend in digital electronics from small-scale to large-scale integration, and then to microprocessor control. The basic operations of equalization, which involve many iterations of the same shift-multiply-add sequence, make equalizers amenable to custom LSI implementa-

tion under software control. Today, equalization is widely employed over telephone lines at data rates of 4.8 and 9.6 kbit/s.

Equalization refers to the process of improving the signal transmission characteristics of a communications system. The term is also commonly used for tone control compensation in music systems, but here its meaning is restricted to the correction of amplitude and phase characteristics of communications channels. Because telephone channel parameters may vary with time, and the user rarely knows the line on which his data is being transmitted, an equalizer at the channel terminal must either be based on some average channel parameters or it must adapt to each particular channel that may be obtained by the user.

The first case is called fixed or compromise equalization. Such equalizers are provided by terminal manufacturers or common carriers and seldom require adjustment. On the other hand, an equalizer that automatically adjusts to each channel obtained is called an adaptive or automatic equalizer.

Before considering the details of adaptive digital equalizers, it is first necessary to understand the channel characteristics and modulation principles that determine the equalization requirements of a data communications network. The analog telephone plant has

1 Typical telephone channel

Cutoff. *Both group delay and gain magnitude (referred to as negative gain in the diagram) prevent a normal telephone cable from passing quality signals above 3 kHz.*

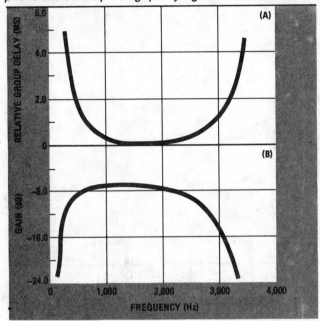

evolved over the past century to transmit human speech in the frequency band of 300 to 3K Hz. Data can also be carried on these lines if it is made to resemble an analog voice signal. For example, a transmitter can generate two audio tones, say 2 kHz for a binary 0 (a space) and 1 kHz for a binary 1 (a mark). Each of these frequencies can easily pass through a telephone channel and be detected by a frequency discriminator in the receiver. Such a basic scheme is called frequency-shift-keying (FSK) and is widely used today for teletypewriter applications at data rates up to 1,200 symbols per second. However, if the two frequencies are switched at higher rates, the data signal spectrum becomes wider than the speech bandwidth for which the channel was designed, and frequency-shift-keying becomes unsatisfactory.

Typical channel
Telephone channels are characterized by their response to sinusoidal signals. This is referred to as the channel frequency response, and is usually represented by two curves: a magnitude response in dB indicates the attenuation of amplitude, and a group delay response indicates the relative time delay for all frequencies of interest. Such curves are shown in Figure 1 for a representative channel.

If a sudden impulse is applied to the input of this channel, the time waveform of Figure 2 results at the output. Formally, this is called the unit impulse response of the channel, and is related to the frequency response by the Fourier transform. It is instructive to analyze this waveform in some detail.

The high frequency oscillation is around 1.7 kHz, which is the center frequency of the channel passband.

The waveform envelope is also dispersed in time over about 5 milliseconds, which is due to both the nonuniform group delay and the band-limiting effect of the channel from about 400 to 2.6K Hz. In particular, the skewing to the right is caused primarily by the group delay characteristic. This time dispersion (called smearing), along with noise, limits the rate at which data can be transmitted. To illustrate, let the rectangular pulse shown in Figure 3A represent a transmitted signal. When it is applied to an equivalent baseband channel (a modulator, a bandpass channel, and a demodulator), the smeared output waveform shown will result. Assume that the bipolar sequence of symbols shown in Figure 3B is transmitted. Because the channel is linear, the received signal will consist of the superposition of delayed and possibly inverted (for binary zero symbols) replicas of the previous smeared waveform shown. This type of distortion is called intersymbol interference (ISI).

If the data rate is increased by making the transmitted symbols shorter, then the ISI becomes more severe and the error rate increases. Thus one way of avoiding ISI is to use a sufficiently low data rate.

Fortunately, it is also possible to greatly reduce ISI by compensating for the channel characteristics that cause it. This is the purpose of equalizing filters. Such filters may be located at the transmitter, the receiver, or along the channel, and they may be digital or analog. Because ISI is essentially a linear distortion, most equalizers are linear filters, although certain nonlinear structures are also feasible.

Reshaping a signal
Equalizers correct for ISI by reshaping the received signal. To understand this process, it is first necessary to understand the Nyquist criterion. If the spectrum of a received pulse at the channel output satisfies certain symmetry conditions, the corresponding time waveform will have zero-crossings at regularly spaced times Three such baseband spectra $H_i(f)$, $i = 1,2,3$, along with the corresponding waveforms $h_i(t)$, are shown in Figure 4A through 4C.

Notice that each spectrum has odd symmetry about

2 Channel impulse response

Smearing. *The time-dependent waveform of a channel is smeared as indicated. This is principally caused by the channel group delay. Smearing limits the data rate.*

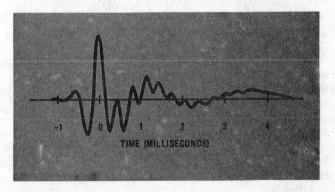

3 Intersymbol interference

Filtering. *Although ISI can be a serious problem in data transmission, it can be corrected, to a large extent, by adding compensating filters to mitigate the channel* *effects that produce it. Such filters can be located at the transmitter, the receiver, or at various locations along the channel. The filters can be either analog or digital type.*

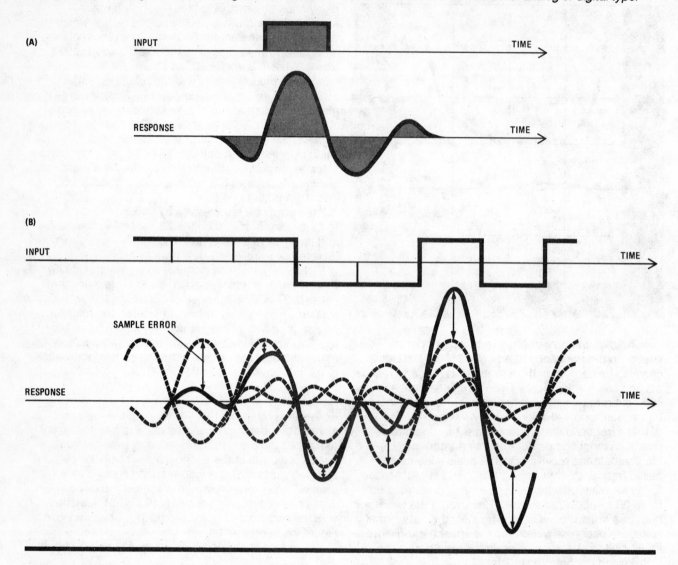

the frequency f_o. Also, all of the corresponding time waveforms have the value zero at all nonzero integer multiples of $T = \frac{1}{2}f_o$. Consequently, if a new data pulse is transmitted every T seconds, the n sample of the received waveform taken exactly T seconds apart will contain no ISI (although there will be distortion between the samples). The figures also illustrate the general tendency for signals with smoother spectral roll-off to have less oscillation in the time domain, a condition that is clearly important if the sample time T cannot be exactly determined or maintained. The minimum bandwidth for which this zero-crossing criterion holds for baseband signals is $f_o = \frac{1}{2}T$, and such pulses transmitted faster than the Nyquist rate of $2f_o$ symbols per second will always have ISI.

A straightforward approach to equalization at baseband is now apparent: filtering should be added to the channel to make the output pulse spectrum satisfy the symmetric roll-off condition of the Nyquist criterion. The data should then be transmitted and sampled at the Nyquist rate. The design trade-offs among bandwidth, data rate, and sensitivity to jitter and timing errors can also be determined and evaluated.

So far, only the equalization of the magnitude spectrum has been considered, tacitly assuming that the phase is zero. However, the telephone plant is designed to transmit speech, and the human ear is relatively insensitive to phase, so the phase or delay distortion on a line is often severe. The group delay characteristic of telephone lines tends to be approximately parabolic as indicated in Figure 1B, and the resulting effect on the impulse response is a skewing of the pulse shape. This type of distortion can be equalized by adding all-pass filters having parabolic delay with the opposite slope. Of course, such filters can also be employed in combination with magnitude-type equaliza-

4 Frequency time relationship

Varying bandwidth. *The impulse response for signals A, B, and C are detailed. Each response is symmetrical about time zero. Smooth roll-off causes less oscillation.*

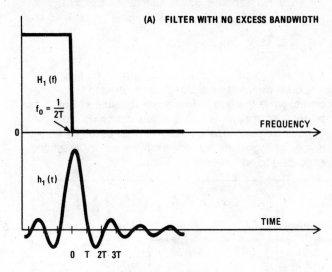

(A) FILTER WITH NO EXCESS BANDWIDTH

$H_1(f)$

$f_0 = \dfrac{1}{2T}$

FREQUENCY

$h_1(t)$

TIME

0 T 2T 3T

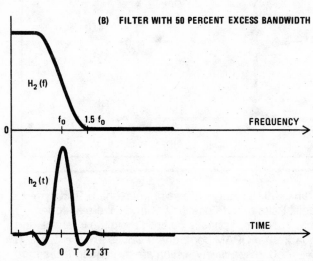

(B) FILTER WITH 50 PERCENT EXCESS BANDWIDTH

$H_2(f)$

f_0 1.5 f_0

FREQUENCY

$h_2(t)$

TIME

0 T 2T 3T

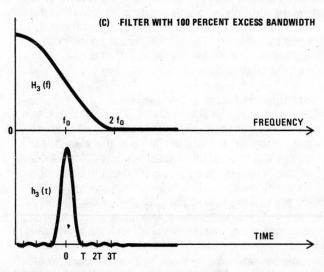

(C) FILTER WITH 100 PERCENT EXCESS BANDWIDTH

$H_3(f)$

f_0 2 f_0

FREQUENCY

$h_3(t)$

TIME

0 T 2T 3T

tion when it becomes necessary to take such action.

Data signals use two or more signal shapes, or states, to represent information during transmission. The signals that we have considered so far all have spectra located near zero frequency (baseband). The channels used in many applications are sufficient to pass the spectra of simple rectangular pulses with little distortion. This is the case, for example, in the internal buses of most computers and electronic laboratory equipment. However, when such signals are applied directly to a communications channel such as that represented by Figure 1, much of the low-frequency energy will not be passed. Although the loss of these low frequencies is of little consequence in voice transmission, for data it results in a weak, distorted output signal at the receiver.

Translating baseband spectra

For efficient transmission, it is necessary for the data transmitter to produce a waveform having a spectrum in the same band as the frequency response of the channel. Such a signal can be synthesized directly, but the common procedure is to translate a baseband signal spectrum up to the center of the channel passband by modulation. Also, two or more independent signals can be modulated on a single channel by placing each signal spectra in a unique portion of the channel bandwidth. This is known as frequency-division multiplexing. For example, data can be transmitted simultaneously in both directions over a telephone line by using the lower half of the bandwidth for one direction and the upper half for the other.

In the past, many different modulation schemes have been proposed for various communications applications. Each scheme has certain advantages and drawbacks for any given application. For data transmission over telephone lines, it is conventional practice to use frequency-shift-keying for data rates up to about 1.2 kbit/s, and some form of linear amplitude modulation at higher rates. The popularity of FSK is primarily due to its simplicity and ease of implementation, but the bandwidth requirements make it attractive only at low speeds. For a fixed-channel bandwidth, higher data rates can be obtained by a combination of four basic techniques.

First, the channel amplitude and phase response can be equalized so that some specific impulse-response requirement is approximated. Called line conditioning, this often takes the form of a flat amplitude and linear phase across most of the passband.

Second, the shape of the baseband pulse can be selected so that after modulation, its spectrum properly matches the expected channel characteristics. For example, the transmitted pulse can be predistorted, or pre-equalized, to correct for the skewing caused by the channel phase distortion.

A third technique is to combine several binary data samples into one transmitted symbol so that, for example, three bits are collected and used to select one of eight possible symbols. This is a form of coding for bandwidth reduction.

A final method for obtaining higher data rates is to

The transversal digital filter

Because transversal, or "tapped delay line," filter structures have no feedback, they are suitable for digital filters. This type of filter is extremely versatile, simple and straightforward to implement, and, except for possible numerical effects, is always stable.

The diagram shows a transversal filter structure, which consists of a digital shift register, adders, and multipliers (often called "taps"). The N tap coefficients are denoted by $c_0, c_1, \ldots, c_{N-1}$, while $x(n)$ denotes the numerical value of the nth sample of input signal $x(t)$. Notice that although the filter has N sections, each is identical to the others, so that efficient implementations are possible that multiplex a single hardware section or use a single software loop. The filter continually computes the weighted average of the data

samples $x(n), \ldots, x(n-N+1)$ contained in the shift register. This is equivalent to performing a discrete convolution of these data samples, with the unit pulse (or impulse) response of the filter given simply by the tap coefficients. The output sample $y(n)$ is then

$$y(n) = \sum_{K=0}^{N-1} c_K \, x\,(n-k)$$

For a transversal digital filter of length N, the frequency response depends on the sampling rate and tap coefficients, while the output is a linear function of both the present input sample and the past samples stored in the shift register. The coefficients can be adjusted by simply changing the contents of N memory locations according to an adaptive algorithm.

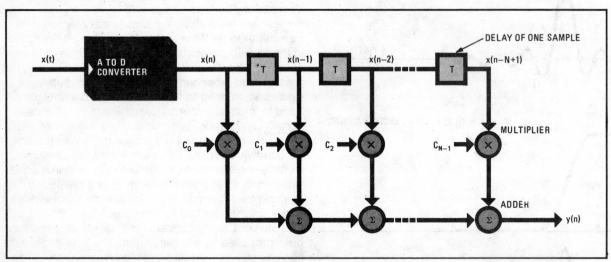

use modulation techniques that afford good bandwidth utilization and noise immunity.

Transmitting simultaneously

Modulation for higher data rates is usually some type of linear amplitude modulation such as vestigal sideband (VSB), quadrature amplitude modulation (QAM) with a rectangular pattern, phase shift keying (PSK), or combined phase and amplitude modulation (QPAM). Because QPAM is widely used and easy to understand, it is focused on here. Furthermore, even though PSK conveys information as discrete phase angles, it can be treated as a special case of QPAM.

Quadrature modulation allows two signals to be simultaneously transmitted at the same carrier frequency. Using double-sideband suppressed-carrier amplitude modulation, the second (quadrature) signal is modulated by a carrier that is 90 degrees out of phase with the first (in-phase) signal carrier. The sum of these signals can be recovered at the receiver by multiplying the received signal by two coherent reference carriers in quadrature that are synchronized with the original carriers, then recovering the two baseband spectra with simple low-pass filters.

Figure 5 illustrates a coherent QPAM system for

transmitting binary data using four-phase PSK symbols. Pairs of data bits, say (1 and 0), are encoded into one of four phases by producing the in-phase and quadrature QPAM component values $a_1(t) = 1.0$, $a_2(t) = -1.0$, respectively, which are then quadrature modulated onto the channel. Notice that the use of four different symbols results in the data bit rate (into the encoder) being twice the symbol rate (into the line). Hence the use of 8, 16, or 32 symbols on the phasor diagram would result in a data rate that is 3, 4, or 5 times the symbol rate, respectively.

Adapting to changing channels

The purpose of equalization is, of course, the reduction of ISI to a point at which the receiver has a high probability of making correct decisions in the presence of noise. It would be ideal to insert an equalizing filter that has the inverse frequency response of the channel. This would make the cascade system have flat amplitude and linear phase characteristics. Although such an ideal situation cannot be exactly realized in either digital or analog form, it can be closely approximated over the signal bandwidth with properly designed equalizers, once the channel frequency response has been determined. In modern data networks, the equal-

5 QPAM system

Combination. *Quadrature phase and amplitude modulation, referred to as QPAM, are actually a combination of phase and amplitude modulation techniques employed* *concurrently. Pairs of data bits are encoded into one of four phases by producing in-phase and quadrature components. The separate signals are then modulated.*

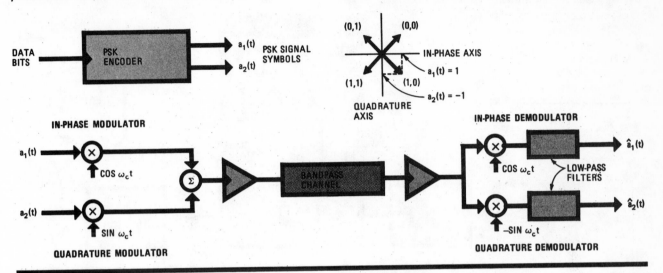

ization problems are usually complicated by the channel being unknown. For example, many networks work in a dial-up mode, where a central location systematically queries remote data terminals by automatically dialing their telephone number. Each such dial-up connection results in a new channel that must then be quickly identified and equalized by the receiver. If this process takes more than a fraction of a second, transmission efficiency suffers. Even if the same line is used repeatedly, its transmission characteristics may vary significantly as a result of changing temperature and weather conditions.

These considerations illustrate the class of problem that a modern equalizer must solve; it must identify the channel and assume a configuration so that its output approximately satisfies the Nyquist criterion for minimal ISI. All of this must be typically done in a fraction of a second by what is actually an adaptive open-loop control system. Such systems obviously involve considerable speed and sophistication. Consequently, they are usually implemented with digital hardware, which now frequently includes microprocessor control.

Adaptive equalization

The definition of an adaptive digital equalizer involves (1) the selection of a performance criterion (or cost function), (2) an algorithm for minimizing this cost function, and (3) a means for implementing the algorithm. The resulting system should be stable, reliable, cost effective, and should first allow for fast initialization and then on-line tracking of variations in the channel and data statistics. Figure 6 is a block diagram of a typical equalizer based on a transversal digital filter . The algorithm uses the error samples $e(n)$ to adjust the filter tap coefficients in order to reduce the cost function iteratively. A decision algorithm estimates the data sample from the equalizer output.

The process can best be clarified by a specific example.

The mean square error (MSE) cost function is defined as the statistical average of the square of the error samples. It can be minimized by incrementally adjusting the tap coefficients in a direction opposite the gradient of the cost function (in the direction of steepest descent). The resulting algorithm for the kth coefficient at the nth iteration is

$$c_k(n+1) = c_k(n) + \Delta c_k(n)$$
$$= c_k(n) - \gamma E[x(n-k)e(n)]$$

Here E denotes statistical average, $x(n-k)$ is the input sample in the Kth shift register stage, and the positive constant γ determines how large the adjustments will be. The third requirement for defining the MSE equalizer is the means of implementation. It is impractical to compute the exact statistical average in real time, so a suitable estimate must be made. A simple, yet effective estimate is to just use the argument $x(n-k)e(n)$ without averaging. The result,

$$c_k(n+1) = c_k(n) - \gamma x(n-k)e(n), k = 0, 1, ..., N-1$$

is known as the LMS gradient algorithm. The samples $x(n-k)$ are readily available, since they are just the shift register contents. However, $e(n) = y(n) - a(n)$ requires knowledge of the transmitted data $a(n)$, which is, in general, unknown by the receiver. This is circumvented in two ways, depending on whether the equalizer is in the initialization or the tracking mode.

During initialization, a known sequence of training pulses is transmitted. It may consist of either isolated pulses with enough time between each for the channel response to decay or of some sequence with desirable spectral properties. Once synchronization is acquired, the equalizer output is compared with a locally generated replica of this initializing sequence to produce the error sample at the receiver. Over many iterations, the

6 Basic adaptive equalizer

Feedback. *A typical adaptive equalizer system uses some form of algorithm to minimize the cost function associated with its realization. Here the equalizer's error* *signal, e(n), is fed back to the algorithm, which then uses the error data to continuously signal adjustments to the transversal filter. The taps are adjusted to compensate.*

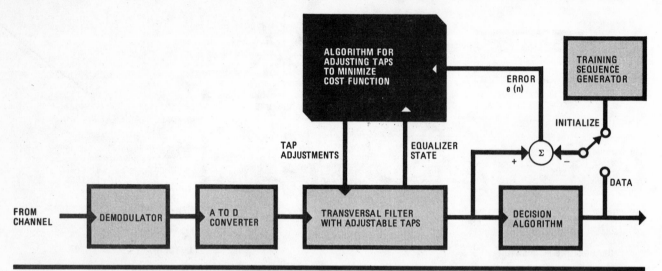

algorithm adjusts the tap coefficients $c_k(n)$ so as to reduce the correlation between each $x(n-k)$ and $e(n)$ until $c_k(n+1)$ is approximately equal to $c_k(n)$. Then the optimal tap setting is obtained. At this point, the equalizer output should closely approximate the training sequence, and $e(n)$ should be very small. The coefficients will be initialized so that the unit pulse response samples of the combined channel and equalizer have minimal ISI. After initialization is completed, the coefficients may be fixed. This is automatic equalization.

If the time of transmission is long enough for the channel to vary, or if the data statistics change significantly, the initial equalizer setting is no longer optimal. Then it is desirable for the equalizer coefficients to slowly track these changes, in which case the equalizer is made adaptive. The error in an adaptive equalizer can be computed by assuming that the receiver decisions for $a(n)$ have a high probability of being correct, and thus can be substituted for the actual values. This is called decision-directed operation (the equalizer algorithm is driven by receiver decisions).

Other choices
The MSE equalizer is currently the most popular for data transmission, particularly for two-dimensional QAM signals. However, many other types and variations are also used. Two important ones are the zero-forcing and decision-feedback equalizers. The basic theoretical work on adaptive equalization, *Automatic Equalization for Digital Communication*, published in 1965, used a cost function called the Distortion, which actually represents the worst case ISI. Minimizing this cost function results in a constrained minimax optimization problem that can be solved iteratively. Intuitively, the taps are adjusted so that there is a large output if the channel unit-pulse response is located at some central tap, and a relatively small output if it is centered

at any other tap. Thus all but one of the output samples within the equalizer are driven toward zero, and for this reason the equalizer is called zero forcing. Extension to an adaptive tracking mode is done in a manner similar to the MSE case, but the error sample is correlated with the equalizer output samples rather than the input.

The decision-feedback equalizer has been the subject of considerable study in recent years because for the same number of taps, it offers potentially better performance than the linear MSE equalizer. It can also provide useful timing information directly. The basic approach is to use a separate transversal filter to feed decisions back so as to completely cancel the effects of those samples preceding the main sample. The usual feed-forward filter is used only for reducing the ISI effects of the next samples. Such equalizers are nonlinear, and because of the feedback, they require careful attention to stability.

A final example is the extension to QPAM of the previous mean square error equalizer. The corresponding equalizers are called two-dimensional (or complex) equalizers. The MSE cost function can be defined, and the gradient algorithm can then be determined in two dimensions, resulting in both in-phase and quadrature tap coefficients.

Most equalizer applications are based on the theory presented here, but there are an infinite number of other possible variations. For example, a great deal of effort has gone into schemes to reduce the number of multiplications. The location of the equalizer in the receiver can also be varied, and many receivers perform equalization in the passband before demodulation. This offers advantages with regard to synchronization, at the expense of dealing with higher frequency.

Other approaches to equalization have also been proposed, such as Kalman filtering, but the costs of such schemes have so far been prohibitive. ■

Communications processors keep networks ticking

Gilbert Held, U.S. Civil Service Commission, Macon, Ga.

Communications concentrators and front-end processors have distinct attributes—each is designed to perform specific tasks

Integral to almost every data communications network—and responsible for much of the smooth gear-like meshing of network elements—are two devices which, although consisting of many similar hardware components, must be recognized and utilized as distinct entities. These two devices are the communications concentrator and the front-end processor. Each device is designed to perform specific applications.

Substantial confusion concerning the utilization of these devices can occur due to the multitude of overlapping functions they perform. A front-end processor, in effect, performs concentration functions by concentrating a number of lines into a few data transfer paths between that processor and a host computer. Likewise, a remote network processor can be viewed as performing the functions of a front-end processor when its high-speed data link is used to transmit data directly into another processor.

To alleviate some of the existing confusion about the utilization of these processors, this article will examine the basic components of the devices and the functions they perform, the characteristics that should be investigated for evaluation purposes, and the placement of these devices within a data communications network.

As a general statement, a concentrator is a device

which concentrates M incoming lines to N outgoing lines, where a number of incoming lines is usually greater than—or possibly equal to—the number of outgoing lines. The incoming lines are usually referred to as concentrator-to-terminal links, whereas the outgoing lines are normally called concentrator-to-concentrator or concentrator-to-host links. Although the concentrator-to-host link implies that such lines from the concentrator are connected to the host processor, in actuality they can terminate at a front-end processor which is, in turn, connected to a host processor or main computer.

Depending on the hardware components and operating software one selects, the concentrator can be used to perform concentration, pure contention, store-and-forward concentration, message switching, and remote network processing. Remote network processing is a term some computer manufacturers use to denote concurrent concentration of low-speed terminals with remote batch processing, all on one processor. (For a detailed discussion of the concentrator's message-switching role, refer to "How concentrators can be message switchers as well," DATA COMMUNICATIONS, April 1977, pp. 51-57.)

In a concentration role, concentrators merge the traffic from several low- to medium-speed lines onto one or more high-speed lines, similar to the function performed by a multiplexer. However, concentrators can be programmed to transmit data only from terminals that are active, as opposed to conventional time-division multiplexers in which a fixed fraction of the multiplexed channel is reserved for each terminal, regardless of whether or not the terminal is active.

Concentrators can also be programmed to make the high-speed link more efficient through data compression. A reduction in the average number of bits transmitted per character is made possible by determining the different occurrence rates of characters, and applying an algorithmic code to denote each character. (See the article, "Data compression increases throughput," Data Communications, May/June 1976, pp. 65-76.) In addition, if the host computer's native code is different from the terminal's codes, code conversion can be performed by the concentrator, relieving the host processor of this burden.

Interfacing with controllers

The typical hardware components included in a concentrator used in a concentration role are illustrated in Figure 1. The single-line controllers (SLCs) provide the necessary control and sensing signals which interface the concentrator to individual data communications circuits. While single-line controllers can be asynchronous or synchronous, the majority are the synchronous type. The preponderance of synchronous transmission is due to the SLC's normally providing only one—or at most a few—high-speed transmission links from the concentrator to another concentrator or to a host computer (front-end processor).

Since the support of numerous lines would be expensive and would take up a lot of space if implemented with single-line controllers, most communications support for the concentrator-to-terminal links are implemented through the use of multi-line controllers. Multi-line controllers (MLCs) can be categorized by capacity (number and speed of lines supported) as well as by operation: hardware- or software-controlled.

Hardware-controlled multi-line controllers place no additional burden on the concentrator's CPU, the hardware MLC requiring much less operating software than the programmed controller. However, programmed controllers have the lowest per line cost by reducing

1 Concentrator hardware

Components. *Typically, a concentrator used in a concentration role is made up of a central processing unit, a multi-line controller, and numbers of single-line controllers.*

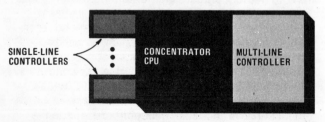

SINGLE-LINE CONTROLLERS

CONCENTRATOR CPU

MULTI-LINE CONTROLLER

2 Groupings by channel

Foursomes. *In this typical multi-line controller arrangement, each of the four channels in a group must be of the same terminal class, having identical bit rates and codes.*

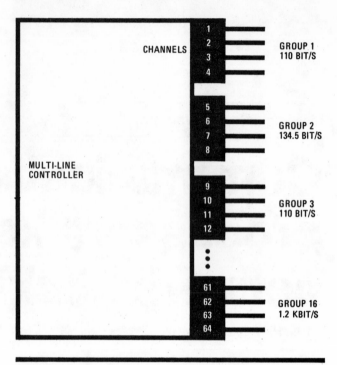

MULTI-LINE CONTROLLER

CHANNELS

1
2
3
4
GROUP 1
110 BIT/S

5
6
7
8
GROUP 2
134.5 BIT/S

9
10
11
12
GROUP 3
110 BIT/S

61
62
63
64
GROUP 16
1.2 KBIT/S

the hardware in the interfaces and the controller to a minimum, although a large burden is placed on the processor. For a programmed controller, all sampling control, bit detection, and buffering is performed by the processor through software control. The amount of processing time required by the operational program is the main factor limiting the number of lines that can be connected to the concentrator via software-controlled MLCs.

To reduce the complexity of circuits in hardware multi-line controllers, as well as to reduce software overhead of programmed controllers, incoming lines are often arranged in groups. These groupings are by bit rate, code level, and the number of stop bits for asynchronous terminal support. Figure 2 illustrates a typical grouping by channel for a multi-line controller. This controller requires a minimum of four channels per group—all four channels of the same terminal class (same bit rate and code). In Figure 2, groups 1 and 3 are of the same class. The MLC may have any mixture of classes, until the number of groups multiplied by four equals the total number of channels supported by the controller (64 in the example).

Although a complete examination of controllers might entail the investigation of up to 50 parameters, Table 1 lists the 13 key types of information that one should ascertain about the different controllers which are supported by a concentrator. Included are those parameters discussed above.

Another area that can have a major bearing on communications costs—and where the cost-cutting implementation is comparatively convenient—are the types of interfaces supported by the controller. If the controller supports directly connected terminals, and the concentrator can be located in the vicinity of a number of the terminals, then connecting those terminals directly to the concentrator will eliminate the cost of installing pairs of line drivers or modems between the concentrator and each applicable terminal. In this case, vicinity means—typically—up to 50 feet for EIA RS-232-C interfacing, or up to about 1,000 feet for a TTY current loop interface configuration.

Pure contention

In essence, a pure-contention concentrator is a port selector. In performing this function, any of M input lines are connected to any of N output lines as one of the N output lines becomes available. The M input lines are commonly called the line side of the concentrator, whereas the N output lines are referred to as the port side—to interface the ports of a front-end processor. The basic hardware components of a contention concentrator are illustrated in Figure 3.

Incoming data on each line of the line side of the device is routed through the concentrator's processor, which searches for a non-busy line on the port side to transmit the data to. The determination of priorities can be programmed so that groups of incoming lines can be made to contend for one or a group of lines on the port side. When all ports are in use, messages can be generated to notify terminals attempting to access the system of the "busy" situation. Through the addition of peripheral storage devices, incoming jobs can be batched to await the disconnection of a user from the system. Then connection to the newly available port side line is made to gain entry to the computational facility, and the stored job is transmitted.

Evaluating the CPU

Although some vendors offer a complete concentration package which includes controllers and CPU, other vendors permit the customer to select the CPU that is to be used for the concentrator. The evaluation and selection of the concentrator's CPU should be accomplished in a manner similar to the evaluation and selection of any stand-alone computer. Both the hardware and software should be evaluated according to user

3 Contention concentrator

Basic hardware. The input lines from the terminals contend for the output lines to the host ports. Both input and output interface multi-line controllers to the CPU.

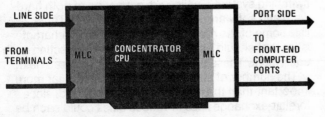

LINE SIDE			PORT SIDE
FROM TERMINALS	MLC	CONCENTRATOR CPU	MLC	TO FRONT-END COMPUTER PORTS

TABLE 1 Controller parameters

Multi-line controller only
Control type—hardware or software
Number of lines supported
Number of lines per class
Maximum throughput

Both single- and multi-line controller
Data codes and speeds supported
Number and grouping of channels
Terminal classes supported
Full-/half-duplex support
Auto-dial/auto-answer interface
Dataset interface
Direct connect interface
Protocols supported
Parity checking

requirements. Thus, if one needs a store-and-forward message-concentration system, emphasis should be placed upon peripheral equipment, data transfer rates, and software appropriate for this particular application. In addition, if the application is critically time dependent, examining hardware reliability by itself may not suffice, and the user will most likely want to consider a redundancy configuration.

As shown in the redundant store-and-forward arrangement of Figure 4, both systems are directly connected to each other by an intercomputer communications unit and share access to incoming and outgoing lines and peripherals via electronic switches. During operation, one system is considered the operational processing or master system, while the other is the slave or standby system, monitoring the master. Upon a hardware failure or power interrupt, the master system signals the slave system to take over processing via the intercomputer communications unit, generates an alarm message, and conducts an orderly shutdown.

Since the slave system has been in parallel processing, it resets all controls and becomes the master system, holding the potential of losing data to a minimum. This procedure can usually be completed within 500 microseconds for processors with a cycle time of 750 nanoseconds or less. In this case, 666 cycles or more (500 microsec ÷ 750 nanosec) are available with that time slot to execute the required instructions to transfer control and effect the orderly shutdown. Actually, just two to four computer cycles are needed for the execution of such instructions.

Switching the message

To effect message switching, incoming data is routed to a central point where messages are concentrated for processing. Then, based upon some processing criteria, messages are routed over one or more lines connected to the system. In message switching, all terminals connected to the system can communicate with every other terminal connected to the system—once the message has been processed and the desti-

4 Redundant message concentration

Store-and-forward. During operation, one concentrator system is considered the master, and the other is the slave—monitoring the master. The slave system operates in a parallel processing mode. When it senses a failure of the master system, the slave resets all controls through the shared ICCU, and it becomes the new master system.

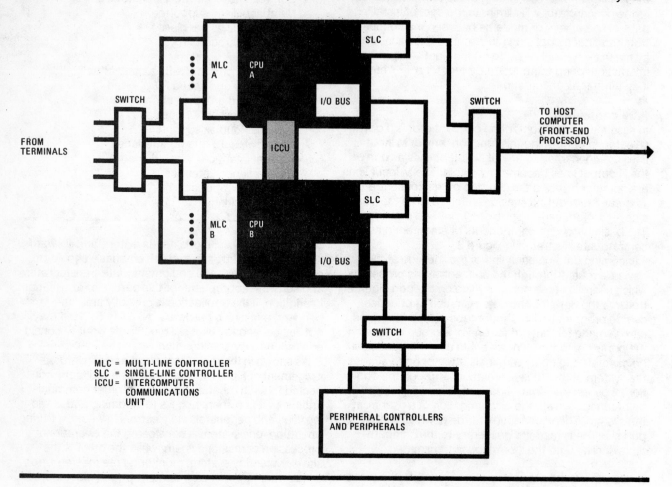

MLC = MULTI-LINE CONTROLLER
SLC = SINGLE-LINE CONTROLLER
ICCU = INTERCOMPUTER
        COMMUNICATIONS
        UNIT

nation data contained in the message is acted upon.

The hardware required for a message-switching system is quite similar to that required by a store-and-forward message-concentration system. The primary differences are the application software, and that incoming messages are not stored, but are processed and then routed over one or more of the incoming lines. And accesses to peripherals such as disks are handled via direct memory access (DMA) channels instead of the lower speed available from data transfers conducted via a processor's I/O bus.

The interface used to transfer data to communications controllers and peripherals is usually determined by the necessary I/O transfer rate. Interfacing may occur at the computer's I/O bus or via such devices as direct memory control (DMC) and direct memory access (DMA). Data transferred on the I/O bus is bit-serial and under control of the program. In the DMC mode, data transfers are effected independent of program control, and data blocks are transferred on a word basis (bit-parallel) to and from any portion of main memory. The DMC mode is used for medium-speed data transfer, and requires a starting and ending

address, as well as the number of characters to be transferred. Although similarly word-oriented and a direct-to-memory medium, the DMA mode requires only the starting and ending address. For high-speed data transfers, the DMA mode is used, but at a cost higher than with DMC. The speed at which DMA permits transfer of data is such that a computer using DMA on a high-speed channel can exchange data with several devices (peripherals) and controllers concurrently on a timeshared basis.

Line and station

In addition to the controller parameters listed in Table 1, the line and station characteristics of the message-switching system—which are a function of both hardware and software—should be determined. Table 2 lists some of the message-switching system characteristics that should be investigated prior to selecting such equipment. These characteristics are discussed next.

The number of stations supported is often far more important than the number of lines supported, since foreign-exchange lines in various cities could each be connected to a channel on the multi-line controller of the message-switching system. This situation would enable a large number of terminals to contend for the foreign exchange line in each city, with each terminal having a unique station code. The station types listed in Table 2 refer to whether full-duplex, half-duplex, or simplex transmission is supported. Message addressing refers to the number of addresses per message, as well as the capability of broadcasting a message to a predetermined group of stations, or to all stations, by using a group code addressing scheme.

Most message-switching software permits several levels of message priority. Examples of priority levels would be Expedite, Normal, and Deferred. A deferred-priority message is transmitted to its destination after normal working hours. A message of expedite priority would preempt any lower priority message being transmitted to an addressee until the expedite message transmission is completed. Depending on the software, some software packages permit any station to assign any message a priority, while other systems can lock out certain stations from assigning one or more specific priorities to a message.

Normally, the maximum length of any message is a function of disk space and system throughput. For all practical purposes, though, users can transmit messages without worrying about their length.

Software for a preferred message-switching system will pre-process the message header as it is entered. Then the user is informed of invalid station codes, invalid group addresses, garbled transmission for both header and text, and any other errors prior to routing of the message. On some systems, a message denoting these errors will also be routed to the message-switching system's operator console, so that the console operator will be able to ascertain user problems as they occur and furnish assistance if required. An example of such assistance is alternate routing, which permits supervisory personnel to route all traffic des-

tined to one station (or group of stations) to some other station. This capability is important if, for some reason, a communications component or terminal becomes inoperative, and there is a station nearby that could handle messages destined for the inoperative terminal.

Line and station "skips" and "holds" supplement alternate routing. The skip command permits the omission of any line or station from the polling pattern. A hold permits traffic to any station or line to be kept from delivery.

Retrieving the message

The journalization characteristic (Table 2) permits every message transmitted from the system to be recorded on journal storage. This storage provides the basis for message retrieval from the journal. However, the type of retrieval permitted varies from system to system. Some systems permit any station to retrieve messages destined only to itself, while other systems permit any station to retrieve any journaled message by sequence number. On some systems the operator can access the journal by either station number, sequence number, or by time of day.

The intercept characteristic permits the central-site operator to have traffic destined for specific lines or stations rerouted to intercept storage. The traffic may then be delivered to the addressed destinations by using a recovery function. The intercept and recovery characteristics are especially important if a large number of lines become inoperative at one time and messages cannot be rerouted to other nearby terminals. Since line losses are of critical importance to a message-switching system, events of this type can normally be expected to cause an alarm message to be generated to a console so the operator can take appropriate action. This action includes notifying the phone company, establishing an alternate route, and notifying

5 Remote network processor

Concurrent processing. *In addition to the standard concentration function, the RNP permits entry of remote batch jobs for transmission to the host computer. Meanwhile, completed jobs are printed on the line printer, and other jobs are being punched out on the card punch. Some RNPs allow downline program load from the host.*

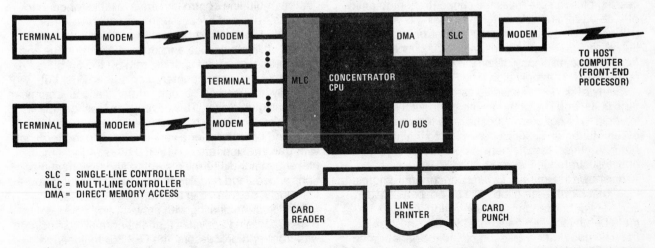

SLC = SINGLE-LINE CONTROLLER
MLC = MULTI-LINE CONTROLLER
DMA = DIRECT MEMORY ACCESS

Host interface. *Although FEPs are similar in design and use components common to those in concentrators, FEPs normally have larger word sizes, faster cycle time, larger* *memory, and permit the interfacing of more communications devices. A local multiplexer is sometimes encountered on FEPs, but is normally not used on concentrators.*

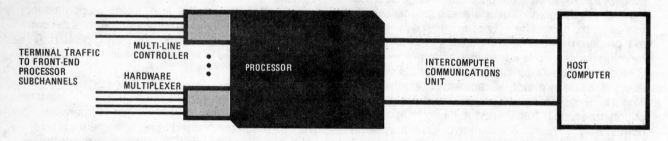

Table 2 Switching characteristics

Number of lines supported
Number of stations supported
Line speeds and codes supported
Station types
Message addressing permitted
Levels of message priority
Message length
Input error checking
Alternate routing
Line and station skips and holds
Journalization capability
Retrieval capability
Intercept and recovery provisions
Alarms and reports

the traffic originator of the actions taken—including where transmissions will be received.

Another form of concentrator is a remote network processor (RNP). Besides concentration, it performs the additional function of remote batch processing, thus providing two distinct functions in one package. Remote network processors vary in capabilities—ranging from basic, single-job-stream remote batch processing plus remote message concentration, to multiple-job-stream remote batch processing combined with remote message concentration. Due to the addition of remote batch processing to the concentration function, the efficiency of line utilization to the host computer is extremely high. The RNP may be serving a variety of devices, including card readers, magnetic tape units, and line printers. This peripheral support is in addition to concentrating the data from a number of remote terminals for transmission to the host computer. A typical remote network processor configuration is illustrated in Figure 5.

As shown in Figure 5, several concurrent remote and local batch processing jobs can be accomplished in addition to the standard concentration function. Remote batch jobs can be entered for transmission to the host computer, while completed jobs are printed on the line printer and other jobs are being punched

out on the card punch.

Some remote network processors have a segment of read-only memory which permits downline loading of operational software from the host computer to the RNP. This is a valuable feature since it permits programming changes for new batch and remote terminal equipment to be performed at the central site, and alleviates the necessity of employing programmers at every RNP installation to effect equipment configuration changes.

By offloading work from the host computer, and by blocking the characters transmitted from each terminal into messages, the RNP permits users to better load-balance their computational equipment. In many instances, this load-balancing can alleviate a costly host processor upgrade or the threat of encountering degraded service.

Front-end processing

A front-end processor (FEP) provides a large volume of network communications power in support of a particular computer system. Although FEPs are similar in design and use components common to those in concentrators, normally FEPs have larger word sizes, faster cycle time, larger memory, and permit the interfacing of more communications devices. A typical front-end processor configuration is illustrated in Figure 6.

More multi-line controllers are available for connection to a front-end processor than to a concentrator. The multi-line controllers are close to being universal in their ability to service a mixture of synchronous and asynchronous data at speeds from 50 to 50K bit/s.

Another device encountered on some FEPs, but normally not used on concentrators, is a local communications multiplexer. This device provides for time-division multiplexing, by character, to and from the front-end processor for a variety of low-speed terminals with transmission rates up to 300 bit/s. A local multiplexer can handle terminals with differing communications speeds and code settings. The character demultiplexing is performed in the front-end processor.

In addition to dealing with network and communications processing activities that one normally associates with front-end processors, the FEP is often used to perform message-switching functions. These functions

7 Integrating into a network

Combining devices. *Location 1 uses a standard concentrator for its 32 terminals. Since location 2 has a remote batch processing requirement as well as connecting 12 terminals to the host, an RNP is used. Location 3 has a redundant store-and-forward operation for its terminals. Location 4's front-end uses a contention concentrator.*

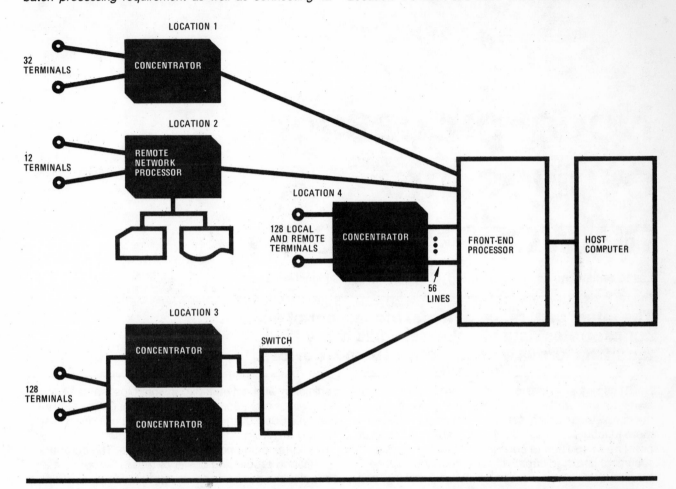

are aided by the FEP's large memory and word size, and by the ready addition of modular software.

Supervising software

The operating system which supervises the overall control and operation of all system functions is the key element of a front-end processor. Although numerous software elements must be evaluated, major consideration should be given to determining supported line protocols as well as supported processor communications. Most vendors divide their supported line protocols into several categories or classes of support. Normally Category 1 refers to vendor-developed and -tested software to support certain line protocols. Category 2 usually references vendor-developed , but non-qualified tested software, which means that the vendor will not guarantee results because the program has not been fully debugged. Category 3 references customer-developed interfaces designed to support certain terminal line protocols.

While the features of front-end processors are similar to those of concentrators, the FEP's reliability and redundancy, as well as its diagnostics, should be more

extensive, since the front-end processor is the heart of a communications network. Figure 7 illustrates a typical data communications network consisting of several different types of concentrators and a front-end processor. This network combines examples of much of what was discussed previously.

At location 1, a standard concentrator is used to concentrate the traffic from 32 terminals onto a high-speed line for transmission to the front-end processor. Since location 2 has a requirement for remote batch processing as well as connecting 12 terminals to the host computer, a remote network processor has been installed to perform these two functions. And since location 3 has a significant number of terminals doing an important application, a redundant store-and-forward message concentrator was installed.

Terminals remaining in the network (location 4) total 128. However, it was felt that at most only 56 would ever become active at any given time. Therefore, to economize on front-end processor ports, a contention concentrator was "front-ended" to the front-end processor, making the 128 channels connected to terminals contend for the 56 front-end processor ports. ∎

Nodal processor evolves into network mainstay

Lee K. Sudan and John A. Fagerberg, Codex Corporation, Mansfield, Mass.

The latest generation of nodal processor not only concentrates data but also assumes many functions formerly handled by separate devices.

Nodal communications processors are vital to almost every data network. As networks have evolved over the years, these processors have assumed more and more functions. Today's new generation of nodal processor—in addition to concentrating data—provides such sophisticated capabilities as least-cost routing, satellite-delay compensation, resource switching, and protocol conversion, all in a single node.

In the past, a nodal processor was essentially only a data concentrator. Concentrators, which are specially programmed minicomputers, meet specific user applications such as multiplexing special protocols, supporting high-speed lines (greater than 9.6 kbit/s), performing protocol intervention and switching, and providing management-oriented reports. But they are not the most cost-effective solution for several reasons. First, minicomputer architectures are not suited for communications functions; rather, they are optimized for data processing applications. Second, the specialized nature of concentrators limits their use to a few communications environments, and their development and maintenance costs must be amortized over a small number of users, resulting in a higher cost of ownership than with a less-specialized device. Third, future network expansion can be a problem unless provided for in the concentrator's initial design. Because of the rapid development of data communications equipment, the network designer often has difficulty envisioning future growth requirements beyond three years.

The new-generation nodal processors, on the other hand, are designed specifically for communications efficiency and network expansion. Most have microprocessor architectures. For example, Codex Corporation's 6050 distributed communications processor (DCP) has from 10 to 70 microprocessors and up to 10 Mbytes of memory in a single node. The computational and processing power of these microprocessors enables the node to perform a multitude of functions that previously needed external implementation or were not possible at all. But beyond the apparent advancements in functionality, the higher intelligence of these nodes enhances network reliability and increases data throughput.

However, there are still certain applications that warrant the use of special-purpose concentrators over the new-generation nodal processor. One is in networks whose terminals access applications in multivendor hosts, requiring mapping and support of host-transport and presentation-layer functions. Other examples are support and switching of terminal speeds higher than 19.2 kbit/s, a direct interface to a host channel and computer bus instead of to a front-end processor, and node programmability by the user via higher-level languages such as Basic and Cobol.

Most networks, though, comprise many geographically distributed terminals accessing various host resources, and these networks can benefit from nodal processors. As shown in Figure 1, nodal communications processors placed at appropriate locations can optimize overall network performance and operation and minimize costs. (Programs available from firms like Network Analysis Corporation and the DMW Group

172

1. Configuration optimization. *Certain programs aid in placing nodal communications processors at sites where they can optimize overall network performance, cost, and* *operation. Performance optimization results in maximum data throughput. Operational optimization maximizes network observability, control, and availability.*

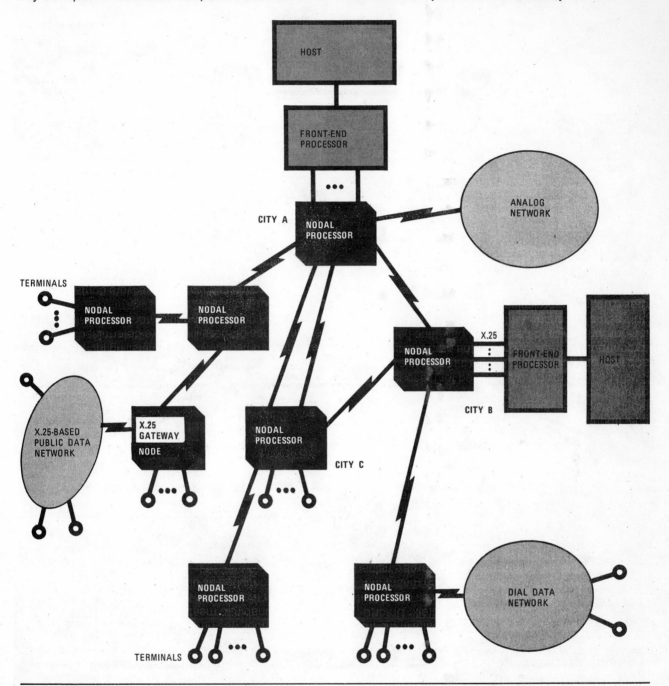

can aid users in placing these nodal processors.) Optimizing performance results in maximum data throughput, with acceptable response times and network costs. Operational optimization means increased network observability (access to parameters such as data flow rate, network degradation, and congestion), control, and availability. This might be achieved by providing backup links or by placing network control centers at appropriate locations to ensure that supervisory information does not overburden the links. To a great extent, the network optimization and availability also

depend on whether the nodal architectures are centralized or distributed.

In network architectures with centralized nodes, the intelligence is located at a single site, with all other nodes either partially intelligent or just tributaries feeding information from the remote sites. These architectures have the advantage of simplicity, but a failure at the central site can paralyze the whole operation.

On the other hand, the distributed architectures made possible by the new processors have intelligence that is equally distributed among all nodes; failure of

2. Two techniques. *In packet switching (A), each packet has address and control overhead on a per-terminal basis. In statistical multiplexing (B), data from many terminals is shared in a single frame. Combining both techniques (C), control information is sent without path-establishment overhead, and the packets use the least congested paths.*

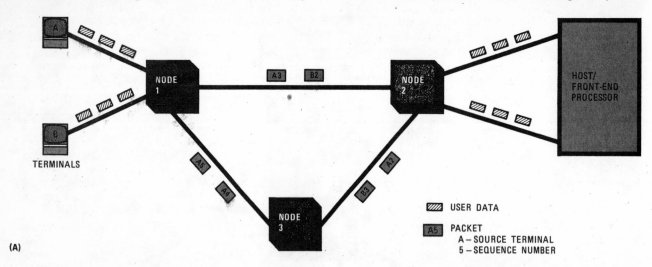

(A)

USER DATA

PACKET
A — SOURCE TERMINAL
5 — SEQUENCE NUMBER

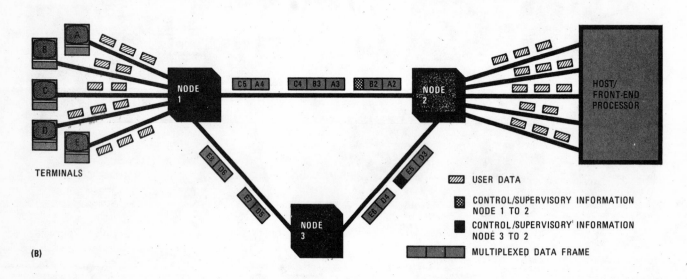

(B)

USER DATA

CONTROL/SUPERVISORY INFORMATION NODE 1 TO 2

CONTROL/SUPERVISORY INFORMATION NODE 3 TO 2

MULTIPLEXED DATA FRAME

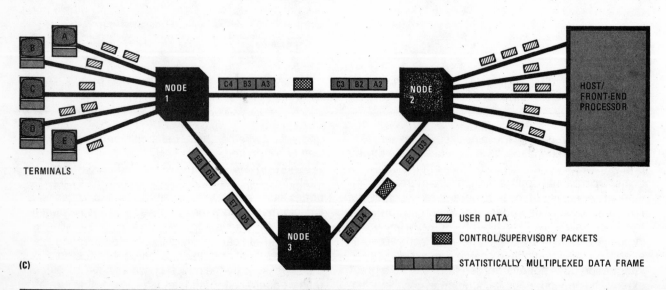

(C)

USER DATA

CONTROL/SUPERVISORY PACKETS

STATISTICALLY MULTIPLEXED DATA FRAME

one node affects communications with only that particular node. Therefore, depending on the network topology, the distributed, intelligent network architectures are generally more reliable than the centralized ones. They also allow improved network response time and higher throughput, since most functions such as error checking, statistics computation, and network diagnostics are performed locally at the node.

The higher intelligence of the new-generation processors also enhances throughput by combining the advantages of data-transport techniques such as packet switching and statistical multiplexing, providing for advanced data-compression schemes, performing protocol intervention, and using efficient internodal protocols. (Protocol intervention means that the node interacts with the users' protocols instead of just passing them transparently.)

Normally, for internodal communications, full-duplex, HDLC (high-level data link control) -like frames are used. These variable-length frames are formed by packet-switching or statistical-multiplexing techniques that dynamically assign the high-speed bandwidth only to active user terminals (Ref. 1). Statistical multiplexing generally yields smaller delays and greater throughput than packet switching.

Multipathing
In packet switching, the nodes form data into packets and send them over the physical links (Fig. 2A). The packets from one source may not use the same path to reach their destination (this multipath capability is packet switching's major feature), and the destination nodes have to be intelligent enough to rearrange any packets that are received out of order.

Also, the node must interact with the user protocol as it forms each packet, resulting in higher overhead, as each packet must have sufficient addressing, error-checking, and control data.

Nodal packet switching is advantageous when terminals have high utilization (70 percent or more), because the nodes can better balance the high-speed link capacities. Since the nodes make packet-by-packet routing decisions, the links are balanced almost instantaneously. Sometimes, if links are unstable, the packets loop between the same nodes, but there are algorithms that correct this situation very effectively.

In statistical multiplexing, each frame may contain data from several active terminals along with supervisory and control overhead (Fig. 2B). The multiplexer establishes a virtual call for each terminal and sends the data frames from these terminals along fixed paths unless link outages or congestion occurs. When this happens, the multiplexer examines alternative paths to the destination and moves the data to the least congested one. As a result, the data always arrives at the destination in the same sequence as it is sent. In addition, since data from many terminals is shared in a single frame, the associated overhead is much lower than in packet switching where each packet has similar overhead (on a per-terminal basis) regardless of the amount of data.

Hybrid nodes are the culmination of packet switching

and statistical multiplexing: Packets are used for supervisory and control communications, and statistical multiplexing is used for data transfer (Fig. 2C). This combines the advantages of both techniques, since supervisory and control information can be sent with minimum delay and without the overhead of path establishment, and data can be sent more efficiently using statistical multiplexing. There is also better load leveling, since packets are routed independently and use the least congested paths.

Data compression and throughput
Two ways to increase transmission efficiency are reducing the frame overheads and using compression techniques. Of these two, data compression is much more effective. Before the new-generation nodal processors, data-compression techniques were limited to a couple of protocols at most, since custom tables were required for each specific protocol. However, the increased nodal intelligence now available eliminates this data-compression limitation.

For some time now, the Huffman coding technique has been used in concentrators and multiplexers for data compression. This technique must be applied to each data stream entering the network, and, to be highly effective, every code table must be tailored to each stream's character probabilities (Ref. 2). As the network grows, this custom tailoring becomes unmanageable. In the new processors, this technique adapts dynamically to the received data.

Under this scheme, when a network connection is established, a standard table is initialized at each end of the network. As characters enter the network, each terminal node monitors the occurrence of characters and adjusts its tables appropriately. Frequently used characters are assigned short (4-bit) code words, and low-use characters are assigned longer (8- or 12-bit) code words. In this way, the nodes adapt to the user's character probabilities for each data stream in the network. These adaptive data-compression techniques can increase throughput up to 45 percent.

A prerequisite for using this compression scheme is that the nodes provide an end-to-end automatic repeat request (ARQ) in the network so that characters are not dropped or duplicated, throwing the compression tables out of synchronization. In end-to-end ARQ, the sending node buffers data from the terminals individually until it receives an acknowledgment from the destination-end terminal ports of the receiving node. If a link outage occurs, the sending node retransmits all unacknowledged frames to the appropriate destination-node terminal ports.

Protocol intervention
Another factor that affects data throughput is the delay experienced in the high-speed links. For example, satellite links have a one-way-trip delay of approximately 250 milliseconds. Also, as networks grow, the increasing number of network links causes a similar delay. In asynchronous-protocol applications, this delay usually does not present any problem, but in binary-synchronous protocols, which require that each block of data

is acknowledged before another block is sent (stop-and-wait protocols), this delay may substantially reduce throughput. To alleviate this problem, some form of protocol intervention is required.

In the case of batch-oriented remote-job-entry (RJE) terminals, this involves local acknowledgment: When a data block is received from the host or terminal, the receiving node buffers the data and acknowledges (ACKs) the block so that another block can be sent immediately. If a block from the terminal is received in error, the node negatively acknowledges (NAKs) that block, and the terminal retransmits it.

Since the acknowledgment is done locally, the actual ACK responses from the destination end are discarded. If the host computer NAKs the data, the sending node retransmits that block, and the destination node delivers it to the host in the correct sequence. The nodal processors guarantee this sequence by measuring the end-to-end round-trip delay and buffering the appropriate number of data blocks.

Higher throughput

This protocol-intervention technique allows multiple blocks of data to pass through the network simultaneously, thereby increasing throughput. The only risk in this form of protocol intervention is if the destination terminal or host aborts the transmission. Then, the network will not be able to deliver the blocks of data in transit, and they will be lost.

Figure 3 shows typical throughput improvements versus terminal speed because of protocol intervention. Performance improves with increased terminal speed because the "wait-for-ACK" time depends on a network's propagation delay and is therefore a larger percentage of transmission time at higher speeds; protocol intervention reduces the wait-for-ACK time to the same minimum at all speeds.

In the case of 3270-type interactive terminals—which are polled by the host—protocol intervention is normally performed by remote nodes polling them. (Figure 4 illustrates this concept in a multihost environment.) This has the effect of increasing throughput by eliminating the polls being passed through the network. In this case, the node connected to the host—the local node—emulates the remote cluster-controller unit (CCU), and the remote node connected to the CCU emulates the front-end processor.

The remote node is loaded with the host's polling list so that it can poll the terminals. All data sent in response to the host's read/write commands is passed on to the destination nodes. The data is delivered to the host the next time it polls that terminal address. Since there can be delays between the host's polling a terminal (or CCU) and its receiving the response data—caused by network delays and differences in poll timing—the local communications node uses delay tactics. These tactics take the form of sending NAKs or EOTs (end-of-transmission signals) to the host and sending messages with parity errors that force the host to retransmit the poll or continue through the poll list. When the local node receives data from the remote node, it delivers it to the host. If under abnormal situa-

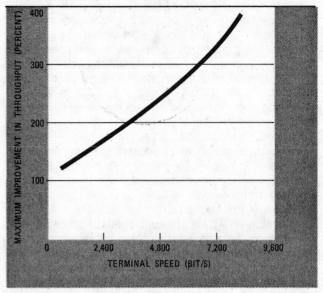

3. Improving throughput. *With protocol intervention, the wait-for-ACK time is the same at all speeds. Shown here are typical throughput improvements.*

tions certain devices cannot be accessed or are not connected, the nodes generate appropriate alarm messages to the host for operator intervention.

The remote-polling technique can be extended beyond the basic terminal support in the host in multi-host-attached networks. All hosts are configured to poll all terminals. The terminal node can then request from the terminal operator the particular host the operator wishes to access before establishing a network connection. This allows each terminal on a controller to communicate with different hosts as required.

Protocol intervention also requires a good end-to-end ARQ mechanism in the network to ensure that data acknowledged by the network reaches its destination intact. Each protocol-intervention function previously was performed by a standalone unit. Today, these features can be built into the node.

Enhanced integrity

Another prime consideration in a communications network is preventing loss of data and delivering error-free data to the desired destination. To accomplish this, the nodes usually rely on ARQ error-protection mechanisms and end-to-end flow control. In addition, they automatically reroute the data if an internodal link fails. The new-generation nodal processors incorporate several alternative routing techniques.

The most basic method is to assign an alternative path in case the primary link fails. The more sophisticated techniques also provide adaptive alternative routing to maintain load leveling. The basic method is used primarily in networks with centralized intelligence, and the alternative-link establishment is either triggered by the central node or host-initiated in certain computer-vendor architectures. Although this method is simple to implement, it has the disadvantages of sluggish response times, reduced transmission efficiencies, and the likely loss of user data if a link fails. Furthermore,

4. Multihost polling. *Both hosts poll all terminals. The terminal node asks the terminal operator which host the operator wishes to access. Therefore, each terminal on* *the same controller may communicate with different hosts. This is an extension of the remote-polling technique as applied to networks accessed by multiple hosts.*

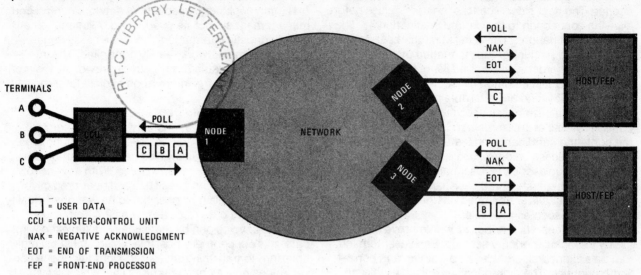

TERMINALS

☐ = USER DATA
CCU = CLUSTER-CONTROL UNIT
NAK = NEGATIVE ACKNOWLEDGMENT
EOT = END OF TRANSMISSION
FEP = FRONT-END PROCESSOR

---

failure of the central-site node or host results in loss of control of alternative routing.

In distributed intelligent nodal architectures, adaptive routing is readily implemented. There are several methods that guarantee that nodes have consistent routing information (Ref. 3), that is, that each node's routing tables are accurate and that they make similar routing decisions. Each node contains configuration information and a routing matrix for the whole network; these are updated periodically to ensure minimum end-to-end transmission delay.

The routing techniques differ for supervisory packets and statistically multiplexed data. The packets are routed from node to node, consistent with packet-switching techniques: Each node examines its routing tables and sends the data to an adjacent node. The statistically multiplexed data uses virtual-circuit switching. Here, the path through the network is selected when the call is established and is changed only if a link fails or becomes congested.

In virtual-circuit switching, congestion can be handled less disruptively: A new path is selected while the overloaded existing path is in use. When the new path is established, the nodes switch to this path and delete the old one; thus, the data flow is not impacted.

The user interface to the network does not give insight to the internal network architecture. For example, the user interface to a network may be X.25, which is a packet-based protocol. However, internally the network may be statistically multiplexing the data and using virtual circuits.

The new nodal processors usually use statistical multiplexing and support transparent and nontransparent networking. Transparent operation allows the network to be implemented without requiring changes to the host software or hardware. Various industry-standard protocols such as BSC (binary synchronous communications), HDLC, SDLC (synchronous data link

control), ADCCP (advanced data communications control procedure), and asynchronous can be accommodated. Transparent networking can also support nonstandard protocols or network expansions in multihost/multivendor environments.

However, in certain applications, such as where data traffic does not justify leased lines, use of X.25-based public data networks (PDNs) is advantageous. This requires nontransparency, since the attached devices must convert user data into packets before transmission. Normally, access to an X.25 PDN is done via a packet assembler/disassembler (PAD). For example, PADs for asynchronous terminals support CCITT X.25, X.3, X.28, and X.29 standards and convert asynchronous data to packets in conformance with X.25 standards. They also provide call establishment, downline loading, and remote control of parameters using X.29 standards. No CCITT standards exist for BSC PADs, but Telenet, Tymnet, and Datapac have agreed to support 3270, 3780, and 2780 BSC terminals.

Supporting both network types

There are several benefits in a nodal processor's enabling both transparent and nontransparent networking. A single entry node allows access to both network types, avoiding duplication of terminals. Also, one node can statistically multiplex both transparent data frames and packet frames into a single, high-speed data frame and statistically interleave the two types of frames. (However, if the network supports only the X.25 interface, it cannot support transparent data.)

X.25 support in nontransparent environments allows users to choose destinations from their own terminals. The intelligent nodes extend this capability to the transparent environment. This allows the formation of closed user groups, each with access to its own group and to a subset of other groups. Closed user groups enhance network security and user segmentation by allowing only a certain class of users to access the specified host resources. The classes are usually defined by assigning mnemonic names or by terminal-speed categories. The host's node checks the user's class before allowing connection to the desired destination.

At the destination (host-access) node, the user calls are answered by hunt groups managed by the same node. In hunt groups, a specified list of host ports is assigned a certain mnemonic resources name—for example, XYZ—and any available port in that group will answer the user call, establish the connection, and confirm the call establishment to the user. In addition, the contention and camp-on features increase the cost-effectiveness by permitting a few host ports to support a large user base. User calls are established on a first-come, first-served basis, and once the port is busy, other calls are camped on until a port in the hunt group becomes available.

The new-generation nodes further improve networking by providing a priority scheme. Each user terminal can be assigned different levels of routing and bandwidth priorities. The high-priority terminal, usually an interactive one, gets its configured bandwidth even when the link is most congested. The routing-priority scheme reroutes the higher-priority users' data first when a link fails. This scheme optimizes network operation by reducing the response times for interactive or digitized-voice traffic.

Multiple management

Management and control are important considerations in designing a communications network. Generally, these functions are centralized for the most effective operation. Consolidating all activities at a central point reduces duplication of valuable technical and human resources. However, in certain operations, it is crucial to have at least one backup management-and-control center in case the main one fails. Also, in multidivisional corporations, multiple control centers are desirable to give each division control of its own subnetwork. To ensure this, each communications node must be accessible from more than one control center.

In nodes where network intelligence is distributed, each node has its own management-and-control collecting-and-computing capability. Any node can become the master site—which controls the whole network—or there can be more than one master site.

Equally important considerations are that the network be manageable, controllable, and diagnosable on-line. This permits changes to be implemented; users to be added; and the networks to be diagnosed for faults without disrupting the operation.

The intelligent nodes generate many important management reports, which let the center operator examine such variables as the node throughputs, data-compression efficiency, network errors, buffer utilization, response times, and processor use. Administrative reports and statistics, such as the number of bytes of data transferred for each call and call-collect and -disconnect times, help in generating billing information for the network users. The diagnostics-oriented reports are generated whenever the network approaches certain critical error or performance thresholds. These reports might show excessive data-error rates, retransmission rates, or processor overloading.

Human engineering aspects of network control and management cannot be overlooked. All management and diagnostic information should be easily understood, and the network readily controlled. The intelligent nodes available today usually provide all the management and control information in plain English.

Integrated voice and data

Most data communications networks have some excess bandwidth that can be used for other functions, such as voice. Conversely, the networks can be designed with this integration in mind. With advanced voice-digitizing techniques such as linear predictive coding (LPC), it is now possible to have a good-quality voice signal at data rates as low as 2.4 kbit/s.

Digitized voice can be statistically multiplexed with data. It is conceptually possible, using statistical multiplexing, to transmit from four to eight telephone conversations on a single 9.6-kbit/s line, which previously could handle only one call. Voice would generally be assigned the highest priority and would get through even under congested link conditions. Conservatively, one or two telephone calls can be transmitted along with data on 9.6-kbit/s (Bell 3002) circuits.

Some intelligent nodal processors, in addition to having the capabilities already mentioned, have security assignment, protocol conversion, and priority-assigned multitask operations. Future generations of processors will have even more sophisticated functions.

As the trend toward added throughput power and functionality continues, multivendor-host applications will demand processors that facilitate communications between dissimilar protocols. Furthermore, the onus will be on the nodal processors to find the desired application program and connect the user to the appropriate machine, process the user task according to a predefined priority scheme, and make communications possible by performing appropriate speed, protocol, and code conversions.

Increased user data and voice support will require T1 (1.544 Mbit/s) carrier support—possibly higher in certain cases. This will require nodal processors with sophisticated functions to provide historical reporting, management reports, statistical analysis, and selective-reporting capability. More functions such as facsimile and message switching will be integrated, and gateways will be provided to computer networks like SNA (systems network architecture) and Decnet. ∎

References
1. G. David Forney and Robert W. Stearns, "Statistical multiplexing improves link utilization," DATA COMMUNICATIONS, July/August 1976.
2. G. David Forney and W.Y. Tau, "Data compression increases throughput," DATA COMMUNICATIONS, May/June 1976.
3. S. G. Finn, "Resynch Procedures and a Fail-Safe Network Protocol," *IEEE Transactions on Communications,* June 1979.

The micro, mini, and mainframe in a DDP network

Terry D. Pardoe, International Management Services Inc., Natick, Mass.

Knowing the capabilities and limitations of the processors available, plus the differences from the DP center approach, should lead to a better DDP design

Network planners and designers have found that distributed data processing (DDP) systems have special equipment needs. To understand these needs, the generic concept of distributed data processing must be examined.

The DDP concept can be defined as "the use of an interconnected family of computers of varying capabilities to supply computational power at all points (geographically or functionally) where it is needed." In contrast to the traditional data processing center approach, the computer is taken to the task rather than taking the task to the computer.

Distributed data processing therefore involves placing computers at end-user locations—such as source-data-entry points, inquiry points, and common-collection points. Since the computational requirements at these points (also called nodes) will vary considerably, full use of the computer spectrum must be made.

The full benefits of a distributed philosophy cannot be realized unless the computational powers placed at each node (or assigned to each function in the case of functional distribution) is carefully examined. This examination should result in a cost-effective match to the requirements, functional expectations, operator-skill levels, data and information needs, and environmental condition of the node.

In many cases, the high-cost mainframe used in most data processing centers is an expensive, overburdened tool that labors to service the computational requirements of both top-level management and bottom-level user. This approach was acceptable when computation costs were high, and data communications costs were relatively low. Today's low-cost micro- and minicomputers, however, make local processing much more practical than moving information unnecessarily to a central point. Distributed data processing is attractive because of the following:

■ It can relieve the burden on existing high-cost, overworked data centers.
■ It provides computational power where it is needed and can be most effectively utilized.
■ It produces a processing structure which is more "in tune" with most organizational structures.

The distributed concept requires, therefore, computational equipment of various levels of processing capability and skill levels. Also needed are flexible and low-cost communications techniques plus the creation of trouble-free complex systems and networks.

The computer spectrum outlined in Figure 1 ranges from simple single-chip microprocessors to the powerful systems found in most large data processing centers. Each of the major categories indicated in the

1 Computer spectrum

Wide range. *The computer spectrum ranges from simple single-chip microprocessors to the powerful mainframe systems found in most large data processing centers.* *Technological advances make it difficult to place absolute definitions on these major classifications. Each could be further expanded to reveal many more computer types.*

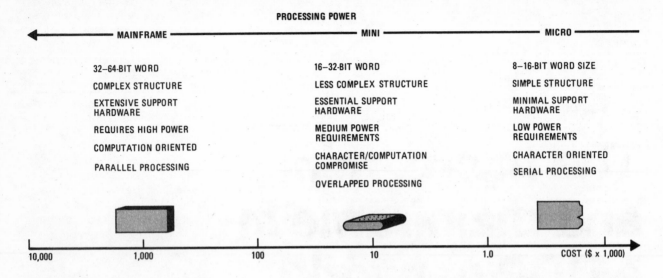

PROCESSING POWER

◀—— MAINFRAME —————————————— MINI ——————————— MICRO ——

MAINFRAME	MINI	MICRO
32–64-BIT WORD	16–32-BIT WORD	8–16-BIT WORD SIZE
COMPLEX STRUCTURE	LESS COMPLEX STRUCTURE	SIMPLE STRUCTURE
EXTENSIVE SUPPORT HARDWARE	ESSENTIAL SUPPORT HARDWARE	MINIMAL SUPPORT HARDWARE
REQUIRES HIGH POWER	MEDIUM POWER REQUIREMENTS	LOW POWER REQUIREMENTS
COMPUTATION ORIENTED	CHARACTER/COMPUTATION COMPROMISE	CHARACTER ORIENTED
PARALLEL PROCESSING	OVERLAPPED PROCESSING	SERIAL PROCESSING

10,000   1,000   100   10   1.0   COST ($ x 1,000)

spectrum diagram could be further expanded to reveal a range of computer types—each with its own advantages, limitations, and costs.

Equipment overview

Major generic types within the broad micro, mini, and mainframe classifications can—and are—being effectively used in distributed systems. Technological advances make it increasingly difficult to place absolute definitions on these major classifications. However, the following guidelines can assist potential users in understanding the significant roles which the various spectrum members can play in a distributed system.

■ Microprocessors and microcomputers. Characterized as low-cost and slow, with limited performance capability and a simple interconnectable structure.

■ Minicomputers. Characterized as medium-cost, fast and flexible in performance, and exhibiting high user and environmental tolerance. In operation, they need limited support from computer "professionals."

■ Mainframes. Characterized as high-cost, efficient in a batch mode, complex, and requiring sophisticated professional support.

These generalized functional attributes, in turn, lead to the spectrum of potential application areas shown in Figure 2. These areas range from the extensive data processing of "batch" in a general-purpose CPU, to the dedicated control of "real time" in a task-oriented microcomputer. As shown in Figure 2, the minicomputer falls somewhere in between—with some applications that overlap the other two categories.

When applying microcomputers and minicomputers, the systems implementer will be able to utilize a broad array of peripheral devices not normally found in the data center environment. Such devices have "grown up" with minicomputers, and provide the flexibility, at comparatively low cost, which has ensured the success of thousands of installations. Estimates of the total number of available mini and micro peripherals range from the hundreds to the thousands, but certain generic types become even more important to the distributed system creator.

Figure 3 presents some of these "mini" peripherals and their major advantages (plus) and disadvantages (minus). The range of peripherals available with minicomputers (and even microcomputers) is not limited to these peripherals, but also includes disks, disk packs, reel-to-reel tapes, card readers, paper-tape readers, serial printers, and line printers usually associated with the recognized "standard" data processing environment.

DDP intelligence

Intelligent terminals and terminal controllers are part of the advertised spectrum of equipment which can be used in the construction of a distributed system. Both devices are normally microprocessor-controlled, and as such can be classified (in functional capability) as microcomputers—or even minicomputers.

An essential aspect of the distributed concept is the interconnection of computers. The use of this communications link type implies the use of a range of data communications tools. These tools extend from acoustic couplers (up to 300 bit/s), through standard leased lines (1.2 to 9.6 kbit/s), to wideband groups (19.2 to 230 kbit/s). Special connections and antennas provide microwave and laser transmission up to two Mbit/s.

It is the breadth and depth of the equipment spectrum available which makes possible the matching of user needs and environment at each node. One node type, the microprocessor, represents the lowest cost computational unit available, and therefore can be placed closest to the user. Its extremely low power requirements allows for maximum portability.

Functions which can be assigned to a microprocessor are:
- Control of terminal formatting;
- Performance of simple data editing;
- Control of communications;
- Front-end computing tasks, such as the decoding of machine-readable information;
- Portable low-level processing.

Portable computing represents the ultimate in DDP, since it allows for computation at variable remote points without any specific geographic limitations imposed by a communications network.

Micro's communications role

In a portable device, not only is the microprocessor used to perform DP functions, but it is also used to control data transfers to other systems, perform protocol generation, and control and carry out code construction or conversion. Microprocessors are also used to add error-detection data, and subsequently check errors and request retransmission if needed.

Minicomputers represent the primary component of any distributed data processing system. As such, they serve several functions:
- Data terminal managers
- Local file builders and managers
- Data field, value and format editing, and file look-up
- Message management and communications control
- Output report generation

Minicomputers are affordable local-level computing systems because of their relatively low cost, software support, interactive processing capabilities, and complete range of peripherals. Minicomputers support local needs and can provide the essential distributed functions of moving data upward through a network, extracting information downward from the network, and providing support on behalf of failed systems above.

Minicomputers can be used for both front-end and back-end processing in conjunction with a mainframe computer. In either case, they are being used to relieve the processing burden of the data processing machine by performing repetitive real-time tasks.

Minicomputers also can handle most data communications tasks. Like microprocessors, they can create message formats, control signal generation, and handle error detection and correction tasks. Their high speed and greater processing power suits them for the additional tasks of message routing and switching, handling of a variety of line disciplines and protocols, and concentration of messages for transmission on expensive high-speed lines.

Minis and the system

The data communications use of a minicomputer provides system designers and end users with a number of advantages. For example they:
- Can considerably reduce the communications and applications burden on a host system.

- Can save money by allowing the use of high-speed lines (lower cost per unit of information transferred).
- Allow error control and response to be close to the message source.
- Can provide extensive message validation.
- Supply interrupt structure for message handling.
- Can be provided with software or firmware (read-only memory) modules for specific message handling routines.

To realize these advantages, the distributed concept requires suitable equipment to be placed at identified processing nodes. These nodes normally can be split into four categories: user, local, intermediate, and central (corporate). Figure 4 indicates the probable equipment type to be used at each node level, their cost ranges, and how they interconnect.

The exact definition of node equipment needs will be controlled by its location and data storage requirements. User-level nodes most likely can be serviced with intelligent terminals or microprocessor-based devices, and need a storage capability suitable for transaction logging and small working files. Such requirements can be supplied by cassette tapes (for transaction logging) and diskettes (for working files).

Local level needs—a plant, an office, or a department—can be met by a small minicomputer with local data files stored either on flexible disks or on a relatively small "hard disk". At the local level, additional (historic) data storage may also take the form of punched cards, magnetic tape, or hard copy.

Whether employed at the user or local level, portable computational systems need to have special consideration given to the duration of independent portable

2 Application spectrum

Mixing batch and real-time. The minicomputer's application area falls somewhere between the batch data processor and the real-time dedicated microcomputer.

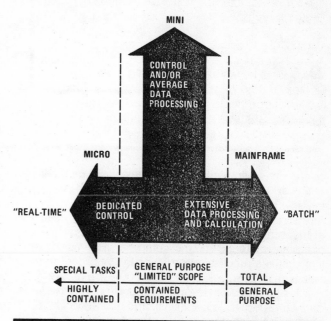

3 Mini peripherals

Pluses and minuses. *Peripheral devices not normally found in the data center environment have "grown up" with minicomputers, providing a high degree of flexibility.*

Shown here are some major advantages (plus) and disadvantages (minus) of these devices. Also available are the "standard" DP units, such as disks and reel-to-reel tapes.

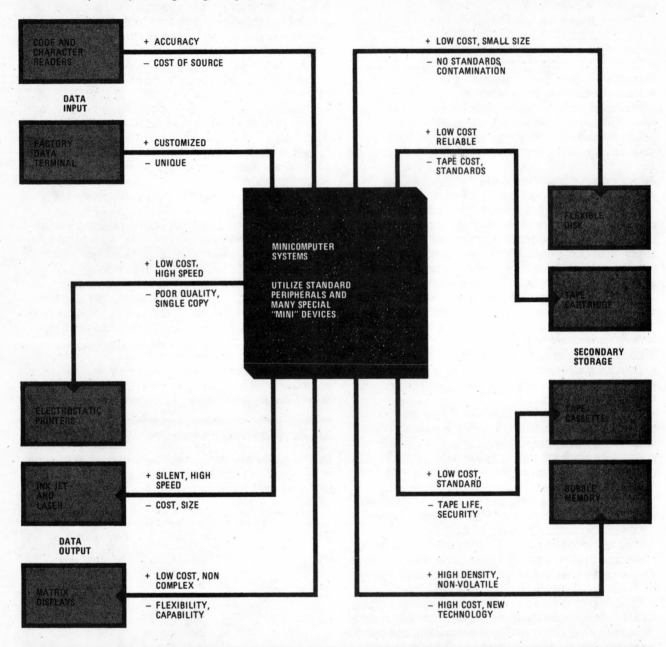

CODE AND CHARACTER READERS	+ ACCURACY / − COST OF SOURCE
DATA INPUT	
FACTORY DATA TERMINAL	+ CUSTOMIZED / − UNIQUE
	+ LOW COST, HIGH SPEED / − POOR QUALITY, SINGLE COPY
ELECTROSTATIC PRINTERS	
INK JET AND LASER	+ SILENT, HIGH SPEED / − COST, SIZE
DATA OUTPUT	
MATRIX DISPLAYS	+ LOW COST, NON COMPLEX / − FLEXIBILITY, CAPABILITY
MINICOMPUTER SYSTEMS — UTILIZE STANDARD PERIPHERALS AND MANY SPECIAL "MINI" DEVICES	
FLEXIBLE DISK	+ LOW COST, SMALL SIZE / − NO STANDARDS, CONTAMINATION
TAPE CARTRIDGE	+ LOW COST RELIABLE / − TAPE COST, STANDARDS
SECONDARY STORAGE	
TAPE CASSETTE	+ LOW COST, STANDARD / − TAPE LIFE, SECURITY
BUBBLE MEMORY	+ HIGH DENSITY, NON-VOLATILE / − HIGH COST, NEW TECHNOLOGY

operation, equipment and communications capability, task load-sharing between fixed and portable elements, and backup redundancy.

The various devices which can be effectively used at the local level include intelligent terminals, microcomputer systems, and minicomputer systems—listed in ascending processing-power order. Intelligent terminals—costing from $2,000 to $8,000—are programmable and can do extensive editing. However, available data storage is usually minimal, and operation with a host will be in contention with other terminals.

Adding secondary storage to an intelligent terminal could hike its price to the $20,000 range. But greater local data handling capability is, of course, gained. Potential disadvantages include less central control and a greater impact when inoperable.

Local-level microcomputer systems—costing up to $100,000—provide a high degree of flexibility at a lower cost than minicomputer systems. But—because of their newness—hardware and software support is limited.

At the local level, minicomputer systems—costing

as much as $400,000—provide another order of flexibility, considerable processing power, and a high degree of software support. Of course, users pay for these benefits. And network operation requires rigorous operational discipline to maintain system control over the mini's potential independent functions.

Intermediate-level (Fig. 4) requirements may take the form of communications processing, or communications and data processing. Either one or both functions can be performed by a minicomputer system. If the system is restricted to the communications task, then computer memory storage may be sufficient. But with any level of data manipulation, hard disk storage (for control files, for example) and magnetic tape (for transaction logging and archiving) will be needed.

Corporate level (Fig. 4) needs normally absorb large amounts of processing power. In organizations which have an existing data processing department with mainframe capability, these needs are adequately met. In applications requiring large amounts of corporate processing and the manipulation of huge files, the traditional CPU cannot be replaced. For less complex central requirements, a large-scale minicomputer can be used—particularly if front-end and back-end real-time tasks (on-line processing) have been delegated to additional smaller minicomputers. The resulting configuration will resemble "parallel processing," implemented to maintain minimum response times.

Since the proper availability, usage, and transfer of data are essential ingredients to the successful operation of a distributed system, careful consideration must be given to data storage and movement. Designers should ask:
- How much should be stored and where?
- How much can and/or should be allowed to accumulate at any one node?
- When should it be transferred, and to where?
- How will it be recovered if damaged, destroyed, or "lost"?

Be prepared for bitters
The distributed concept is not without its problems. The potential system designer, purchaser, or user should be fully aware of them, and take adequate precautions to limit their impact on successful network implementation and operation. In general, most problems fall into one of three categories: technological, functional, or commercial.

The major technological problems are those of compatibility, communications protocol utilization, and speed. Throughout the equipment spectrum, different manufacturers use different interface methodologies, so that random equipment interconnection may not be as easy as it appears on the surface. The biggest single problem exists in the interconnection of minisystems to mainframe computers. This problem is compounded by the absence of a standardized communications protocol between vendors. Designers and users can best protect themselves from these problems by carefully examining available technologies and protocols, and extensively questioning users as well as suppliers to ascertain what combinations work.

4 Node equipment

Levels and costs. *Individual end users in a distributed system operate with four node categories of interconnected equipment: theirs, local, intermediate, and central.*

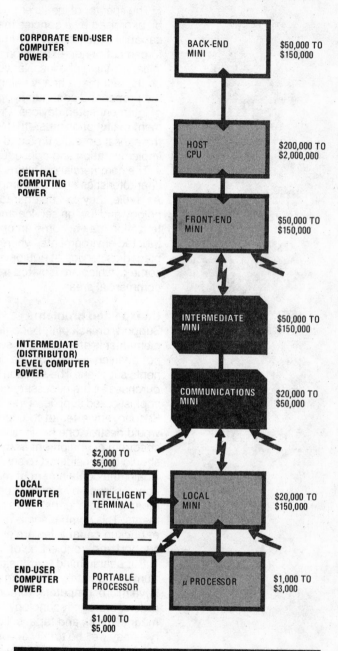

Telecommunications techniques can be expensive. While they are sufficiently fast for most tasks, they appear as a slow element in a distributed system. The efficiency—from a time utilization point of view—of a distributed network may well be limited by the data transmission speed of the communications lines. This type of limitation can be minimized by careful evaluation of data movement requirements and priorities.

Functional problems are associated with either the equipment type used at a particular node, or the total network itself. Use of micro- and mini-based systems at a particular node will limit that node's processing capability. Micro- and minicomputers are, fundamentally, relatively fast (in processing) and flexible (in application), but they are easily overloaded by too much data and slowed by too many tasks.

The specter of inefficient nodal processing can only be exorcised by a concise matching of computational capabilities to node requirements, and rigorous enforcement of non-expansion rules set up during the initial planning phases. Network problems are based on the fact that a heavy reliance must be placed on the proper and continuous operation of a complex set of interconnected devices. Protection against equipment malfunction must, therefore, be designed-in at the earlest possible time and validated at all stages of implementation and consequent operation.

The commercial problems are limited to the natural characteristics of small-computer-systems suppliers. As a rule, they can be characterized as high on technology and low on service and support. This characterization may become an operational problem in distributed environments, where heavy reliance may be placed on service of equipment in multiple locations— some of which are isolated from the traditional major commercial areas.

Unexpected problems

Support, or lack of it, becomes an issue when the implementer is attempting to solve problems which have not been envisioned by the original system components suppliers. The solution does not lie in a plan to purchase all the necessary equipment from a single sophisticated supplier. First, no such supplier exists. Second, any attempt to become this type of supplier would destroy one basic distributed concept: the total spectrum of equipment from all suppliers can and should be considered to service the needs of any node. Again, the containment of this problem area can be accomplished by a careful comparison of the equipment suppliers' capabilities and the nodal requirements. This comparison is needed to ensure that proper backup capabilities are employed, guaranteeing support and trouble-free operation.

But bear in mind that the computer equipment spectrum is continually changing and expanding. Today we have microcomputers; tomorrow it may be picocomputers. Storage technology—currently restricted to magnetic disk and tape, solid state and core memory—may well be totally eclipsed by improvements in bubble memory technology and new amorphous and molecular methodologies.

Consequently, users must be alert to technological advances and be ready to seize innovative opportunity. Users, however, must also beware! The equipment spectrum is broad, and the choices are many. But equipment alone does not a distributed system make. Successful distributed systems consist of equipment plus software, plus management control, plus operational procedures, plus many other important operational tasks. All of these elements must be combined into the most productive and cost-effective package obtainable. ■

Henry J. Miller, State University of New York at Buffalo

The month-to-month implementation of a private network

Despite tight budgets, vendor problems, and operating headaches, this manager orchestrated a cost-effective network.

The necessity of keeping communications costs down and operating capabilities up mothered the inventive design of a large university network. The following is the manager's account of how he, his staff, and the equipment vendors met the successive crises during planning and implementation.

The State University of New York at Buffalo (SUNYAB) is split into three campuses: the Main Street campus located just inside the Buffalo city limits; the Amherst campus, a sprawling facility in the suburbs; and the Ridge Lea campus, a temporary facility situated between the other two. University Computing Services (UCS), located on the Ridge Lea campus at the University Computing Center (UCC), houses two mainframes: the Academic Computer System, a Control Data Cyber 173, and the Administrative Computer System, a Sperry Univac 1106.

In the early autumn of 1977, we used several dial strings, or hunt groups, to provide host and speed selection along with contention for the host resources. A dial string is a group of phone numbers daisy-chained such that if the first number in the group is busy, the caller "falls through" to the next number until a free line is found or until the end of the group is reached, which causes a busy signal. These dial strings were arranged by host and port speed. For example, the user accessed the 300-bit/s ports on the Cyber by dialing the first phone number in the dial string connected to these ports. The contention was simply, first come first served.

This method required the user's terminal to have a Bell-113-type originate modem or an acoustic coupler. New York Telephone Company (Telco) charged a flat rate per phone call—regardless of length—based on the message unit. Occasionally, rumors surfaced about a new rate structure using the timed message unit, but that was almost always several years away.

After some terminal speeds changed from 110 and 134.5 bit/s to 300 bit/s in November 1977, we re-evaluated our contention groups and determined that the dial strings should be broken up and reconfigured to reduce the number of host ports at 110 and 134.5 bit/s and increase the number of 300-bit/s ports. Because this was rather expensive ($100+ per phone line), we invited the Telco business agent to a meeting at the computing center to discuss possible alternatives. He advised that we might want to reconsider our position because the phone company planned to implement timed-message-unit (TMU) charges on nonresidential phones in selected areas in New York State on Jan. 1, 1978. Buffalo was one of the chosen areas.

Some quick calculations of total connect time per month to both host systems and the projected TMU charges (approximately 7 cents for the first 5 minutes and 1.1 cent for each additional minute) showed a cost increase to the university of between $15,000 and $18,000 per month—or $180,000 and $216,000 per year—for data communications alone. Suddenly, our thoughts about possible alternatives to the Telco offering jumped from informal conversation at lunch to a top-priority project at UCS and the university.

After continuous dialog with Telco representatives into January 1978, it was clear that Ma Bell did not have an inexpensive solution to our problem. UCS personnel would have to come up with its own answer.

First, we had to determine exactly how many terminals accessed the computers. This information had not been maintained in the past, so the computing

185

center initiated a detailed survey. All persons accessing the computers were instructed to contact the UCS engineering lab in order that detailed survey forms could be completed. Information was needed about terminal speed, type, and location, and which of the two hosts was being accessed.

Secondly, we had to find some means of connecting terminals located in buildings other than the computing center's. Any connection method would have to have fixed costs and support 300-bit/s transmission speed at the very least.

Finally, we had to provide contention, formerly supplied by the Telco dial strings. There were approximately three times more terminals than host ports, so an equitable means of sharing access among all users was an absolute must.

1978
February–March

As we investigated current communications technologies, the solution began to take shape. Time-division and frequency-division multiplexing and concentration were considered, but no one solution fit all our needs. It became clear that a nodal approach was a must because of the three separate campuses.

Each node would have to support all terminals on its campus, and the nodes at Main Street and Amherst would have to connect to the node at UCS over a four-wire Bell 3002 voice-grade circuit with a minimum of special conditioning. To accommodate all anticipated terminal speeds—including CRT terminals operating at 1.2 kbit/s—statistical multiplexing would be required to squeeze the data through a 9.6-kbit/s communications line connecting the nodes.

Telco was the obvious choice for connecting the terminals to their nodes. But conventional means meant either continued TMU charges or extra extensions to the university's Centrex telephone system, both relatively expensive. Through an investigation of other offerings, we discovered that Telco had closed-property-loop (CPL) circuits that were available for a continuous piece of property. These circuits came in various "flavors," such as two types of security-grade lines and a private (leased) line. The beauty of them was that all had fixed monthly costs: about $5 a month per pair or $10 a month for a four-wire circuit.

Further inquiry revealed that these circuits could be driven by a relatively new product, the limited-distance modem (LDM). LDMs operate over circuits with d.c. continuity at distances dependent on transmission rates, and they clearly fit into the low-cost category when compared with Bell-113-type modems and the 1.2-kbit/s kinds used on dial-up phone lines.

We also learned that terminals located in the same building as the mux nodes could be hard-wired directly to a node without employing any modem. A few terminals were operating satisfactorily while wired directly to computers, even though some connections were substantially longer than the 50-foot maximum in the RS-232-C interface specification. In fact, one line was close to three times the specified length.

April–August

During this time period, we drew up our specifications, and on June 27, 1978, we submitted to the state a request for a proposal (RFP) for multiplexing equipment and modems. This detailed the basic attributes of the communications network. Some of these were:

■ The contention group(s) that each terminal would be allowed to access had to be field-programmable.
■ The network had to support a minimum of 32 contention groups at each node, and, if a group were full, a terminal's request for access would be placed in a queue until a host port became available.
■ The network had to support statistical multiplexing over the trunk lines connecting each node while being transparent to any terminal.
■ Each node had to support a minimum of four statistically multiplexed links and supply usage statistics such as channel and buffer use.

Several vendors submitted bids ranging from about $200,000 to $650,000. A committee was established to evaluate the various proposals, and after a week or two, it announced the selection of vendors. Prentice Corporation of Palo Alto, Calif., was selected for the modem section of the RFP, and another vendor (unnamed for reasons later explained) was selected to provide the statistical multiplexing equipment.

Prentice modems were chosen not only because they cost less but also because they are slot-transparent, meaning the modem circuit boards can plug into any modem slot. All modem boards fit in both a card rack (for mounting in a standard 19-inch electrical-equipment cabinet) or a standalone enclosure. This gave us the capability of having P113 modems, LDMs, and SLDs (synchronous line drivers), interchangeable in the equipment cabinets.

As an aside, Prentice frowns on its product's being called a limited-distance modem. It is really an asynchronous line driver (ALD) that relies on current changes to carry the intelligence from point to point. The ALD can operate at speeds up to 19.2 kbit/s over any of our unloaded telephone lines (loading refers to the coils placed in a telephone circuit to reduce the apparent capacitance of the circuit) and up to 4.8 kbit/s over our loaded circuits.

The Prentice P113 modems are registered by the Federal Communications Commission so they can connect directly to the modular phone-line jack without the data-access arrangement provided by Telco. We needed both originate and answer modems. The latter

187

allow off-campus users to dial into the system, and the former let UCC personnel dial into remote nodes to verify operation of the network.

It should be noted that the Prentice devices have light-emitting diodes showing the status of the RS-232-C control lines and transmit and receive signals. This proved extremely helpful in diagnosing difficulties.

The multiplexer vendor met almost every point in the RFP, such as a node at each of the three campuses, statistical multiplexing, and queuing. After appropriate processing by state procurement agencies in Albany, the university issued purchase orders.

September–December

During these months, we maintained a continual dialog with Telco to evaluate the options for interconnecting the ALDs (terminal-to-node). The price of these metallic circuits floated up from roughly $10 to about $30 per month. With 120 of these lines, this comes to approximately $40,000 per year—a substantial sum.

In light of the 200 percent increase in CPL costs, we began to study the possibility of running our own cable throughout the university campuses. To represent the longest-haul situation, we pulled a test cable between one of the buildings that would house a mux node and another building on the same campus—some 4,000 feet. Four-wire cable from a terminal room was connected to each end of the trunk.

As an experiment, we wanted to see what the real limits were with a direct (no, or "null," modem) RS-232-C connection. We placed a CRT terminal at each end of the run on the four-wire cable and connected them in a null-modem arrangement. Bit-error-rate testers were connected to the remaining pairs in the trunk line to simulate traffic and test for crosstalk. Unfortunately, these tests failed at rates in excess of 1.2 kbit/s but worked for 110 and 300 bit/s, which meant that the ALDs would still be required. This exercise helped us understand the problems to be encountered in pulling cable and in operating distances.

The experiment also proved the feasibility of hard-wiring all buildings on the campuses. The trunk lines were mapped out, and material estimates were made. For about $60,000, we could purchase cable, connectors, and other pieces of hardware that had four times the line capacity of the Telco equipment we planned to order. Leasing a similar facility from Ma Bell would cost about $160,000 per year. Even with the cost of labor, the project would have a remarkably short payoff period of about one year.

After careful review, we decided for reasons of safety and lack of equipment to handle large spools of cable to contract the trunk portion of the hard-wiring. The interior wiring was to be done by part-time help available at the university. An RFP for the trunk lines was drawn up, and a preliminary estimate showed the cost to be about $200,000. But even when we matched this with Telco installation charges and ongoing monthly costs, the idea still seemed reasonable.

Before an RFP is released, it must be approved by the responsible state agency in Albany. During the process of requesting this approval, we had an interesting revelation. This agency was using the type of Telco circuits we desired, but the cost—while slightly more than $10 per month—was nowhere near the latest Telco quote of $30 per month.

We arranged another meeting with our Telco data representative to clear up the confusion about the actual price of these circuits and to discuss an installation schedule. The price of the lines was now stated to be $10.96 per month per four-wire circuit. They were called metallic circuits for data and were an untariffed offering. The specifications were that the lines have d.c. continuity, be unloaded, and have no more than 1,000 ohms end-to-end resistance.

We were once again talking about a relatively inexpensive circuit and getting a commitment from Telco that the lines would be installed by Jan. 31, 1979, so we scrapped our own hard-wiring plans. Vendors received purchase orders for the multiplexer and modem equipment, and delivery dates were established. The modems were promised in early December and the multiplexing equipment in early February 1979.

It was mentioned earlier that the terminals located in the same buildings as their multiplexer nodes could be hard-wired to them. Two computer center employees installed about 40 of these lines over two months. The lines were run through existing conduits, over dropped ceilings, and, in one case, in an elevator shaft.

We gained much experience from this operation. We discovered that the original time estimate to complete the hard-wiring was about half of what was actually needed, but, working overtime, we completed the job well ahead of schedule nonetheless.

While work was in progress, we heard that the multiplexer vendor was having problems, and that he would be unable to meet his commitment. With assurances from the supplier that these rumors were untrue, business continued as usual.

1979 January

By the end of this month, Telco completed the metallic-circuits installation, as promised. Computer center personnel immediately began installing jacks on the terminal ends of these lines. (We determined at an earlier date that local labor could more economically install the four-pin jacks.)

Things progressed well until we were contacted by the mux vendor, who desired a meeting with key UCS personnel at the earliest possible time. The vendor would not discuss the purpose of the meeting over the phone, so speculation ranged far and wide.

On Jan. 17, the meeting took place. Our earlier suspicions were confirmed: The vendor announced that delivery of the multiplexing equipment could not be scheduled until September 1979 and, worse, gave no assurances that the date would not slip again. The most jarring fact was that the company offered no short-term alternative to our problem. We were left facing the start of the fiscal year (April 1) with a large unfunded expense—timed-message-unit charges.

Within one week, we contacted the next-lowest bidder, Digital Communications Associates (DCA) of Norcross, Ga. DCA was presented with the problem and informed us that it could guarantee delivery of a statistical multiplexing network 30 days after receiving the order. Unlike the first vendor, DCA already had networks installed and operating in several locations. And an operational remote diagnostic service was available, whereby DCA would interface to one of its on-site units to help troubleshoot its problems.

Within a few days, we completed evaluation of DCA's proposal, cancelled the first vendor's order for failure to perform, and sought approval to replace that order with DCA equipment. The Office of General Services and the Division of the Budget gave approval within two weeks, which reflects the high degree of cooperation on the part of responsible state agencies.

By the end of the month, DCA had been given updated information about the network (terminal types, speeds, and host contention groups). The network it offered met all major items in the RFP except the camp-on or queuing section. Also, the firm offered no accounting package. DCA's philosophy differed from the original vendor's in that its system performed the basic functions we desired, but some of the additional functions we requested were regarded as special applications and our responsibility.

February

As soon as the telephone-line installation was completed, we set a date for Prentice to install the modems. One Prentice technician, with the assistance of UCS engineers, installed the ALDs at all sites in four days. This involved going to the terminal locations, installing the ALDs, and then stopping at the mux node locations to connect the rack-mounted modems to the appropriate four-wire line. Each line was checked with a bit-error-rate tester (BERT) for operation up to 4.8 kbit/s. The two job foremen and several installers from the local Telco office did a remarkable installation job. Almost every one of the more than 120 lines they installed worked properly, and the few that did not were corrected promptly.

The entire Prentice ALD installation went more smoothly than anticipated. Only three units out of almost 250 ALDs were dead on arrival, and the few line problems that existed were quickly identified with the aid of the line drivers' LEDs.

The network consisted of four DCA System 150s. Each 150 node consisted of a Digital Equipment Corporation (DEC) PDP-8 minicomputer with 32K words of memory, modified with a "core window" to allow the access of eight words of memory at a time, thus increasing throughput and addressing range. The PDP-8 bus connected to the circuit-card files containing DCA modules that interfaced terminals or host ports.

Network details

Each 150 can support up to 128 ports, depending on the number of trunk lines and if a log port is in use. Each DCA module supports two ports, so a full 150 would have 64 module boards. The log port tracks the time a terminal connection is established and broken, providing network connect time.

Also, each 150 is controlled by a customer-supplied console terminal. This console acts as the PDP-8 front panel, allowing its operator to implement such functions as EXAMINE MEMORY, DEPOSIT INTO MEMORY, and to manually enter data bits into storage. By entering the proper commands, the user can examine a listing of trunk-error counts, the amount of remaining buffer space, or the configuration attributes of a particular terminal or host port. It is also possible to dynamically reconfigure the 150, changing port attributes as necessary. The trunk lines are handled by Z-80 microprocessor-based protocol processors. The maximum number of protocol processors in a 150 is five, limiting each node to five trunk lines.

The figure shows the staged layout of the network. The 150s are labeled A,B,C, and D. A and B are located on the Ridge Lea campus, in the machine room. C is located on the Amherst campus, and D on the Main Street campus.

A is connected to C, and B to D via 9.6-kbit/s synchronous modems and a 3002 voice-grade circuit with D1 coditioning. A and B are also connected via a null-modem 4.8-kbit/s cable so that data, if need be, can be transferred between mainframes.

The host ports—56 from the Cyber 173 and 59 from the Univac 1106—are divided almost equally between the two 150s. The staff and public terminals located in UCS are directly connected to system B, and the 13 dial-up lines (to serve off-campus users) and Ridge Lea terminals not in UCS are connected to system A via Prentice P113 modems and ALDs. Hard-copy terminals are connected to A and B and function as the 150s' consoles. A dual 8-inch floppy disk is switched between A and B for system loading.

System C at Amherst supports roughly 60 terminals, and system D at Main Street supports about 75. Each system is down-line loaded from Ridge Lea: C by A, and D by B. To perform a down-line load, the remote 150 must first be called by the console terminal at the UCC assigned to C and D.

The hosts are divided into eight contention groups, five on the Cyber and three on the Univac. The groups were selected for terminal speed and type. For example, a 1.2-kbit/s minicomputer port was established on the Cyber, and a few ports were allocated to UCS staff terminals only. Minicomputers were restricted to one port because the nature of these data transfers is obviously different from those of an interactive terminal. (The mini's continuous data stream cannot be statistically multiplexed.) This contention group has proved to be extremely popular at the university.

The terminals connected to the network could be of two logical types: system select or nonsystem select. A system-select terminal is one that can choose the contention group(s) it will access. A six-character system-select code followed by a CARRIAGE RETURN is entered, and the 150 connects the terminal to the proper host port, if available. If not, it sends a canned message back to the terminal stating, CONTENTION GROUP BUSY. A nonsystem-select terminal is allowed access to only one contention group. The user merely strikes the carriage-return key and is automatically mapped through to the host. If that group is busy, the terminal is sent the group-busy message.

March-May

The only thing holding up the DCA installation was the lack of a handful of integrated circuits for the protocol processors. Fortunately, UCS was able to borrow sufficient quantities of these chips to send to DCA to complete production. On Monday, March 19, DCA arrived on site to start the installation.

The 150s were uncrated and connected to the trunk modems. Technicians ran diagnostics on each 150 and, after successful completion of testing, began the changeover from the switched telephone network to the DCA network. This was a staged operation, so first the groups of host ports were switched and then the terminals that accessed these ports. The morass of interface cables from host front ends to modems had to be untangled and connected to DCA cables and their respective 150s. Each cable was carefully labeled, to ensure easy recognition for the future, and neatly coiled under the raised flooring.

When a sufficient number of host ports was switched over, a team went to the remote campuses to connect the ALDs to the 150s and the terminals to the other end of the line. Servicemen left instruction sheets detailing how to access the hosts on every terminal and, where possible, personally instructed users on the new access methods.

Within a period of 10 days, the switchover was completed. Most of our users were pleased with the end result, expressing delight over the ease and coordination of the change.

While things were looking rather good, we encountered several problems during installation. For example, during light-load conditions, terminals that were connected to the same 150 as the host port they were accessing received garbled characters during continuous output from the host. "Breaks" (output-interrupt signals) were sometimes transmitted in error from word processing terminals to the host they were accessing, causing some confusion to users. Also, a nonerror condition in the protocol processors triggered a major

alarm in the network at irregular intervals and rendered useless the aural alarms, on which we depended to notify operators of network faults. The majority of these types of problems have been corrected, and several minor ones are still being evaluated.

Also, due to a misunderstanding between us and DCA, host flow control was not installed in our network. This function allows the 150 to suspend data flow from the hosts if its buffer storage exceeds a predetermined threshold. To implement this option, we would have to install different cables between the 150s and the host ports, requiring the system to be off-line for about 20 hours. Because the lack of this option was not having an adverse effect on network operations, we decided to defer installation until a low-usage period.

The network was in use for several weeks when we realized that minor adjustments to the configuration were required. The hoped-for ease in reconfiguring the network became a reality. Terminal speeds and contention groups were readily changed from a system console, and new floppy-disk storage was created. Reconfiguration on a single 150 required about half an hour to plan and 15 minutes to install.

During the early part of this period, the network was stable and we had very little downtime. But suddenly toward the end of April, the B-to-D link started to experience stops and auto-restarts.

Soon, possible sources of the B-to-D problem were reduced to either the synchronous modems or the 3002 phone line between the two. B and D were shifted to a 7.2-kbit/s trunk used by a remote-job-entry (RJE) terminal collocated with the remote 150. The RJE was connected to the 150's 3002 line and modems. At this point, we entered into a common user dilemma: finger-pointing. Telco said the modems were at fault, and the modem company said it was the phone line. This difference of opinion was not resolved until mid-June, when the modem vendor sent a technician with line-testing equipment and proved once and for all that the 3002 phone line was out of specification.

June

As mentioned earlier, the network was designed to support expansion to connect to other sites. The time for this had arrived. We installed an experimental Bell 3002 leased-line link to SUNY at Binghamton. It used a DCA System 115, which is a scaled-down version of a 150 (see figure). The 115 is Z-80 based and supports up to 32 ports: one console port, 15 terminal ports (Binghamton terminals to Buffalo hosts), and 16 host ports (Buffalo terminals to the Itel 6 computer in Binghamton). The 115 connects to node B's 150 through a protocol processor and acts as a slave system, its configuration being stored in the 150. During the summer months, this link would be available only to staff terminals, but access would be expanded. The Itel host in Binghamton offers software packages not available at Buffalo, and the Cyber 173 offers its number-crunching capabilities to Binghamton. The link's data rate is

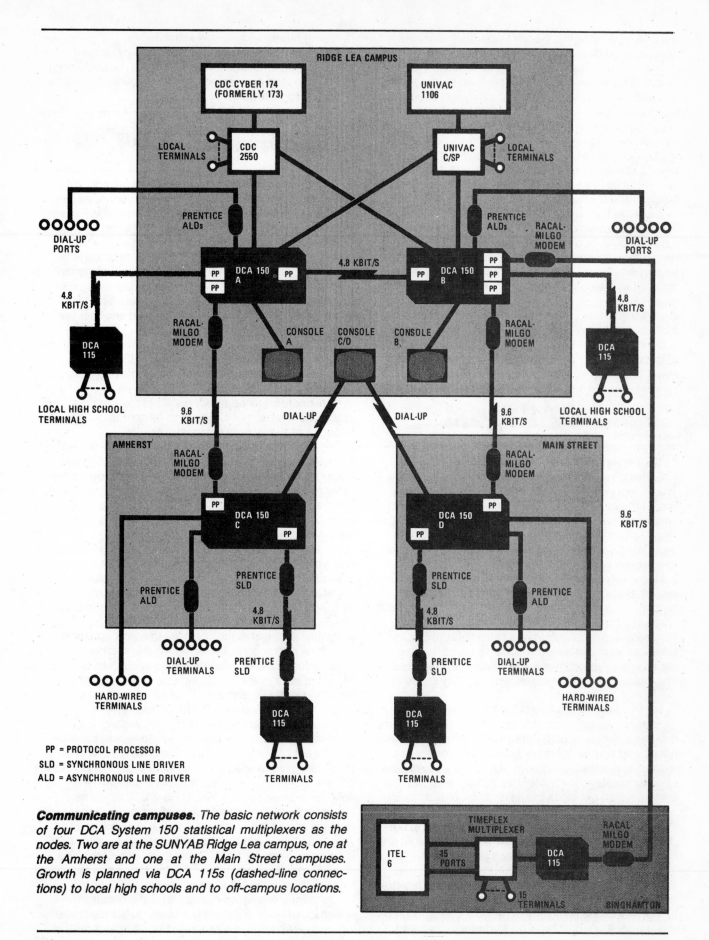

Communicating campuses. *The basic network consists of four DCA System 150 statistical multiplexers as the nodes. Two are at the SUNYAB Ridge Lea campus, one at the Amherst and one at the Main Street campuses. Growth is planned via DCA 115s (dashed-line connections) to local high schools and to off-campus locations.*

9.6 kbit/s, although 2.4-kbit/s operation is feasible without degrading service.

The first few weeks of the Binghamton link were interesting. The modems we had planned to use were delayed, so we pressed a pair of old synchronous modems into service. Although checked out prior to delivery to Binghamton, the modem failed within a week of installation. A spare modem was promptly shipped to the site. Shortly after, the link again failed, and this time the problem was traced to an intermittent connection in the modem cable. By the end of the month, the Binghamton link had stabilized.

Just after the Binghamton hookup, the A and B nodes showed an occasional "system hang"; that is, a node would stop executing code. When this happened, the operator had to manually restart the node, forcing all users of that node to reconnect through the network to the desired host. Also, an occasional stop-restart would occur in a node. In this situation, the software would detect an unrecoverable error, such as no more buffer space, and restart the software from scratch. Users were understandably getting upset about the number of times they were interrupted as a result of these problems.

July–August

At the beginning of July, a DCA customer engineer (CE) installed field changes in the protocol processors. These changes were made with a minimum of disruption to the network. However, the very next day, local terminals connected to system B began receiving "garbage" characters. Fortunately the CE was still in the area. Within hours the problem was traced to an intermittent bus cable within the 150.

More problems developed: terminals connected to system B appeared to "hang," and the "garbage" problem returned. We ran many tests and tried various hardware configurations in order to isolate the faulty component. This problem was extremely difficult to solve because just a restart could temporarily clear the problem; sometimes it was days until it recurred. The cause was finally discovered in a faulty board in the PDP-8 processor.

Early in August, DCA installed two more field changes in the protocol processor to correct problems that were experienced by other customers. The system hangs and stop-restarts became more frequent as the month progressed. The hangs were broken down into two classes: one, the system would halt, and two, the system would get stuck in an infinite loop. Both cases required operator intervention to restart.

During June and July the load is typically light, but during the month of August the load starts off light and builds to one of the highest usage periods of the year. Twice a year—from the end of August through the middle of September and in January—on-line registration takes place at the university. We were very concerned about the instability of network operation and the impact this would have on students adding and dropping courses for the fall semester.

By the end of August, not a day went by without some sort of network interruption. Node A would hang, or B would stop and restart. We were now in the middle of on-line registration.

September–October

September saw a severe degradation of network reliability. Stop-restarts and system hangs continued to plague users. The registration process was disrupted, causing students to endure long waiting lines.

We established an almost daily dialog with DCA, reporting failures and any observations. After considerable discussion, DCA recommended the installation of host flow control. Recall that in March, due to a mutual misunderstanding, it was not installed. Now we all believed the problem was too much load and that the data from the host had to be controlled.

Host flow control was installed in September. By removing the clear-to-send (CTS) RS-232-C signal, the 150 could suspend output from a host port until the buffers were back to satisfactory levels.

Network reliability degraded still further. We now requested a customer engineer to be sent to our site to augment the remote diagnostic service.

The DCA customer engineer arrived on site and within 2 hours, one of the nodes hung. He quickly ran some diagnostic tests and determined that the protocol processors were lacking a field change. This change was installed, and in the following days the number of system hangs was significantly reduced. But the stop-restart problems continued.

By now we had determined that the restarts were caused by a low buffer-space condition. Some staff members suspected that a minicomputer or block-transfer terminal was transmitting a continuous stream of 1.2-kbit/s data into one of the nodes. We had been sending dumps (storage readouts) after a stop to DCA, and some of these dumps pointed to a port commonly used by a microcomputer as the trouble source.

The micro's owner was contacted and asked to send blocks of data to the host computer in an attempt to make the network overload. If we could duplicate the cause, we could find a cure. Out of three attempts, only one failure occurred—hardly conclusive.

Another potential source of the stop-restart problem was thought to be the Prentice line drivers. Almost all these devices are energized 24 hours a day. Thus, each driver is continually sending and detecting carrier signal. The request-to-send (RTS) RS-232-C signal was strapped in its "on" condition in all modems at the terminal end of the circuit, to meet DCA requirements. This option was selected because, otherwise, some terminals do not assert RTS until they have data to send. Under this condition, when the terminal was turned off (with the transmit-data circuit "floating"), the modem transmitted a space over the circuit. A space looks like a constant line break to the multiplexing node—and that is a problem since a space creates constant interruptions in the node. Prentice was notified of this condition, promptly evaluated the problem, designed a field change for a "mark hold" on all modems, and set a schedule to modify the modems.

At this point, DCA committed itself to making the 150 more defensive. One step to this end was called load shedding. When the buffers start filling up, there is flow control to stop output from a host. But if a terminal is the source, flow control is inoperative. Load shedding would disconnect any terminal that continued to send data after the buffer reached a fixed threshold. The arrival of this software was to coincide with the arrival of a DCA software expert on Oct. 23.

By the end of the day, he had found a software bug in system A. If a terminal connected to either A or C requested a host port and that port was not available in A (all busy), the request was supposed to cross over to B. If a port was available there, it would then be connected to the requested host.

Apparently a blockage existed from A to B. Any characters entered at a terminal would enter A but not be passed along to B. The characters, having no place to go, occupied buffer space in A. Frustrated users would tap the carriage-return key on their terminals and not get a response—then tap some more. Each character they sent ate up buffer space until a stop finally occurred. A quick program patch to temporarily correct the problem was installed.

The next day, the hang problem was back in A. The expert quickly found a bug in the patch and, the next day, sent us a clean copy of the program.

November-December

The major problems we had experienced in past months had been solved. The network was stabilizing, and new problems were quickly resolved by DCA and UCS personnel. DCA pointed out that the extent of our network troubles were far from typical of most of the company's implementations.

One problem was particularly interesting and had us briefly worried. Node A would go into the load-shedding mode and stay there. Each terminal that tried to enter data into the node was disconnected. This was reminiscent of our stop-restart days but not nearly as frequent. DCA customer support, by dialing into the node, discovered that the log port was generating data but had no physical port through which to output. So it was slowly filling up the buffer space with connect and disconnect (log) messages. When the available buffer space exceeded the threshold, load shed would be turned on. But the stored data could not be flushed, so the buffer just stayed in load shed, and the node program had to be reloaded.

This problem was solved almost as soon as reported. A module card was inserted to give the appearance—to the program—that there was an output port in use. Since the data did not have to be saved, nothing was actually connected externally to this port.

We prepared for on-line registration—scheduled immediately after the Christmas break—with weekly preventive maintenance. The entire network was now functioning according to our expectations.

Another bug was uncovered in the software that initialized the links to remote nodes. This had not caused much inconvenience because the reload had become so infrequent. A simple change to one word in core corrected the problem.

A power failure caused a nodal hardware failure that was quickly corrected. That was the last problem recorded for January. In spite of the extremely heavy load, the network met all expectations.

The Cyber 173 was upgraded to a Cyber 174. The number of host ports on the Cyber will be increased to 120. This represents roughly a 30 percent increase in host ports in the network.

The untariffed metallic circuits we are leasing were finally tariffed by Telco. The rate for these lines is now $47.20 per month. We are again investigating replacing the Bell circuits with our own.

Our approach to adding terminals will be to use 115s wherever there are large clusters of terminals in buildings not housing a main node (150). This will eliminate not only the installation costs and the monthly leasing of many phone lines but also the need for a pair of ALDs per terminal. Instead, we will use one metallic circuit and Prentice synchronous line drivers to connect the 115 to the 150.

Two more 115s will be used by two local high schools to access the Cyber. Our initial eight contention groups will be increased to 12 to accommodate research users and the high schools. The single port for minicomputers is being expanded to two ports (one for each remote campus).

We have also discovered an inability to gather and analyze the usage data available from the console and log ports of each node. To completely monitor each 150 would require eight terminals. The method currently in use monitors only the console ports on nodes A and B in the computing center. A third terminal is available to dial up the remote nodes for error analysis. A plan, in its infant stages, will use a microprocessor to monitor the output of all log and console ports.

This system has run since November without any major failure. Total system availability has exceeded 98 percent, and production-time interruptions are minimal. In general, everyone is now happy with the performance, and the network has proved to be as cost-effective as we had originally planned. ∎

Scott G. Abbey*, David N. Bertollo, and Joseph R. Geller,
Rockland Research Institute, Orangeburg, N.Y.

Necessity is mother of homegrown DDP network

Some users were dissatisfied with offerings from top vendors, so they built their own multilevel architecture.

The evolution of distributed data processing (DDP) technology has reached the point where major vendors are announcing and delivering actual DDP hardware and software packages. At the network-software level, such products include IBM's systems network architecture (SNA), Digital Equipment Corporation's Decnet and digital network architecture (DNA), Tandem's Non-Stop System, Prime's Primenet, and Burroughs's network architecture (BNA). They provide various types of application-to-application communications protocols. Several of the major database-management-system (DBMS) vendors, such as Cullinane—with its integrated database management system (IDMS)—offer software packages that link a number of different computers together. Communications have gone far beyond AT&T's limited offerings and now include such enhanced services as GTE's Telenet and Tymshare's Tymnet, with AT&T's Advanced Communications Service expected soon.

Regardless of how far technology has come, serious problems exist for the user who must construct a DDP network using a variety of computers from different manufacturers. The value-added networks of Telenet and Tymnet are adequate for asynchronous or X.25 protocols, but not for binary synchronous communications (BSC). None of the vendor software packages such as SNA or Decnet will suffice. (They deal with data transfer, but not with the data's information content.) The standards proposals of the International Organization for Standardization (commonly known as the ISO) in its open systems interconnection (OSI) reference model would help solve these problems for the user. Unfortunately, none of the OSI proposals exist as standards yet. The user must develop the software

to allow application-to-application coupling.

The Rockland Research Institute, in Orangeburg, N.Y., has come to grips with this problem, however. The Institute has operated, for more than 10 years, a batch database configuration, the multistate information system (MSIS), that offers applications developed primarily for mental health and mental retardation programs. These include admission and census programs, drug ordering and monitoring programs, patient service recording programs, and patient billing programs. A variety of clinical, evaluation, and treatment-planning applications are available. More than 200 organizations ranging in size from major inpatient hospitals to small-community mental health centers currently use the MSIS through IBM's remote-job-entry (RJE) program. Most users have installed programmable intelligent terminals to provide local interactive data entry and editing (Fig. 1). The Institute has also exported MSIS to four other states and three foreign countries that operate their own networks.

The Institute has recently worked with the Office of Information Systems of New York State Department of Mental Hygiene to design, develop, and implement an interface between an IBM 4341 computer located at the Institute and a DDP network consisting of seven local data centers and more than 200 terminals throughout the state (Fig. 2). The data centers contain Burroughs B1860 processors, each supporting up to 10 of the 52 inpatient sites operated by the Department of Mental Hygiene.

To understand the architecture of such a network, it is useful to divide the functions it performs into layers. Basically, one layer serves the layer above it and depends on the layer below. The interface between each layer is well defined, and each need not understand the internal functioning of its neighbor in order to serve it or be served by it. In addition, other layers may exist farther

*Now with Morgan Stanley & Company, New York, N.Y.

194

removed from a given layer.

The number of layers in current architectures ranges from three to nine or more, with the necessary functions differently partitioned within the layers of each. However, all layered architectures recognize the existence of pairs of control elements (part of the network software), one at each layer in each network node. The crucial point in the design of a layered network architecture is to permit each control element to communicate with its peer in another node through the next lower layer.

Storing the data

The design of the Department of Mental Hygiene Information System (DMHIS) permits day-to-day operational data to be stored at the local data centers, and interactive updates to that database made by each user site. Clinical data such as psychological evaluations and drug regimens are processed and stored on the Institute's host computer in Rockland. A patient's demographic data and location (building and ward) are stored at the host for use with the clinical data and for distribution of reports. Sex, ethnic group, occupation, and religion are used for statistical research.

The functional design addresses these critical needs:

■ Updating of both local-data-center and host-computer databases from one input transaction.

■ Maintaining concurrency of both databases.

■ Allowing DMHIS to be developed using new techniques and data items, yet allowing DMHIS to take advantage of the existing MSIS applications.

■ Maintaining transparent connections among the processors to reduce the complexity of the network as seen by the user.

The Institute was given the task of implementing the network portion that connects the local data centers with the IBM host. The first issue that had to be resolved was the choice of a network architecture. After a review of the literature and the functions available on the selected computers, a four-layer architecture was chosen:

1. Communications message protocol (CMP)—transfers data across the transmission subnetwork (the phone lines) and routes incoming or outgoing data to the correct location within the node.

2. Network services protocol (NSP)—establishes and maintains each logical path between nodes, verifies passwords, and performs other validation functions.

3. Message store-and-forward (MSF) subsystem—collects transactions for transmission or processing at a later time.

4. Presentation services (PS)—the user-written or user-defined application that either processes the data at a node or interacts with the user at a terminal to present or obtain data.

Each architecture layer is dealt with independently, so long as it maintains the appropriate interface to the next layer. The choices for the layers are limited by the differences between manufacturers involved (Burroughs and IBM) and the desire to avoid custom building and duplication of effort. A synchronous protocol handles the high-speed transmission (up to 9.6 kbit/s) of batched data. Therefore, IBM's BSC protocol was

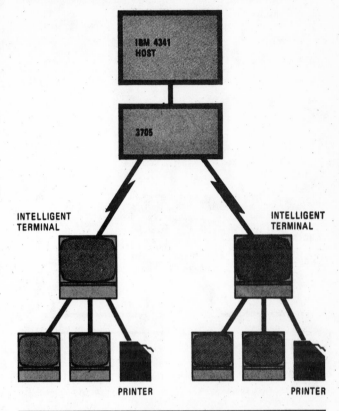

1. Batching the data. *Most MSIS users access the 4341 host with programmable intelligent terminals, to provide the capability for local interactive data entry and editing.*

chosen for the CMP layer, and the HASP (Houston automatic spooling priority) and RJE/3780 protocols were selected for the NSP layer. The PS and MSF layers were developed by the Institute's staff.

Protocol functions

The CMP level (Fig. 3) transfers data across an inherently noisy transmission medium, such as a telephone line, and routes each incoming data packet to the appropriate NSP level within the node. It also collects outgoing data packets from all NSP levels within the node and transmits them over the appropriate transmission link.

Note that the CMP level consists of compatible pairs on the ends of the transmission link (the same is true at each layer). At the host end, the CMP level's instructions are executed by an IBM 3705 communications controller in emulation mode. The 3705 is programmable and, therefore, can handle many different CMPs; in this case, the CMP is in BSC. At the local data center, a Burroughs nonprogrammable standard synchronous communications adapter is used. The two CMPs are symmetric: Data flows equally well in either direction. The unit of communication is a data block.

The NSP level establishes a link between the nodes, and presents passwords and identification information from the local data center and verifies them at the host. It also assembles outgoing data into packets and disassembles those incoming. At the host, HASP is used.

2. A DDP interface. *A network of local data centers, featuring Burroughs 1860 processors, interfaces user terminals to the host. A center supports up to 10 user sites.*

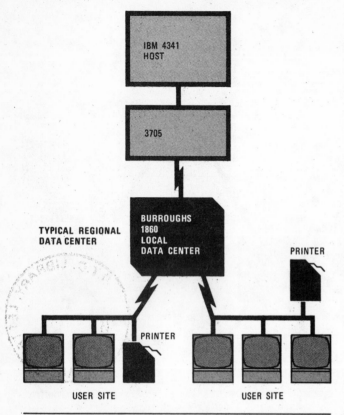

The local data center runs either a HASP workstation or an RJE/3780 program. The NSP pair cooperates in other ways by compressing and decompressing packets and transmitting data between the CMP and a spool (storage) file within their nodes. The NSPs are mostly symmetric: Punched-card images (80-column blocks) can flow in either direction, but print lines (data intended for a printer) can flow only from the host to the local data center (Fig. 4). The unit of communication is referred to as a "job."

Because the host's database is designed for batch application, the MSF subsystem at each node acts to collect transactions into successively larger batches for later processing. In particular, it builds the files that the NSP processes for outgoing data and accepts and stores the files that the NSP receives from another node. It also interfaces with the appropriate portion of PS to collect or process the transactions.

The MSIS front-end programs perform the MSF function at the host, and the interface performs it at the local data center (Fig. 3). The MSF subsystems are not symmetric but are complementary. The interface collects transactions from the presentation services and forms card images, transmits them to the host (through CMP and NSP), and receives print lines back. It then separates each job for each user and presents them to the PS. The MSIS front-end programs, on the other hand, receive card images from the network services protocol and pass them on to the PS (Fig. 5, A and B). The unit

of communication is a batch.

Presentation services is the applications programming needed to connect the user to the network. The user can be a person sitting at a terminal or a database management system. The PS speaks the language of the user: at the host, translating the card-image transactions—admissions, drug orders, or treatment—into a series of calls to the DBMS to update the database. These host presentation-services application programs form the MSIS.

At the local data center, PS communicates with the data-entry clerk's terminal to elicit input (to be transferred to the MSF), or to transfer reports from the MSF to the line printer. These PS applications of the local data center are part of the DMHIS. The presentation services at each node complement each other (Fig. 6, A and B) and communicate transactions.

Vendor restrictions

The choice of vendors not only restricts the choices for both the network architecture and necessary components; the choice mandates certain components. For example, the communications-message-protocol layer required installing a standard synchronous adapter on the local data center's Burroughs B1860 and additional line sets on the host site's IBM 3705.

The network-services protocol was implemented on the RJE/3780 program supplied by Burroughs on the B1860 and by updating password and remote-configuration tables in HASP on the IBM host. The message store-and-forward subsystem required a major amount of work on the B1860, but no work was necessary on the IBM host. The MSIS front-end was capable of handling all of the necessary functions. On the B1860, the interface had to be written.

The interface consists of:

1. Print collector—handles print streams created at the host and transmitted to the local data center through the RJE/3780 program. Among its other functions, the print collector must ensure that reports sent back to the center from the host are accessible only to authorized users. This function should probably be part of the NSP, but the RJE/3780 program as provided by Burroughs—and its entire printer spooling application—left a great deal to be desired.

2. Data batcher—collects update transactions, report requests, and miscellaneous card images from the database maintained by the interface and formats them into jobs suitable for transmission to the host. It must obey protocols established by HASP on the host and the MSIS front-end for data submission.

3. Utility programs—"clean" old data out of the interface database; retransmit a batch, if a failure occurs during transmission, by creating another job containing it; update and maintain various user-security and configuration-parameter tables, such as applications in use and the transmission schedule.

4. Scheduler—automatically invokes the data batcher, RJE/3780, and the print collector.

Most of the host presentation-service layers have been in place since 1975, when the multistate information system started operating. But modifications to the

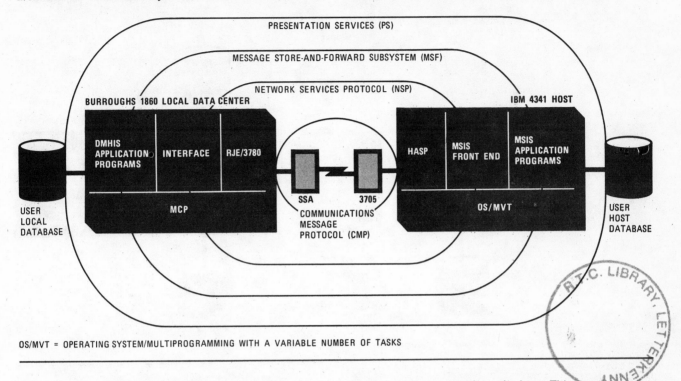

OS/MVT = OPERATING SYSTEM/MULTIPROGRAMMING WITH A VARIABLE NUMBER OF TASKS

admission/termination and census programs were made to speed up processing. DMHIS ensured that all these transactions were correct before they were transmitted; therefore, less editing was required.

User-site programs
For the local data center, several classes of programs were written:
1. Programs to interact with users at terminals for collection of data to be processed at the host. Examples are drug orders and incident reports.
2. Programs to spin off data from the local database to transmit to the host. Examples are admissions, releases, census movements, and name changes.
3. Programs to interact with users for entry of retrieval report requests to be processed at the host.
4. A program to control printing output reports produced at the host and stored in the interface database.
5. A program that allows the entry of any card-image data from terminals, to handle all transmission not covered by 1, 2, or 3.

MSIS users enter their requests to the Burroughs computer in one of two ways. In the one, most applications data and report requests are handled by screen-processing programs. Otherwise, to enter data for which no screen processing program exists, or to enter program source code or special data, a general card-input program is used. This program permits users to enter data in 80-column card format and provides maintenance and submission of these card streams to the host.

A special screen program, the print controller, provides printed output from the host. This program displays, at the user's CRT, the status of all print streams that have been received for printing at a given user site. It also allows the user to select print streams from the list presented to him. Users may also delete print streams when they no longer need them. Print streams not manually deleted by the user are automatically deleted after a given period of time by the data cleaner.

To illustrate from the user's viewpoint the flow of a typical collection of data through the network, the example of entering drug-order data is examined. The user first logs on to the local data center. Then the drug-system input-screen program is called up by entering the command RUN DRUGS. The program first presents a menu listing the possible input screens. As the user has drug-order transactions to enter, he selects and enters ORDER into the function area of the listing. This will cause the order screen to be presented. Drug orders can now be entered as required.

The program edits the syntax of all fields, checking numerics and correcting format. The program also edits the context on some fields, correcting chronology. Errors are presented in reverse video. The operator then corrects them. This process continues until all data has been entered correctly.

The correct data is then stored on the interface database for later processing by the data-batcher program. A new data-input screen is presented, and when no more data is to be entered, the user enters a blank screen to return to the menu screen. Entering the command END terminates this session.

The user takes no part in the actual transmission of this data to the host. At a fixed time each day, the data

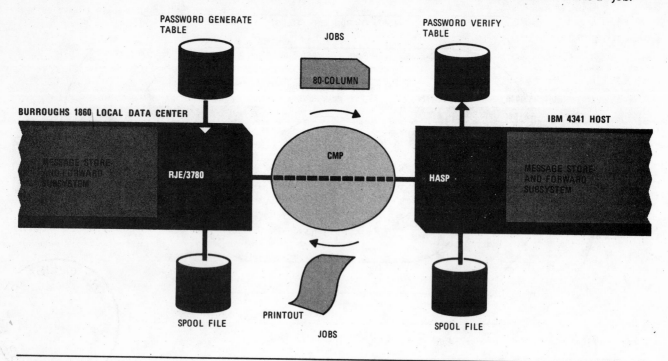

4. Servicing the network. *The NSP pair—the RJE/3780 and HASP programs—cooperates in compression and decompression of data packets and in data transmission between the CMP and storage files. Punched-card images flow in either direction, but print lines can flow only from the host to a center. The communication unit is a "job."*

batcher is automatically executed by the scheduler to collect all data entered during the day and to produce a file of batch-update jobs from the collected data. This job file is then input to the RJE/3780 program (also started automatically), which does the actual data transmission to the host.

As all database updates to the host are run overnight, the user looks for printed output from the drug program the following day by first logging on to the local data center, then by starting the print controller program. This program displays the status of all of a user's print streams. One print-stream report, "Drugerr," for drug-error analysis, indicates the number of copies desired next to the print stream name on the screen. The copies are produced on a line printer.

Earlier, the actual print stream containing the drug-error-analysis report is transmitted to the Burroughs machine by the RJE/3780. After this program completes its task, the print collector program automatically starts. This program divides the single print-stream file created by RJE/3780 into sequential files. As each sequential file is created, an entry is placed into a print-catalog database containing various data about the print stream, such as the user it belongs to and the host application that created it. This catalog data is then input to the print-controller program. Report request and card images, including their job streams and data streams, are transferred between computers several times a day for one-day delivery to the user.

Because many users are connected to the local data center at any given time, it is important to provide easy access for users' input data, job streams, and print streams. But because most patient-related data is highly sensitive, security must take priority.

Security is provided at two levels. The first level is in the Burroughs operating system, the master control program (MCP). MCP checks user identifications with physical terminal addresses and only allows a user to log on at specific terminals and to reach specific files.

The second level of security is provided by the presentation-services programs. Within each program accessible to users (screen applications and the print controller) is code which verifies that this user, with a password, is allowed to use this application. It does this by comparing the combination of unique user code, application password, and application name with entries in a security file. If such a record is not found, the local data center supervisor receives a message on his screen and the session is terminated.

More user clearance

In addition to providing program-access security, the security file allows the print collector and the print controller to determine which user-code-and-password combinations may request the printing of specific print streams, as well as receive status information about them. For example, a supervisor may decide that any user may see the status of any print streams directed to his site, but only a user with clearance for the "Drugs" password may print drug reports.

DMHIS and MSIS allow users to specify many processing options. A parameter file provides all processing rules pertaining to a site trying to retrieve information located at the local data center. These rules cover editing options, database names, and transmission schedules. There is one parameter record maintained

5. Storing, forwarding. *In A, the MSF interface collects transactions from the PS for the host. In B, the MSIS front end receives card images from the NSP for the PS.*

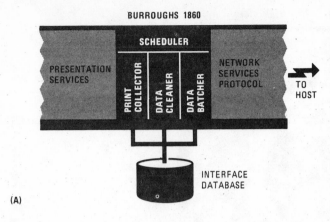

BURROUGHS 1860

SCHEDULER

PRESENTATION SERVICES | PRINT COLLECTOR | DATA CLEANER | DATA BATCHER | NETWORK SERVICES PROTOCOL

TO HOST

INTERFACE DATABASE

(A)

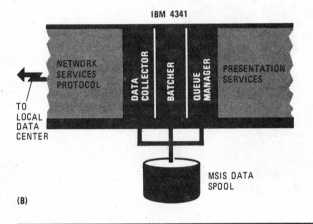

IBM 4341

NETWORK SERVICES PROTOCOL | DATA COLLECTOR | BATCHER | QUEUE MANAGER | PRESENTATION SERVICES

TO LOCAL DATA CENTER

MSIS DATA SPOOL

(B)

for each site-and-application combination.

Editing options include specifying required versus optional data fields as well as screen formats that are site specific. The MSIS-host-database name for each site is maintained in the parameter file. Transmission schedules ensure that update data will only be transmitted to the host as necessary.

Program functions

Data is entered through screen application programs. Each major application has screen programs that process user data, edit the data for syntax, and place the resulting host transactions onto the interface database for later processing by the data-batcher program. The user has no control over this data after it is entered.

To allow the entering of transactions for which no screen applications exist, and for entering special report requests, compiles, and tests, a special screen application program, "Job," is provided. "Job" allows data to be entered to the host as though the user entered it through a standard RJE terminal. This program provides for the creation, editing, submission, and deletion of "Job" files. These files are maintained on the interface database but are only transmitted to the host

when the user submits a "Job" file for transmission. RJE files are in 80-column card-image format.

To simplify common report requests, a "Report" program offers the user a menu of common host reports. Report requests are placed on the interface database and transmitted periodically.

All data transmissions to the host are initiated by the data-batcher program, started automatically at intervals during the day. It will optionally select only report requests, "Job" files, or data-update requests in any combination for transmission. The usual procedure for report requests and "Job" files requires that their transmission occur during all executions of the data batcher, with all data-update requests sent only once at the end of the working day.

As each collection of data is selected for transmission, it is assigned a batch number that is reported to the local-data-center supervisor. By using the retransmission program, the operator sends selected data batches at a later time if there is a communications failure during the actual transmission, or if the data is lost at the host (because of a site failure) and must be retransmitted. For update data, these batch numbers are recorded at the host as well.

The data-batcher program writes all selected data to a sequential file. When the data batcher completes its work, the RJE/3780 program is automatically started. RJE/3780 does two things: First, it begins transmission to the host of the sequential file created by the data batcher. Second, it receives print streams that the host has spooled (placed in temporary file storage), writing them off to a sequential spool file.

When RJE/3780 has completed its processing, another program, the print collector, is started. This program takes the spool file created by RJE/3780 and creates one sequential file for each print stream present. As each file is written, an entry is made in the interface database. This entry shows an identifying name, date and time of file creation, and the estimated number of print lines that the file contains.

The final program run on a regular basis is the database cleaner. None of the programs mentioned so far actually remove data from any of the database files; they merely mark the appropriate records as deletable. The database cleaner actually removes this data. Also, in order to prevent data from cluttering the interface database, the cleaner program checks the last time the record was referred to, and deletes all records that have not been referred to within the number of days specified in the site-parameter record.

With a reasonable amount of work, it is possible to implement a distributed data processing network across a variety of different computers. The development activities described took less than four man-years. A prime factor in the success was recognizing the existence of control-element pairs at each architecture layer in each network node. By ensuring that these pairs communicate successfully, the hard part of the network was completed. In fact, most of the problems that arose during the development occurred in the attempt to make HASP (on the host) and RJE/3780 (at the local data centers) communicate.

6. User interface. *At a center (A), PS elicits inputs from the user terminals for the MSF. At the host (B), card-image transactions are translated to update the database.*

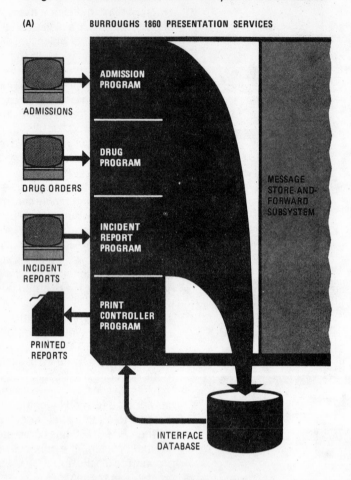

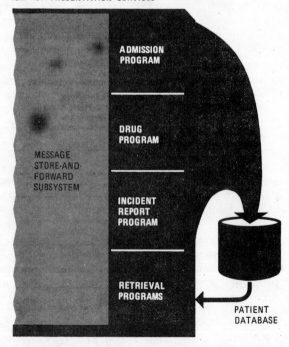

3 Network Management

5 basic principles for achieving high availability

Don Mueller, Tran Telecommunications Corp., Marina Del Rey, Calif.

Downtime can affect the overall efficiency of a data communications network, so it is essential that the user know what factors keep availability up

Availability is a key parameter used in specifying modern data communications networks. But what exactly is availability? How does it relate to the actual operation of a network? What factors affect it?

Availability may be defined as the probability of a system operating at some required time. Simply stated, if a system has an availability of .999, there is a 99.9 percent chance that it will be operational when needed.

Mathematically, availability A may be calculated by the following equation:

$$A = \frac{MTTF}{MTTF + MTTR}$$

where MTTF is the mean time to failure and MTTR the mean time to repair—which includes the time to detect the failure, administrative waiting time, diagnosis, and actual repair.

Here are some practical principles that may be applied to improve operating availability.

Corporate commitment. Probably the single most influential availability factor is corporate commitment—commitment by both the user and the supplier. Several commitment factors have an impact on availability. Most of them cost money on an ongoing basis, without any immediate and direct return—except that when the data communications network is used, it works; it is available.

The corporate commitment, then, is a willingness to take charge of the situation from the start, rather than wait for trouble and simply react to daily disasters.

Performance measurement. Before trying to improve availability, the user must know what it is. Surprisingly, many sophisticated corporations do not measure availability. This is like trying to drive an automobile at 55 mph without using a speedometer.

The user must have quantitative performance feedback. It is unwise to wait until the payroll can't run because the network is down. Availability should be measured continuously and reviewed weekly. Performance degradation must be detected and fixed.

Availability is measured by recording downtime. The operations people must develop a way to do this. Sometimes an indirect approach is best. A designated person can simply record the fault condition that occurs on a network and assign a mean time to clear each fault—perhaps 15 or 20 minutes. Although this method does not provide a precise measurement, it has proved effective in estimating availability.

 Network topology and architecture. Because trunk lines go down, network topology should be designed to provide alternate paths to major nodes. Take a simple three-node configuration (A, B, and C), for example. With node B connected to both A and C, it is important that A and C are interconnected. In this arrangement, a trunk could fail without disabling communications between any two nodes. However, if there were no connection between A and C, a single trunk failure would isolate a node, cutting it off from the other two.

Assuming a good topology, is the architecture of the communications equipment designed to handle it? Does this architecture allow for redundancy of major switching nodes?

Allowing for redundancy both in the network topology and nodal switching equipment has the effect of reducing the MTTR figure to the time it takes to detect the failure and switch in the redundant system. Of course, the probability of a double failure has a second-order effect that can become significant if the MTTR of the spare system is excessive.

Quality assurance. The quality assurance function of both the supplier and user organizations can have a profound effect on the network availability, especially during the first six months of operation. The supplier organization must do the proper testing before delivery. Of greatest importance is burn-in (operating) testing, at both the component and finished-equipment levels. At least a 48-hour burn-in—under load—is needed at the equipment level.

The user organization should develop a functional test to be run before accepting the network. The user should develop this test and be responsible for implementing it. He bought the equipment, so he must know what he wants it to do.

The user should require 30 days of acceptance tests after delivery. If he expects a .999 availability figure, he should operate the network and carefully record downtime. Of course, a 30-day sample is not very large, so he must allow for a confidence factor in the results. Nevertheless, the network should be accepted only after it has been demonstrated—on site—that the availability goals can be met.

Maintainability. The user should select a network that provides a healthy dose of effective diagnostics. Effective diagnostics monitor the network in real time; if something goes wrong, they not only indicate the problem but also what to do about it. Diagnostics allow tests such as channel loopbacks from a centralized site. They also enable determination of the most likely geographical location of a problem before dispatch of repair personnel.

Once the trouble is isolated, how long does it take to repair? Are the modules easily replaceable? Are there spare modules available—and can they be used as replacements? A common pitfall in data communications maintenance is the lack of operating spare modules at a site. Remember, a communications network is geographically distributed. It is difficult enough to isolate the trouble. But all diagnostics are wasted if—after pinpointing the problem at a remote location—there is no spare module. Spares must be operationally cycled on a regular basis—preferably on a standby test system.

In addition, strict inventory control must be maintained over these spares. They tend to disappear. A procedure should be established so that when a spare is used at a remote site, a replacement for it is mailed at once. This calls for a centralized store of parts that can be sent to a remote site immediately.

In effect, spares should be maintained at the remote sites and duplicated at a central one. This is called a like-for-like spares program and has proved very effective in large data communications installations.

What about preventive maintenance? Certain things can be done in this area, such as power supply adjustments and diagnostics during off hours. But, in general, if it's working, do not touch it. Preventive maintenance is important, but it should be limited to activities that can't significantly upset the network. If a technician shuts equipment down and removes modules, he will create more problems than he will solve.

 Customer service and training. What kind of customer service organization does the supplier have? What training is available to the user? The competence of the personnel involved in the maintenance of the gear is crucial. It is the final ingredient to high availability.

The user should make sure the vendor's customer service organization has an effective procedure for calling in its top technical people if a problem cannot be solved by the customer engineer.

The user's technical people should be sent to maintenance-training classes before installation time. And the 30-day test should be used not only to evaluate the supplier's servicepeople but also the user's maintenance personnel.

Depending solely on a supplier to provide maintenance is shortsighted. True, it is a good idea to employ the supplier's service organization, but the user should also be able to identify problems and provide support where and when it is required.

The six principles discussed here do not constitute a foolproof blueprint for a successful availability program. There will be many difficulties along the way. One should never sit back and relax when things are going well. Constant diligence and effective action are required to run a data communications network at utmost efficiency. ∎

David L. Lyon, Intertel Inc., Burlington, Mass.

How network control curbs downtime

As an interactive data network grows, so does the cost of outages. This cost is reduced with an effective network-control system.

The primary purpose of network control is to minimize—or better, avoid—downtime. And downtime affects nearly everyone: daily users, company management, and network managers. For example, in the United States, most financial transactions are logged in, cleared through, and checked out by several types of distributed data processing (DDP) networks. Modern commercial airlines use interactive computing systems not only to coordinate ticket reservations but also to schedule flight crews and equipment, select and recall seat assignments, and specify the most comfortable and fuel-efficient route for the aircraft. Consider what would happen if any part of these systems failed.

As computers and communications equipment become faster, more efficient, and more functional, the price/performance ratios improve. However, there is another price to pay as an interactive network delivers increasing benefits through growth. This price is figured in downtime. And unless efficiently treated, downtime can be the undoing of large DDP networks.

The network operations manager is responsible for keeping all terminals up and running uninterrupted as long as possible, that is, minimizing the terminal hours lost to downtime. Why is this already difficult job becoming harder? There are several reasons, some mathematical (which are explained in the section, "Analyzing downtime"), and some intuitive.

First, the more complex a network grows, the greater its probability of failing. Imagine that more and more terminals, remote processors, and concentrators supplant their less-complicated counterparts in a processing network: intelligent concentrators replace dumb multiplexers, or intelligent terminals replace simple teleprinters. The result is more-frequent failures, simply

Rosenblum.

because the network has more basic components—such as semiconductors and switches—each with its inherent failure rate.

Second, as the network grows, so does the time needed to identify the cause of a problem. Since there are more pieces to distinguish among, the delay before a repair increases because it takes longer to identify the true problem area. Compare the relative simplicity of identifying a "streaming" terminal condition on a point-to-point line with the complexity of pinpointing the same condition on a multipoint line equipped with a dozen remote stations. (Streaming occurs when a terminal's request-to-send, or RTS, signal is locked in its "on" condition, causing the associated modem's carrier signal to remain constant. This interferes with transmissions from other terminals on that line.)

Finally, the time to cure any particular problem grows as the network expands, because the distance between the terminal sites and the locations of spare equipment is greater.

On the other side of the network, the users suffer from the inconveniences and from declining availability. Thus, each minute of terminal downtime costs the network's operators that much more in terms of lost business and loss of customers' good will. Since it is too expensive for each installation to maintain sufficient manual backup techniques, the network will sustain only short periods in the manual backup mode before the user experiences further inconveniences.

Is there any plan that allows a network to grow without imperiling terminal availability? Several sectors of the data communications industry have addressed this issue and have designed technical-control techniques

as well as network-control systems in attempting to alleviate problems.

The earliest and most basic approach to managing a network starts with equipment that resides at the central site. The network manager must first provide access to both the digital and the analog interfaces of all modems in the network. This can mean either jack fields and patch cords, of both analog and digital varieties, or, more recently, sophisticated switching arrangements utilizing semiconductors and computerized control. Regardless of the tool, the aim is the same: to allow the central-site operator to directly access any analog (telephone-line) interface or any modem-terminal interface. [The central-site (CS) operator, equipped with modern diagnostic and control devices, can replace the technician in many on-line functions.]

What is the purpose of providing access? Two reasons are most important: the ability to monitor signals for measurements and the ability to intercept and substitute signals for testing.

In the analog domain, the CS operator may need to measure signals at the access points. For example, using only the data signal patterns normally present on the lines, he can measure the signal level, or he may connect a particular analog signal to a loudspeaker or an oscilloscope for extended examination.

For making analog-parameter measurements requiring standard signals originating at one location for measurements at another, the central-site access is insufficient, and coordination with the remote sites is necessary. Say that a CS operator measures the received-signal level on the inbound (to the CPU) two-wire link connecting a remote site to the central site (Fig. 1). Although he can easily attach a power meter to the analog wires as they appear on his centrally located jack field at B, a problem arises when he tries to excite only the data transmitter at remote site A. For that, he needs a conveniently placed confederate to ensure that the modem transmitter at A is turned on and is sending a randomized data pattern. Of course, if the centrally located operator could remotely and selectively trigger the modem to send a randomized data pattern, then measuring signal levels on multipoint links would be more convenient. But, as later discussed, this remote-control capability at the modem is the cornerstone of network-control systems and is not part of technical control as normally defined.

Consider the advantages of centrally located equipment that can monitor and display digital traffic without requiring remote personnel. When the network operates with relatively few transmission errors, then the data signals passing the central modem-computer interface reflect the transactions of all remote sites. (A high error rate on the high-speed, or trunk, line negates the benefits of central-site monitoring.) Referring again to Figure 1, that means that data bound for, or returning from, any remote site on a multipoint line must pass the interface labeled C. Of course, the same data, in analog form, also passes point B. But more can be learned about software- and protocol-related problems by monitoring the digital form at point C.

Using a device for capturing and displaying the dig-

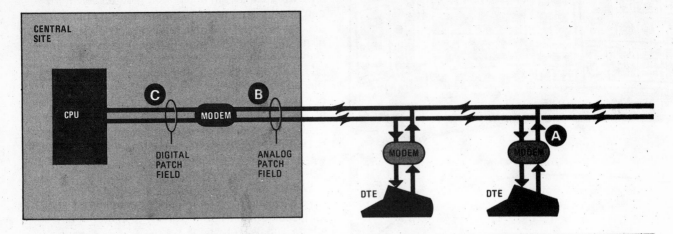

1. Measuring from afar. With the transmitter on only at A, the control-site operator measures the incoming signal level with a power meter at the analog patch field, B. By monitoring the equivalent digital data at the digital patch field, C, the operator can learn more about software- and protocol-related problems, after some training.

ital data at the central site, a trained CS operator can identify network faults by observing how the data messages are structured. With a more intelligent data monitor, the operator can program the device either to ignore all messages except those with a particular address header or to trigger only on a particular response code. In this manner, protocol or software faults can be diagnosed relatively quickly.

The step beyond data-content monitoring is data emulation, which is similar to using standard test signals in the analog domain. Here, the CS operator composes and then substitutes test-data patterns in place of the normal traffic. By observing the network's response, he can further diagnose and solve problems.

Content monitoring and emulation are commercially available today, but they have weaknesses that are not obvious on first examination. These techniques are vulnerable to transmission faults and cannot discriminate among error sources. For example, if a CS operator monitors a particular line, and numerous parity

errors appear, then he might correctly infer a severe problem somewhere in the computer-modem-line-modem-terminal series. However, a data monitor cannot distinguish between data bit errors caused by a faulty modem, by an out-of-tolerance telephone line, or by an intermittent terminal. Furthermore, if the errors occur too frequently, the monitor will cease to give any useful information whatsoever. These same objections apply to network-control systems that are based strictly on main-channel data.

Another shortcoming of centrally located monitors and emulators (as well as analog patching and measuring equipment) is their inability to provide useful service for outlying sites in multitiered networks. As Figure 2 shows, data crossing point A is not necessarily related in any simple fashion to data passing points B and C, because the remote network node may represent an entirely independent processing function.

However, network managers may insist on maintaining one diagnostic and control facility in this architec-

2. Multitier monitoring. In this network, data crossing point A is not necessarily related in any simple fashion to data passing points B and C, because the remote network node may represent an entirely independent processing function. But the continued demand for one centralized diagnostic and control center is expected.

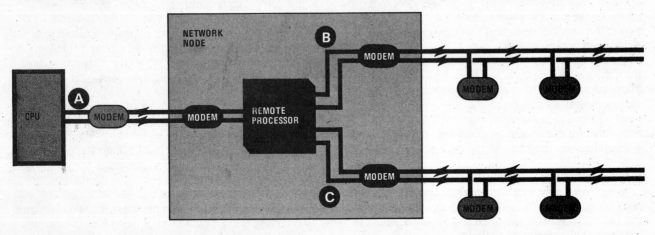

ture. In fact, in future multitiered networks, the only distinguishing characteristic of the central site may be the network manager's office. Computers and analog subnetwork centers may be spread all over the countryside in future meganetwork configurations, while management insists on having only one network-control center responsible for overall operations management—no matter how incongruous it may appear.

Clearly, a technical-control center based on centrally located access, test, and control devices—and lacking remotely controllable equipment—is insufficient to handle total network control, especially in multipoint and multitiered networks. The most effective way for a network manager to hold downtime in check is through a unified network-control system.

Keeping availability up

To meet the objectives of a good network-control system and thus control the network's downtime, management should:

■ Place comprehensive diagnostic, test, and control facilities in the hands of the network manager.
■ Allow these facilities to be centrally controlled but implemented at any remote site in the network.
■ Make these facilities sufficiently independent of the other network components so that the network manager, and not his vendors, can arbitrate field service issues ("fingerpointing").

During the mid- and late 1970s, several modem vendors shared in establishing the network-control system as a practical reality. As networks have grown bigger and more complex, most users have realized the worth of network control in terms of lower downtime and generally happier customers and upper management. What are the elements of a network-control system as it has evolved?

The first element is a tool to gain remote access from a central site: the out-of-band test channel. Modem vendors are in the unique position of bridging the analog and digital domains at every network site. They are, therefore, well set to create a special test channel in both analog and digital domains, in addition to the normal main data channel that the modem supports. Figure 3 illustrates how the main and test channels are separated and shows their relative signal amplitudes and spectrum positions. Thus, it is both technically and economically feasible for the modem vendor to supply an entire multipoint or multitiered subnetwork that operates over the same transmission facilities as the main-channel application. The test-channel subnetwork has exactly the same configuration as the main network—be it point-to-point, multipoint, multitiered, or some combination thereof.

The second element of the network-control system is the test module that resides at every remote modem and communicates over the test channel. This test module must recognize its own address when instructed, then accept commands and perform required functions (Fig. 4). Of course, it must have sufficient access to—and control of—internal and external modem signals to perform an accurate diagnosis and test and sufficiently powerful remedial control functions.

The test module replaces the roving field technician in these functions. In the earlier example of the analog measurement of a received data signal, the test module and subchannel would serve several useful purposes. Operator commands would travel over the subchannel to a number of receiving test modules. A signaled module would recognize its address and go into an active mode, accepting the command and acting on it. In this case, it would activate the modem transmitter to send a standard, pseudorandom data pattern. Receiving units at nodal sites would handle measurement.

The network-control system's third element is the control console and its centralized intelligence, which forms the interface between the CS operator and the distributed portion of the network. The central site has evolved greatly from its relatively simple beginnings, when it consisted of manual keyboard input and hardcopy or CRT readout. Most vendors of network-control systems now offer both manual and automated central-site facilities, some with arrays of processors and peripherals that rival the complexity of the main application. Depending on network size and purpose, management can now choose central-site equipment for its degree of automation, complexity, and price.

Two key questions about network control systems remain: What are the features of such a system? and What tests and remedial controls can a user expect in a state-of-the-art network-control system?

To select a good network-control system, the user should consider the three design elements just described: (1) the test channel, (2) the remote addressable test module, and (3) the central-site controller. (A general rule is that the user should strive to find a modem vendor who can supply both his network-control equipment and modems. Splitting suppliers here could later cause grave problems of incompatibilities and incomplete coverage.)

Adapting to the channel

In considering the test channel, the user should study the flexibility of the implementation. How many different types of modems and network configurations can the test channel accommodate? Ideally, it should handle a broad range of modems and accessories from the same vendor. Since four-wire private- (leased-) line applications are the rule for interactive configurations, the user should check that the vendor's private-wire modems meet all required data rates. (The full range is 1.2 to 9.6 kbits/s for voice-grade channels.)

If a user's network configuration is more exotic than a simple four-wire multipoint or point-to-point layout, he should find out which network-control vendors supply modems and remote test capabilities for these applications. As an example, consider multitiered networks which contain several serially embedded layers of analog links interspersed with digital hubs. Can the test channel be successfully routed around the remote processors, and to what level of hubbing can addressing be applied?

A good network-control system handles multitiered networks as easily as point-to-point ones with respect to user interfacing and control. It should accommodate

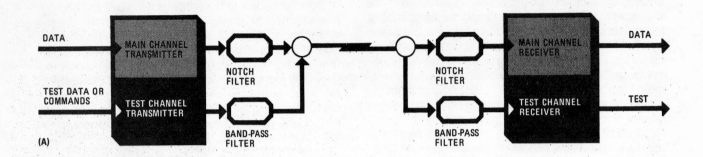

(A)

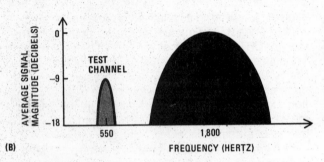

(B)

3. Bridging the band. *Modems are in the unique position of bridging the analog and digital domains at every network site. In addition to the normal main data channel supported by the modems, they create a special test channel in both domains. Main- and test-channel signals are separated and flow as shown in A. The test channel is used for network-control functions, when its frequency is positioned as in B. Note the main-channel position.*

a minimum of four or five levels of serial hubbing in case a future application requires unusual multiplexing and routing patterns.

For unusual configurations such as two-wire serial links used in the new wave of IBM banking and point-of-sale systems, network control needs test-channel capability designed to handle the routing requirements of two-wire loops. The needs here are especially acute, because multiple links routed in series with one another can seriously threaten network uptime.

Having considered flexibility of addressing and rout-

ing, the user should next examine the remote test module's functions and carefully investigate which features are available on which modem models and for which network configurations. It is best to break down the functions into subdivisions related to visibility to the main data application. The "Network-control checklist" lists the test features that represent test and control functions currently available in the industry.

The primary divisions in the checklist are nonintrusive tests, intrusive tests, remedial functions, and analog measurements. As the name implies, nonintrusive tests

4. Communicating modules. *The modems' test modules communicate over the test channel (dashed line). These modules take the place of the roving field technician in*

coordinating tests and exerting control. Each test module recognizes its own address when instructed, then accepts commands to perform its assigned functions.

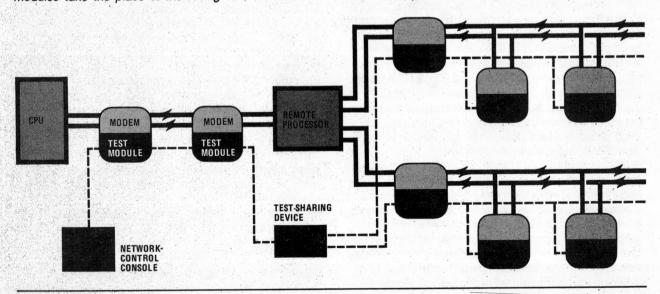

are executed by the network-control system without interrupting main-channel data. The operator can therefore run a complete battery of these tests, including an inspection of DTE/DCE (data terminal equipment/data circuit-terminating equipment) interface-lead states, without coordinating with the main application or the associated personnel.

Several of the nonintrusive tests deserve some additional comments. DTE streaming refers to a condition described earlier, where a terminal device seizes the request-to-send function and holds it continuously active. On a multipoint line, this causes a remote modem transmitter to stay on and renders the entire line useless for further polling and data transfer. A good network-control system can detect the streaming condition, initiate automatic or manual shutdown of the streaming RTS lead, then detect the presence of the resulting streaming-disabled condition.

Another noteworthy nonintrusive test is the signal-quality sensing at the modem receiver. A properly designed network contains modems with sensing circuitry built into the receivers to judge the degree of distortion in demodulated analog signals. These circuits indicate "out-of-tolerance" when the signal quality falls below the predetermined bit error rate. Although the acceptable threshold in error rate changes with the type of distortion encountered, the circuit will warn that the demodulated data signal is declining (change-of-state measurement). This, in turn, may point to degrading telephone or modem equipment and will prompt the user to perform further quantitative testing.

Intrusive tests generally cause some interruption in the main-channel data traffic. In exchange for this inconvenience, these tests render precise information about the high-speed operation of modems and the quality of the whole transmission channel.

A complete network-control system will have both steady-state as well as switched-carrier error-rate tests. These two types of tests are necessary to check out all of a modem's operating circuitry, as well as to fully test the telephone channel. Steady-state tests should have variable run-time lengths from 10^4 to 10^7 bits. This allows the user to test for sporadic "hit" phenomena that may occur at irregular and widely spaced intervals. Switched-carrier tests generally use fixed-bit-length blocks but should have variable numbers of blocks specifiable.

Fixing the fault

Remedial functions are extremely important in helping to directly control downtime by reducing the repair time for several kinds of failures (see "Analyzing downtime"). Good network-control systems can eliminate DTE streaming, replace faulty modems, and bypass faulty private-line facilities. Replacing modems with on-line "hot" spare units generally requires that the user install two complete modems at a site plus a remotely controlled switch placed at the DCE/DTE interface. Changeover to the hot spare is actuated manually by the central network-control (NC) operator as quickly as the faulty modem is identified.

Dial backup of a private line requires that the user install an auto-answering adapter at the remote node, as well as two dial telephone connections to the device. At the master modem, an analog bridging arrangement is needed to recombine the private-line and dial-line signals so that the backed-up site will operate as a normal member of the multipoint environment.

Analog measurements can provide further quantitative information about signal strengths and signal degradation. Some of these measurements may be intrusive, such as those that substitute a test tone for the main-channel data signal. Others, although nonintrusive, may, in fact, be approximations of residual signals measured in the modem receiver while data is flowing. Estimated signal-to-noise ratio is an example of this nonintrusive type of measurement. The user must never assume that these estimates are exact, but rather use them more to spot and track network trends.

Finally, after considering the test-channel routing and the test and control functions, the user must decide what level of sophistication and computer power he requires at the network-control system's central site. Several systems now combine reasonable cost with a relatively high degree of automation and data management, thanks mainly to the rapid evolution of microcomputer applications.

The test-module cost per remote site ranges from

Network-control checklist

Nonintrusive tests
Terminal-related
☐ DTE powered and connected
☐ DTE/DCE interface-lead states
☐ DTE streaming
☐ DTE streaming disabled
Channel-related
☐ Channel continuity
☐ Level of received analog signal
Modem-related
☐ Modem powered?
☐ Quality of received signal
Intrusive tests
Quantitative
☐ Steady-state error rate
☐ Switched-carrier error rate
Qualitative
☐ Modem self-test
☐ Analog and digital loopback control
☐ Transmitter control
Remedial functions
☐ Disable streaming terminals
   (automatic or remote manual)
☐ Switch to hot spare modem
☐ Dial-backup of private-line facilities
Analog measurements
☐ Data-signal levels
☐ Test-tone levels
☐ Relative quality of data signal (estimated)
☐ Signal-to-noise ratio (estimated)
☐ Phase jitter (estimated)
☐ Hit phenomena

$500 to $800. The central-site cost depends on the amount of computer power and mass memory desired. A minimum, manual central-site configuration costs from $3,000 to $7,000; additional automated functions could bring the price to $25,000 and beyond.

A good automated network-control-system controller does the following:

- Automatically executes the nonintrusive tests at all remote sites
- Flags changes in the nonintrusive test results
- Schedules intrusive testing based on time of day and particular network addresses
- Maintains hard-copy or magnetic storage of the intrusive test results and their changes of state ■

Analyzing downtime

Defining and analyzing downtime are the important first steps in deciding which features of network-control systems will most efficiently increase reliability. As with any other product, trade-offs exist between price and performance. Here they are measured in differences in average terminal downtime.

We define the downtime quotient as the ratio of terminal operating time lost because of failures to the network's total number of available terminal hours. Thus, average downtime d is the mean fraction of terminal operating time lost to failures. For the total cost of network downtime, we calculate d for each terminal and add the results.

Assume, for example, that in a multipoint network, each device's reliability can be described with an exponential function exp of time. That is, the probability P that device i does not fail in an interval of duration t can be written

$$P \text{ (no failure in t)} = \exp(-\lambda_i t) \tag{1}$$

where λ_i is the failure rate of device i, whose inverse is the mean time between failure (MTBF) of device i.

Since the average failure rate is λ_i, then by knowing the average time to repair such a failure, M_i, we can calculate the average fraction of time device i is down by multiplying the two.

$$\lambda_i M_i = \frac{\text{Number of device } i \text{ failures}}{\text{Unit time}}$$

$$\text{X Average time to repair device } i \tag{2}$$

Another way to view this expression is that in every unit of time, $\lambda_i M_i$ units are lost because of failure.

By assuming that device failures occur independently, we can extend equation 2 to calculate the average downtime fraction d for general network designs. Remembering that the basic definition is

$$d = \frac{\text{Terminal operating time lost to failures}}{\text{Total terminal operating time}}$$

$$= \frac{T_{OTL}}{T_{OT}} \tag{3}$$

we derive the exact expression for d as follows.

Each device, when it fails, can cause a certain number of terminals to go out of service. For a failure of the ith device, assume that J_i terminals go down. Thus—in unit time—the amount of terminal time lost because device i failed is the product

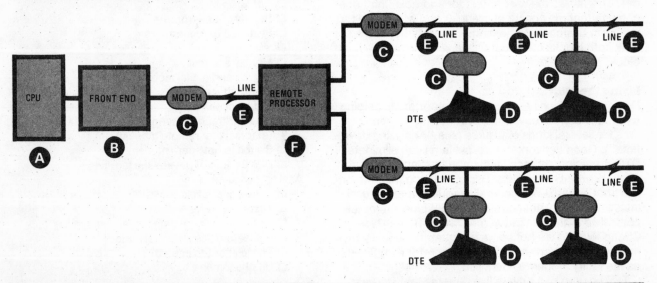

5. Downtime derivation. *The six major network components are assigned letter codes A through F. The downtime fraction, d, is derived from the failure rate and aver-age time to repair each component type. The correctness of the calculations and results depends on whether the number of sites per multipoint line is an average or exact.*

Downtime with and without net control

	FAILURE RATE λ_i (HOURS^{-1})	REPAIR TIME (HOURS)			
		BASIC	WITH NETWORK-CONTROL SYSTEM (NCS)	WITH PROCESSOR BACKUP (PBU)	WITH NCS AND PBU
A CPU	1.4×10^{-3}	2.0	2.0	0.1	0.1
B FRONT END	4.6×10^{-4}	2.0	2.0	0.1	0.1
C MODEM	5.7×10^{-5}	$4\sqrt{S}$	0.1	$4\sqrt{S}$	0.1
D DTE	1.1×10^{-4}	$4\sqrt{S}$	4.0	$4\sqrt{S}$	4.0
E LINE	4.6×10^{-4}	$4\sqrt{S}$	0.1	$4\sqrt{S}$	0.1
F REMOTE PROCESSOR	2.3×10^{-4}	4.0	4.0	0.1	0.1

$$J_i \times \lambda_i \times M_i \qquad (4)$$

Now, if we assume that all failures are completely independent, then the amount of lost terminal time in unit time is equal to expression 4 summed over all devices in the system that might fail.

$$T_{OTL} = \sum_i \times J_i \times \lambda_i \times M_i \qquad (5)$$

In unit time, if there are N terminals in the network, then there are N units of terminal operating time.

$$T_{OT} = N \qquad (6)$$

Thus, for typical multipoint or multitiered networks under the prior assumptions, the average system downtime is

$$d = \frac{\sum_i \times J_i \times \lambda_i \times M_i}{N} \qquad (7)$$

We next apply equation 7 to the simplified model of the distributed data processing network shown in Figure 5. First, we assign letter codes A through F to the six major network components. Next, we consider how many terminals are affected by any one component failure. After some arithmetic, we arrive at this equation for the downtime fraction:

$$d = \lambda_A M_A + \lambda_B M_B + 4\lambda_C M_C + \lambda_D M_D$$
$$+ \lambda_E M_E \left[\frac{S}{2} + \frac{3}{2} \right] + \lambda_F M_F \qquad (8)$$

where S is the number of sites per multipoint line.

Note that the calculations and results are generally valid for a large network with many remote processors and remote lines, as long as the site distribution per multipoint line is S. The results are approximate for networks that simply average S.

To further evaluate equation 8 and derive quantitative results for the multitiered network, we must settle on a set of numbers for failure rates and repair times

(λ_i, M_i)—both with and without a network-control system (NCS). In the table, NCS refers to a network-control system that is fully equipped with dial backup and hot-spare-modem switching. Processor backup (PBU) refers to full alternate-equipment backup of all central and remote processing units.

Figure 6 shows the resulting downtime fractions as a function of S. Note from the table that some repair times are also stated as functions of S, meaning that the time to repair gets longer as remote sites are added. Note also that the curvature of the Basic and PBU plots—on the logarithmic scale used—is caused by a strong probability of line outages, whereas with NCS the probability is greatly reduced.

In Figure 6, the single most striking attribute of the downtime curves is its insensitivity to S when a network-control system is present. Using hot spare modems—meaning with power on and ready to be substituted—and backing up private-wire links with dial-connection capability can drastically reduce a network's downtime. When these measures are combined with processor backup, the overall network downtime statistics can shrink impressively.

6. Network control is better. *Without network control, downtime increases rapidly with the number of drops per line because of the increased probability of line outages.*

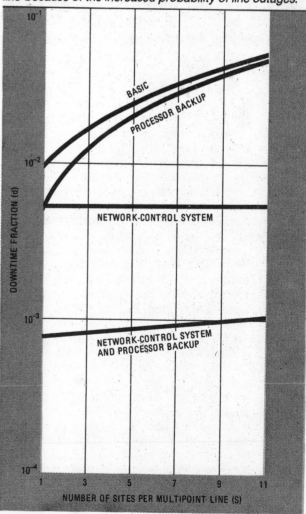

Troubleshooting short- and long-haul analog lines

David Levin, Netcomm Inc., Westport, Conn.

Excessive lead times for receiving digital service caused one company to switch to analog lines and to learn techniques for maintaining them.

In spite of the major advantages of digital transmission, most common carrier services today are analog. In fact, only 40 percent of AT&T's total facilities in the United States are digital. Regardless of the telephone company's massive campaign to upgrade, the change-over to digital is slow and costly, resulting in excessive lead times for delivering digital service to users. These excessive lead times forced Donovan Data Systems, a data communications service bureau for the advertising industry, to replace existing digital channels with analog equivalents and to develop effective analog-measurement and -repair techniques.

In 1978, Donovan Data Systems, which subscribed to AT&T's Dataphone Digital Service (DDS), was preparing for the growth of its then-125-line network to its present 300-line data communications network. Part of this upgrade involved physical preparation for 60 to 75 digital circuits.

Dataphone Digital Service, operating in 100 major cities in the U.S., provides synchronous data channels at 2.4, 4.8, 9.6, and 56 kbit/s, with lower error rates and greater accessibility than conventional analog-transmission channels. The DDS network uses pulse-code-modulation (PCM) techniques over a combination of local distribution facilities, intermediate-length regional lines (T1 and T2 carriers), and long-haul microwave facilities.

Before Donovan's expansion, 66 percent of the firm's long-haul leased data lines were Bell DDS circuits and only 33 percent were analog (Bell unconditioned Type 3002 voice-grade circuits). Data transmission within the organization was over copper quad (four-conductor, 24-gauge cable), and citywide transmission was over New York Telephone's four-wire, unconditioned leased circuits terminating in telephone-company 42A blocks with telephone-company 829 channel-interface devices. The 829 devices used at each end of a Bell data line contain the amplifier that controls the signal strength at the line-termination point. They also house a 2,713-Hz detector, which, when activated, trips a relay and connects the transmit pair to the receive pair.

As the total number of Donovan's data lines grew from 125 in 1978 to more than 200 in 1980, the shortage in available digital facilities completely changed the mix of digital and analog circuits within the network. The move to analog lines was inevitable: Donovan's clients who were forced to move their offices on short notice could no longer simply add new drops to existing digital circuits—that would take 45 business days. Adding a completely new analog circuit takes only 18 to 21 business days. The lead time for getting new digital circuits or increasing the speed of existing digital circuits is 90 business days. Furthermore, changing a 2.4-kbit/s DDS circuit to a 4.8-kbit/s line requires a completely new circuit, not simply changing the telephone company's Data Service Unit (DSU), as many people believe. Speed changes require that Bell allocate a new time slice (the user's interval of time that is sampled and multiplexed with other subscribers' intervals) on its T1 carrier system. The digital-line delivery delays left Donovan no choice but to replace the

212

Bell DDS circuits with Bell 3002 voice-grade circuits.

By 1980, only 25 percent of the company's leased lines were digital; 75 percent were analog. Donovan had disconnected 33 digital lines during this period and added 108 analog lines. Suddenly, analog-line maintenance was Donovan's most serious concern.

Doctoring ailing lines

Donovan could easily provide redundancy for the network's hardware. A typical client's cluster installation consists of a control unit (an ITT Courier Terminal Systems multistation adapter) and from three to six terminals (ITT Courier Executerms) served by a line and modems connected to an NCR Comten 3691 front-end processor. The ITT Courier controllers have redundant logic circuitry for backup. A modem that fails within New York City can be replaced with a working unit within a couple of hours. But line outages sometimes take several days to correct. Therefore, it was paramount that Donovan technicians be able to deal intel-ligently with telephone-company technicians on a day-to-day basis.

Knowledgeable technicians contribute significantly to the quality of repair service on data circuits. In many instances, telephone-company repairmen look at the wrong circuits. In other cases, they do not provide sufficient depth of testing to find an impairment.

The volume of existing circuits that might need repair, as well as the volume of new circuits requiring acceptance—an official O.K. from the user that a new line meets specifications—calls for an important relationship between the on-site telephone-company technicians and the user's technicians. If a Donovan technician can describe precise symptoms when reporting a problem or pinpoint the faulty drop or circuit segment, a telephone-company test-board attendant merely verifies the symptom, enabling quick and effective service dispatch. Over a period of time, a sophisticated user builds a record of accurate repair reports and learns what to check for at the time of line

Table 1   Rating line-testing instruments

TYPE OF INSTRUMENT	TYPE OF MEASUREMENT			
	OPEN CIRCUIT	CONSISTENT LOW LEVELS	CONSISTENT EXCESSIVE NOTCHED NOISE	INTERMITTENT IMPAIRMENTS
(A) FOR POINT-TO-POINT ANALOG LINES				
DIGITAL LINE MONITOR	P	I	I	I
INTERACTIVE DIGITAL LINE MONITOR	G	I	I	P
BIT/BLOCK-ERROR-RATE TESTER (BERT)	G	I	I	I
CONVENTIONAL NUMERIC TEST INSTRUMENT (UTILIZING THRESHOLD DETECTORS)	G	G	G	G
SUPPRESSED-TONE-PHASOR-DOMAIN MEASURING TECHNIQUE	G	G	G	G
VOICE-FREQUENCY LINE ANALYZER IN CONJUNCTION WITH ADDRESSABLE LOOPBACK DEVICES	E	E	E	E
(B) FOR MULTIDROP ANALOG LINES				
DIGITAL LINE MONITOR	I	I	I	I
INTERACTIVE DIGITAL LINE MONITOR	P	I	I	I
BIT/BLOCK-ERROR-RATE TESTER (BERT)	P	I	I	I
CONVENTIONAL NUMERIC TEST INSTRUMENT (UTILIZING THRESHOLD DETECTORS)	P	P	P	P
SUPPRESSED-TONE-PHASOR-DOMAIN MEASURING TECHNIQUE	P	P	P	P
VOICE-FREQUENCY LINE ANALYZER IN CONJUNCTION WITH ADDRESSABLE LOOPBACK DEVICES	E	E	E	E

P = POOR CAPABILITY OF MEASUREMENT   G = GOOD MEASURING CAPABILITY
I = INCAPABLE OF MEASURING IMPAIRMENT   E = EXCELLENT MEASURING CAPABILITY

Table 2 Selected voice-frequency testers

VENDOR	SIMPLE INSTRUMENTS	INTERMEDIATE-LEVEL INSTRUMENTS	SOPHISTICATED INSTRUMENTS	REMOTE DIAGNOSTIC DEVICES
BRADLEY TELECOM LEONIA, N.J.			X	X
ELECTRODATA BEDFORD HEIGHTS, OHIO	X			
HALCYON SAN JOSE, CALIF.			X	
HEWLETT-PACKARD PALO ALTO, CALIF.			X	
HEKIMIAN LABS ROCKVILLE, MD.		X	X	
LEDEX CONTROL SYSTEMS VANDALIA, OHIO				X
T-BAR DANBURY, CONN.	X			X
TEKTRONIX BEAVERTON, ORE.			X	

acceptance.

Donovan technicians developed analog-troubleshooting techniques that not only improve the use of facilities but also aid in accepting new facilities. Proper knowledge and instrumentation enable intelligent line acceptance and guarantee good facilities. Marginal facilities can be refused with authority. When it comes time to complete a terminal installation, a good line will usually ensure a smooth installation.

Analog instrumentation
Table 1 illustrates the relative effectiveness of various types of instruments in measuring line impairments on point-to-point and multipoint lines. The simplest instrument (included in most all-voice-frequency line analyzers) for analog channels is a speaker that is bridged across the line. The speaker enables listening to white noise, cross-talk, dial pulsing, and other impairments on a circuit. A speaker can also be used in a more sophisticated mode, called notched-noise measurement: A reference tone is suppressed, and only the disturbance is heard.

Digital devices are widely used to troubleshoot analog facilities. Looping a remote modem enables a bit-error-rate test (BERT) of the facility. Several value-added networks use only BERT tests when accepting local loops from the telephone company. But in spite of their wide acceptance, digital line monitors, even

Table 3 Features of selected testers

	BRADLEY PB1C	HALCYON 520B	HALCYON 701A	HEKIMIAN 41-01	HEKIMIAN 42-10	T-BAR 5911
FREQUENCY MEASUREMENT	X	X	X	X	X	X
AMPLITUDE-LEVEL MEASUREMENT	X	X	X	X	X	X
NOISE MEASUREMENT	X	X	X	X	X	X
SIGNAL/NOISE MEASUREMENT	X	X	X	X	X	X
FIXED-OR VARIABLE-SIGNAL GENERATOR	X	X	X	X	X	X
AUDIO MONITOR	X	X	X	X	X	X
PORTABLE	YES	YES	YES	NO	YES	NO
PRICE	$3,700	$10,900	$1,700	$1,500	$2,000	$1,500

interactive digital line analyzers, do not effectively measure analog channels. Other equipment is required.

Table 2 shows the relative sophistication of several vendors, analog test equipment, and Table 3 compares the measuring capabilities of selected products. The most simple devices include a combination signal-level and frequency meter with a speaker. Intermediate-level instruments incorporate additional features such as a 2,713-Hz tone launch used to activate the loopback feature in telephone-company 829 devices, a 1,004-Hz tone launch used in testing signal levels, and a variable-frequency tone generator used to measure tariffed circuit parameters.

Addressable diagnostic devices can be installed on remote ends for added analog diagnostics. These units are addressable either by tone or by digital schemes and enable testing of multipoint lines in the same way point-to-point lines are tested. Additional codes command the remote unit to loopback the drop (connect the transmit to the receive pair), quietly terminate the drop (disconnect all other remote equipment on the line) into the Bell-standard 600-ohm load, or launch a test tone back to the central site. These devices are invaluable in diagnosing multidrop lines since each drop can be controlled individually. However, when using these testers, users must never try to activate the telephone-company 829 devices on a multidrop circuit, because users can never be sure exactly how many devices are activated. Precautions, such as filters, ensure that the 829 devices are not triggered inadvertently. In many cases, some devices will not revert back to their original state, and the telephone company must correct the condition (a billable repair). Addressable devices are manufactured by T-Bar, Ledex Control Systems, and Bradley Telcom as standard products and are custom-made by Dynatech Data Systems.

The addressable diagnostic device is used in conjunction with a central-site instrument or touchtone pad, enabling it to perform a comprehensive set of diagnostics and measurements. The remote-tone-launch feature of, say, the Bradley TTL 15 touchtone addressable loopback device is particularly effective in diagnosing noise-level problems that cancel out in a typical loopback measurement. Donovan uses these devices on some of its New York City point-to-point circuits, some of which have chronic impairments because of their age.

Line access and measurement
Donovan uses a customized technical control center to access and maintain its analog facilities (see "How to troubleshoot network problems through tech control," DATA COMMUNICATIONS, March 1980). A T-Bar multiple-access switching system (MASS) breaks the signal path of any analog line and terminates the line with an instrument or bridges the instrument onto the circuit without disturbing the circuit. The unit's single-bus architecture allows access to only one analog line at a time. Multiple-bus architectures are available at an additional cost.

A T-Bar selector switch is used to connect one of up to four test instruments to the selected line. One

port accepts a central-site-modem substitution switch. Testing the digital and analog sides of the same data line entails substituting a standby modem from the central technical-control site into the regular data flow. This is a quick and effective test of a suspected failure in a central-site modem.

The Bradley PB1C voice-frequency line analyzer is the heart of the analog-measurement facility at Donovan. The unit costs approximately $3,800 and includes a speaker, a signal-level/frequency meter, an oscilloscope-like display, and a variety of electronics used in generating and filtering test tones. The device's suppressed-tone phasor-domain measurement technique allows displays of real-time-signal representations. This instrument is not limited by predefined threshold detectors or time-averaged numeric meters. (Numeric meters must use detector circuits with specific limits and specific durations of the impairment. Bell occasionally changes these thresholds when it redefines specific impairments.)

Donovan uses the Bradley addressable loopback device on all multidrop leased data circuits. The central-site controller, which includes a speaker, costs $1,500, and each remote unit sells for $450. Status lights in the control unit indicate which remote devices have been activated. The Bradley remote devices have a tone-launch feature not included in other units.

The basic voice-grade circuit
Bell's unconditioned voice-grade circuit is presently the most commonly used data circuit (see "Types of Bell data lines"). Donovan employs it almost exclusively for local communications within New York City because of its low cost (less than $100 per month, depending on length), its ease of installation (provided by the telephone company within 18 to 21 business days in all high-rise office buildings), and its reasonable installation rates of from $100 to $300.

Most short-haul circuits are prone to several significant line impairments:

1. Envelope delay distortion
2. Excessive loss variation
3. Poor signal-to-noise ratio

A standard voiceband data channel has a signal-attenuation specification within certain frequency ranges. This measurement refers to the strength of the signal once it has passed through the channel. Between 500 and 2,500 Hz, attenuation distortion must be between −2 and +8 decibels (dB). Within the 300- to 3,000-Hz range, attenuation distortion may vary from −3 to +2 dB.

Since different frequencies travel through a channel at different velocities, a signal composed of different frequency tones transmitted simultaneously into a channel will be received at different times. Bell specifies a maximum of 1,750 microseconds of variation between 800 and 2,600 Hz. However, measurement of frequency-tone delay, known as envelope delay distortion, is only possible using some of the most sophisticated instruments available (for example, the Halcyon

Bell's line offerings

Bell's telephone lines for data transmission are available in many varieties. The Type 3002 voice-grade private line is the most common for high-speed (2.4 kbit/s and greater) data traffic. Even the Type 3002 channel is available in several flavors: It may have C- or D-types of conditioning or it may be unconditioned.

The unconditioned circuit usually contains repeaters at specific intervals, as well as loading coils and echo suppressors. In addition, local telephone companies, such as New York Telephone Company, offer what is called a straight copper circuit, which comprises pairs of copper wires terminated at each end by Bell 829 channel-interface devices.

This type of circuit is available only when the entire circuit is within the same telephone-company central office. In essence, the straight copper circuit is composed of two local loops connected at the central office. Since there are no repeaters and no loading coils in the signal path, the user can, in most cases, use the less-expensive limited-distance modems. Limited-distance modems may also be used on standard Type 3002 unconditioned channels, depending on the length of the circuit and the data rate. Modem manufacturer can supply the specific details.

C conditioning. Five types of C conditioning are available from Bell. C1 and C2 conditioned lines may be ordered for point-to-point, multipoint, and switched configurations. C3 conditioning, which is similar to C2 conditioning, applies only to private switched networks with a maximum of four trunks and two access lines in tandem.

C4 conditioning can be ordered in two-, three-, and four-point circuits only. C5 conditioning can be ordered only in point-to-point circuits and is similar to C2 conditioning. C5 conditioning is primarily intended for overseas channels. The 3002-type channel with C conditioning has specific limits on attenuation distortion and on envelope delay distortion that exceed those for a 3002 unconditioned channel (see Bell's technical reference Publication 41004 for exact specifications). Since Bell charges a premium per conditioning type per termination point, the telephone company is required to keep line impairments from exceeding the limits set in the tariff.

When transmitting digital data, it is necessary to transmit many state-changes per second. Attenuation distortion describes the extent to which a signal traveling through a channel is affected as the frequency of the signal changes. The higher the data rate, the more changes per second the channel must handle. The ability of a channel to handle these changes is called high-frequency response. Good high-frequency response is the same as low attenuation distortion. C conditioning improves the high-frequency response of the basic 3002 channel.

Envelope delay distortion occurs because the amount of signal delay is not constant at a particular frequency. High-frequency signals are delayed differently from low-frequency signals. Since data signals are transmitted by pulses, it is important that a channel preserve the pulse shape. In a channel with excessive delay distortion, various parts of the pulse arrive at different times and cause the reception of a distorted version of the original pulse.

Since data transmission involves successive pulses spaced closely over time, the envelope delay distortion causes pulses to spill over into each other. This phenomenon is called intersymbol interference. C conditioning limits the permissible amount of envelope delay distortion within specific frequency ranges.

D conditioning. D conditioning, available in two types, specifically limits noise and harmonic distortion. D1 conditioning is offered for point-to-point channels, and D2 for two- or three-point channels. Bell charges for D conditioning on a per-circuit-per-month basis rather than per termination point per month. Minimizing noise and harmonic distortion is critical to data transmission because these impairments interfere with the accurate reproduction of the transmitted pulse shapes. Once these impairments change the original signal shape, a modem receiver is unable to recreate the signal shape regardless of its sophistication. To combat this problem, modem manufacturers maximize the differences between various pulse shapes. A signal that uses four voltage levels to define 2 bits per pulse is more resistant to noise and harmonic distortion than one that uses eight levels to define 3 bits per pulse. High data rates such as 9.6 kbit/s on voice-grade circuits require the best protection against these impairments.

D-conditioned channels must meet the following specifications:

1. Signal to C-notched noise: 28 dB
2. Signal to second harmonic distortion: 35 dB
3. Signal to third harmonic distortion: 40 dB

Most 99 kbit/s modems operate satisfactorily with lines meeting only the basic 3002 specifications for noise and harmonic distortion. By minimizing these major impairments, modems can tolerate a greater number of other impairments, which makes D conditioning worthwhile.

Model 520B2 test set). In addition, automatic adaptively equalized modems can compensate for this impairment, so the typical user does not get involved in measuring envelope delay distortion.

The 1,004-Hz loss variation is a significant specification. The initial Bell installation specification (– 16 to ± 1 dB) is considerably more stringent than the later, ongoing specification (– 16 to ± 4 dB), and it is important that a user require Bell to bring a new circuit into specifications at the installation stage so there will be less chance that the quality of the circuit will deteriorate. At Donovan Data Systems, a circuit is not accepted until a technician has verified that it meets all of the appropriate initial Bell specifications.

A 1,004-Hz loss variation is an important specification. Most users measure this loss variation from a central site using the loopback feature of the telephone company's 829 channel interface. The 829 devices are provided free of charge by Bell but must be requested when the circuit is initially ordered.

When the central-site end of the leased line is terminated with a voice-frequency test set employing a signal-level meter, a 2,713-Hz tone is launched toward the remote end on the transmit side of the line. The remote 829 device senses the 2,713-Hz tone and activates a relay that connects the transmit and receive pairs, creating a loopback.

A 1,004-Hz, 0-dBm test tone is then launched. The test tone travels from the central site down the transmit side of the line, through the 829 device, and back to the central site on the receive side of the line. The signal-level meter is monitored, and the decibel scale is read. This is called a loopback test of the 1,004-Hz signal loss. Either excessive attenuation or excessive amplification will cause modem failure. This measurement technique does not detect the compensating-gain errors on the transmit and receive pairs that may cancel out in a loopback measurement.

Measuring maximum noise

C-message noise is the noise on the circuit in relation to a reference level of -90 dBm (this measurement is also known as zero dBrnC in Bell nomenclature) after passing through a C-message filter. A circuit from New York to San Francisco would fall in the 2,501- to 4,000-mile range and should have a maximum noise level at the modem receiver of 44 dBrnC, according to Bell specifications.

In measuring C-message noise, users read the meter with the test instrument on the receive leg only. (On the Bradley PB1C, the meter selector should be in the noise position.) This measurement should be made with and without the 30- to 300-Hz filter. Although the telephone company is not responsible for impairments in the 30- to 300-Hz band, power-line disturbances fall in this range and may be significant.

When C-message notched noise is measured, a test tone is sent down the channel. The signal-to-noise ratio is measured with the tone notched, or filtered out. The specification for a standard Bell voice-grade line is at least 24 dB below the received 1,004-Hz test-tone power. The specification for a D1 conditioned channel is at least 28 dB below the test-tone power.

Signal strength still strong

With the line in loopback, a 1,004-Hz, 0-dBm test tone is produced. The meter selector is placed in the notched-noise position, and the dBrnC scale is read. On the Bradley PB1C, typical readings for copper circuits within New York City are greater than 40 dBrnC, which pins the meter off the scale. This indicates that the circuit's signal-to-notched-noise ratio is excellent.

Besides the major line impairments found on short-haul circuits, additional impairments occur—but these usually are insignificant. There are, however, some other impairments that typically occur on long-line voice-grade circuits.

The basic Bell Type 3002 unconditioned voice-grade circuit is the Bell System's most popular offering for long-distance communications. Donovan has more than 50 such circuits—both point-to-point and multidrop (typically fewer than five drops). These circuits represent the backbone of the company's long-haul network, and their use is steadily increasing because of the shortage of digital alternatives.

The Bell specifications for long lines are basically the same as for local lines, although telephone-company equipment, such as loading coils, repeaters, and compandors (devices that compress a signal's components) introduce additional impairments. The PB1C voice-frequency line analyzer is useful in demonstrating the presence of these subtle impairments through use of suppressed-tone-phasor-domain measurements.

A test tone in two dimensions can be represented in various ways. The amplitude can be placed against the time representation of a sine wave, as viewed on an oscilloscope. The same wave can be viewed as amplitude versus frequency on a spectrum analyzer. The phase of the sine wave can also be viewed as amplitude versus quadrature, which would appear as a vector rotating around the origin. In the suppressed-tone-phasor-domain measurement technique, the vector is filtered out and only the tip of the phasor is visible. A perfect circuit would have a suppressed-tone-phasor-domain representation of a dot circling the origin. At a predetermined sampling rate, the phasor will appear to be in the same position each time it is viewed. Variations in the signal's amplitude will cause the phasor tip to deviate vertically. Variations in the signal's phase cause the phasor tip to deviate horizontally (actually, variations are along an arc rather than a horizontal line). In this way, the technique fully represents all impairments on a line in a real-time representation and simplifies making go/no go decisions on the facility regarding parameters that affect modem operation.

Additional impairments affecting long lines

In addition to being susceptible to the impairments discussed for the short-haul circuits, long-line channels may have other ailments:

1. Single-frequency interference
2. Excessive white noise
3. Phase hits, gain hits, and dropouts
4. Impulse noise
5. Amplitude and phase jitter
6. Nonlinear distortion (harmonic distortion)

Single-frequency interference (such as 60-Hz interference from 110-volt a.c. power sources) must be at least 3 dB below the C-message noise limits, according to telephone-company specifications. It is read on the Bradley PB1C scope with the meter selector in the vector-notch mode.

A dropout is a sudden and large reduction in signal level (greater than 12 dB and typically lasting 4 milliseconds or longer). The noise on the facility can be heard suddenly fading in and out. This usually affects modem operation since all signals present on the channel also

1. *Line report. This evaluation-report form, known at Donovan Data Systems as a benchmark sheet, is used for noting repeated measurements taken at predetermined intervals. It helps identify not only channels needing immediate repair but also trends that indicate deterioration. In general, the sheet provides the history of a channel.*

AGENCY _____ LINE NO. _____ P/P _____

LOCATION _____ ID/TC _____ M/D _____

_____ 829 NO. _____ TTL NO. _____

_____ LINE SPEED _____ BIT/S

TEST	TOTAL POWER RECEIVED	TOTAL POWER ON LOOPBACK	C-NOTCHED NOISE		WHITE NOISE		IMPULSE NOISE (COUNT/10 MINUTES)		PHASE HITS (COUNT/10 MINUTES)		PHASE JITTER		HARMONIC DISTORTION		GRATICULES USED TO SKETCH DISPLAY PATTERN
DATE			REC'D 1004	LOOP-BACK	REC'D TERM	LOOP-BACK	REC'D 1004	LOOP-BACK	REC'D 1004	LOOP-BACK	REC'D 1004	LOOP-BACK	LOOP-BACK		LOOPBACK
BY	DBM	DBM	DB		DBRNCO		HITS		HITS		DEGREES		2nd	3rd	

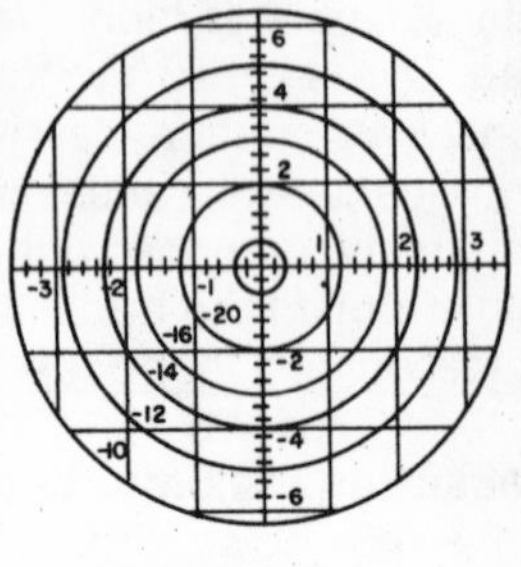

SCALE X
VECTOR UNNOTCHED

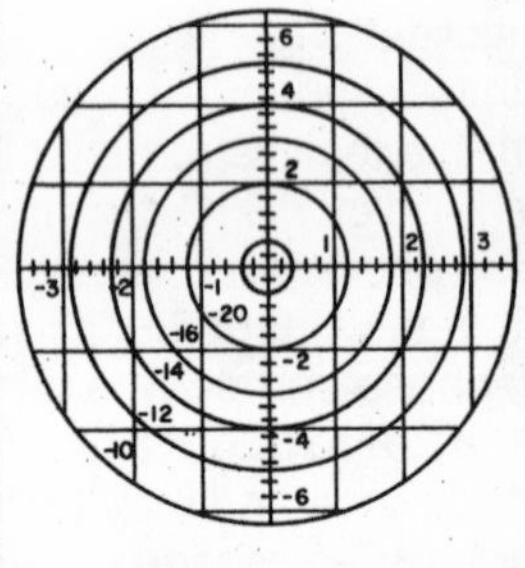

SCALE X
VECTOR NOTCHED

---

fade in and out. When a dropout is viewed on the PB1C scope, the phasor tip suddenly travels off the graticule scale and then quickly reappears.

Impulse noise consists of sudden, short, and dramatic increases of noise. Presently, Bell does have a specification for impulse noise, based on the maximum number of occurrences in 15 minutes that exceed a particular threshold with respect to the received 1,004-Hz test-tone power.

A signal's phase at any instant in time may oscillate—a phenomenon called phase jitter. At low data speeds, this is usually not significant. High data speeds (4.8 kbit/s and higher) are accomplished through various forms of multilevel coding and various modulation schemes. All schemes currently used, such as quadrature amplitude modulation (QAM), are susceptible to different line impairments, of varying severity.

Phase jitter is read on the PB1C scope display, with the meter selector in the vector-notch mode, as the user observes the horizontal variations of the phasor tip. The graticule scale on the PB1C scope display is calibrated in degrees. The magnitude of the horizontal excursions to the right is added to the magnitude of the horizontal excursions to the left. To be within specifications, the combined magnitude should not exceed 10 degrees, peak to peak, in a 15-minute period.

Amplitude jitter is similar to phase jitter except that the variation is in amplitude (the vertical scale on the PB1C scope display). Bell currently has no specification for amplitude jitter. Phase and amplitude jitter also can be measured on the Halcyon Model 545A test set and the Bradley Model 75 LMA test set.

Various components presently used on voice-grade channels can distort a data signal by reproducing unwanted harmonics. By placing a frequency analyzer's meter-selector switch in the second or third harmonic position, the strength of the unwanted harmonic can be compared to that of the original signal.

Getting it on paper

The polar scale of the PB1C scope display is used to measure harmonic distortion. The operator must recognize the scale multiplier and factor this into the reading. The Bell specification for second harmonic distortion is a minimum 25-dB difference in amplitude from fundamental to second harmonic. A minimum 30-dB difference from the fundamental frequency's amplitude to the amplitude of the third harmonic is also part of this specification. Harmonic distortion can be measured on a Halcyon Model 520B2 test set.

Figure 1 shows a facility-evaluation report used to benchmark data lines at Donovan. Benchmarking is the practice of taking repeated measurements at predetermined time intervals to identify channels needing immediate repair, as well as those exhibiting a trend toward deterioration. It is a tool used to track the condition of a data line, including each side (transmit and receive) and each leg (in multidrop lines).

One benchmark sheet should be maintained for every point-to-point analog circuit, as well as for each leg of multidrop data circuits. Background information should be initially entered for each circuit. This information should include client name, address, and contact names; the telephone-company line number; the line identifier and technical control center address (ID/TC); the number of the central-site 829 devices in the telephone-company cabinet; the type of line [point-to-point (P/P) or multidrop (M/D)]; the modem speed; and the activation code of any touchtone addressable loopback device (TTL).

The bottom of the benchmark sheet is used to record observations. Each time a technician measures the circuit, he records the data and initials it. He then completes all applicable entries across the page. The graticule-scale reproductions are used to sketch the scope representation of the circuit in the vector-notch and second and third harmonic modes.

Significant observations should be noted on the back of the sheet, along with the date of observation. This information would include the presence of line hits, crosstalk, single tones, or dialing noise. A special Polaroid camera may be modified to take photographs of the scope display. Although Polaroid film is somewhat expensive, this method of recording introduces none of the operator inaccuracies inherent in sketching the display pattern.

The advantages of using a facility-evaluation report to benchmark analog circuits are obvious. The facility-evaluation report, along with the log of a circuit's trouble calls, provides an effective historical record of the channel. It facilitates intelligent management and control of a very important resource.

Donovan Data Systems uses this technique to determine which of a client's existing data lines are best suited for high-speed data traffic. The technique helps in isolating repair problems. ■

DBMS takes on network management

David L. Lyon, Intertel Inc., Andover, Mass.

Network-control systems integrated with database management systems constitute a new generation of highly automated network management.

Data communications network managers now face the same problem that data processing managers have long battled—an information explosion. How can they organize and exploit the mass of data generated by a modern automated network-control system (NCS)?

Database management provides the necessary tools. Integrated in network-control systems, database management systems (DBMSs) can methodically and automatically file network-related data and simplify procedures for machine generation of statistical reports.

The resulting network-management systems (NMSs) streamline operations: Paperwork disappears in favor of magnetic storage and machine generation of reports; performance measures such as downtime, which previously could not be quantified, can now be accurately tracked; varied forms of statistical and trend analyses are performed on collected data; troubleshooting and restorative techniques become more automated, reducing the time to repair faults.

DBMSs are just beginning to be used in innovative network-management applications. One such application is automated recovery from hard and soft failures. (A hard failure causes a complete operational outage. A soft failure causes degraded service but does not fully block operation.) Another is trend analysis of parametric information such as signal levels and response time. The DBMS can also be an efficient means of adding and editing records.

To understand how a DBMS functions in an NMS, we must examine its structure. Basically, a DBMS stores information, recalls it in response to user inquiries, generates statistics, and produces reports. It is an electronic filing system complete with an automated "clerk/typist" that does the storing and retrieving. In fact, DBMS files are structured similarly to those in a clerk/typist's hard-copy filing system. An electronic file has a name and contains many individual records. Every record comprises a number of fields, each of which has a name or description associated with it. A field may be filled with data or be blank. The data format is flexible: It may vary in length, comprise alphanumeric characters, and have prescribed, embedded delimiters such as blanks or parentheses.

Figure 1 illustrates these concepts in a trouble-ticket file. Most on-line networks use the trouble ticket as their primary means of recording operational problems. It is normally kept on paper, one trouble to a sheet. The network operator is responsible for initiating a ticket for any event that causes terminal downtime.

In DBMS jargon, the entire group of trouble tickets constitutes the trouble-ticket file. Each created ticket corresponds to a separate record within the file. Each data entry within a record is a field that has a name such as "site address" and "problem description."

The records themselves do not have names. The identity of each is determined by the contents of its fields. This means that to extract information from a DBMS, the user must enter his needs, exactly stated, in quantitative form. Then, the DBMS sorts through the available records in the indicated files and collects those that match the user's requirements. The order of the sort—the relative importance of each data field

1. DBMS jargon. *The entire group of trouble tickets constitutes the trouble-ticket file. Every ticket is a separate record within the file. Each data entry is a field.*

```
TROUBLE TICKET NO. _____

NAME _____

ADDRESS _____

TELEPHONE NO. _____

SITE ADDRESS _____

TIME OF OCCURRENCE _____

PROBLEM DESCRIPTION _____

VENDOR CONTACTED _____

TIME OF CONTACT _____

NCS SYMPTOMS _____

ACTUAL CAUSE _____

GUILTY VENDOR _____

TIME OF RESTORAL _____

COMMENTS _____

_____
```

average duration. He wants the information first on his CRT, and then he may decide to produce a printout. What must he tell the DBMS, and how does it retrieve, reduce, and report the data?

To enable the DBMS to collect the relevant records, the user must establish limits or a set of "match strings" on the data of certain fields in the records. (A match string is a group of characters for which a search is to be conducted.) A test, then, is composed of numeric checks on limits or searches for string matches or both. If data in a field falls within the specified limits or fits the match strings, that record is kept in a temporary collection subject to further sorting. If the test on the field fails, that record is excluded from the collection for all subsequent tests and reports.

Filling the fields

Specifically, in the search for trouble tickets, the user must set quantitative limits or specify match strings for these fields: (1) time of occurrence, (2) site address (either as an alphanumeric name or as an assigned numeric value), and (3) guilty vendor. For example, the user may specify (1) all hours of March 10, 1981, (2) all sites with numeric port addresses under 10, and (3) Fly-by-Night Electronics Inc.

Next, to enable the DBMS to put in sequence the trouble tickets for reporting, the user specifies the order of the fields, that is, which field will be treated as the primary key, or factor, and which as the secondary. (Generally, the DBMS vendor provides a predefined order of keys and, further, assumes first-to-last ordering both numerically and alphabetically.) The user may wish to see the trouble tickets arranged primarily by site address (according to the user's criteria) and secondarily in order of occurrence. Thus, several records with the same site address are further arranged chronologically for presentation.

Finally, the user states his needs for statistical summaries: a count of the pertinent records and the largest and average values of the difference between "time of restoral" and "time of occurrence"—that is, the maximum and average durations in this collection. Then, a single command is usually required to send this structured report to a CRT or printer.

There is a lot of work involved in setting up many files with complete record definitions. Even more effort can go into defining, sorting, and reporting records, and compiling statistical procedures. If the user were responsible for all of this, his headaches would be many. However, vendors of network-control equipment have begun attacking these DBMS problems and applying their solutions to network management. Results from this work are only now coming into use.

The DBMS contains sets of interrelated files (see "Necessary files"). Every network manager maintains at least two types of files to keep network operations moving from day to day: a network directory and a log of trouble tickets. The network directory is generally a compendium of relatively static information about each network site. One record may contain such items as logical addressing, street address, contact's name and telephone number, names of key personnel, descrip-

in determining sequencing—must also be specified.

Once the collection is formed and the sequence established, the user can instruct the DBMS to calculate statistics summarizing numerical data found in various fields. Finally, the user requests that a hardcopy or CRT-based report be generated, sometimes having to define the format of the report and the peripheral devices that will produce it.

Managing the database

In the trouble-ticket example, the user might want a report that summarizes the performance of a vendor on a particular day in one part of the network. Furthermore, the user would like to know the number of problems encountered, the duration of the longest, and the

tions of equipment and applications, and telephone numbers for dial backup of private-line telephone service. In most central sites today, the network directory is kept on paper, and one or two copies are available in loose-leaf binders or pasted on the wall. The network address is often used as the primary key for sequencing the individual records describing sites.

The trouble-ticket log contains the records of problems observed by the network operator. Each ticket serves two purposes—one operational and the other historical. During the time a problem is open (unsolved), the operator refers to the trouble ticket to gauge how long the problem has existed. The operator also uses the ticket to obtain critical information for advising vendors of the nature of the problem. Some trouble tickets have sections for updated reports of a problem's status, so that the problem-solving process and restoral of service can be tracked. Once the problem is resolved, the completed trouble ticket becomes a historical record, potentially useful for quantifying the performance of the network and its vendors.

Like the network directory, most trouble-ticket files are today stored in hard-copy form in loose-leaf binders. But there are many problems with hard-copy storage. Tickets or directory records can be effaced or lost. Operators can neglect to complete an open ticket unless specific checking routines are enforced. Data retrieval and the incorporation of new information is tedious. Sorting is especially inflexible, since only one or two copies of the records exist, and these are usually needed for on-line operation.

Networks that use a network-control system put out several other forms of information that might also be filed. This data is usually automatically generated by the NCS and, in the absence of a DBMS, is printed onto paper or transcribed onto tape or disk. The network operator must then set this data into the proper groups and produce meaningful reports.

The first category of machine-generated records is exception reports. They are produced by an NCS while it operates in its automatic-monitoring mode: The central-site NCS periodically polls remote network sites on a secondary communications channel to check for changes in conditions. The changes are detected by remote test modules (RTMs) that coexist with the remote-site modems (see "How network control curbs downtime," DATA COMMUNICATIONS, July 1980, p. 52).

Taking the network's pulse
The RTMs perform a battery of tests, collect the results, and determine changes that occur from one poll query to the next. Tests performed are noninterfering so that automatic monitoring can proceed as a background activity simultaneously with the main channel application. The secondary path over which the diagnostic information flows is logically separate from the main data path. It is often created as a frequency-division-multiplexed channel on the same analog telephone circuit or, less often, as a time-division-multiplexed channel on the same link.

A typical set of noninterfering tests performed in the automatic-monitoring mode—more for pass/fail flag-

---

Necessary files
Network directory
Created by keyed input.
Contains addressing, contact information, descriptions of equipment and applications, telephone numbers, and circuit numbers.
May contain free-format section for critical operator comments.
May contain threshold information for exception or performance reporting or both.
Trouble tickets
Created by keyed input.
Contain descriptions of problems observed by the network operator. May include times, locations, status reports, descriptions of problems and resolutions, and identities of involved parties.
Are closely related to exception reports.
Exception reports
Machine-generated by network-control system.
Contain descriptions of faults discovered by NCS, including times of occurrence and resolution, nature of problems, and network locations.
Measurement data
Machine-generated by NCS.
Contains quantitative results of scheduled tests on the network. May include results of analog-parameter tests, error-rate tests, measurements of terminal/CPU response time, and link utilization.

---

ging than for analysis—include: Is data terminal equipment (DTE) powered and connected? Is DTE streaming (request-to-send locked on)? Is channel continuity unbroken? What is the analog receive level? Is modem powered? What is the receive-signal quality? In the near future, NCS designers are expected to add tests related to terminal-response-time statistics and to the rate of incorrect-flag or -check characters.

The exception reports have a relatively simple form. In DBMS terms, each record has a few fields, such as the time of occurrence of a failed test, the location of the failure, the nature of the test that failed, and the time the problem was cleared and the test began to show a pass condition. This information is similar, but not identical, to that tracked by trouble tickets. The trouble ticket is operator-generated and contains much more information about background material (addresses and problem descriptions) and follow-up activities (vendors contacted and actions taken).

Another type of file that an NCS with DBMS can automatically generate is measurement data. This includes results of quantitative tests performed and recorded by the NCS. These tests can be interfering or noninterfering and can generally be scheduled by the network operator as a function of both network address and time and date.

Tests that produce useful quantitative data fall into three broad categories:
1. Interfering tests that measure error-rate performance of particular communications links. Interfering may mean that the main channel is completely cut off

on the links tested or that a sizable fraction of the normal bandwidth is not available.

2. Tests of analog line parameters that may be interfering or noninterfering. These may include measurements of signal-to-noise ratio or signal level using either the main-channel signal (noninterfering) or a specific tone (interfering) as the test signal for the channel. Other analog measurements are harmonic distortion, phase jitter, frequency offset (carrier-frequency change), amplitude and delay distortion, and hit phenomena (see "Why the line acts that way—and what can be done," DATA COMMUNICATIONS, January 1978, p. 63).

3. Tests of the data content of the main channel. These are usually noninterfering and can include measurements of response time, poll-to-poll times, link utilization, and computed message-error rates. These tests are only now becoming available in the NCS context.

The measurement-data records are potentially more complicated than those for exception reporting, mainly because many different types of results must be stored. The simplest organization includes the test time, the site address, the type of test, and the numerical results. Another organization casts the different tests as distinct fields, and each numerical result resides in its corresponding test field. This kind of structure is preferable if the NCS tests are fixed and are relatively numerous (at least six), so that many results would be tagged with the identical time and location.

Cross-referencing

The DBMS should be capable of cross-linking its files in ways that will accommodate the user when new records are being generated or reports created. Ideally, information from any existing file should be available for inclusion in a new report or record.

An example of cross-linking is shown in Figure 2. The network operator is creating a new trouble ticket. Once the site address is defined, the DBMS inserts relevant data from the network-directory record for that site in the new ticket. Similarly, once the location and time of occurrence are established, the DBMS links the symptoms reported automatically in an exception report (if applicable). This allows for very rapid and accurate generation of new records. The same type of file cross-linking can speed the creation of reports that summarize activities recorded in different files.

What can the network operator do with the data stored in these files? This depends on the network-management task. That is, there are no fundamental limits on the flexibility of DBMS; the kinds of reports and statistics are limited more by the user's imagination than by physical constraints.

Certainly, if the user places stringent demands on the DBMS response time while requiring a high degree of versatility, the technical problems of implementation become greater. Thus, if a user wants 5-second response in sorting a 20,000-record file based on fields normally not considered sorting keys, the DBMS designer must make certain trade-offs. The most obvious—and costly—is the increased need for additional storage to house multiple directories, each based on separate fields of the records. Less obvious, the real-

2. Cross-linking. *The network operator creates a new trouble ticket by combining the pertinent portions of the network-directory and exception-report records.*

time performance when storing records will suffer, since every new file entry will trigger the creation of entries in the multiple directories.

However, if the DBMS designer understands the network operator's needs, intelligent design choices will yield satisfactory response time and flexibility at reasonable cost. For example, a report that summarizes a month of performance data and yields numerous graphic plots probably will not need extremely fast response time. Here the designer would not create multiple directories but would save the disk space and suffer several-minute delays between the time the commands are given to the DBMS and the time the reports are generated as hard copy.

On the other hand, certain DBMS functions may

require fast response times to keep pace with real-time network events. An example is the creation or modification of a trouble-ticket record. A network operator cannot wait even 1 minute to fetch an open trouble ticket for inspection or modification. Sufficient cross-referencing directories must be maintained in memory to facilitate instantaneous recall of trouble tickets.

Timely functions

Good network management requires two kinds of DBMS functions. "Non-real-time" functions are not time-sensitive; their value is not dependent on short response times to operators' commands. "Real-time" functions are time-sensitive and would diminish greatly in value if response to commands or to conditions were not virtually instantaneous. The table lists the envisioned DBMS functions.

In the non-real-time category, the DBMS performs primarily as a report generator. The reports can be listings of whole records, parts of records, or "super-records" made up of pieces of records from different files. They can be statistics derived from collections of records, which include counts of records, maximum or minimum field values, average values, and variances of particular fields. These statistical operations might also be applied to differences between fields, such as the duration of events figured as the difference between times of occurrence and resolution.

Report generation can be profitably applied to the network-performance data. In each type of performance file, certain fields present themselves naturally as valuable sorting keys. For trouble tickets, these sorting fields would include "guilty vendor," "site address," "time of occurrence," and "type of fault." For exception reports, the same fields—except vendor information—would be useful. For measurement data, the important fields are the site address and virtually all quantitative test-result fields. Often a user wants to inspect all records showing where particular tests have exceeded user-selected thresholds.

Keeping track of trends

Several new applications for network-management systems are emerging. One is trend analysis of performance data. It is, in some ways, equivalent to report generation coupled with statistical analysis but can be more useful because it foretells serious problems. Communications networks, especially long-haul communications links, typically have many kinds of faults that develop slowly over time. By graphically displaying analog-parameter measurements and error-rate data, an NMS can help the user spot the development of a potentially hard failure while the network is still in its soft-failure mode.

Trend analysis of data-content parameters can be used to track potential problems in software or in the network configuration. By watching response times gradually increase, for example, a network manager may predict when network components must be replaced or added. Conversely, a dwindling utilization statistic might prompt the contraction of services to some locations.

DBMS functions

NON-REAL-TIME

REPORTS ON NETWORK PERFORMANCE

- LISTINGS OF SORTED RECORDS FROM TROUBLE-TICKET, EXCEPTION-REPORTS, MEASUREMENT-DATA FILES
- STATISTICS DERIVED FROM SORTED COLLECTIONS

TREND ANALYSIS OF PERFORMANCE

- TABULAR OR GRAPHICAL PRESENTATION OF STATISTICS VERSUS TIME

REPORTS ON THE PHYSICAL NETWORK

- LISTINGS OF SORTED SITE RECORDS
- ASSET MANAGEMENT

REAL-TIME

NCS OPERATIONS

- PROVISION FOR STORAGE AND SOURCE OF AUTOMATIC-MONITORING THRESHOLD VALUES
- STORAGE AND TRANSMISSION OF MEASUREMENT TEST SCHEDULES

RECORD CREATION AND EDITING

- SIMPLE, FLEXIBLE MEANS FOR CREATING NEW RECORDS
- MEANS FOR EDITING OR ADDING TO EXISTING RECORDS

PERFORMANCE ALARMS

- MESSAGES TO THE OPERATOR INDICATING NETWORK FAULTS
- REMINDERS OF OPEN FAULTS

TROUBLESHOOTING AND RECOVERY ROUTINES

- AUTOMATED ROUTINES FOR DIAGNOSIS AND RESTORAL
- PROMPTS TO LEAD OPERATOR THROUGH STRUCTURED SEARCH FOR CORRECT ACTIONS

Since reports on the physical network are essential for sound financial management, an obvious network-management-system application is the tracking of equipment at particular network sites. This requires structuring the network-directory records to include information fields such as model names, serial numbers, dates of acquisition, and costs, and even management of vendor warranties and service contracts.

The real-time functions of a DBMS are far less related to reports and statistics and much more concerned with the moment-to-moment operation of the main-channel application and the network-control and diagnostic functions. The emphasis is on quick recall and transmission of small data batches. In some cases, this data is useful for particular operator activities, such as recovery from a fault. In other instances, the data is used to signal the NCS about some change of conditions, such as modified test thresholds at RTMs.

The DBMS helps control and modify these NCS operations. Schedules of quantitative tests used to collect measurement data are stored in the DBMS as part of the network directory. The initiating commands are then launched from the central site as the DBMS signals for them. In a similar fashion, thresholds for exception reporting of test results are stored in the network directory. The DBMS manages the remote signaling when the network operator modifies these values at the console.

Record creation and editing are functions that require fast response, sometimes for operational reasons (such as with trouble tickets), but more generally because human operators cannot tolerate repeated, lengthy delays between keyed input and displayed response. A good DBMS must provide a simple yet flexible means for adding and editing records. This need has already been met by the vendors of text-editing equipment in the office environment, and these solutions can serve as models for NCS designers.

Alarms based on performance data help the network operator keep faults under control. The DBMS should signal the operator at the first indication of a new fault and at regular intervals as long as a problem exists. A particular fault alarm to the operator could be accompanied by structured statements that permit the operator to diagnose a problem by simply answering "yes" or "no" to a series of questions posed by the DBMS. Once the trouble were identified, the DBMS would prompt the operator to take specific actions for recovery. An extension of these functions includes completely automatic recovery wherein the network-management system itself initiates dial backup or similar preprogrammed remedial activities.

Hardware organizations

The flexibility of a network-management system depends most on its software implementation. However, the organization of the hardware, especially the processors and memory, also affect performance. Several arrangements are possible, and two have been implemented commercially in the recent past.

Perhaps the most obvious hardware arrangement is the totally centralized configuration (Fig. 3A). The processor is unique in the network, and all NMS devices are attached to or driven by it. This includes the mass memory on disk, operators' CRTs, printers, and physical interfaces to the network's RTMs.

A second structure includes two processors: one to maintain the DBMS and a second that runs the network-control activities (Fig. 3B). A link between the two provides the necessary information flow to tie together the different sets of functions. The DBMS processor has control of the mass memory, whereas the NCS processor has a smaller amount of memory attached, consistent with its real-time functions.

A third structure involves multiple computers spread throughout a shared-resource network (Fig. 3C). Here, the exact structure of each computer is not as important as the wide distribution of the database files themselves. This third scheme is the least practicable at the present time because of the novelty of distributed database technology. However, as the fundamental problems in programming these applications are solved, this approach for network management will become

3. Hardware organizations. *The setup in A is totally centralized. In B, each CPU has its own function. The shared-resource network (C) is not yet practicable.*

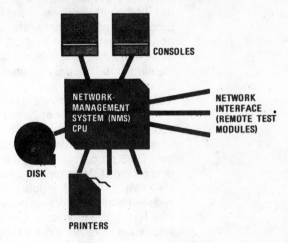

(A) CENTRALIZED

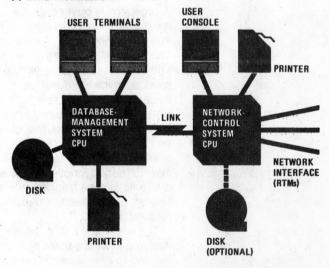

(B) DUAL PROCESSORS

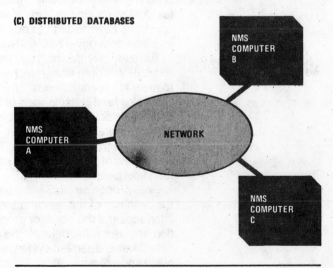

(C) DISTRIBUTED DATABASES

more viable and more attractive.

Each of the first two hardware structures has advantages that recommend it. The centralized approach has a smaller number of central-site components, which can result in higher overall reliability and simpler use for the network operators. Furthermore, the single processor and its peripherals can be relatively more powerful (faster, more extensive instruction set) than those in the two-processor approach and still maintain the same total cost. By combining DBMS and NCS activities in one processor, the response time of the real-time DBMS functions is potentially shortened.

The dual-processor approach has two potential advantages. With the proper software design, the NCS function can be made operationally independent of the DBMS processor. Then, if a failure causes downtime on the DBMS side, the basic NCS functions are still available. Also, the dual processors can be tailored in speed and peripheral capacity to individually match their respective functions. This flexibility is most beneficial when there are extraordinary demands placed on either the NCS or the DBMS functions.

The consumer's guide to NMS

A prospective buyer and user of a network-management system incorporating DBMS and NCS might ask, Will NMS bring the promised benefits, or are there hidden "hooks" that will prevent the gains in productivity and accuracy? To answer these questions, the user must examine the descriptions of functions and files to determine if they have sufficient breadth and capability. The relatively basic functions are automatic filing of real-time NCS data, machine generation of statistical and trend data, maintenance of network-directory and trouble-ticket files, and cross-linking of all available files. Extended functions that are only now becoming available include tracking of results from data-content testing, automated troubleshooting, and automated restoral routines.

The user must also consider the advantages promised and measure them against the time and effort needed to assimilate and use the system. He should question a product that demands extensive customer programming or customer modification of standard features to accommodate his needs. Most network operators have enough to do keeping the network up, let alone debugging new software applications.

The user may decide to accept the burden of customization, or the NMS may have sufficient flexibility to meet his specific needs. The next questions are: What skill level is demanded of an operator? Can functions be selected by menu choices or simplified commands, or are subroutine-like programs required for the execution of commands? These questions are critical in view of the dwindling numbers of available good technical people.

Finally, once an NMS has been qualified based on the definition of the files and functions, the operator interface, and the need for programming customization, the user must balance the performance of the network-management system with the acquisition costs and upkeep. ∎

Richard B. Freeman, IBM Corporation, Research Triangle Park, N.C.

Net management choices: Sidestream or mainstream

One technique depends on externally derived, processed data; the other feeds data internally to application programs residing in the network's central-site CPU.

How does the user perceive the quality of a network and its remote computers? How well the network is managed will inevitably influence the user's perception of the quality of service he receives. "Sidestream" and "mainstream" network management techniques can affect user perception in different ways. The sidestream methods view the network primarily from a physical interface perspective, while mainstream solutions analyze from within using both a physical and a logical view of the network.

When discussing network management, clear definitions are required of the different network elements and the disciplines associated with managing the network, as well as of the basic characteristics of mainstream and sidestream management. The individual elements of a network, from a user's perspective, typically include everything between himself and an application program executed in the host CPU. Quite simply, the user defines the network to be "everything behind the tube." This includes:

■ Terminal hardware and microcode
■ In-house wiring
■ Local, intermediate, and remote controller hardware and software
■ Telephone company (Telco) circuits
■ Local and remote modems
■ Host CPU access-method software
■ Application programs

There are six distinct disciplines associated with managing the components of a network.

Problem determination is the process of identifying the failing element of a network so that the proper vendor and service organization may be contacted. Distinct from maintenance and service procedures, problem determination pinpoints what caused the failure — not necessarily why the failure occurred.

Performance analysis measures the network's response time and availability. Other functions include the measurement of delays across network components and a set of data collectively called traffic, or "tuning," statistics.

Problem management concerns the reporting, tracking, and resolution of problems that affect the user's ability to communicate with his chosen host application program. Problems may be documented manually via pencil and paper, semi-automatically by manual entry into a database, or automatically via program-to-program communications with performance-analysis and problem-determination application programs.

Change management consists of reporting, tracking, obtaining approval for, and verifying the implementation of changes in one or more network components. Change management may be done by pencil and paper or by manual entry into a database.

Configuration management means creating a database that keeps an inventory of the past, present, and future physical and logical characteristics of network elements. For example, a database describing a terminal would contain machine type; serial number; SDLC, BSC, or start/stop station address; features installed; logical network name of the device; and original cost. The configuration database should also contain connectivity information.

Operations management supports the remote manipulation of various network elements. During normal network operation, this typically involves the remote control of a processor, controller, or other programmable element connected to the network. During the process of network reconfiguration, this management function supports the remote loading of microcode, software, or an optional configuration into the affected network elements.

227

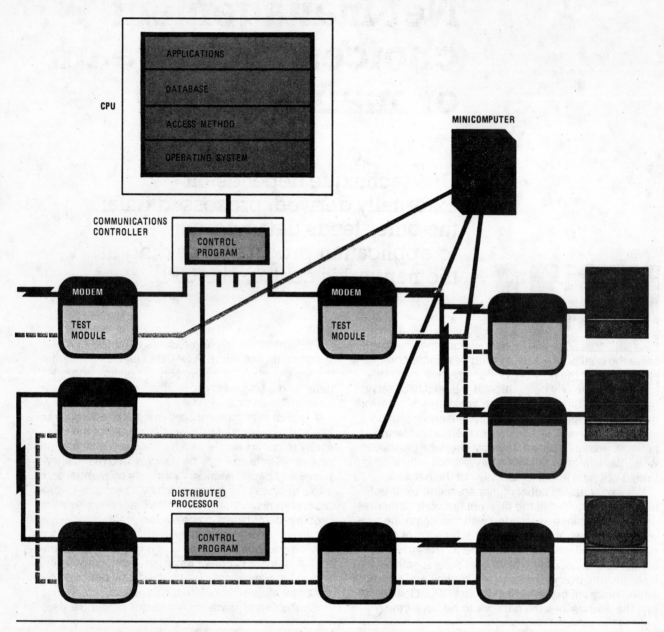

1. Doing business on the side. *By attaching to the "side" of various network elements, sidestream management derives and analyzes diagnostic data. One method* *involves the use of a modem secondary "test" channel, which is frequency-division multiplexed onto the same circuit being used by the primary data channel.*

As the name implies, sidestream network management requires probes that attach to the "side" of data communications network elements. These probes sample and analyze data from physical interfaces within the host CPU and at the RS-232-C interface between a local communications controller and modem. Additionally, the sidestream technique derives data about modems and Telco circuits by the use of a modem's test module and its secondary channel, which is frequency-division multiplexed onto the same circuit being used by the primary data channel (Fig. 1).

Via attachment to various points in the CPU hardware (Fig. 2), sidestream management typically measures CPU and channel use, cache memory accesses, I/O interrupt counts, and virtual-memory paging rates

(transfers to and from real storage).

Sidestream's performance monitor probes at the local-modem interface to measure various traffic statistics and user response times. Typical traffic statistics generated include line use, data-link-control error rates, productive and nonproductive poll counts, and characters transmitted and received.

Response-time measurements are typically calculated on a per-terminal, physical-address basis. The technique monitors inbound data (to the CPU) for the appearance of an "enter" character code and then monitors the outbound data for characters sent to the same terminal address.

The secondary-channel intelligent modems alert network operations personnel to certain types of prob-

2. Looking for trouble. *One sidestream technique has probes attached to the CPU hardware and to the RS-232-C interface between a local controller and modem.*

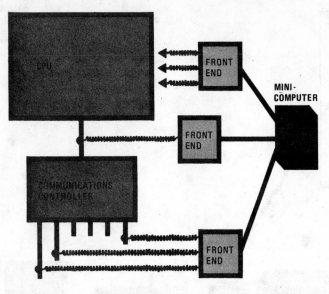

lems without interfering with the normal primary-channel data traffic. The problems detected include modem or terminal power failure, specific analog parameters above or below a threshold value, and no response from the modem's secondary channel when polled.

Troubleshooting net components
Secondary-channel modems also perform several user-initiated modem- and line-problem isolation tests that fall into two categories: those that do and those that do not interfere with primary-channel data traffic. For noninterfering tests and commands, the modems:
- Measure analog parameters
- Test remote RS-232-C modem-to-terminal interfaces
- Disable a remote tributary modem's transmitter on a multipoint line
  The interfering tests are typically:
- Analog and digital loopback "data-wrap" tests
- Local-to-remote and remote-to-local data transmission tests
- Local or remote modem self-tests
- Multipoint polling tests

The problem-bypass facilities included with secondary-channel modems are semi-automatic switched-network dial-backup and automatic spare-modem switchover control.

The configuration database supported by most sidestream methods is typically keyed to physical addresses that can be observed at the interface into which the sidestream device plugs. Secondary-channel modems invariably use the physical address of the secondary channel. Performance monitors use the physical data-link-control address of the terminals being monitored.

The configuration database maintains a record for each modem and terminal that contains physical location, serial number, associated Telco circuit number, contact name and address, vendor name and address,

and switched-network-backup telephone numbers.

The sidestream problem-management database function supports the creation and update of problem records ("trouble tickets") that describe modem and line problems. The elements of each problem record usually include time and date of problem awareness, Telco circuit number, modem type and serial number, technician reporting the problem, remarks about the nature of the problem, time and date the problem was resolved, and installed status of modems.

Feeding the host
Mainstream network management—in contrast to sidestream—consists of incremental hardware and software additions implemented among existing network components (Fig. 3). These additions feed data on problem-determination, performance, and configuration to a set of application programs residing within the host CPU. Associated with these dynamic functions are additional administrative application programs that track problems and changes.

Problem-awareness messages are asynchronously transmitted within the network as normal data traffic. Information contained in the heading of these "alerts" is used by various software components to route the messages to the appropriate network-management application program. Problems reported via a mainstream alerting mechanism may include:
- Noncatastrophic terminal failures
- Terminal-to-controller in-house wiring failures
- Remote, intermediate, and local controller problems due to noncatastrophic hardware and microcode failures, software application failures, and controller I/O-device failures
- Remote and local modem failures
- Telco circuit problems due to poor line quality and line failures
- Host CPU access-method software failures

Usually the mainstream alerting mechanism is sufficient for isolating a problem to a particular component and thus does not require further problem-isolation tests. On detection of a failure or recoverable failure threshold, the mainstream software that provides network management automatically initiates any required isolation test and then generates an alert message.

Reconfiguring the network
Problem-bypass functions of mainstream management are contained within the host CPU access-method software. They allow the dynamic reconfiguration of local controllers, switched-network-backup Telco circuits, and leased-line Telco circuits between intermediate controllers and terminals.

The most important measurements of mainstream performance analysis are user-perceived terminal response time and network availability. Data for these measurements is obtained from within the terminal and reported to the host CPU performance application on demand. The response-time interval is usually defined as the period from the "enter" key depression until data is returned to the terminal. Availability is basically the intervals of time during which a terminal is not

3. Flowing to the host. *Mainstream network management consists of incremental hardware and software additions implemented among existing network components.* *Problem-determination, performance, and configuration data are routed to host application programs. Administrative application programs track problems and changes.*

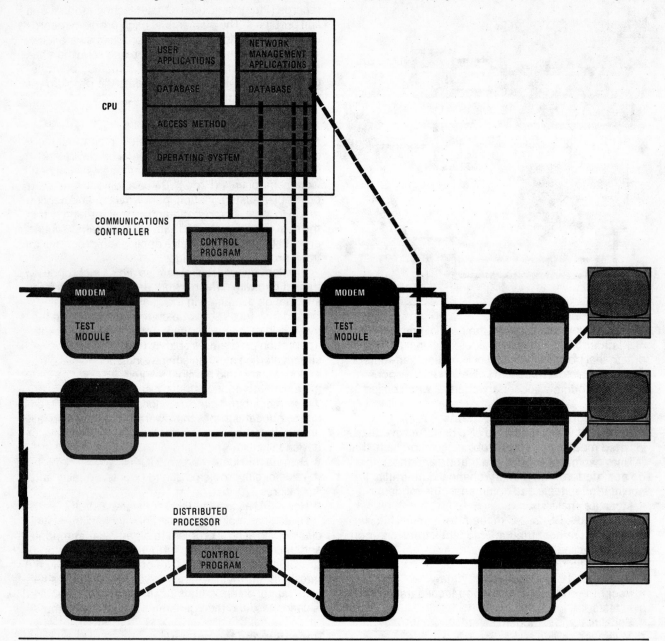

polled, measured over a period of time.

To further isolate and correct performance problems, the host CPU performance-analysis application can solicit a set of statistics from all network components. These statistics include the following for each terminal, controller, and access method:
- Processor and line utilization
- Characters and messages transmitted and received per unit time
- Characters and messages received in error per unit time
- Software queue lengths and buffer counts

Mainstream problem management consists of a host CPU application program that has program-to-program links with configuration, problem-determination, and performance-analysis application programs. The elements of the problem record may include the technician reporting the problem, his department, and telephone number; time and date of problem awareness; logical (software) names of the network and the affected network element; target date and time for problem resolution; problem status (such as new, vendor called, closed); assessment of the problem's impact on CPU, network, and device; physical location of elements reporting the problem; and remarks about the nature of the problem.

The **program-to-program** links may be used to automatically ''fill in'' certain fields of the problem record—

for example, the time and logical names of the affected processor and device. Additionally, the problem description originating from the problem-determination and performance-analysis applications may be automatically inserted into the remarks section of the problem record.

The complete record
The mainstream configuration database is keyed to the logical name of each network component as known to the processor software. For each network element, a record is maintained that may include the component's logical name, physical type, model and serial numbers, order number, ship date, lease start and end dates, microcode change level and installed/uninstalled status, associated network and node logical names, physical location, description remarks, vendor name and phone number, depreciation information, and rental and purchase prices.

The database may also contain records describing the physical and logical paths connecting any two network elements. For example, the path between Terminal A and Application X may be described as:

- Logical terminal name Terminal A attaches to
- Logical controller name CTLRB, which attaches to
- Remote modem 38640023, which attaches to
- Telco circuit 4FD232927, which attaches to
- Local modem 38640024, which attaches to
- Local controller port 3705021B, which is logically attached to
- CPU and channel SYS1CH00, which is logically attached to
- Subsystem program CICS0001, which is logically attached to
- Application program Application X.

Access to the connectivity information is via a command in which the operator specifies the "from" and "to" components of the desired path information.

Mainstream's change-management component consists of an on-line application program controlling a database. Each change to the network is recorded on the database with fields that describe the person responsible for effecting the change and his department and telephone number; date and time of task assignment; coordinator's name, department, and telephone number; status (open, pending, completed); planned times and dates of change initiation and completion; estimated manpower effort; risk assessment; and co-requisite and prerequisite changes.

Comparing techniques
The first phase of problem determination is awareness that a problem exists—ideally before the user calls to complain. If a network problem is due to a modem, an analog Telco line, or a terminal refusing to turn off "Clear-to-Send," secondary-channel modems (a sidestream element) provide a rapid means of alerting network operations personnel.

Mainstream operation, because it is part of the hardware and software that constitute the network, is aware of any problems in the network components. It provides network-operations personnel with information

about a wider range of problems affecting user communications than does sidestream because alert messages may be received from the local controller, the modems, the intermediate and remote controllers, and the terminals. The controllers report all attached-circuit problems, whether analog or digital types. The modems report associated Telco analog-circuit problems. Remote controllers report on behalf of in-house wiring. Microcode or supervisory software within the controllers report failures in application software executing within the same machine. And terminals report their own problems.

The second phase of problem determination involves isolating the problem to a particular network component so that the proper service organization may be contacted. On a nondisruptive basis, sidestream modems identify changes in various analog parameters, such as phase jitter and signal level, which may be used to pinpoint the reason for a particular analog-circuit failure. Further problem isolation consists of executing one or more disruptive tests, which specify either a failing modem or analog Telco circuit. For the duration of these tests, which may take minutes, the circuit is unavailable.

The results of these tests are usually definitive for local-modem failures, but ambiguous for line- versus remote-modem failures and for analog-parameter disturbances. This ambiguity results from the fact that the secondary channel is the only means of communications between local and remote modems that can be initiated by the microprocessor controlling the secondary channels. When the remote modem suddenly stops responding on the secondary channel, the central-site modem has no alternative means of attempting communications with the remote modem to pinpoint the failure.

Where does the trouble lie?
Measuring analog parameter variations, without knowing the extent to which the modems are correctly transmitting and receiving on the primary data channel, may falsely indicate a line problem where none exists. State-of-the-art modems accept a wide variation in parameters such as phase jitter, signal level, and signal-to-noise ratio. If, however, an analog parameter is grossly out of range (40 degrees phase jitter, for example), the analog parameter measurement most likely identifies the source of the problem.

Mainstream problem isolation is based on the analysis of error records that have been generated throughout the hardware and software components of a network. The records are asynchronously forwarded to the central site for program analysis and reporting to network operations personnel.

For local-controller problems, error records indicate whether a failure is due to hardware, software, or microcode. In addition, the controller assumes responsibility for reporting problems associated with attached modems, Telco circuits, and remote "dumb" terminals. Specific modem and line tests are scheduled by the controller software as part of its normal error-recovery procedures, as though they were user-data transmissions. Thus these tests result in an apparent 10- to 15-second network delay as viewed by the user. If the mainstream "intelligent" modem uses both primary and secondary signaling channels to the remote modem, the distinction between a failing line and a failing remote modem is made apparent.

Remote terminal failures are detected by the local controller when violations of the data link protocol occur. Failures are also occasionally detected when the terminal or remote controller responds to a poll sequence with a status message indicating an abnormal condition. Typical problems that may be isolated with these functions include no response to a poll, terminal hardware failure, terminal-to-controller in-house wiring failure, and controller hardware failure.

Remote intelligent processors, controllers, and terminals asynchronously transmit an alerting message to the central site. This message defines the source of a failure as a particular field-serviceable unit of the message-generating device. The records specify the source as hardware, software, attached I/O, microcode, or some other element of the device.

The primary difference between sidestream and mainstream problem isolation is the span of control. If the reported problem cannot be localized to the line, modem, or terminal, the sidestream method provides no direct support or linkage to other facilities that help to isolate these failures. Controller and terminal hardware problems and, in general, any software problems are unobserved.

Less disruptive tests
Mainstream techniques provide a more organized view of network problems, regardless of their source. If tests are required as part of the isolation process, they may be scheduled as normal data traffic, and therefore users sharing a common element of the network feel a minimum impact.

A reduction of the total problem-isolation time is also achieved because of mainstream management's correlation of logical, or software-naming, conventions with those of the network's supporting physical elements. This contrasts with the sidestream modem's use of a unique binary address, which has no relationship to other network naming conventions, for each modem element.

The final phase of problem determination is temporarily bypassing failing network elements while permanent repairs are effected. Sidestream management compensates for failing point-to-point and multipoint lines by patch panels that convert a leased-line modem temporarily into a switched-network one. Central-site operations personnel perform a direct-distance-dialing operation manually—typically twice, to establish the backup equivalent of a four-wire circuit. The modem at the other end of the failing line automatically answers its incoming long-distance calls, and the remote controllers and terminals are returned to service.

For failing Telco circuits used in a loop configuration, sidestream methods employ secondary-channel signaling to invoke a switched-network-backup operation in lieu of the patch panels used for point-to-point and multipoint circuits. A second element that may be bypassed by use of sidestream modems is the modem itself. This requires that each modem have a "hot-standby" companion modem that may be switched onto the circuit in place of the failing one.

Doing it with software
The problem-bypass functions of mainstream management are based primarily on the network's software elements. Switched-network-backup operations are performed by a supervisory operator issuing a command to the access-method software. The access method performs a logical version of the sidestream patch-panel physical operation by redefining the failing controllers or terminals. The failing devices appear as switched-network terminals attached to an alternate line on the same or an alternate local controller.

From the user's viewpoint, both techniques allow a quick network restoration if the problem happens to be a failing Telco circuit. Mainstream management also is capable of bypassing local and intermediate controller hardware and software but cannot, unlike sidestream management, bypass failing modems. User perceptions of these functions will be influenced primarily by the extent to which modem or controller failures create network outages.

Measuring performance
The cornerstone of any on-line network-performance analysis is the measurement of response time as perceived by the user. Sidestream methods measure precisely the response time of the central site. By monitoring the local modem interface, the sidestream device starts a timer when an "enter" character is detected in the inbound data stream. The timer is stopped when data is detected in the outbound data stream destined for the same terminal address.

The network portion of response time is estimated by the sidestream monitor keeping a record of the time interval between previous polls to the terminal. Typically, one half of the poll-to-poll delay is then assumed to be the average time between the user depressing the enter key and the arrival of a poll message at the terminal. These two values (host delay and half the poll-to-poll time) are then added to produce an approximation of user response time.

Response-time measurement via mainstream techniques is performed in the terminal, as close to the user as possible. The terminal records the time interval between enter-key depression and the first subsequent display of data on the terminal's screen. Periodically—perhaps once an hour—a program in the host CPU solicits response-time statistics from all terminals. This program appends to the collected statistics information that describes use of the terminal over a certain time period. For example, the information could include the logical name of the line used by the terminal, the names of any intermediate controllers and lines, the name of the local controller, and the name of the host CPU application being accessed by the user.

Once response-time data has been accumulated, both mainstream and sidestream store the data on a

Sidestream support

ELEMENT	SUPPORTED BY SIDESTREAM
TERMINAL HARDWARE	NO[1]
IN-HOUSE WIRING	NO
REMOTE CONTROLLER HARDWARE	NO[1]
REMOTE CONTROLLER SOFTWARE	NO
REMOTE CONTROLLER MODEMS	YES
INTERMEDIATE CONTROLLER HARDWARE	NO[1]
INTERMEDIATE CONTROLLER SOFTWARE	NO
INTERMEDIATE CONTROLLER MODEMS	YES
LOCAL CONTROLLER HARDWARE	NO
LOCAL CONTROLLER SOFTWARE	NO
LOCAL CONTROLLER MODEMS	YES
ANALOG TELCO CIRCUITS	YES
DIGITAL TELCO CIRCUITS	NO
ESTIMATED END-USER RESPONSE TIME	YES
ACTUAL END-USER RESPONSE TIME	NO
END-USER AVAILABILITY	NO
LINE UTILIZATION	YES
CHARACTER COUNTS	YES
MESSAGE COUNTS	YES
TRANSMISSION ERROR RATES	YES
QUEUE LENGTHS	NO
BUFFER UTILIZATION	NO
PROCESSOR UTILIZATION	YES

NOTE: ALL ELEMENTS ARE SUPPORTED BY MAINSTREAM

(1) IF A FAILURE CAUSES REQUEST-TO-SEND TO BE HELD UP, SIDESTREAM METHODS CAN ISOLATE THE CONDITION

historical database and provide on-line displays of this data. The objective of viewing this response-time data is to give the central-site operations personnel the same information known already by the user so they can determine whether or not previously committed service levels are being achieved.

The sidestream estimate of network delay yields an imprecise response-time measurement. For small, single-CPU networks, this error may be small; for large, multi-CPU networks, it may be quite large.

Mainstream measurements of response time, since they are performed right at the user interface, are uncontestable evidence of the entire network's performance as viewed by the user. Since the mainstream

Comparing cost and availability

Two major considerations in assessing whether to implement mainstream or sidestream management are the functions available to network operations personnel and the cost of purchase and maintenance. The initial cost of mainstream consists of a portion of the mainframe CPU, software license fees, and "features" for various network components. The initial cost of sidestream consists of a complete minicomputer configuration, software license fees, line or interface probes, and per-modem secondary-channel features.

The ongoing cost of the two types is primarily software maintenance. By definition, when CPU software is generated, mainstream network-management software is updated to reflect the addition or deletion of components within the network. Thus mainstream software maintenance consists primarily of installing new program releases. In contrast, sidestream software must be updated each time the host network adds or deletes a terminal, a controller, a line, or a probe point. Sidestream software maintenance requires duplicate updates as well as the installation of new program releases.

Sidestream's availability, unlike that of mainstream, is unaffected by host CPU outages. When a mainstream host CPU goes down, the network management tools are inoperative. Sidestream then has an apparent advantage over mainstream from an availability perspective—or does it? When a host computer that drives a network goes down, the primary objective is to get it operational again as soon as possible. Executing tests on modem secondary channels and monitoring the performance of various lines and interfaces are comparatively purposeless in this situation.

The key resources required by mainstream management are CPU cycles, memory, and a portion of the network's transmission capacity. This portion is typically insignificant, consisting of less than 100 bytes per hour per terminal or controller.

The extent to which virtual storage and CPU cycles are consumed is directly proportional to the size of the managed network. With contemporary operating systems that support multiple virtual machines, mainstream management techniques may be generated so that they execute in their own virtual machine. Thus the storage constraint of mainstream management techniques is the limit of all components that must concurrently fit into one virtual machine's address space.

The CPU cycles consumed by mainstream management are determined primarily by the number of records that flow through the network in support of the management software. This traffic load is user-determined as part of software-generation procedures. Once the software is generated, the user has the option of blocking certain classes of messages either at their source or as they arrive at the network-management database.

data is associated with a particular line, controller, or application program, isolating the cause of poor response time is an easier task for operations personnel.

The network's up-time

The second most desirable performance-analysis measurement after response time is network availability as perceived by the user. That is, how often does the user see the network fail, and, when a failure occurs, how much time does it take before the network is up again? Response time and availability together usually form the contractual agreement between users and the central site.

The differences between mainstream and sidestream observances of network availability are basically the same as those of response time. Sidestream methods accurately record outages of the central-site CPU and local controllers, but have no knowledge of outages occurring within the network. Mainstream measurement of availability performed within the remote terminal can accurately record all outages and again provides uncontestable evidence of the entire network's performance as viewed by the user.

If response time falls below a committed service level, traffic and various node statistics must be analyzed to determine what improvements are needed. Sidestream methods provide a complete set of line-traffic statistics but little, if any, information about the internal performance of the various network software elements. Mainstream methods provide both line-traffic statistics and software-performance data, such as queue lengths and buffer and controller utilization.

Quick fixes to poor response time are based on "tuning" various software parameters. Changing traffic patterns to achieve the same objective may take longer. Thus if there is to be any short-term impression on the user as a result of monitoring traffic statistics, it will likely come as a result of modifying parameters observable by mainstream management.

Take your choice

The overall effectiveness of mainstream and sidestream methods depends on their ability to isolate problems that the user sees. A listing of the various network elements addressed by the two techniques for problem determination and performance management is shown in the table. All the elements are supported by mainstream techniques. It should be noted that modem-bypass and loopback-test functions are unique to sidestream techniques.

The table indicates that sidestream management yields a much smaller span of control than does mainstream management. And it is more costly to maintain, with no actual gain in availability (see "Comparing cost and availability"). Furthermore, the use of sidestream management does not preclude the necessity of mainstream management (and, to some extent, the opposite is true). ■

How to keep terminal users honest

Alan Berman, Citibank, N.A., New York City

Locks and keys are a nuisance. Lip prints are messy. Perhaps the best method is a new software approach—virtual passwords.

Successful terminal security—being able to identify a user and control his or her activity—involves more than hardware and software. It requires knowing what security equipment will best fit into the user's data processing environment. Especially difficult is setting up a security system for on-line configurations that have multiple applications and several operators on any given terminal during a normal working day.

There are two basic means to identify terminals and their operators: physical devices and software devices (passwords). In security circles these methods are generally referred to as "something you have" and "something you know," respectively.

Physical devices take on several forms. The most common is the key-operated terminal. A key is required to turn on the terminal and keep it on. Remove the key and the terminal is inoperative. It is easy to identify those terminals equipped with key "protection"; the key is in the terminal 24 hours a day, 7 days a week.

From keys we progress to magnetic-strip readable cards. By inserting the card in the attached reader, the user can access the network based on some preset control restrictions. If the card is lost, somebody else can use the terminal as he pleases.

Chaos reigns when a key or card is lost or stolen. The card must be invalidated and replaced, locks removed, and new keys issued. Obviously, these security devices are not very sophisticated.

A new product introduced by Intelsec Corporation of Santa Fe, N. Mex., has brought computer technolo-

235

gy to terminal security. The device, TAC II, consists of a control unit placed in a secure location up to 1,000 feet from the terminal and connected to a remote unit at the terminal. The remote unit is cabled either to enable or to block serial data transmission from the terminal. The control unit generates a random challenge word to the remote unit, which returns an authentication as long as the terminal-access-control (TAC) printed-circuit card is inserted in the remote unit. The authentication is then compared with the control unit's own answer: if there is no match, the control unit interrupts the terminal's transmission.

This challenge-response pattern continues at a rate of approximately once a second. Should the terminal operator remove the card from the remote unit, the connection is broken. An optional alarm can be installed to warn if the card is removed from the premises. When a card is either lost or stolen, the matching-pattern section of the card is removed from the control unit, and a different pattern segment and access card are substituted.

But physical security is not limited to the use of removable devices. Fingerprint identification, used for data center access control, is now being tested for

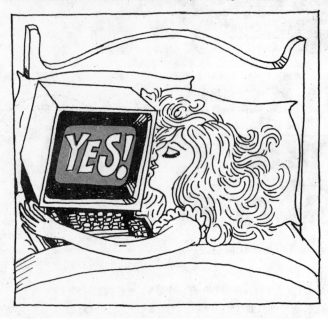

terminal identification. In addition, other parts of the anatomy have been tested for that purpose. Lip prints were considered, but it was feared that kissing a terminal every morning would foster a love-hate relationship. Several operators donned helmets connected to terminals to investigate the possible use of phrenology to identify users.

The major problems with physical security are the expense of additional equipment and the need for stringent controls of physically removable devices, such as cards and keys. Many organizations find these requirements too complicated and too expensive, so they opt to use passwords.

Passwords are cheap and easy to produce. Anyone can create a password identification system, and almost everyone does. But there are problems inherent in this approach. First, conventional passwords exist on a file and are relatively easy to compromise. Depending on the degree of security at a site, anyone from the mail clerk to the systems programmer may have access to any and all passwords. This situation does not promote an attitude of responsibility for protecting user identifications and passwords.

Additionally, changing conventional passwords is cumbersome and often ties up the data processing area and its personnel when updates, recompilations, and reloads are necessary. The end product of all this activity is a password system that may have been compromised at any of several levels and requires data processing support for maintenance.

An alternative to conventional passwords is a new approach called virtual passwords. Virtual passwords are not contained in any files and are created at the time the user identifies himself to the system. Implementing a virtual password identification system requires an authorized on-line user file, which contains such identifying items as name, employee number, social security number, and department number. One additional field should be set aside for the password-generation number. This number determines the starting point from which to calculate a user password and may have any value from 1 on.

Generating the password

For the sake of this discussion, let us examine a unique five-digit employee number and a nine-digit social security or equivalent number. The 14 digits are arranged in a predetermined sequential pattern of columns, resulting in a number table of single digits:

E1	S6	S3	S2
S9	E3	S2	E2
S8	S5	E5	E3
E2	S4	S1	S7
S7	E4	E1	S4, etc.

where En = digit of employee number
Sn = digit of social security number

Consider employee number 57598 and social security number 014-97-6247. Thus, E1 = 5 (the first digit of the employee number), and S9 = 7 (the ninth digit of the social security number). This pattern can be arranged as desired.

After deciding on a pattern for the numbers, we select a pattern for the alphabetic characters. Two sample tables, one for consonants and the other for vowels, are shown below.

CONSONANT TABLE			VOWEL TABLE
X	Q	J	E
Z	M	P	I
B	C	K	U
F	N	S	O
Y	H	R	A
L	D	W	
V	G	T	

Three-character passwords are recommended because they are short enough to remember and, hence, do not have to be written on terminals, on desks, or on pieces of paper taped to the bottoms of desk drawers. Even easier to remember are consonant-vowel-consonant constructions that make up short, pronounceable passwords.

We then consider the algorithms necessary to generate a number that will point to an entry in the consonant-vowel tables. This number is referred to as an offset, subscript, or displacement, depending on the preferred programming language. If possible, three separate programs or subroutines should be written by three different programmers and then linked together for execution. Additionally, the numbers table and letters table should be kept separate to provide a greater degree of security through independent software components.

Here is an example of the use of three algorithms. Each yields a quotient and a remainder.

$$\text{Algorithm 1: } \frac{N + (N + 1) + (N + 2)^2}{21}$$

The remainder + 1 = the pointer to the first letter in the consonant table.

$$\text{Algorithm 2: } \frac{N + (N + 2)}{5}$$

The remainder + 1 = the pointer to the second letter in the vowel table.

$$\text{Algorithm 3: } \frac{N^2 + (N + 2)^2}{21}$$

The remainder + 1 = the pointer to the third letter in the consonant table.

N, the start position of the number table, is the generation number. The contents of the number table indexed by N is substituted into each algorithm.

Using the above information, we can construct a password. Assume that the generation number is 1. Thus, N points to the first position of the number table (E1, the first digit of the employee number), which in our example is 5. Therefore, N + 1 points to the second position of the number table (S9, the ninth digit of the social security number), which is 7. And N + 2 points to the third position of the number table (S8, the eighth digit of the social security number), which is 4. So, substituting the actual numbers from the number table, the results of the three algorithms are:

$$\text{Algorithm 1: } \frac{5 + 7 + 4^2}{21}$$

Adding 1 to the remainder gives us 8. (A 1 is added to forestall a meaningless remainder of zero.) The offset (subscript, displacement) into the consonant table is 8. This yields a first letter, "Q."

$$\text{Algorithm 2: } \frac{5 + 4}{5}$$

Adding 1 to the remainder gives us 5. This offset into the vowel table yields a second letter, "A."

$$\text{Algorithm 3: } \frac{25 + 16}{21}$$

Adding 1 to this remainder gives us 21. This offset into the consonant table yields a third letter, "T."

We can then issue a first generation password of QAT for employee 57598. This method of deriving passwords is simple and straightforward, which is reason enough to install such a system. But there is another advantage to this approach.

In most environments, passwords are changed periodically or on request, but there is no reference kept of previously issued passwords. This may not be very important in batch systems, but in on-line systems reference to previous passwords provides a tool to identify an unauthorized user.

Illegal entry

The following scenario illustrates this point. Employee A (whose employee number and social security number are those in the previous example) feels his password has been compromised. He notifies his supervisor, who in turn notifies the data security officer (DSO), who decides that a new password should be issued to employee A. The DSO uses his on-line terminal to request an operator-profile update on his screen, and he updates the password by simply placing a "Y" in the appropriate field (see figure).

Internally, the generation number is incremented by 1, and the newly generated password is compared to the prior one. If they are the same, the generation number is again incremented until a unique password emerges. Externally, the DSO does not know the password, and there is no intervention by data processing staff members or operations personnel. The update occurs instantly without anyone's knowledge.

Now the data security officer requests that the employee sign on in a secure area, so that no one else may observe the new password. (This is usually done under the DSO's direct supervision or while in telephone contact with him.) When employee A signs on, he sees his new password, which, based on our tables and algorithms, is "RAJ." This password will not be displayed again.

The scenario is complete when employee B (who has compromised employee A's password) attempts to sign on using A's identification and password. When employee B enters the password QAT (in a nondisplayable mode), the system recognizes that this is not the current password. However, instead of rejecting it and issuing an error message, which is the common procedure, the system internally reduces the current generation number (2) by 1 and generates the user's previous password. If the previously issued password matches the one entered, a message to the DSO's on-line printer informs him of the violation and the terminal's location. The system then allows the unauthorized operator to sign on but restricts him to nonsensitive inquiry-only information. This gives security personnel time to confront the unauthorized user while he is still at the terminal.

For a security system to work this well requires a

knowledgeable and conscientious data security officer. This individual is generally responsible for monitoring terminal activity, issuing new passwords, and assigning employee identification. The DSO usually has an on-line terminal station to execute his various duties. It is relatively easy for him to monitor the direct-line local terminals and even the leased-line remote ones (which are in actuality extensions of direct-line terminals). There is a logical address associated with each one of these terminals, and this can be translated into a physical location, such as a building, a floor, a department, a group, and a position.

Security with dial-ups

However, a different problem is associated with location of dial-up terminals. All dial-up terminals should be equipped with an answerback capability (generally an option) to let them send precoded identifiers with data transmissions—even automatically when the modem's carrier-detector signal is first received. Even though the precoded identifier may not pinpoint the location of the terminal, the equipment is identified for future investigation.

In addition to deciding on password methodologies

Screened employee. To update a password, the data security officer requests the operator's profile on his on-line terminal and places a "Y" in the proper field.

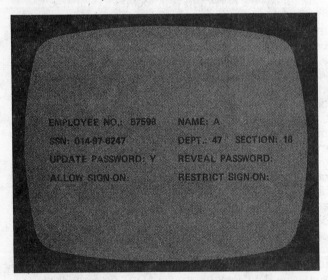

and physical devices, the user must decide whether to control the terminal operator or the terminal itself. Are certain transactions allowed only from terminal XYZ or only by employee Jo Doe? This is not an easy question to resolve.

Restricting the entry of transactions to predetermined terminals works if the environment involves low-volume, highly sensitive transactions, but it may require the additional expense of backup terminals to ensure continuous processing. By tightly constraining terminal use, the network planner risks designing a terminal security system that will directly conflict with the move toward the "universal" terminal. This approach also jeopardizes a terminal operator's productivity by forc-

ing him to move to the appropriate terminal to accomplish a task. But even so, some staff members will feel secure only in this type of environment.

The alternative to the secured terminal is to control the operators and allow them to use any terminal that is convenient and available. This method is feasible, but it requires, above all else, a belief that the security system—whether physical, password, or a combination of both—can identify a terminal user with a high degree of accuracy.

It is important that management define every operator's job responsibility and authority. This information can then be made a part of the operator's profile, which is retained on the same file that is used to control passwords. There should also be a mechanism to continually update the profile on-line.

Degrees of control

This operator-control approach supports the universal-terminal concept, reduces the need for backup equipment, and lends itself to greater flexibility and productivity. Even with these positive points, there may still be a real need to have some highly secure terminals. How is this apparent dilemma resolved?

The solution is to combine both approaches for maximum benefit. That means, for very sensitive transactions, requiring entry from selected terminals and restricting the entries to certain individuals, and, for high-volume, less sensitive transactions, allowing other operators to input data from any available terminal.

There are additional programming requirements. A terminal-restriction file must be available on-line, and the file entry associated with a particular terminal must be combined with the profile of the operator (from the operator file) who is using the terminal on the premises.

A proper evaluation of the user environment is necessary before designing a security system. If terminal security directly interferes with a production area, personnel will naturally resist it. On the other hand, if a system has minimal impact upon productivity, the staff will show little or no opposition. ∎

Hal B. Becker, Advanced Computer Techniques Corporation, Phoenix, Ariz.

Data network security: Everyone's problem

It has never been easier for network vandals to penetrate and damage or destroy sensitive and costly databases.

The ease with which information networks and their resources can be penetrated was illustrated by the widely publicized access of a Canadian computer system by students at the Dalton Preparatory School in New York City (DATA COMMUNICATIONS, June 1980). While the motivation in this case appears to be primarily intellectual and the incurred loss minimal, the event will likely stimulate additional attempts by more-determined penetrators.

A number of organizations, recognizing their vulnerability, are taking steps to protect their installations. Unfortunately, other installations that should be concerned have exhibited a considerable degree of apathy. With the necessary level of awareness, involvement, and support, however, data communications managers can reduce the possibility of a major penetration occurring on their networks.

Prior to the middle 1970s, most installations were centralized; that is, their processing and database resources were configured at a single, centrally located site. This simplified some aspects of the security issue. Now, the increasing use of distributed functionality—multiple, geographically separate sites with information processing and database capabilities—makes information potentially accessible to the growing user community and creates new security problems.

An often overlooked aspect of the increasing user dependency is the cost to an organization of a major, lengthy outage. Disaster preparedness and recovery plans frequently receive their first test when the disaster occurs. In most cases, these recovery plans are discovered to be inadequate.

The potential for unauthorized or fraudulent access of automated information-management systems has not gone unnoticed during the previous decade. While accurate statistics reflecting the true picture are not readily available, those professionals studying the security aspects of modern information-management systems and their networks generally agree that the problem's complexity cannot be overstated.

Even now, it has become obvious that efforts to append security measures to existing installations are, in themselves, a potential risk. The lack of a comprehensive approach, integrated to sufficient depth within existing system-design, implementation, and operation methodologies, often results in a false sense of security. Successful resolution of the security issues will require increased levels of awareness, involvement, and support by the user and vendor communities alike.

The environment to be protected encompasses four

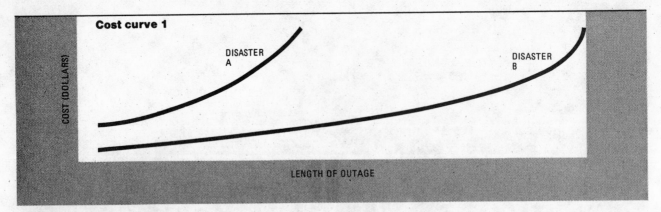

Cost curve 1

COST (DOLLARS)

DISASTER A

DISASTER B

LENGTH OF OUTAGE

sets of resources: components, information, personnel, and services. Components include all information processing and database equipment configured at the central and at satellite locations. Also in this category are the terminal devices, the network hardware, and the links used to connect them with the processing and database resources.

Analyzing the risks

Information includes anything prepared for entry into the system, contained within the system, or produced, as output, by the system. Each of these three categories consists of the procedures and programs for handling and processing the information as well as the information itself.

Personnel extends to all levels of management with access to the system or to sensitive information: the system administrators, developers, builders, and operators, on to the, usually larger, end-user community. Services encompass the various utilities necessary to support the installation (such as electric, water, gas), communications facilities (voice, radio), delivery services, plant protection, and physical security, and the facilities-management organization (janitorial, maintenance, and so on). A realistic approach to the security issues must include the identification and analysis of the risks that exist across these resources.

System penetration may involve any one of these four sets of resources or combinations of any or all of them. The objectives of penetration can be structured into four categories: retrieval, alteration, destruction, and utilization. The penetration possibilities may be identified by relating the four resource sets, called targets, with the four penetration objectives, as shown in the table. With the exception of the retrieval of personnel and services, all combinations represent possible system penetrations and must be considered.

Terminals and other components may be retrieved (borrowed, stolen) either for sale or for use in accessing the processing and database resources for the retrieval of desired information. This information is then used to initiate additional levels of penetration or may be sold to interested parties. Realistic scenarios involving the retrieval of personnel—with the possible exception of kidnapping—or services are unlikely.

Alteration can occur across all four target areas. Components can be altered to facilitate unauthorized access. Personnel may be bribed or induced to alter

a normal procedure, thereby contributing to the success of the penetration attempt. Various services may be altered—through electrical fault or interruption, for example—which opens a vulnerability window (the time during which the system is susceptible to penetration). Following any or all of these, a penetrator can alter information for his benefit.

The partial or wholesale destruction of any or all targets is also possible. Undetected, the unauthorized use of a combination of the targets can provide a penetrator with many profitable possibilities. The extent of the destruction and the methods used to achieve it depend on the penetrator's motivation. Similar or greater levels of destruction may result from natural disasters, such as flood, fire, earthquake, or explosion. A thorough analysis of the risks associated with the many penetration possibilities involves evaluating the motivation, the vulnerability window, the system's operation, possible physical access, event frequency and methodology, and additional resource requirements.

Motives

There are three classes of motivation: financial, emotional, and intellectual. Financial motivations include the creation or diversion of cash, checks, negotiable instruments, raw or finished materials, and others. Emotional motivations result from treatment perceived as unfair (to the penetrator), management or political encounters, and personal problems. Intellectual penetrations frequently show an inability to resist either the challenge ("This is a secure system!") or an urge to simply prove that penetration can be done.

What is needed

The vulnerability window associated with various means of penetration ranges from minutes to months. Some windows appear once, while others appear periodically or are open continuously.

System knowledge required to achieve penetration can be relatively little or considerable, but it usually includes knowing the physical aspects: location, configuration, accessibility, scheduling, and others, and the logical aspects: content, format, access algorithms, priorities, passwords, and procedures. System developers, builders, operators, and administrators will naturally have considerable knowledge of the system. End users and outsiders will have correspondingly less.

Some penetrations require physical access to one

or more sets of targets. Other penetrations can be accomplished from a distance and without physical access. The frequency of penetration and associated methods span from single events executed overtly (by the time it is discovered, the perpetrator is gone) to multiple events occurring covertly over a considerable time span (perpetrated by an insider). The additional resources required for the penetration, beyond physical and/or logical knowledge of the resource set, include test and diagnostic equipment, means of access to a site, finances to acquire penetration means, personnel, and adequate time.

Three rings

Generally, insiders (an organization's personnel) are granted considerably greater levels of access than service personnel, who, in turn, have greater access than many of the end users and the outside world. Thus, physical access control alone is not sufficient to inhibit penetration, since penetrations are not always from the outside.

Physical access to targets is controlled by maintaining three concentric rings, or shells, of protection. The outer ring is the perimeter of the site containing the target. The middle ring is the building within the site, and the inner ring is the room containing the target.

Three parameters have evolved for controlling physical access to targets—something carried, something known, and physical personnel characteristics. These in conjunction with various degrees of surveillance (physical and/or optical) present several advantages and disadvantages that must be evaluated in selecting an appropriate level of control.

The perfect solution to the identification of personnel entering a target area will be small, inexpensive, 100 percent positive, tamperproof, and provide multiple levels of control and hard-copy documentation of all entry and exit activities. Unfortunately, this device does not yet exist.

Preparation and recovery

The growing dependence of the user community on information-management systems is illuminating an area that has, in many large installations, been overlooked. Two phases and, correspondingly, two sets of procedures are being recognized: (1) the steps to prepare for a disaster at the resource sites and (2) the procedures to follow after a disaster occurs.

The initial steps in the disaster-preparedness phase involve the generation of a set of curves (Fig. 1) that relate the cost of a major outage (loss to the organization) to its length. These indicate the maximum available recovery time before irreparable damage is done and the organization faces financial failure. Another set of curves (Fig. 2) relates the cost of disaster recovery to time. Generally, the shorter the desired recovery time, the higher the cost.

These two sets of curves are integrated (Fig. 3), to derive a minimal total cost to the organization and an anticipated outage time. The results must then be adjusted to reflect the level of user service necessary to restore the system to its predisaster state and to accommodate the increased user requirements that may occur during the recovery time.

Figure 4 illustrates the step-function service level that results when equipment is upgraded to meet growing user requirements. Assuming a major disaster and an acceptable outage-recovery time, the increase in user requirements (normal growth and/or processing backlog accumulated during the outage) must be considered in the recovery plans. Failure to include this may result in unnecessary and undesirable congestion and possible saturation of resources during later stages of the recovery process.

Essential backup

The first stage of the recovery plan involves the acquisition of and transition to the backup resources. The restoration of service on the backup resources will occur on a priority basis. Some nonessential services may not be provided on the backup facility, since these would only contribute to the processing backlog.

Efforts to restore the damaged resources will be initiated and pursued in parallel with the transition to the backup facility. When the restoration of components, information, personnel, and service capability is achieved, the restoration of service to the user community—also by priority—can begin.

It is essential that the disaster-preparedness and recovery plans cover all resources and are completely documented. All personnel should be thoroughly familiar with them and trained in their responsibilities. The recovery plan should be periodically tested in as realistic an environment as possible. Both plans—preparedness and recovery—should be continuously maintained and updated to reflect the many changes

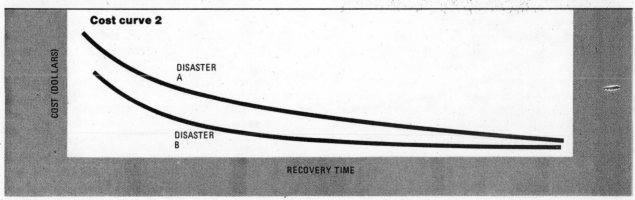

Cost curve 2

COST (DOLLARS)

DISASTER A

DISASTER B

RECOVERY TIME

in the system resources and user requirements.

Some penetrations are achieved using physical methods, while others are accomplished with combinations of physical and logical penetration. Still others are the result of logical methods alone, and these are usually perpetrated by insiders aided by physical access.

Insiders can use the greater levels of physical and logical knowledge of the system to effect countless types of logical penetration. Awareness of application development, implementation, and operational methodologies will frequently reveal weaknesses. Although some weaknesses exist only when the network is operating, others exist prior to or following run time. Some involve procedural knowledge, while others require procedural and content (information) knowledge. In the absence of adequate protection measures, weaknesses can be built into a system and later exploited during testing or cutover periods.

The communications function presents a set of physical and logical penetration possibilities that are different from those associated with the information and database processing sites of the installation. Physical access control or surveillance measures are more difficult to implement due to the addition of geographic parameters associated with the links interconnecting the various sites.

The evolving encryption technology (see following article) currently offers the greatest degree of protection against the tapping of links for monitoring, retrieval, and alteration of information flows. Two forms of encryption are of interest—link and end-to-end, and their costs, complexity, and protection levels should be examined.

P, F, and L analysis
The definition of a realistic set of physical and logical security measures involves a series of events that begins with the identification of the penetration possibilities. Three factors are then derived: the probability (P) that a penetration attempt will be successful, the frequency (F) that the penetration is attempted, and the loss (L) to the enterprise from a successful penetration. P, F, and L are then correlated from the penetration objectives and the risk-analysis parameters examined earlier.

The summation of the product of these factors for each penetration indicates the existing exposure within the system, which is then compared with a previously determined acceptable exposure. If the existing exposure is greater than the acceptable exposure, the communications management must take action.

The first step in reducing the existing exposure to acceptable limits is to rank identified risks in descending order. These risks are then evaluated to determine what combination of reduction of P, F, and L will bring the existing exposure down to or less than the acceptable exposure. Any proposed course of action must then be correlated with its impact on the performance of the system, its availability to the entire user community, its costs, its ease of use, and its maintainability.

Challenges remain
The user community, increasingly aware of the growing dependence on automated information-management systems and the sensitivity and relative accessibility of information stored within, is applying pressure to computer and related technology vendors. Terminal populations are growing rapidly, information and database processing resources are being distributed over larger topologies, and sophisticated terminals and other access methods that utilize a growing variety of readily available carrier services are becoming commonplace. These and other factors contribute to the growing complexity of the security problem.

Users—significantly those intent on penetration— are discovering that the security measures used for years in centralized installations with reasonable success are inadequate when extended to the distributed environment. The appearance of mature distributed operating systems and database architectures can contribute significantly to the resolution of this problem if, and only if, the security issues are considered and appropriately implemented during the design. The separation of the information and database processing functions and the emergence of freestanding, independent database processors will facilitate the improvement of security in both arenas.

User identity
The positive identification of devices and users attempting to access system resources is at this time neither workable nor cost-effective. A reasonable solution to device-identity problems will appear first. Discrete, random algorithmic code generators under mi-

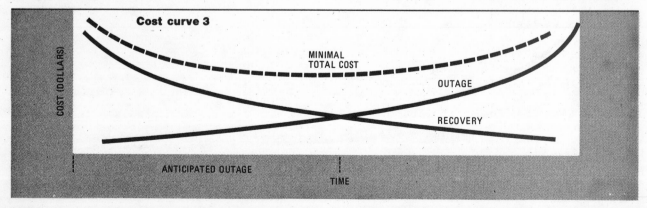

COST (DOLLARS)

Cost curve 3

MINIMAL TOTAL COST

OUTAGE

RECOVERY

ANTICIPATED OUTAGE

TIME

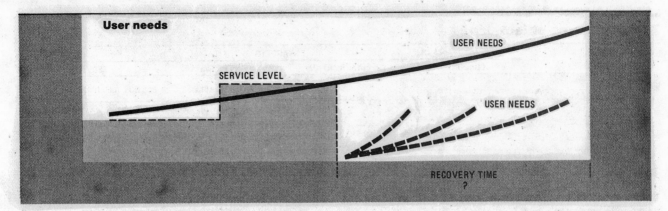

Figure labels: **User needs** · USER NEEDS · SERVICE LEVEL · USER NEEDS · RECOVERY TIME ?

croprocessor control, integrated within the device at reasonable cost, are under development. Work on this technology appears to be progressing in parallel with encryption devices and will eventually be integrated into terminals and other access devices.

Positive physical identification of users will occur neither as easily nor as soon. Currently available methods can usually be compromised, and those that are difficult to defeat—voice-print analysis requiring entry of a randomly selected series of words, for instance— are prohibitively expensive.

Commercial positive user-identification techniques present an additional problem: the identification of acceptance/rejection thresholds. If the limits are narrowed, the device rejects all unauthorized personnel and a percentage of users authorized for access. Broader limits that ensure that all authorized users are accepted also allow access to a percentage of unauthorized users. The trade-off is one of inconveniencing authorized users (rejected on one or more attempts) versus accepting a percentage of unauthorized users and relying on information and/or database processing measures to prevent further penetration.

The mobility of terminal devices and users compounds the security problem. If access is to be granted from various, or possibly all, areas of the system topology, complications in security measures will emerge in the information and database processing functions as well as in the data communications resources.

It must be assumed that users will continue to exchange passwords and other access codes. So, until positive physical user-identification technology produces a workable, unambiguous, cost-justified solution, information/database processing security measures and frequent, random changing of passwords will be the primary defense.

Test and diagnostic facilities
As users become more dependent on the network, they demand higher levels of system availability. Problems or failures must be quickly identified, located, and resolved. Yet the very sophisticated equipment that helps maintain higher availability levels also greatly facilitates penetration of the system, particularly through the data communications function. Although security methods have not yet appeared in this technology, encryption techniques can offer considerable resistance to this type of penetration. However, en-

crypted links also offer considerable resistance to test and diagnostic procedures using this technology. Encryption must then be included in the test and diagnostic equipment, and the encryption-key-management problem takes on added complexity.

A number of social and legal problems exist relative to information-system security. Many organizations are reluctant to publicly expose system penetrations and frauds that are detected. Whether perpetrated by employees or outsiders, they are always embarassing, and it is assumed that public confidence in the organization will be shaken if such weaknesses are exposed.

Inadequate laws
Of the small number of reported system penetrations, an equally small percentage are brought to the attention of lay enforcement agencies for prosecution. Part of this is attributable to the inadequacy of the laws to deal with this type of offense. Trial judges and prosecuting attorneys are readily intimidated by the technological aspects of the action. Further, laws frequently cannot be interpreted to distinguish between the value of the information (a program or sensitive data) and the intrinsic value of the media through which the information was obtained (for example, a reel of magnetic tape or disk pack).

Existing laws do not adequately cover the fraudulent use of the new technologies that information systems bring to contemporary management practice. Major areas of difficulty involve the definition of fraudulent use and the admission of evidence in the prosecution of such use.

Prosecutions resulting in conviction are relatively rare and typically result in extremely light sentences when related to the magnitude of the loss sustained. Thus, to the penetrator, the risk is relatively low and the reward is potentially very great.

Activity is under way in a number of states and at the federal level to correct these deficiencies in the legal system. However, considerable time will pass before adequate, enforceable laws are in place.

Encryption technology
Encryption technology, while promising, exhibits problems that must be resolved before it becomes an integral element of information sytem security. The cost of the more secure versions is still relatively high. The addition of end-to-end encryption to existing installa-

Targets versus objectives

OBJECTIVES	TARGETS			
	COMPONENTS	INFORMATION	PERSONNEL	SERVICES
RETRIEVAL			NOT APPLICABLE	NOT APPLICABLE
ALTERATION				
DESTRUCTION				
UTILIZATION				

tions requires significant redesign of data communications processor software.

Encryption presents equally difficult problems for existing information processing and database installations. Truly secure installations involving encryption of data communications traffic, databases generated and maintained in encrypted mode, and the information processing itself executed in encrypted mode may appear by the end of this decade.

The generation, distribution, changing, and management of encryption keys may present significant problems. If encryption keys are to remain secure, they cannot be transmitted through the network from the generation location to the nodes requiring them. Cost and time to distribute new encryption keys thus become significant.

Auditing the computer environment

The growing awareness of the security risks inherent in many installations is extending to the area of corporate/organization auditing practices. The classical auditing techniques, developed long before computers and information networks became such an integral element of business practice, are frequently found to be incapable of detecting penetration and fraudulent use of the resources.

Knowledge of the classical auditing methods and the accessibility of information system resources makes the production of documentation that will pass many of the audit tests relatively easy. A number of major accounting/auditing firms, large users, and industry consultants are redefining procedures to the computer environment. It is not a trivial task, and evolving an adequate set of procedures will take years.

A question, relative to auditing in the computer environment, is frequently asked: since people with both skills (auditing and information systems) are extremely rare, should auditors be trained in the information system skills or should information system experts be trained as auditors? The latter approach appears to be more realistic.

Application-development methodology

Early, and to a surprising extent, contemporary system/application-development methodologies do not include adequate security techniques. Many installations, having recently become aware of potential or existing security risks, have attempted to implement appropriate security measures as an afterthought. The often-predictable result is a false sense of security.

The development methodologies must be reexamined and restructured, if necessary, to include adequate security considerations and measures in every phase. The process must begin with the initial definition of the user requirement (the problem) and continue through the various design, testing, implementation, operation, and maintenance phases (the solution). The procedures must be documented, understood by all personnel involved, and enforced.

The complexity of the process and the overhead incurred are obviously related to the level of security required. The more secure implementations will naturally be more expensive.

Security measures implemented in an installation should be periodically and realistically tested. System-knowledgeable personnel should attempt penetration by any and all means to test the effectiveness of the implemented security measures. It is obviously less traumatic to discover a weakness through a test than through an actual penetration, which receives wide publicity. Outside consultants are also useful in testing installations for their resistance to penetration of all forms. The fact that they are unknown to the installation personnel results in a level of objectivity and thoroughness difficult to achieve internally.

Education

Awareness and support of the need for improved security measures is required at many levels. Much of the "security" in contemporary installations is the result of an implicit trust between the nontechnical management and staff and the technically skilled information systems management, systems designers/builders/operators. Further, both groups tend to implicitly trust the larger remote user community, skilled and unskilled. Experience indicates that weaknesses do exist in information systems, and people do take advantage of them for a variety of reasons.

The plant-security organizations in a number of large corporations are beginning to take an active role in establishing and maintaining adequate information system security precautions. Education and training is obviously a significant element of these efforts.

The legislative and judicial bodies must be educated relative to the security issue and encouraged to enact and enforce realistic laws that will greatly increase the risk of prosecution and conviction of perpetrators of computer fraud. The security risk and its visibility are continuing to grow. Unfortunately, legislative and judicial action is not progressing at the same rate. ∎

Network Economics

Dos and don'ts of network planning

Albert J. Seedman, Bunker Ramo Corporation, Trumbull, Conn.

There was a time when network planners looked at the geographical distribution of terminals, noted their distances from the central computer site, estimated the density of planned data traffic, and chose, based on those findings, either a private or a dial-up telephone line. With the emergence of time-division and frequency-division multiplexing and the implementation of front-end processors at central sites and data concentrators at remote sites, with host processors freed from their communications burden and numerous long-haul lines reduced, complex networks grew. So did the complexity of network planners' jobs. Nowadays they weigh the benefits and drawbacks of network architectures, of leasing control equipment from the telephone company or of buying it from a modem vendor.

Not long ago, modem manufacturers began introducing the network-control concept with a secondary channel that allowed central-site personnel to monitor and control remote modems. And the CRT dataline monitor became the basic tool to isolate and identify problems.

For a while, it might have seemed that the central-site planner was gaining some degree of control. He could suggest using the monitor to check the network-control system. But then the ubiquitous microprocessor entered the planner's life, bringing programmability in its wake. The time-division multiplexer became a programmable device, advancing to take in statistical multiplexing, data compression, error detection, and retransmission. Now the dataline monitor can even simulate a computer terminal.

On the software side, today's planners must build true duplex operations with error protection through retransmission and bit-oriented high-level data link controls. There are even further planning considerations with the budding acceptance of the X.25 protocol and the growth of packet switching. What makes matters more difficult, planners are faced with communicating office equipment, although the hardware and suitable software is three to five years off.

Even in the face of change, wise network planners adhere to guidelines that remain relatively changeless. Here are some definite dos and time-tested don'ts, both technical and administrative, for creating a cost-effective network.

Technical

1. Attend common carriers' sales presentations.
2. Give carriers your network requirements so they can tailor their proposals to your purposes.
3. Use a consultant for those areas in which you lack expertise.
4. Work out a maintenance scheme at the start. Record all outages and failures, and know where the prime offenders lie.
5. Establish regular review sessions with carriers to confer on all problems.
6. Consider using a backup carrier for lines with heavy traffic.
7. Plan meetings between central-site communications personnel and the carrier's operations personnel. Learn about each other's facilities.
8. Use the RS-449 interface.
9. Look for carriers who assume end-to-end responsibility for network operation and maintenance.

10. Don't underestimate future expansion. Every network grows beyond initial expectations.

11. Don't cut costs with jury rigs or inexpensive, unproven hardware.

12. Don't underestimate software tasks.

13. Don't use equipment that does not conform to accepted standards.

14. Don't stock the central site with test equipment left over from the initial installation.

15. Never commit to an unrealistic schedule, regardless of pressure and in-company demand.

16. Don't pick hardware without talking to other users. Listen to their experiences.

17. Don't overlook leasing time-division multiplexers from the Bell System. Consider lease-purchase plans for equipment you may upgrade in speed or capacity.

18. Don't wait until the end of the schedule to select communications hardware and expect the vendor to make up for lost time.

19. Don't overlook the limited-distance modem for low-cost, high-speed local distribution.

20. Don't run a network without a CRT dataline monitor with recording capability.

21. Don't overlook multiplexing digitized voice in a 2.4-kbit/s channel.

22. Don't forget to reevaluate network layout and costs after a tariff change.

Administrative

1. Conduct network-planning review meetings. Invite participants from user departments. Develop a master network plan and make a point of discussing it at this meeting.

2. Gear terminal selections to users' jobs so that occasional terminal users can easily learn operating procedures.

3. Make up an honest schedule, setting milestones and noting their achievement. This is easier than trying to enforce unrealistic objectives.

4. Include department managers in deciding on terminals and who will use them, response-time requirements, line speeds, and traffic studies and simulations. Tell the managers that you are working for them and ask for their cooperation.

5. Pick the host-processor location based on economics, convenience, power, personnel, and the like. Corporate headquarters is often the worst location for the host computer.

6. Establish procedures for network administration. These should include tracking, verifying, and billing network users; recording failures and outages; scheduling moves and installations; and noting the supplies inventory.

7. Include the private branch exchange in the communications plan.

8. Develop a return-on-investment presentation so that management can see the plan's value. Show potential savings in operating costs.

9. Where costs will be charged back to several departments, allocate costs according to traffic activity. Don't initiate a charge-back scheme based on bit rate or bandwidth alone. If a plan to allocate costs does not exist, suggest it, and you may get a bigger budget to work with.

10. Write your plan for the user. Relate functional requirements to users' jobs.

11. Compare present jobs and services with new jobs and services available under your plan.

12. Don't consolidate corporate data communications needs in a single step. Establish a planned integration that treats each department and manager individually and with care.

13. Don't overestimate or underestimate security requirements. Either can prove costly.

14. Don't forget to check user satisfaction and to measure response time. Conduct a user survey after the network is operating.

15. Don't reduce voice communications with increased capacity for data. Remember that, where economical, digitized voice can be multiplexed with data.

16. Don't be discouraged or misled by satellite-propagation-delay figures. Let the satellite-network operators show how a network can be designed to account for delays.

17. Don't centralize data processing if it will overburden the computing facilities. Consider disaster planning and power failures. Use distributed processing for local and regional data.

18. Don't modify office procedures and structure with the network plan. Keep present operating procedures intact.

19. Don't standardize on the choice of terminals. Base the selection on application. Several types of terminals may be suitable for various uses.

A software aid to network reevaluation

Gilbert Held, U.S. Office of Personnel Management, Macon, Ga.

How one government agency constructed a tool for monitoring user activity, assigning costs, and facilitating network redesign.

Rapidly changing telecommunications makes it necessary for the data communications manager to both select the most suitable transmission methods and constantly reevaluate them to ensure the best price-performance ratio. For the United States Office of Personnel Management (OPM), this reevaluation led to the successful in-house development of a computer-based monitoring tool known as the Remote User Report. The report evaluates data traffic patterns according to geographical region, types of processing jobs, central site activity, and computers accessed. It is based on information extracted from OPM's computers' accounting data.

The Remote User Report is a least-cost software package, which takes a minimal amount of time to develop. Although its details are unique to the OPM application, its design concepts can be used in any data communications network to curtail problems associated with changing user activity. For example, significant changes in the pattern of network use can render the original transmission means (In-WATS lines, foreign exchange lines, value-added carriers) economically unsound. Or bottlenecks can arise—such as busy ports or the user's inability to access a multiplexer channel—that the network manager does not foresee.

OPM, a small government agency, was forced to develop the Remote User Report to monitor altering user patterns at existing network sites. Its Macon, Ga.-based data communications network, built around a Honeywell 66/80 triple processor and two Hewlett-Packard HP 3000 computers (see "Lots of data processing"), had become too complex—and had too much traffic to be monitored by existing commercial software or hardware.

The changing user activity at the various OPM network sites could not be predicted accurately enough from the usage estimates that users must provide to the network manager. What is more, with the exception of feedback from value-added carrier services, no convenient means are available to recognize altering user patterns. Since varying network traffic can put a strain on both the transmission medium and the network components, including multiplexer channels, port selector channels, and front-end-processor channels for the Honeywell system, and computer controller channels for the Hewlett-Packard computer, finding a method of measuring such activity was considered important. So, OPM investigated vendor-furnished monitoring equipment for its network.

Normally, manufacturers' equipment can accurately monitor network-usage patterns, since it provides statistics down to the character and second. However, OPM found that the acquisition of such equipment posed two problems. First, maintaining monitoring equipment full-time was not considered cost-effective if this were the only function it performed. Although the equipment could be leased for a specific time period, it would not have generated the statistics necessary for a long-term evaluation of the network's activity. Second, the equipment was limited in capability and could normally measure the activity on only one channel at a time. Thus, either a large number of monitors would be needed, or only a very small portion of the network could be analyzed at any given time.

OPM also eliminated the option of acquiring special software, since the lead time for its development was unacceptable. Furthermore, a customized software package would have required a considerable amount of personnel coordination and operational tailoring to monitor every application at every site, and the one-time cost of purchase was prohibitive.

The groundwork
Before developing the software, OPM determined the minimum statistics necessary to monitor the change in network usage. It also investigated what resources were available to assist in obtaining the required information. OPM hoped that a portion of the existing network might furnish some of the data and thus minimize the software-design effort.

To satisfy OPM requirements, the parameters that the software measured and reported had to include both communications-usage time and the number of data characters transferred. These parameters were categorized according to the originating location, the offices or bureaus within OPM, and the function or task. This was a challenge because some tasks use the Honeywell computer, while others reside in the Hewlett-Packard system.

The statistics required to provide the usage data are the sign-on and sign-off times for each terminal session and the number of data characters transmitted and received during the session. Once OPM determined these parameters, it had to decide on the frequency of a report and the locations to be included. OPM answered these questions by examining each computer's accounting information.

Billing information was generated by both the Honeywell 66/80 and the HP 3000. However, the information was not compiled in a format conducive to geo-

---

Lots of data processing

The mission of the Office of Personnel Management is recruitment, examination, and personnel administration of government employees. Because of this, OPM is a large user of data processing resources. Its Macon, Ga., network includes one Honeywell 66/80 triple processor and two Hewlett-Packard HP 3000 computers. Each Honeywell processor has 524,288 thirty-six-bit words of central memory, 9.6 billion characters of on-line disk storage, and twenty-four 1,600-bit-per-inch tape drivers. Four Datanet 6678 front-end processors, each with 65,539 nine-bit bytes of memory, complete the package. The Hewlett-Packard units have 320,000 eight-bit bytes of memory. One has 238 million characters of on-line storage, and the other has 550 million. Both HP 3000s have additional peripherals such as magnetic tape drives, high-speed printers, and optical character readers.

A port selector is a front end for both the Honeywell front-end processors and the Hewlett-Packard HP 3000s. It not only handles port contention but also performs automatic computer selection. This is based on keyboard-controlled routing indications provided by terminal operators (see figure). In this way, the port selector permits a common network to provide users access to different computers (see "Controlling the mushrooming communications net," DATA COMMUNICATIONS, June 1980, p. 97).

Since 1975, the number of remote sites connecting users to OPM's network has increased to about 60, and more are planned. Remote users can access the port selector in Macon in various ways. For example, most network-access points in the continental U.S. use multiplexers that are connected either to dial-in lines with automatic-answering modems or directly to terminals at various remote locations. However, a mixture of foreign-exchange lines, In-WATS lines, and value-added carriers are also employed in OPM's network. Which transmission method links a remote user into the OPM network depends on economic and performance factors.

For foreign-exchange-line users, remote terminals are normally connected to a multiplexer. In contrast, for selected locations outside the continental U.S., network access is via In-WATS lines connected to the nearest multiplexer in the U.S. For OPM offices with a small transmission volume, it is cost-effective to use a value-added carrier.

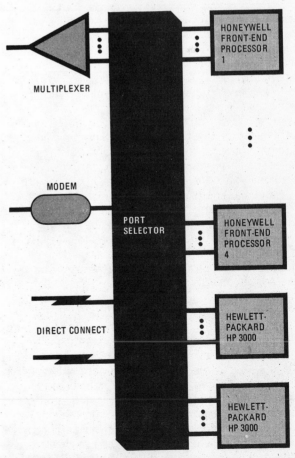

---

graphic analysis, since only the account number, user ID, processing time, and terminal-connect time are printed. This was a drawback: Unless the location ID can be equated to a particular user at that site and the account code to a particular project, it is tedious and time-consuming to match applications at remote sites to user IDs and account codes. Moreover, although the statistics could have been garnered manually to produce a representative report of connect time, they would not provide any data on the transmission and reception of data by characters. In addition, the time required to categorize connect times by location would have been substantial.

Collecting a file

Since the billing reports were produced by programs that accessed a statistical collection file on both the Honeywell and the Hewlett-Packard computers, OPM further analyzed the data in these files. In the Honeywell 66/80, a logical record is written to the statistical collection file by the Honeywell General Comprehensive Operating System under certain conditions, which include activity termination, input or output of a job by a computer, occurrence of particular peripheral errors, or log-off of a timesharing subsystem.

One record generated in the statistical collection file provides connect-time and data-character statistics (Table 1). This record has thirteen (0 to 12) 36-bit words. Words 4 through 7, words 11 and 12, and the first 18 bits of word 8 were used to develop the stat-

Table 1   Data statistics record

WORD NUMBER	CONTENTS
0	FILE AND RECORD CONTROL WORD [N/A]
1	RECORD TYPE INDICATOR [SORT KEY]
2	COMPUTER IDENTIFICATION [N/A]
3	MONTH 0100 = 10 DAY (IN BCD NUMERICS) 0211 = 29 [SORT KEYS] YEAR 0711 = 79
4 AND 5	USER ID GIVEN AT LOG-ON TIME (12 BCD ALPHANUMERIC CHARACTERS) [GEOGRAPHIC LOCATION DETERMINATION]
6	TIME OF DAY (CLOCK PULSES IN BINARY COUNT) END OF SESSION [CONNECT TIME]
7	TIME USER ENTERED COMPUTER (CLOCK PULSES IN BINARY COUNT) BEGINNING OF SESSION [CONNECT TIME]
8	NUMBER OF TERMINAL CHARACTERS HANDLED (UPPER 18 BITS ÷ 8) [DATA TRANSMISSION RATES]
9	MEMORY X TIME [N/A]
10	CALCULATED COST ON CPU [N/A]
11 AND 12	ACCOUNT CODE GIVEN DURING LOG-ON (12 BCD ALPHANUMERIC CHARACTERS) [FUNCTION, APPLICATION]

N/A = NOT APPLICABLE
BCD = BINARY-CODED DECIMAL

Table 2   Sample user IDs and locations

WORD NUMBER	CODE			TRANSLATION		
	CITY	SITE	USER	CITY	SITE	USER
1	DA	0	JCD	DALLAS	AREA OFFICE	JOHN C. DOE
2	SA	0	ATJ	SAN ANTONIO	AREA OFFICE	ALAN T. JONES
3	SF	0	AMS	SAN FRANCISCO	REGIONAL OFFICE	ANN M. SMITH
4	SF	0	JRM	SAN FRANCISCO	AREA OFFICE	JAMES R. MILLS
5	NY	0	ABC	NEW YORK	REGIONAL OFFICE	ALBERT B. CEE
6	PH	0	BBB	PHILADELPHIA	AREA OFFICE	BEN B. BELL
7	WA	X	JLM	WASHINGTON	CENTRAL OFFICE	JEAN L. MOSS

istics that form the basis for the Remote User Report.

Words 4 and 5 contain the user identification, which can have 12 alphanumeric characters. The user ID is assigned by the database administrator's office within OPM. The first three letters of the user's identification code refer to his geographical location (Table 2). This assignment permits OPM to distinguish Los Angeles multiplexer users from those in San Francisco or Hawaii. The coded information is keyed in during the sign-on procedure.

Words 6 and 7 in Table 1 contain the connect and disconnect times in a binary count of clock pulses. There are 64 clock pulses per millisecond, and therefore the elapsed time can be readily calculated. With this approach, connect time can be quoted in hundredths of a second.

The first 18 bits of word 8 is a binary count (divided by 8) of the number of data characters handled by the timesharing terminal. Even though this count does not contain communications overhead characters, a satisfactory estimate of this overhead can be made from the data in the record. Finally, multiplication by 8 generates the number of data characters that are inputted at the terminal.

OPM next had to decide how often to gather the data generated. It also had to determine how much of the overall task was already accomplished by other work groups within the agency. Each night, at a specified time, the statistical collection file was written onto a tape. The production-control personnel then used these tapes as input for the billing report. Each week, these tapes were merged to form a composite tape file. Four of these composite weekly tape files were in turn merged to form a monthly, or billing period, tape

Table 3 San Francisco bureaus' network use*

*CALCULATED DURING 1-MONTH BILLING PERIOD

	PROJECT 1	PROJECT 2	PROJECT 3	PROJECT 4
STAFFING SERVICES				
ACCOUNT CODES	LOGO	XO8C	XOCD	XOCF
TOTAL CONNECT TIME (HOURS)	0.045	0.345	125.451	6.339
TOTAL DATA CHARACTERS HANDLED	1,624	16,016	3,956,040	71,184
AVERAGE CHARACTERS HANDLED PER HOUR	36,088	46,423	31,534	11,229
AVERAGE CONNECT TIME PER DAY (HOURS)	0.001	0.014	5.227	0.264
AVERAGE CHARACTERS PER DAY	67	667	164,835	2,966
WORK FORCE EFFECTIVENESS AND DEVELOPMENT				
ACCOUNT CODES	LOGO	XO8A	XO8B	XO8D
TOTAL CONNECT TIME	0.178	28.303	101.978	13.516
TOTAL DATA CHARACTERS HANDLED	2,856	838,336	1,127,352	170,432
AVERAGE CHARACTERS HANDLED PER HOUR	16,044	29,620	11,054	12,609
AVERAGE CONNECT TIME PER DAY	0.007	1.179	4.249	0.563
AVERAGE CHARACTERS PER DAY	119	34,930	46,973	7,101
OTHER BUREAUS				
ACCOUNT CODES	LOGO	XO8E	XOYG	
TOTAL CONNECT TIME	0.007	0.026	2.898	
TOTAL DATA CHARACTERS HANDLED	232	1,352	60,832	
AVERAGE CHARACTERS HANDLED PER HOUR	33,142	51,999	20,991	
AVERAGE CONNECT TIME PER DAY	0.000	0.001	0.120	
AVERAGE CHARACTERS PER DAY	9	56	2,534	
GRAND TOTALS FOR SAN FRANCISCO OFFICE				
TOTAL CONNECT TIME		279.086		
TOTAL DATA CHARACTERS HANDLED		6,246,256		
AVERAGE CHARACTERS HANDLED PER HOUR		22,381		
AVERAGE CONNECT TIME PER DAY		11.628		
AVERAGE CHARACTERS PER DAY		260,260		

file. The billing information was processed from this file, passed to the various users, and incorporated in the Remote User Report.

Structuring the report

The Remote User Report contains four separate information sections to satisfy OPM data requirements: (1) account codes and bureau-usage data for each OPM location, (2) a summary of usage by geographical region, (3) a section for Washington, D.C., where a majority of OPM's data traffic originates, and (4) a brief ratio analysis of the network usage by the Honeywell and Hewlett-Packard computers.

An extract of data for OPM's San Francisco office (Table 3) shows an entry for each bureau that transmitted data to either Macon computer system during the one-month billing period. This report section provides information about network usage for individual OPM locations and summarizes the types and amounts of data activities within the bureaus. If this report section is compared with corresponding sections of previous reports, changes in activity levels can be traced to a particular bureau and activity.

OPM's network users are required to keep the data communications section informed of new activities and any expected growth or contraction of existing activities. However, a steady increase in use might not be noticed until excessive busy conditions are encountered by users dialing a network access point. Thus, the data in the first section of the Remote User Report can be used as a guide to anticipating specific network problems and making changes to prevent their occurrence. This report section also facilitates decision making about equipment requests, such as additional terminals at a particular OPM location. By examining projected terminal usage in conjunction with existing transmissions, the network designer can determine if the communications facilities at the remote location are adequate or need expanding.

The second report section summarizes geographic data for OPM's offices for a particular billing period. As Table 4 shows, this section provides OPM with the information to perform a segment-by-segment economic analysis of its network. Once the cost and throughput on the existing network is known, alternate means of communicating from each city to the Macon facilities can be examined and the costs projected. For example, Dayton shows 50.4 hours of connect time and 2,433,032 characters transmitted during a billing period. Although a foreign exchange line connects Dayton to Chicago, alternate routes that include value-added carriers, dial-up lines to Chicago, and dial-

Table 4 Geographic breakdown of network use*

	REGION TOTALS BY OFFICE AND BUREAU									
	HONEYWELL 66/80						HP 3000			
	STAFFING SERVICES		WORK FORCE EFFECTIVENESS AND DEVELOPMENT		OTHER		OPM's NATIONWIDE EXAMINATION		TOTAL	
BUREAU LOCATION	TOTAL CONNECT TIME (HOURS)	TOTAL CHARACTERS	TOTAL CONNECT TIME	TOTAL CHARACTERS	TOTAL CONNECT TIME	TOTAL CHARACTERS	TOTAL CONNECT TIME	TOTAL CHARACTERS	TOTAL CONNECT TIME	TOTAL CHARACTERS
ANCHORAGE	8.005	128,688					21.780	849,304	29.785	977,992
ATLANTA	105.505	2,092,776	9.437	124,600	8.261	173,720			123.203	2,391,096
CHICAGO	353.334	7,972,872			16.126	269,256			369.460	8,242,128
DALLAS	125.834	1,776,160	0.384	9,136	2.633	101,632			128.851	1,886,928
DAYTON	0.000	0					50.400	2,433,032	50.400	2,433,032
DENVER	40.943	669,824	0.959	29,544	54.256	1,124,072	62.600	4,473,816	158.758	6,297,256
WASHINGTON, D.C.	0.000	0					170.630	4,367,640	170.630	4,367,640
HONOLULU	31.943	491,216					37.380	1,751,112	69.323	2,242,328
LOS ANGELES	20.123	265,432					137.580	5,525,992	157.703	5,791,424
NEW YORK	125.778	4,245,448			13.562	160,776			139.340	4,406,224
OKLAHOMA CITY	0.000	0					29.470	2,567,104	29.470	2,567,104
PHILADELPHIA	99.928	1,886,272	6.684	32,152	1.566	62,624	45.730	5,706,984	153.908	7,688,032
PHOENIX	21.113	250,216							21.113	250,216
SAN FRANCISCO	132.180	4,044,864	143.975	2,138,976	2.931	62,416			279.086	6,246,256
SAN JUAN	11.403	82,848							11.403	82,848
SEATTLE	115.196	908,648			3.695	115,528	54.980	2,839,624	173.871	3,663,800

*CALCULATED DURING 1-MONTH BILLING PERIOD

up to Macon could be added if necessary.

Since a change in usage from one billing period to another would not cause a change in a particular location's method of communicating, this section of the report merely serves as a warning flag for data communications personnel. If there is a flag, OPM personnel contact users to determine if a particular job, such as a rescheduling of the Professional and Administrative Career Examination from one month to another caused the shift. Although many factors could affect usage, often a steady increase or decrease is the result of gradual operator workload buildup or operator experience permitting a job to be run faster each day. For such situations, the data in the geographical-usage report section permits alternate communications to be selected quickly and efficiently.

The high concentration of personnel and a greater usage of the communications network by users in Washington, D.C., necessitated a different format for this location. The total connect time and total characters transmitted are tabulated for each bureau. Since the third section of the Remote User Report breaks down network usage by Washington bureaus, it is simple to compute communications costs from Washington to Macon for each bureau. Although data communications are currently centrally funded for Washington,

D.C., users, policies could change. Should this happen, usage information would be readily available as a decision-making guide.

The last portion of the Remote User Report contains a ratio analysis of network use for each computer. This section is broken down into three separate categories called Regional, Washington, and HP 3000. Regional and Washington contain those regions' connect times and transmitted characters for the Honeywell 66/80 only, while the Hewlett-Packard 3000 figures reflect the combined regional and Washington, D.C., overall level of activity. The statistics can also be plotted to indicate network-usage trends.

Verifying the billing
Billing verification is an unanticipated application of the Remote User Report. Since several In-WATS lines, cross-connected to OPM multiplexers, are used only by selected offices, it is possible to compare telephone company bills with computer-generated use figures. In one year, over $5,000 of erroneous charges were found. This amount, which is approximately equal to OPM's in-house software-development cost for the Remote User Report, was a positive surprise. The Remote User Report was an analysis tool that had quickly paid for itself. ■

User studies value-added-network response times

Michael P. Rose and J. Patrick O'Keefe, Paccar Inc., Renton, Wash.

One test of carriers in thirty-two North American cities links performance to message size and distance.

During 35 days in May 1979, a minicomputer in Renton, Wash., near Seattle, generated more than 26,000 messages in an effort to measure the performance of three packet-switching networks: GTE's Telenet, Timeshare's Tymnet, and Bell Canada's Datapac. A two-man study team from Paccar Inc. of Bellevue, Wash., identified the relationship between message size and network response time for 32 cities throughout the United States and Canada.

Paccar, a major manufacturer of trucks, railway freight cars, and mining equipment, was planning on-line access to a centralized database to 300 locations across North America for order processing. The company ran this test to determine which value-added carrier, Telenet or Tymnet, might perform more efficiently in the projected application. The study team also tested Datapac, the Canadian carrier, because Paccar's Canadian dealers could not gain access to Telenet or Tymnet without first requesting a respective gateway from Datapac.

For the test, the team members picked 32 test cities with value-added-network access ports. They used an IBM Series/1 minicomputer located in Renton to act as an automatic send-receive teleprinter and communicate with an IBM System 370/158 mainframe, also in Renton. The Series/1 was chosen because, in addition to emulating the teleprinter the test team had in mind for its eventual network (a Teletype Corporation 33/35), it was powerful enough to process data. It could function as if it were an intelligent terminal lo-

cated in each test city, though it remained close to the mainframe in Renton. During the test, the Series/1 gained access to a carrier's port in Los Angeles, Boston, Omaha, Calgary, Halifax, or any test city, then called the 370 host in Renton to place an order. Yet, acting in its normal capacity, as a minicomputer, the Series/1 processed test data that measured the time it would take a terminal in, say, Boston to send a message on Telenet or Tymnet to Renton and receive a positive acknowledgement.

The team added another element to the test: direct-distance dialing (DDD). Whenever the value-added-carrier access ports were busy, or blocked, the Series/1 called the host directly through an automatic dialer, the Bell 801C. It also handled host and network log-on functions. And although the Series/1 used DDD lines to call access ports in all test cities, the DDD delays were negligible compared to the measured network-response times. Besides, the test team subtracted DDD times from network measures to isolate carrier response time. In the planned Paccar scheme, intelligent terminals at the access-port sites would eliminate the need for DDD connections.

To conduct the test, the study team:
■ Equipped the Series/1 with prototype, machine-independent software
■ Added software to generate messages of differing sizes to gauge the effect of size on response time
■ Received and echoed asynchronous messages from the 370 host (Echoing means that the host software

1. Layout. *Messages emerge from the Series/1 minicomputer for testing Telenet, Tymnet, and the Canadian carri-er, Datapac. They are received at the host computer and bounced back along the same paths for verification.*

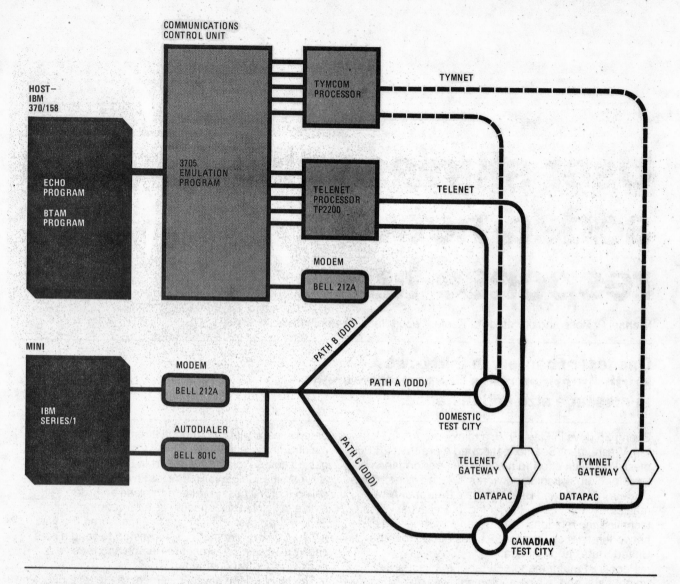

COMMUNICATIONS
CONTROL UNIT

HOST—
IBM
370/158

ECHO
PROGRAM

BTAM
PROGRAM

3705
EMULATION
PROGRAM

TYMCOM
PROCESSOR

TYMNET

TELENET
PROCESSOR
TP2200

TELENET

MODEM

BELL 212A

PATH B (DDD)

MINI

MODEM

BELL 212A

PATH A (DDD)

IBM
SERIES/1

AUTODIALER

BELL 801C

DOMESTIC
TEST CITY

PATH C (DDD)

TELENET
GATEWAY

TYMNET
GATEWAY

DATAPAC

DATAPAC

CANADIAN
TEST CITY

receives messages from the Series/1, then, to verify receipt, retransmits them to the same Series/1.)
■ Measured dialing time, network log-on time, transaction response time, and network log-off time
■ Stored all details in a database for later analysis, including the percentage of "blocking," that is, the number of times the Series/1 called a carrier's access port and received a busy signal

Layered software

To allow for expected changes in Paccar's planned operation, as well as in common-carrier offerings and mainframe capabilities, the test-team member who wrote the software designed machine-independent, layered architecture for the Series/1. The designer did not know which intelligent terminal Paccar would eventually choose. He then wrote the application instructions on the highest level of the software layers. This layer controlled the editing and formatting of what

would become user data in the planned network and communicated only with its application-layer peer at the host. The next software layer, designed for terminal identification and for log-on and log-off, communicated only with its counterpart, the teleprocessing monitor.

Beyond that was the layer for value-added-network dialog and log-on, terminal identification, host connection, and any unsolicited value-added-network messages. It also contained dialog modules for Telenet, Tymnet, and the Datapac-Telenet and Datapac-Tymnet gateways, each of which required different dialog code sequences. Further, this layer had the ability to abort a dialog if the network was blocked and to call another. Failure to reach the host through Telenet, for instance, might result in a Tymnet connection, without user intervention. A linked list of the available networks provided such contingency moves. The last resort was always access by direct-distance dialing through the modems or the automatic dialer. The lowest software

254

Table 1   Comparison of domestic carrier response times

CITY	BLOCKING PERCENTAGE (IN SECONDS)		25-CHARACTER RESPONSE TIME (IN SECONDS)			NETWORK RESPONSE TIME (IN SECONDS)	
	TELENET	TYMNET	TELENET	TYMNET	LOCAL	TELENET	TYMNET
SEATTLE	1.6	0.0	3.62	2.78	2.01	1.61	0.77
LOS ANGELES	0.0	6.8	3.84	4.26	2.01	1.83	2.25
CHICAGO	4.4	4.6	4.08	4.20	2.01	2.07	2.19
NEW YORK CITY	2.2	4.6	4.10	4.32	2.01	2:09	2.31
BOSTON	0.0	2.3	4.74	4.83	2.01	2.73	2.82
DALLAS	2.2	16.2	3.90	3.87	2.01	1.89	1.86
WASHINGTON, D.C.	0.0	2.3	4.33	3.60	2.01	2.32	1.59
ATLANTA	4.5	2.3	4.25	4.13	2.01	2.24	2.12
PHOENIX	2.2	0.0	3.87	4.06	2.01	1.81	2.05
DENVER	0.0	0.0	3.99	4.25	2.01	1.98	2.24
ST. PAUL	0.0	2.3	4.17	4.06	2.01	2.16	2.05
OMAHA	4.5	0.0	4.31	4.57	2.01	2.30	2.56
OKLAHOMA CITY	0.0	11.9	4.03	4.40	2.01	2.02	2.39
PORTLAND	4.5	0.0	3.51	2.93	2.01	1.50	0.92
HOUSTON	4.6	2.4	4.00	3.87	2.01	1.99	1.86
SALT LAKE CITY	0.0	0.0	3.57	4.17	2.01	1.56	2.16
NASHVILLE	2.3	–	4.19	–	2.01	2.18	–
PHILADELPHIA	2.3	0.0	4.08	4.28	2.01	2.07	2.27
CINCINNATI	9.3	0.0	4.13	4.32	2.01	2.12	2.31
INWATS	–	0.0	–	3.17	2.01	–	1.16
NETWORK-WIDE AVERAGE	2.5	3.3	4.04	4.00	2.01	2.03	1.99

Table 2   Comparison of Canadian-link response times

CITY	BLOCKING PERCENTAGE (IN SECONDS) DATAPAC		25-CHARACTER RESPONSE TIME (IN SECONDS) DATAPAC			NETWORK RESPONSE TIME (IN SECONDS) DATAPAC	
	TELENET	TYMNET	TELENET	TYMNET	LOCAL	TELENET	TYMNET
VANCOUVER	5.7	0.0	5.10	4.57	2.01	2.56	2.56
PRINCE GEORGE	7.1	7.3	5.22	4.53	2.01	2.52	2.52
CALGARY	7.5	9.7	5.21	4.49	2.01	2.48	2.48
EDMONTON	14.6	19.5	4.39	4.60	2.01	2.38	2.59
REGINA	9.7	12.1	5.40	4.63	2.01	3.39	2.62
WINNIPEG	12.1	2.5	5.21	4.42	2.01	3.20	2.41
OTTAWA	7.6	13.5	5.09	4.58	2.01	3.08	2.57
SUDBURY	13.5	13.5	5.01	4.58	2.01	3.00	2.57
TORONTO	13.5	8.5	5.02	4.59	2.01	3.01	2.58
QUEBEC CITY	5.7	8.8	5.40	4.86	2.01	3.39	2.85
MONCTON	11.7	5.8	5.24	4.78	2.01	3.23	2.77
HALIFAX	0.0	3.1	5.16	4.67	2.01	3.15	2.66
ST. JOHN'S	3.1	0.0	5.23	4.72	2.01	3.22	2.71
NETWORK-WIDE AVERAGE	9.5	8.9	5.21	4.61	2.01	3.20	2.60

layer contained the device-emulation functions (automatic send-receive or ASR 33/35 emulation) plus the device-control functions for the Bell 801C autodialer and the Bell 212A modem.

The programmer wrote the procedures for the network comparison into the application layer. This allowed interactive transactions consisting of a sequence of characters transmitted to the host and echoed to the terminal from the echo code residing in the host. To test for errors, each echo was compared with the message transmitted. Data were gathered on a magnetic disk, which amounted to an electronic journal, for later analysis. Phone numbers for access ports were noted in the software. Additional codes located in various software layers referred to the time taken to perform specific activities, including start and stop times for access-port telephone numbers dialed, for network log-on, for each terminal-to-host and echo transaction, and for network log-off. In addition, the study team recorded all network busy (or blocked-access-port) signals, network log-on failures, host-connection failures, and transmission errors.

The study team defined a test sample as five messages transmitted and echoed. Pilot tests had shown that three messages pushed the response times to within 1 percent of their final values. At the end of each test run, details of the transaction were noted in the journal. Sixty journals, mirroring 60 test runs, were compiled during the study, producing a database of performance measures for 26,000 transactions.

Test procedures
The study team used one test procedure for domestic cities and another for Canadian cities. Test runs were completed for each hour between 7 A.M. and 6 P.M. Pacific Daylight Time and for each day during the 35-day testing period.

For domestic cities, the Series/1, through a modem or the autodialer, called the Telenet access port for the test city. Five messages were sent and echoed. Immediately after, a direct-distance call was made to the host, and the same five messages were sent and echoed. Then the Series/1 called the Tymnet access port, logged on, and sent and echoed the messages. After all test-city access ports were dialed, networks logged on, and messages sent and echoed, the test run was complete.

There was a slight variation for Canadian cities. The Series/1, acting as a remote intelligent terminal, dialed a Datapac access port for the Canadian test city and requested a network gateway for Telenet or Tymnet; that is, the message traveled from the Canadian city to Datapac to the network gateway to Renton, Wash., and back. The other procedures were the same as for domestic cities, including direct dialing to the host.

Figure 1 shows the test configuration. Although synchronous interfaces were available through Telenet and Tymnet, they would have required changes in the host's operations and could not be run concurrently in one 3705 communications control unit. Therefore, asynchronous interfaces were used. As shown, the data paths for domestic cities began at the Series/1

and flowed through the Bell 212A modem onto the direct-dial network represented by paths A and B. For the Telenet test, messages emerged from the Series/1, passed through the modem, went down path A to the test city, and emerged from the network at the Telenet processor, the TP 2200. This device emulated the ASR 33/35 teleprinter in 300-bit/s asynchronous transmission to the IBM 3705. The 3705 emulation program then passed the messages to the host IBM 370/158, where the basic telecommunications access method (BTAM) echoed the messages to the 3705, to the TP 2200, then back along Telenet, through the test city, and ultimately to the Series/1.

For direct-dial response-time measurement, the messages used path B from the Series/1 straight to the 3705, which again passed them to the 370 as well as to the BTAM and echo programs. The echoed messages were then retransmitted to the 3705, to the modem, and back to the Series/1.

The Tymnet test run was similar to the Telenet run, using path A to the test city. The messages traveling along path A to the test city, however, emerged from the network at the Tymcom processor, a Tymnet device emulating the ARS 33/35. The return path to the Series/1 reversed the inward path.

Echoes of Canada
The direct-dial test run for the Canadian cities remained the same as well. However, the Canadian test for Telenet and Tymnet, using Datapac, was more complex. For a Telenet test, for instance, the messages traveled from the Series/1, through the Bell 212A modem, down path C to the test city. Through Datapac, users requested a Telenet gateway to gain access to the Telenet network. The messages were then sent on to the TP 2200. The path to the 370 remained exactly as it did for the domestic test, and the echoed messages went from BTAM to the 3705, through the TP 2200, to Telenet, to the gateway, and back along path C to the Series/1.

In the Canadian test for Tymnet, the procedures and echoed-message verification stayed the same, except that messages entered the domestic network access

---

7. Relationship. *For this test, measured response times were compared for message lengths of 16, 25, 50, 70, and 130 characters, each carrier against direct-dial.*

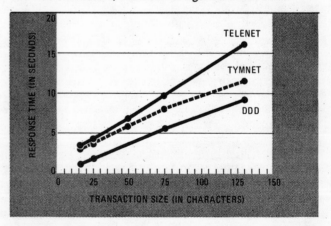

Table 3   Sample of test-city performance

TELENET	SEATTLE
MEAN RESPONSE TIME	3.619 SECONDS
STANDARD DEVIATION	0.402
COUNT (TOTAL TRANSACTIONS OVER 35 DAYS)	225
MEAN CONFIDENCE RANGES FOR RESPONSE TIME	
90% RANGE	3.574–3.663
95% RANGE	3.566–3.671
99% RANGE	3.549–3.688
STANDARD DEVIATION CONFIDENCE RANGES FOR RESPONSE-TIME VARIATIONS	
90% RANGE	0.380–0.429
95% RANGE	0.374–0.437
99% RANGE	0.363–0.453
NETWORK ACCESS BLOCKED 1 OUT OF 60 ATTEMPTS	1.6%
TRANSMISSION ERRORS 0 OUT OF 225 ATTEMPTS	0.0%

ports through a Datapac-Tymnet gateway.

The bulk of the data was based on the echo of a 25-character message, which is approximately the size of Paccar's anticipated application message. Gathering the same amount of data for other message sizes would have been costly and taken longer than 35 days.

Response time was defined as the time from the beginning of the first character transmitted to the end of the last character received. Tables 1 and 2 present the four components used in evaluating network performance: test city, blocking percentage, 25-character response time, and network response time. The blocking percentage shows how often the Series/1 was blocked from gaining access to test-city ports. The response time given for each respective test city is based on a 25-character transaction. The network component indicates the response time attributable to the use of a value-added network in lieu of direct dial. To arrive at that figure, the test team subtracted direct-dial time from the 25-character response time.

Table 1 compares Telenet and Tymnet. The 25-character response time columns contrast the performance of direct dial from Series/1 to the host, in addition to the respective performances of the two carriers. The rate of availability, shown under block percentage, varies widely. Telenet cities show blocking rates from zero to 9.3 percent with an average of 2.5 percent; Tymnet cities, from zero to 16.2 percent with an average of 3.3 percent; and Datapac cities, from zero to

19.5 percent with a 9.2 percent average. Table 2 adds the Datapac element, that of Canadian cities gaining access to the Telenet and Tymnet networks. Gateway delays are included in the response-time measures.

Figures 2, 3, 4, 5, and 6 show probability distributions for the conditions tested. On the horizontal axis are the measured response times. The vertical axis is the percentage of the total direct-dial sample at a given response time. While the response-time data had a resolution of 1.0 millisecond, the graphic representation uses 100-millisecond resolution.

Figure 2 shows direct-dial performance, which is the measure showing the greatest consistency, with a steep distribution, a peak, or mode, at 1.9 seconds, and a mean at 2.0 seconds.

Figures 3 and 4 depict Telenet and Tymnet domestic performance. Telenet shows a broader distribution, with a mode at 3.9 seconds and a mean at 4.0 seconds. The vertical line labeled 90 percent indicates that 90 percent of all measured transactions fall to the left of the line, or 90 percent of all 25-character echoes were received in less than 4.3 seconds.

The Tymnet distribution in Figure 4 is broad in comparison to Telenet's. The mode is 4.0 seconds, the mean is 4.0 seconds, and 90 percent of the transactions were verified as correct in 5.7 seconds or less. Figure 5 places the mode of Canadian performance for Datapac-Telenet at 5.1 seconds, the mean at 5.2 seconds, and 90 percent of all transactions at 5.9 seconds or less. Figure 6 shows the Canadian performance for Datapac-Tymnet: the mode is 4.2 seconds, the mean is 4.6 seconds, and 90 percent of all transactions fall below 5.3 seconds.

The results indicate that Tymnet is more responsive to terminal-to-host proximity than Telenet. There are clearly fewer Tymnet nodes, for instance, between Seattle and Portland, Ore., than there are between Seattle and Boston. This would have been reversed, of course, had the host computer been located in New York City, rather than in Renton.

Figure 7 shows the relationship of message size to response time. Datapac was omitted from this because too few data were acquired to plot the relationship. For this measure, response times were plotted not only for 25-character messages but also for message lengths of 16, 50, 75, and 130 characters. Direct dial is compared to Telenet and Tymnet response times for each message size.

Tymnet maintains a nearly constant response-time difference throughout the message range, while Telenet does not. This may occur because Tymnet, which employs a multiplexer for user data within its packets, creates a fixed path for the data stream between terminal and host, while Telenet, with its virtual circuits of no fixed path, must instead assemble and disassemble packets for message delivery.

The study concluded that the significant performance differences between Telenet and Tymnet depend more on geography than on technology. Network-wide differences were measurable, but in the planned setup they would be imperceptible to the user, except in transmission of the lengthiest messages.

2-6. Plotting. *These graphs show probability distributions for the conditions tested. The vertical axes show the percentage of the total sample at given response times, including the times for direct-dial access to the carrier. The horizontal axes present the measured response times. While the test response-time data had a resolution of 1.0 millisecond, these graphs use 100-millisecond resolution. Figure 2 shows direct-dial performance. Figures 3 and 4 present transmissions on Telenet and Tymnet, respectively. Figures 5 and 6 depict the domestic carriers' performances with the addition of Datapac, the Canadian carrier, for access to domestic-carrier gateways.*

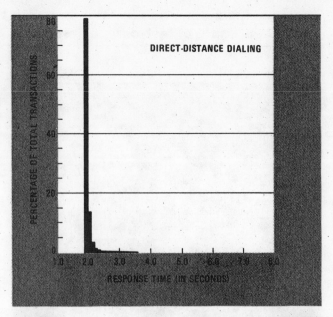

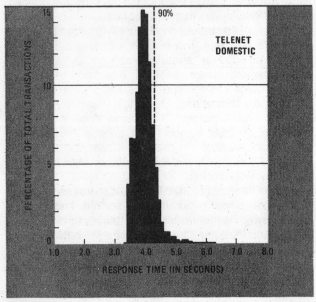

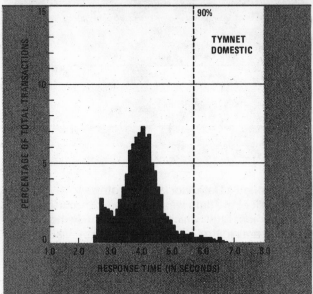

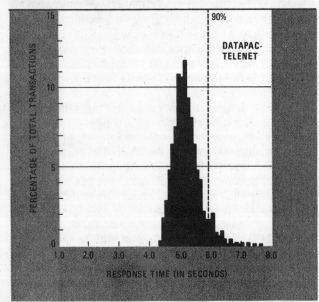

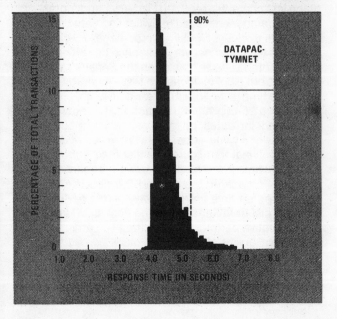

Comprehensive plan rates equipment, eases decision making

Gilbert Held and Robert Abey, U.S. Office of Personnel Management, Macon, Ga.

Here is a simple, step-by-step approach for determining which vendor's product is best for you

As a result of rapidly changing technology, developing needs of organizations, and interacting costs of equipment and personnel, today's data communications manager is faced with the complex task of developing a comparison format for equipment selection.

The United States Office of Personnel Management (OPM) has devised such a procedure and is using it to review its existing communications network on a periodic basis to determine if new technologies and possible price differentials can be used to the advantage of the organization. Recently, OPM used the procedure to evaluate the high-speed 9.6-kbit/s modem market. This program was initiated in order to determine if a better price/performance ratio could be obtained in the event that the existing communications equipment needed to be replaced. This evaluation will serve as a model description of the procedure.

With the establishment of OPM's data center in Macon, Ga., several years ago, one vendor's 9.6-kbit/s modems were obtained on a lease basis. This procurement decision was made on the basis of short installation and delivery time, the then-permissible two-hour on-call maintenance requirements, and the fact that the quantity of remote batch terminals and the terminal workloads that the modems were to support had not been finalized.

Thus the initial procurement decision was to lease readily available modems, and little consideration was given to human engineering and data transfer performance limitations of the modems. As OPM's workload expanded and the procurement of new remote batch terminals was delayed, questions arose regarding the possibility of increasing data transfer rates through the utilization of alternate high-speed modems. An investigation of the high-speed-modem human engineering features was deemed warranted when the eventual procurement of new remote batch terminals and the expansion of OPM's network to areas lacking trained personnel became a reality. Considering these factors, OPM decided to conduct an evaluation of the high-speed 9.6-kbit/s modem marketplace to determine the high-speed modem availability based on human engineering, data-transfer capability (technical performance), and cost.

Before the actual evaluation, each of six modem manufacturers submitted a pair of demonstrator modems along with pricing and operational data sheets. This enabled OPM personnel to conduct a limited performance analysis based on the agency's anticipated use of the devices. A weighted scoring technique was developed to evaluate and compare modems on the quality of their engineering, technical performance, and cost. The scoring was based on a maximum of 100 evaluation points, with 25 points assigned to human engineering, 25 points to technical performance, and 50 points to the cost evaluation. This scoring reflected the OPM priority factors, where human engineering and technical performance were judged to be of equal importance, while economic factors were judged to be twice as important. Other analysis plans can assign different weights to the data to reflect different considerations. In a highly critical network, where,

259

for example, the information being communicated has to be nonstop, the technical performance might outweigh the importance of personnel and cost considerations.

Although many companies manufacture modems, OPM contacted the six that met its criteria. For a vendor's modem to be considered in the final evaluation, three requirements had to be met. First, the supplier had to have maintenance available in both Washington, D.C., and Macon, Ga. Second, the modems had to provide 9.6-kbit/s data transfer rates. Finally, analog and digital loopback capabilities were required.

Although six manufacturers met the criteria and were contacted by OPM, in the interest of brevity only the ratings assigned to three of the vendors are used for this evaluation.

Human engineering

The evaluation of each modem's human engineering factors—based on ease of operation—was conducted by personnel of OPM's technical control center. This was done because they could best judge the degree of ease or difficulty users would encounter in running diagnostic tests based on technical control center guidance. The technical center personnel maintain continuous contact with the OPM network users and respond when problems arise. Other human engineering factors were also considered. The type of indicators on the modem, access to the modem switches, and the physical size and mounting requirements of the modem were included.

Three-person evaluation

Switch and toggle button access was thought to be extremely important, because at some OPM locations, modems would be rack mounted, and switches on the modem's rear panel would require personnel to move behind bays of equipment when running diagnostic tests. Similarly, the modem's physical size and mounting requirements would determine if existing racks were suitable or if a rearrangement of cabinet shelves were required, as would be the case if, for example, horizontally placed rectangular modems were replaced by modems that required vertical mounting, even if the modems were similar in size. Although more vertical modems of the second type can be installed on a shelf, distances between shelves must be increased significantly to permit the increased height clearance as illustrated in Figure 1.

For the human engineering evaluation, three members of OPM's technical control center completed evaluation forms similar to those detailed in Figure 2. Each modem being considered had a separate sheet. Because each human factors category was rated on a zero to 10 scale, using three persons for the evaluation permitted a maximum possible rating of 120 points (4 x 10 x 3). To convert the rating into evaluation points, each rating was divided by the maximum rating of 120 and the result multiplied by the maximum 25 evaluation points allotted to the human engineering phase as illustrated in Table 1.

In order to evaluate the technical performance of the

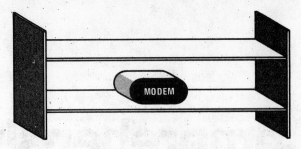

1. Packing. *Among the human engineering factors involved in equipment selection is hardware positioning. Shelf sizes vary for the two modem configurations.*

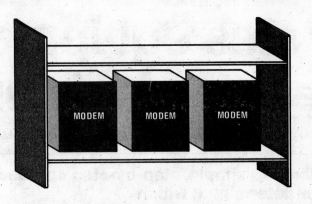

2. Scorecard. *An evaluation sheet is necessary to rate each of the human engineering categories. Similar sheets are used for other aspects.*

MODEM EVALUATION SHEET

VENDOR _____   DATE _____

HUMAN FACTOR   RATING

1. EASE OF OPERATION

2. FEATURES

3. DIAGNOSTICS

4. SIZE AND MOUNTING

                    TOTAL:

RATE ZERO TO 10

modems, a computer benchmark program was prepared to closely simulate the way the modems would be used in normal operating conditions. The benchmark program was a system output (sysout) data file that was representative of the type of output the remote batch terminals handle throughout the day. For the test, two modems were connected on the analog side, with a cable used to simulate a telephone leased-line connection. The digital side of one modem was connected to the remote batch terminal, while the digital side of the second modem was connected to one port on the front-end processor. The circuit block diagram is shown in Figure 3.

During the benchmark test, blocks of data were pulled by the remote batch terminal. At the end of each received block, a longitudinal redundancy check (LRC) was performed and the result compared with the transmitted LRC character. If the computed LRC matched the transmitted LRC, the line was turned around and a positive acknowledgment was transmitted from the terminal to the front-end processor, signifying that the terminal had received the block correctly and that the front-end processor could now transmit the next block of data. If the computed LRC did not match the transmitted LRC, a transmission error had occurred, and the line was configured for the terminal to send a nega-

1. The best time would receive 25 points.
2. Any time between 2.5 to 5 percent slower would receive 20 points.
3. Any time between 5 to 7.5 percent slower would receive 15 points.
4. Any time between 7.5 to 10 percent slower would receive 10 points.
5. Any time between 10 to 12.5 percent slower would receive 5 points.
6. Any time 12.5 percent slower or more would receive 0 points.

Based on the results obtained in the benchmark program test, the technical performance evaluation was completed as shown in Table 2.

Price evaluation

The final category in the evaluation process involved the economic impact of obtaining and operating each vendor's modems for the projected three-year life span of the project. To reflect the operating philosophy and budgetary constraints of OPM, it was assumed that the equipment would be leased for the first year and purchased at the beginning of the second. Thus pricing for the second and third years was based on maintenance and operating costs. Pricing for the first year was calculated on lease and operating costs, because maintenance was included in the lease costs.

To determine the purchase cost of the equipment at the beginning of the second year, the equipment

Table 1 Human engineering

MODEM	RATING	RATING/120	HUMAN ENGINEERING EVALUATION POINTS
A	73	0.608	15.21
B	76	0.633	15.83
C	90	0.750	18.75

3. Operation. *The most important evaluation in a procurement program is operational. It is best to devise the simplest test configuration which takes into account all or*

most of the equipment used in the actual network. The equipment being tested should be easily removable, and the equipment in the test link should be highly stable.

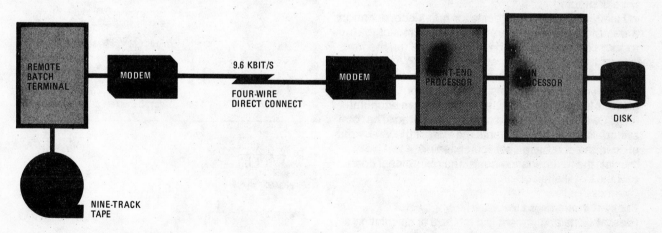

tive acknowledgment to the front-end processor. The front-end processor, in turn, retransmitted the previously sent data block to the terminal.

By transmitting the same benchmark data under identical conditions (with the exception of the connected modems), a detailed timing analysis could be made to determine if there were any significant differences in the internal delay times of the modems or if differences existed in their ready-to-send/clear-to-send delay time. The criteria used to assign evaluation points for this portion were:

accruals were computed and subtracted from the purchase price of the modems:

Equity = Rental × % Accrual × 12 Months
Purchase cost = Purchase price − Equity

Because rental payments included maintenance for the first year, the computation of maintenance costs for the second and third years of ownership were based on each vendor's maintenance price schedule. The operational costs for each modem was computed for the total three-year system life based on the power

Table 2 Technical performance

MODEM	TIME (MINUTES: SECONDS)	EVALUATION POINTS
A	4:58	25
B	4:59	25
C	5:00	25

Table 3 Price

PERIOD	COSTS	PVIF
BEGINNING OF YEAR ONE	INSTALLATION	1.00
END OF YEAR ONE	LEASE FOR ONE YEAR PURCHASE COSTS OPERATION	0.909
END OF YEAR TWO	OPERATION MAINTENANCE	0.826
END OF YEAR THREE	OPERATION MAINTENANCE	0.751

consumption of each device. Because the modems would operate continuously 24 hours a day, seven days a week, and because some of them used low-power consumption, large-scale integrated solid state devices, significant cost differences in this category were computed.

Finally, the installation costs for non-Macon locations were obtained. These were computed to reflect that vendor personnel would be used to install the modems in remote sites where the cost of using OPM technical control center personnel was greater than that of employing vendor technicians. In the situation where OPM personnel could install the equipment more economically, OPM installation costs were computed. The total system-life cost then became the sum of the year/rental cost, the purchase cost (purchase price less accruals), the maintenance costs, the operational costs, and the installation costs.

Present value adjustment
Present value adjustment is a method of calculating a future payment or stream of payments at today's value. Present value (PV) is nothing more than the reverse of the compounding principal. It determines how much a dollar received or spent at a later date is worth at the present time if invested at a given interest rate. PV is calculated by multiplying the principal amount at the end of "n" periods (Pn) by the present value interest factor (PVIF).

$$PV = Pn \times PVIF$$

PVIF is the inverse of 1 plus interest to the nth power, where n is the number of periods in which the interest is compounded.

Table 4 Adjusted costs

VENDOR A

n	COST	PVIF	ADJUSTED COSTS
0	$ 300.00	1.00	$ 300.00
1	4,822.84	.909	4,383.96
2	390.84	.826	322.83
3	390.84	.751	293.52

TOTAL ADJUSTED SYSTEM COST: $5,300.31

VENDOR B

n	COST	PVIF	ADJUSTED COSTS
0	$ 200.00	1.00	$ 200.00
1	6,936.84	.909	6,305.59
2	298.84	.826	246.84
3	298.84	.751	224.43

TOTAL ADJUSTED SYSTEM COST: $6,976.86

VENDOR C

n	COST	PVIF	ADJUSTED COSTS
0	$ 400.00	1.00	$ 400.00
1	8,979.14	.909	8,162.04
2	421.14	.826	347.86
3	421.14	.751	316.28

TOTAL ADJUSTED SYSTEM COST: $9,226.18

$$PVIF \frac{1}{(1+i)^n}$$

therefore:

$$PV = Pn \times \frac{1}{(1+i)^n}$$

where i = interest rate, n = time periods.
For example, the present value of $400 needed to meet a commitment two years from now—if the going interest rate for long-term investment is 10 percent—is computed as follows:

$$PV = \$400 \times \frac{1}{(1 + 0.1)^2}$$

$$= \$400 \times \frac{1}{1.21}$$

Table 5 Scorecard

VENDOR	HUMAN ENGINEERING	TECHNICAL PERFORMANCE	COST	TOTAL
A	15.21	25	$50.00	$90.21
B	15.83	25	37.98	78.81
C	18.75	25	28.72	72.47

PV = $400 × 0.826

PV = $330.40

In terms of today's economic situation, $330.40 invested at 10 percent interest is basically the same as $400 two years from now.

OPM used the present value method of adjusting costs to put all vendors' costs on an equal basis. The present value adjustment was made for every year over the three-year network life span for each vendor. For this procurement, Table 3 lists the periods, the costs included in each period, and the PVIF for each—which was based on an interest rate of 10 percent, the cost to the government for short-term borrowing.

The costs and PVIFs listed in Table 3 form the basis for Table 4, which lists the total adjusted costs.

In assigning the evaluation points based on economic factors evaluated for each modem, the following formula was used:

$$\text{Points} = 50 \times \frac{\text{Lowest adjusted system cost}}{\text{Evaluated adjusted system cost}}$$

Thus the evaluation points based on economic data resulted as follows:

$$\text{Modem A} = 50 \times \frac{5300.31}{5300.31} = 50 \text{ points}$$

$$\text{Modem B} = 50 \times \frac{5300.31}{6976.86} = 37.98 \text{ points}$$

$$\text{Modem C} = 50 \times \frac{5300.31}{9226.18} = 28.72 \text{ points}$$

Overall results

After each vendor met the minimum requirements, and tests had been completed in the three areas of evaluation, the evaluation points awarded to each vendor were totaled to determine which modems should be selected. Table 5 lists each vendor considered, the evaluation points assigned to each category, and the total number of evaluation points.

Based on OPM's evaluation, the best performance for the price was demonstrated by Vendor A.

The equipment acquisitions detailed here was conducted using General Services Administration (GSA) schedule contracts and followed all the existing GSA guidelines and regulations concerning their use. ■

Gilbert Held, U.S. Office of Personnel Management, Macon, Ga.

Why taxes matter in selecting equipment

Recessionary times are forcing users to acquaint themselves with available tax options when buying or leasing data communications gear.

Reduced to the barest, there are only two ways to obtain data communications equipment—purchase and lease. Yet the methods of structuring the lease or purchase agreement and of calculating equipment depreciation can yield sizable differences on an enterprise's balance sheet. Although most organizations have tax and accounting counsel to advise the communications specialist on appropriate procurement methods, all

communications professionals should be aware of the basic economic and legal principles of equipment transactions.

When equipment is purchased, the title and resulting ownership pass from the vendor to the buyer. Generally, the responsibility for maintenance also passes to the buyer, who may have to negotiate a service agreement with the vendor or a third party. Although buying equipment usually requires a large one-time outlay, as opposed to the many smaller payments for leased equipment, there are ways to reduce the expenditure. A buyer may borrow funds and amortize payments over a period of time. He may purchase half of the required equipment on the last day of the year and the remainder on the first day of the next year, thereby spreading the expenditure over two years. The advantage is that the buyer can obtain tax deductions and tax credits for the investment in and the depreciation of owned data communications equipment.

A multiplexer with a useful life of at least, say, five years is an example of equipment eligible for the investment credit. The investment credit varies according to the expected life of the asset, as denoted in Table 1, and could reduce a purchaser's tax liability by up to 10 percent. The investment credit reduces the tax obligation dollar for dollar, whereas a tax deduction lowers adjusted net income on which taxes are computed. Thus, if a firm that otherwise would have a $150,000 tax bill purchased $40,000 worth of multiplexers, each with a useful life of five years, it would receive a tax credit of $2,664 (6.66 percent of $40,000), and its adjusted tax bill would be lowered to $147,336. In other words, the tax credit lowers the effective purchase cost of the multiplexers to $37,336.

Depreciation, another way to lessen the tax liability, allows deductions for the obsolescence of equipment because of technical change or wear and tear. A company can deduct for depreciation when computing federal income taxes. The larger the depreciation, the larger one's deduction; the larger one's deduction, the lower one's net income and, hence, actual tax liability.

There are several depreciation methods for equipment tax purposes, among them, straight line, sum of the years' digits, and double-declining balance. Accelerated depreciation, which includes each method but straight line, reduces taxes in the early years of an asset's life because the deductions are larger during those early years. This can increase the cash available for reinvestment. Selecting a particular method depends not only on certain federal rules and regulations but also on corporate policy and generally accepted accounting practices.

To examine each depreciation method, assume that the multiplexers purchased for $40,000 and with a life expectancy of five years have at the end of that period an estimated salvage value of $5,000. For straight-line depreciation, we determine the annual amount by dividing the equipment cost less the estimated salvage

value by the years of the equipment's economic life:

$$\frac{\$40{,}000 \text{ cost} - \$5{,}000 \text{ salvage value}}{5 \text{ years}} = \$7{,}000/\text{year}$$

The declining-balance method requires applying a constant depreciation rate each year to the undepreciated value of the asset at the close of the previous year. The most commonly used declining-balance method is double declining balance, or DDB, as it is known in financial circles. Since the straight-line rate is 1 divided by years of equipment life, the DDB method results in twice that, or a rate of 2 over useful years. Returning to our example, the straight rate is 1 over 5, or 20 percent; hence, the DDB rate is 40 percent, which is applied to the multiplexers' full purchase price without any allowance for salvage value. Thus, depreciation under the DDB method is $40,000 × 40 percent = $16,000 for the first year, $40,000 − $16,000 × 40 percent = $9,600 for the second year, and so on, as the undepreciated balance declines and the original cost is absorbed.

Using the sum-of-the-years'-digits method, a sliding scale accepted by accountants and the Internal Revenue Service, we can figure the yearly depreciation allowance by first computing the sum of the years' digits, which in our example is year 1 + year 2 + year 3 + year 4 + year 5 = 15. Next, we divide the remaining years of the equipment's economic life by the sum of the years' digits and multiply the resulting fraction by the depreciable cost, which is the equipment cost minus the asset's salvage value. Returning to the multiplexer example, the depreciation for year 1 would be 5 ÷ 15 × (40,000 − 5,000) = $11,667, while for year 5 the amount would be 1 ÷ 15 × (40,000 − 5,000) = $2,333. Table 2 compares each depreciation method as it is applied to the $40,000 multiplexer with a $5,000 salvage value and a five-year lifespan.

Time and money

In selecting a depreciation method for purchased equipment, an organization must consider its current and projected tax rate and the value of money by time. Current and expected marginal tax rates are important since they translate the depreciation deduction into actual tax dollars saved. (Marginal tax rates are derived from and usually equal a company's tax bracket.) For example, an organization with a marginal tax rate of 50 percent would save $1 in taxes for every $2 of depreciation deduction per year.

Understanding the time value of money is critical to comparing an uneven series of payments or benefits, and its computation requires a technique known as present-value discounting. To understand present-value discounting, it is easier first to consider the compounding of money. If we deposit P_0 in a savings account earning interest at a rate i and leave the money in the account for one period of time, the principal and compounded interest P_N at the end of that period N becomes

$$P_N = P_0 (1+i)^N$$

If we deposit $100 at an interest rate of 10 percent

Table 1   Investment tax credit

EQUIPMENT'S LIFE EXPECTANCY (YEARS)	CREDIT AS PERCENT OF PURCHASE PRICE
3 OR MORE, BUT LESS THAN 5	$3.33
5 OR MORE, BUT LESS THAN 7	6.66
7 OR MORE	10.00

Table 2 Depreciation methods
($40,000 asset, $5,000 salvage value, 5-year life)

YEAR	DEPRECIATION METHOD		
	STRAIGHT LINE	DOUBLE DECLINING BALANCE	SUM OF THE YEARS' DIGITS
1	$7,000	$16,000	$11,667
2	7,000	9,600	9,333
3	7,000	5,760	7,000
4	7,000	3,456	4,667
5	7,000	2,074	2,334
TOTAL	$35,000	†$36,890	‡$35,001

†ACTUAL DEPRECIATION IN FIFTH YEAR IS $2,074 - $1,890 ($36,890 - 35,000), BECAUSE THE TOTAL CANNOT EXCEED THE ASSET MINUS THE SALVAGE VALUE.

‡THIS IS ROUNDED OFF TO $35,000.

for two years, at the end of that period it would grow to

$$P_2 = \$100 (1 + .10)^2 = \$100 (1.21) = \$121$$

To determine today's value of tomorrow's payment or receipt, we must find the present value of the future payment or receipt. The present value P_0 and its relationship to a payment or receipt at a time period N is expressed as

$$P_0 = \frac{P_N}{(1+i)^N}$$

As an example of the use of present values, consider the difference between receiving $110 today or $121 in two years. If we invest that money at a 10 percent interest rate, we want to compare the present value of $121 discounted at 10 percent with the $110 we could receive today. To find the present value, we calculate:

$$P_0 = \frac{P_N}{(1+i)^N} = \frac{121}{(1 + .10)^2} = \frac{121}{1.21} = \$100$$

Since the present value two years hence of $121 at 10 percent is $100, it is preferable to receive $110 today. To assist in present-value computations, many financial publications and books contain tables of the term $1 \div (1+i)^N$ for various values of i and N. This term is known as the present value interest factor (PVIF). To cite an example, a tax savings of $1,000 due in five years would have a present value of $620.90, assuming a 10 percent interest rate. Table 3 is an extract from a financial table showing PVIFs for a 10-year period for selected interest rates. The present value P_0 is the product of P_N and PVIF, and the table simplifies the computation for standard periods and rates.

Lease arrangements

Unlike an equipment purchase, leasing results in no transfer of title to the lessee. Thus, although lease pay-

ments are ordinary deductible business expenses, the lessee can neither depreciate the equipment nor use the investment tax credit to reduce his tax obligation.

Under most lease arrangements, the lessee is obligated to pay a fixed amount per time period, usually monthly, for using the leased equipment. Maintenance is often provided by the lessor and is included in the lease cost. Once a lease expires, the lessee and lessor must come to terms on a new lease unless the original lease contains a renewal clause. The lessee, before renewing a lease, should consider other equipment, current corporate requirements, any new lease terms imposed by the lessor, and other products available from the current lessor. If the lease is not renewed, the lessee's obligation may range from packaging and returning the equipment to paying a fee if he violates a multiperiod lease clause.

If we exclude the time value of money and equipment maintenance costs, we can determine the simple lease versus purchase break-even point, which is

$$N = \frac{P}{L}$$

where P = Purchase cost
L = Monthly lease cost
N = Number of months needed to break even

Thus, if equipment costs $5,000 and the lease costs $250 per month, the break-even point is 20 months. This means that equipment ownership is preferable if equipment use is expected to exceed that period of time. Table 4 summarizes the key criteria of lease versus purchase decisions.

Two common lease variations are lease with option to purchase (LWOP) and lease with ownership. Under the first contract, a portion of each monthly payment is set aside and applied toward the purchase price of

Table 3 Present dollar value of payment

YEAR	INTEREST RATES		
	9.75%	10%	10.25%
1	.9112	.9091	.9070
2	.8302	.8264	.8227
3	.7565	.7513	.7462
4	.6893	.6830	.6768
5	.6280	.6209	.6139
6	.5722	.5645	.5568
7	.5214	.5132	.5051
8	.4751	.4665	.4581
9	.4329	.4241	.4155
10	.3944	.3855	.3769

the equipment. Under the second agreement, ownership passes to the lessee upon the last lease payment. Because no leasing company can be expected to give something away for nothing, it is reasonable to assume that the monthly lease cost of these two variations will usually exceed the payments required under the terms of a conventional lease agreement.

Hedges

LWOP permits a firm to decide if it should purchase the equipment while it builds equity with each payment. Other advantages include permitting the lessee to hedge on quantities and to later return excess equipment. Also, since a company avoids a large cash outlay, it can use LWOP as a cash-management tool; that is, the firm continues lease payments until corporate funds are available to pay for the purchase price less the payment accruals for the equipment.

Four areas of an LWOP plan deserve special attention: the required monthly payment, the percentage of each payment that is accrued toward the purchase price of the equipment, the maximum percentage of the equipment purchase price that can be accrued, and the purchase price of the equipment. Once we determine these factors, we can compute the number of months required to reach the maximum accrual. This is important because lease payments after that time are treated as conventional lease payments, and equity buildup stops.

For example, consider a multiplexer with a purchase price of $1,120 and monthly lease cost of $80. We must do more than merely divide the purchase price by the monthly payment. Assume that 50 percent of the lease payments can be credited to the purchase price up to a maximum of 75 percent of the purchase price. The number of monthly payments *M* until the maximum accruals are reached can be expressed as

Table 5 LWOP conversion costs

TIME (MONTHS)	ACCRUED CREDITS	MAXIMUM CREDIT	COST TO PURCHASE
1	$80 × 1 × 50% = $40	$840	$1,120 − $40 = $1,080
6	80 × 6 × 50% = 240	840	1,120 − 240 = 880
12	80 × 12 × 50% = 480	840	1,120 − 480 = 640
24	80 × 24 × 50% = 960	840	1,120 − 840 = 240

$$M = \frac{P \times MAR}{L \times LAR}$$

where P = Purchase price
MAR = Maximum accrual rate
L = Monthly lease cost
LAR = Lease accrual rate

Plugging in the numbers, we obtain

$$M = \frac{1120 \times .75}{80 \times .50} = 21 \text{ months}$$

Thus, the first 21 monthly lease payments of $80 will yield $40 credit each month toward the purchase of the multiplexer. Table 5 shows tabulations of several purchase costs based on the conversion of the lease to purchase at different time periods. The figure illustrates the interrelationship of total lease payments, accruals, and the purchase cost of the multiplexer upon conversion of the lease to purchase over time.

In analyzing the differences between leasing and purchasing equipment, a company must consider many factors, including tax-credit eligibility, the depre-

Table 4 Lease versus purchase

DECISION CRITERIA	LEASE	PURCHASE
TITLE	WITH LESSOR	PURCHASER
PAYMENTS	LOWER BUT REPETITIVE	LARGE ONE-TIME
MAINTENANCE	USUALLY INCLUDED	SEPARATE AGREEMENT
TAX CREDIT	NOT AVAILABLE	AVAILABLE
DEPRECIATION	NOT AVAILABLE	AVAILABLE
DISCOUNT POTENTIAL	NONE TO MINIMAL	HIGHER
REPLACEMENT	END OF LEASE OR ANYTIME WITH PENALTY	MORE DIFFICULT BECAUSE OF INVESTMENT
PRICE RISE (TAKES INTO ACCOUNT INFLATION)	CAN OCCUR AT LEASE RENEWAL TIME	PURCHASE RESULTS IN FIXED COST

Lease changes. The graph shows comparisons of lease payments, accruals, and the cost of the multiplexer upon converting a lease to a purchase agreement.

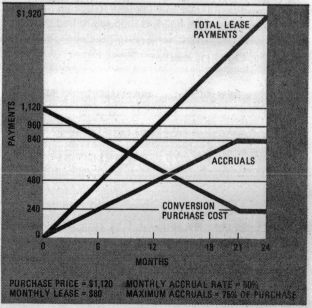

PURCHASE PRICE = $1,120 MONTHLY ACCRUAL RATE = 50%
MONTHLY LEASE = $80 MAXIMUM ACCRUALS = 75% OF PURCHASE

Table 6 Computing lease cost

YEAR	PAYMENT	LEASE COST AFTER TAX [LEASE COST x (1 – .5)]	10% PRESENT VALUE INTEREST FACTOR	PRESENT VALUE OF COST OF LEASING
1	$960	$480	.909	$436
2	960	480	.826	396
3	960	480	.751	360
		TOTAL PRESENT VALUE OF COST OF LEASING		**$1,192**

ciation schedule, the corporate tax rate, and the time value of money. For simplicity, assume that we lease a multiplexer for $80 per month but can make one payment of $960 at the end of the year. This permits us to use three yearly PVIFs for a three-year lease instead of 36 monthly PVIFs. To compute the present-value cost of leasing, we must first determine the lease cost after tax and then multiply that number by the appropriate PVIF for the period under consideration.

If we assume an interest rate of 10 percent, we can compute the lease cost as shown in Table 6. Here the lease cost after tax is simply the lease cost multiplied by 1 minus the firm's marginal tax rate. The marginal tax rate is 0.5, which means that the lease cost after tax is one-half the lease payment. As Table 6 depicts, after considering the tax deductibility of leasing and the present value of future payments, we get $1,192 for the three-year present value of the cost of leasing. Note that the maintenance cost included in a lease is a separate chargeable item when equipment is purchased. For comparison, assume that the purchase price of the multiplexer is $2,400 and a three-year maintenance contract costs $240 per year. A zero salvage value is assigned to the multiplexer, and straight-line depreciation will be used for tax purposes. Table 7 shows tabulations for the applicable cost of ownership. The company's total tax deductions each year are multiplied by its marginal tax rate to obtain the yearly tax savings. This figure is then multiplied by the

Taxing phrases

Accelerated depreciation. A catchall term that describes accounting methods allowing deductions during the estimated *useful* life of equipment, as opposed to its pure physical life.

Accrual. Recognition on the books of incurring expenses (in contrast to prepaid). An accruing item on the books might be the monthly payments toward the eventual purchase of leased equipment.

Declining balance. A depreciation method that applies a fixed percentage to the original cost of a piece of equipment and to the following balances. Say, a multiplexer originally costs $100, constant depreciation is 10 percent, balance is $90; the following year, 10 percent is applied against the $90 with the new balance becoming $81, and so on, until the balance is absorbed.

Salvage value. The estimated scrap value of, say, a terminal at the end of its useful life. It is usually gauged when the equipment is new.

Straight-line depreciation. An almost universal expense computation based on the assumption that a modem, for instance, has a limited useful life. In this basic method, the cost is viewed as a prepaid expense spread over the modem's operating life, less its salvage value.

Sum of the years' digits. A declining-balance variant for determining the annual depreciation percentage. It is derived from placing the estimated useful life as the numerator and the declining sum of those years as the denominator.

appropriate present value interest factor, producing the present value of taxes saved by depreciation, known as cash inflows, that have resulted from ownership. The savings from the investment tax credit is added, and this new sum is subtracted from the purchase price to obtain the net cost of ownership. Based on this example, ownership is more favorable. ∎

Table 7 Cost of ownership

YEAR	DEPRECIATION	MAINTENANCE	TOTAL TAX DEDUCTIONS	TAX SAVINGS [(1 – .5) x TAX DEDUCTIONS]	10% PRESENT VALUE INTEREST FACTOR	PRESENT VALUE OF CASH INFLOWS
1	$800	$240	$1,040	$520	.909	$473
2	800	240	1,040	520	.826	430
3	800	240	1,040	520	.751	391

SUBTOTAL: $1,294

INVESTMENT TAX CREDIT
$2,400 x 3.33% 80

TOTAL CASH INFLOWS $1,374

ADJUSTED EQUIPMENT COST
PURCHASE PRICE $2,400
LESS CASH INFLOWS 1,374
NET COST $1,026

Index

Index (cont.)

IMPORTANT:

HERE IS YOUR REGISTRATION CODE TO ACCESS

YOUR PREMIUM McGRAW-HILL ONLINE RESOURCES.

For key premium online resources you need THIS CODE to gain access. Once the code is entered, you will be able to use the Web resources for the length of your course.

If your course is using **WebCT** or **Blackboard**, you'll be able to use this code to access the McGraw-Hill content within your instructor's online course.

Access is provided if you have purchased a new book. If the registration code is missing from this book, the registration screen on our Website, and within your WebCT or Blackboard course, will tell you how to obtain your new code.

Registering for McGraw-Hill Online Resources

TO gain access to your McGraw-Hill web resources simply follow the steps below:

1. USE YOUR WEB BROWSER TO GO TO: **http://www.mhhe.com/hall4E**

2. CLICK ON **FIRST TIME USER**.

3. ENTER THE REGISTRATION CODE* PRINTED ON THE TEAR-OFF BOOKMARK ON THE RIGHT.

4. AFTER YOU HAVE ENTERED YOUR REGISTRATION CODE, CLICK **REGISTER**.

5. FOLLOW THE INSTRUCTIONS TO SET-UP YOUR PERSONAL UserID AND PASSWORD.

6. WRITE YOUR UserID AND PASSWORD DOWN FOR FUTURE REFERENCE.
KEEP IT IN A SAFE PLACE.

TO GAIN ACCESS to the McGraw-Hill content in your instructor's **WebCT** or **Blackboard** course simply log in to the course with the UserID and Password provided by your instructor. Enter the registration code exactly as it appears in the box to the right when prompted by the system. You will only need to use the code the first time you click on McGraw-Hill content.

Thank you, and welcome to your McGraw-Hill online Resources!

* YOUR REGISTRATION CODE CAN BE USED ONLY ONCE TO ESTABLISH ACCESS. IT IS NOT TRANSFERABLE.

0-07-246204-3 HALL: BASIC BIOMECHANICS, 4E

MCGRAW-HILL
ONLINE RESOURCES

REGISTRATION CODE

magdeleine-63975830

Mc Graw Hill **Higher Education**